THE PAUL CARUS LECTURES

EIGHTH SERIES

1949

NATURE, MIND, AND DEATH

Published on the Foundation
Established in Memory of
PAUL CARUS

Editor of The Open Court and The Monist
1888–1919

Photograph by Imogen Cunningham.

NATURE, MIND, AND DEATH

by

C. J. Ducasse

Professor of Philosophy in Brown University

THE OPEN COURT PUBLISHING COMPANY

LA SALLE   ILLINOIS

1951

Printed in the United States of America
for the Publishers by
Paquin Printers

Preface

The nature of the relation between mind and body, which is what this book ultimately attempts to clarify, has generally been discussed on the basis of criteria of mentality and materiality little if any sharper than those governing the employment of these two categories in ordinary conversation or literary writing. In the more or less stereotyped contexts in which the terms "mental" and "material" occur there, these unanalyzed criteria are good enough to guide application of one or the other term; but they are much too vague to be directly of much use for theoretical purposes — for instance, to enable one to decide whether sensations or so-called sensa are to be classed as mental events or on the contrary as physical, or perhaps as neither. Yet this question turns out to be of crucial importance in connection with the problem of the nature of the mind-body relation.

The criterion that determines whether a given event is mental, or belongs to the material world, is what Chapters 13 and 14 attempt to discover. They are therefore in a way basic for the argument of the whole book. The other chapters of Part III devolop the implications of the outcome of these two chapters and of Part II, as concerns the nature, the constituents, and the operations of a mind, and the nature of the knowledge a mind has of material and other objective things and events.

The question whether the category of Substance is applicable to minds is one that inevitably crops up in discussions of the mind-body relation — even if, perhaps, that category is then only dismissed as (allegedly) made obsolete by a "functional" conception of what a mind is. But there is no need either to accept naively the conception of Substance inherited from philosophical tradition, or, equally naively, to reject that category because it or the traditional conception of it seems to have no relevance to certain questions, and these are the only ones, perhaps, which one is interested to ask about minds. Rather, the proper philosophical course is to analyze empirically the category of Substance, and thus find out whether one is not perhaps using it unawares and perhaps without respecting some of its implications, even when one speaks explicitly in "functional" terms.

But when the needed empirical analysis of the category of Substance is attempted, one quickly discovers that the task requires prior analysis of the category of Causality. In Part II of this book the analysis of both of these basic notions and of certain closely allied others, such as those of telism, of determinism, and of freedom, is undertaken.

It is only after these various analyses have been performed that one really understands just what it is he asks when he asks whether a mind, or a piece of wood, or a living body, etc., is or is not a "substance"; or asks whether something concretely given — whether it be more particularly a substance, a function, an event, an operation, or something else — is to be reckoned as "material" or "mental." Such questions, of course, may have no bearing or no obvious bearing on certain problems, which may happen to be the only ones in which some philosophers are interested. But this nowise entails that those questions are illegitimate, obsolete, or unimportant. They may on the contrary be crucial in connection with certain other problems, in which other philosophers are interested — for instance, that of the mind-body relation — and the results of the analyses mentioned may well show that these other problems are genuine not pseudo problems, and may well also make solution of them possible.

The numerous analyses which the aim of this book thus turns out to require cannot, however, be arbitrary ones — such as purely conventional definitions of terms can only supply — but must be empirical, and therefore so far as they go authoritative, analyses. But just what sort of process analysis of this kind is, and what the data for it may consist of, is anything but immediately obvious. To answer this question adequately amounts to formulating a conception of the method of inquiry that is capable of yielding knowledge properly so called as to philosophical matters; and to outlining a conception of the subject matter and the kinds of problems distinctive of the enterprise called philosophy. This task is undertaken in Part I of the book. In Part IV the conclusions which the three preceding parts appear to warrant concerning the nature of the mind-body relation are then set forth; and the implications are examined which those conclusions have as to the possibility or impossibility that a mind, or some part of it, survives the death of its body.

During the past thirty years various of the ideas which the schema of this book integrates developed in the writer's mind to some extent independently of one another. Some of them, in such shape as they had reached at the time, were published as chapters in books or as articles in philosophical journals. Some of the main features of the conception of Causality formulated in Part II appeared in a monograph, *Causation and the Types of Necessity* (Univ. of Washington Press, 1924); in a paper, "On the Nature and the Observability of the Causal Relation" (*Journal of Philosophy,* Feb. 4, 1926); and in two discussions in *The Philosophical Review*: "Of the Spurious Mystery in Causal Connections" (July, 1930) and "Of the Nature and Efficacy of Causes" (July, 1932). The notion of the nature of telism also presented in Part II was first sketched in an article, "Explanation, Mechanism, and Teleology," in the *Journal of Philosophy* (March 12, 1945). The view of the subject matter and method of philosophy, set forth in Part I, is a summary restatement, with elaborations of some points and certain revisions, of that contained in the second part of my book *Philosophy as a Science* (Oskar Piest, N. Y. 1941). Chapter 6 of the present work includes portions of my University of California Howison Lecture for 1944, entitled *The Method of Knowledge in Philosophy* (Univ. of California Publications in Philosophy, Vol. 16, No. 7).

Chapter 13, which as already stated is a basic one in the book, is in large part identical with the essay, "Moore's 'The Refutation of Idealism'," which I contributed to Vol. IV of "The Library of Living Philosophers," Evanston, Ill., 1942, entitled *The Philosophy of G. E. Moore*. This essay itself developed out of ideas which first appeared as an article in *Mind* (April 1936) entitled "Introspection, Mental Acts, and Sensa."

Chapter 15 is a revised statement of ideas contained in a paper, "Objectivity, Objective Reference, and Perception," published in the journal *Philosophy and Phenomenological Research* (Sept. 1941). Chapter 16 is based on my presidential address to the Association for Symbolic Logic, "Symbols, Signs, and Signals," (*Journal of Symbolic Logic,* June 1939). In Chapters 19, 20, and 21, I have reproduced a number of passages from an address entitled "Is a Life After Death Possible," which I delivered at the University of California as the 1947 Agnes E. and Constantine E. A. Foerster Lecture on the Immortality of the Soul.

I wish to express my grateful thanks to the editors and publishers of these various publications for their kind permissions to incorporate in the present work such portions of my papers as seemed to me appropriate.

I must also thank my colleague, Professor R. M. Chisholm, who was good enough to read the manuscript of the book, and whose penetrating comments enabled me to remedy a number of defects. Needless to say, he has no responsibility for those which undoubtedly remain. I have profited much also from oral discussions of some of my contentions with graduate students in seminars, and with present and former colleagues at Brown and elsewhere. Especially to be mentioned among them are Professors R. M. Blake, V. A. Tomas, and Mrs. N. R. Chatalian of Brown; Professors C. A. Baylis of the University of Maryland, I. McGreal of Southern Methodist University, F. C. Dommeyer of St. Lawrence University, E. J. Nelson of the University of Washington, and J. W. Robson of the University of California at Los Angeles. As stated in a footnote in the text, criticisms by Dr. Dickinson S. Miller and by Professor Robson, of earlier statements of some of my views regarding Causality led me to reformulate and argue them at some length in Chapter 9.

This account of my obligations, incomplete as it is bound to be, would be inexcusably so if it did not mention, and express my great appreciation of, the practically ideal conditions of work which, as a result of the policies of the Administration of Brown University, I have enjoyed as a member of its faculty.

C. J. D.

Providence, R. I.,
October 1, 1949.

CONTENTS

PART I

PHILOSOPHY: ITS SUBJECT MATTER, METHOD, AND UTILITY

PART II

FUNDAMENTAL CATEGORIES

PART III

NATURE, MATTER, AND MINDS

PART IV

THE MIND-BODY RELATION AND THE POSSIBILITY OF A LIFE AFTER DEATH

PART I

PHILOSOPHY: ITS SUBJECT MATTER, METHOD, AND UTILITY

Chapter 1

METAPHYSICS, KNOWLEDGE, AND THE
MIND-BODY PROBLEM

The chief problems to be investigated in this book are that of
the relation between nature, mind, and matter; that of the relation
between the individual's mind and his body; and that of the implications these relations may have as to the possibility that this
mind, or some part of it, survives the death of the body. These
problems, as well as most of those implicit in them that we shall
also discuss, belong to metaphysics.

Metaphysics, however, is a branch of philosophy rather in dis-
repute today. Henry Margenau, a physicist who does not himself
share the animus against it, notes, for example, that among the
taboos of our time there is to be found "the broad convention that
the word *metaphysics* must never be used in polite scientific
society."[1] Among philosophers themselves John Dewey, whose
views have been widely influential, speaks of "vain metaphysics
and idle epistemology,"[2] notwithstanding that many of his own
writings deal with questions philosophers generally would call
metaphysical and epistemological. Another philosopher, Rudolph
Carnap, whose views are influencing many, holds that there is no
way to verify or confute the solutions metaphysicians have offered
of the problems they discuss, and hence that these are but pseudo
problems.[3] And metaphysics is hardly enhanced in repute, but

---

[1] Henry Margenau, "Metaphysical Elements in Physics," in *Reviews of Modern Physics*, Vol. 13, No. 3, July 1941, p. 176.
[2] Dewey, J., *Reconstruction in Philosophy*, p. 124.
[3] Carnap, *Philosophy and Logical Syntax*, Kegan Paul, London, 1935, pp. 15 ff.

occasions for legitimate attack upon it rather afforded, by those contemporary protagonists of its importance who have persuaded themselves that the metaphysical views of Aristotle or of St. Thomas represent, not as in fact they do, precarious speculations, but principles established firmly enough to be now employed, without further questioning, as shapers of our educational and other social policies.

1. The Genuine Problems of Metaphysics Important and Solvable

The slight regard in which metaphysics is commonly held today is ultimately traceable to the fact that what has gone by the name has too often been little more than masses of assertions "vague, pretentious, and very badly reasoned."[4] I do not believe, however, that metaphysics has to be this, nor that all its problems are pseudo problems, nor that any of those which are genuine are humanly insoluble. And I do not think that the genuine ones, however abstract they happen to be, are unimportant. On the contrary, it seems to me that they are tied up in the end with certain of the plain man's most concrete tribulations as truly and in much the same logical way as that in which, for example, the likewise abstract problems of theoretical physics are linked with certain others of the plain man's practical difficulties. As often has been pointed out, every man has a metaphysics — a set of beliefs as to the nature of reality, and as to the nature of man, his destiny, and his welfare. These beliefs, it is true, are seldom, or but in minor degree, original with the individual who holds them; and they are seldom either clearly formulated or critically scrutinized by him. But — and perhaps on this account all the more rigidly — they govern the whole policy of his life. Moreover, dismissal *a priori* — as by some scientists or some self-styled practical men — of the

---

4 D. W. Gotshalk, *Metaphysics in Modern Times*, University of Chicago Press, 1940, p. 1. Gotshalk gives this as one of the meanings the word metaphysics has in popular thought.

questions these beliefs concern, on the ground that they are insoluble or unprofitable, does not mean that even these men get along without tacit beliefs of this kind; for such dismissal itself constitutes acceptance in practice, but unawares and without examination of its merits, of a particular set of metaphysical beliefs. It is true that just as men could not have put off eating until vitamins had been discovered and the principles of nutrition established, so they cannot put off living their lives until the metaphysical assumptions on which they tacitly base them have been brought to light and critically scrutinized. But this does not entail that inquiry into the problems of metaphysics is unimportant or futile; it only entails that, unless it is carried forward in a scientific manner and its results applied, men will go on living blindly and as blunderingly as before.

But although I believe the genuine problems of metaphysics are as soluble as those of the natural sciences and even more important, I also believe that metaphysical problems — and in particular that of the nature of reality — have in most cases been so badly stated that, in the form in which they were stated, they were not genuinely soluble. Also, I am convinced that, if they are to be solved, the mode of investigation used must be purged of the glaring defects which have so often rendered it barren and have brought philosophy discredit — avoidable defects such as looseness of inference, ambiguity of terms, confusion of issues, and inadequate testing of hypotheses.

These convictions rest on a conception of the nature of philosophy, of its distinctive subject matter, of its proper method, and of its functions, which was set forth in some detail in an earlier work.[5] An outline of it, however — embodying a number of important clarifications and revisions — must be presented here, since it underlies the method of this book and implicitly defines

[5] Ducasse, *Philosophy as a Science, Its Matter and Its Method*, Oskar Piest, New York, 1941.

the sort of contribution its pages attempt to make to the solution
of the ancient problems they discuss.

2. Philosophy a Search for Knowledge, Hence by Intent a Science

The major premise of that conception of philosophy is that it
is not guesses, snap judgments, gratuitous opinions, articles of
faith, or wishful beliefs, that philosophers seek as solutions of the
questions they ask, but answers that will have as genuine a title
to the name of knowledge as the answers sought and found — to
questions about other things — by the natural, the formal, or the
social sciences.   Knowledge, however — even the sort of knowledge analytical clarification gains us — consists in *belief based on
evidence rationally adequate to support it;* and philosophers are
therefore no more at liberty than other seekers after truth to
accept an idea as true just because it happens to have come into
their heads.   They too are under obligation to proportion their
assertions to the grounds they are able to offer for believing them
true or more probably true than others.

This is not to say that speculation has no place in philosophy,
for speculation is but the making of hypotheses, and this is as
necessary in philosophy, and has the same function there, as in
other knowledge-seeking enterprises.   But the philosopher no less
than the physicist or biologist has the duty to test the hypotheses
that occur to him; and to test them in a manner genuinely capable
of proving them false if they happen to be false, and of proving
those he puts forward more probably true than their rivals, if they
are so.   Philosophers are not pets of God, favored with a private
entrance into the storehouse of truth.

In many cases, of course, man learns not through personal
investigation, but through testimony.   But he has reason to accept
as fact what testimony reports only in so far as he has evidence
(*a*) that the person whose testimony he accepts was qualified to

investigate the matters as to which he testifies; (*b*) that he actually did investigate them; (*c*) that he is not only an informed witness but also an unbiassed and truthful one; and (*d*) that what is offered as his testimony is indeed his and not perhaps only something alleged to have been testified by him. These conditions of the validity of testimony are binding even when one chooses to label with the august name "God" the witness whose purported testimony one quotes.

That knowledge, not mere opinion — and indeed, systematized knowledge — is what philosophy aspires to gain about the matters it studies entails that philosophy is, by intent even if not as yet fully in fact, a science, and that it must therefore proceed in essentials like any other science; that is, by searching in a certain manner, called Scientific Method, for the answers to questions of certain kinds, which we may call Epistemic or Scientific Questions, asked about the facts it is interested in.

The general method of inquiry, called scientific, is so in the etymological and broad sense of the word, namely, *knowledge-yielding.* It is the kind of method which automatically confers on the answers it yields the status of *probable knowledge* as contrasted with that of guesses, dogmas, or inadequately grounded opinions. The general nature of the methodological precautions which, for each of the several kinds of scientific questions, insure that result irrespective of the particular kind of subject matter concerned, is familiar to all students of scientific method and need not be recited.

The questions here referred to as scientific are so in the sense of *science-fashioning* or *science-constructing;* that is, the answering of them furnishes and organizes the content of the sort of human creation called a science. Some of them are as to what likenesses and differences are observable among the observable facts included in the initial subject matter of the particular science concerned; others are as to the connections detectable among them; others call for inductive generalization of regularities observed, or of the results of experiments. Others yet call for the framing of theories capable both of accounting for the empirical laws inductively detected, and of predicting other laws not yet detected. Others demand that the investigator test the theories in respect to these capacities. And, throughout, it is demanded that observations, experiments, inferences, hypotheses, and procedures, shall be formulated in language precise enough and otherwise adapted to communicate them to other investigators who may wish to repeat or verify them.

Now, the fact that what philosophy seeks is knowledge and indeed systematically organized knowledge means that the questions it attempts to answer about the facts constituting its subject matter are of the same logical forms, just described, as those which any science raises concerning the facts it studies. And it means also that the method of inquiry philosophy shall employ to answer its questions must be as genuinely scientific as that of any other science; for notwithstanding the claims sometimes made for "intuition" or for "revelation," evidence is still lacking that knowledge, as distinguished from merely belief, can ultimately be gained — whether about nature or about man's relation to the universe — otherwise than through the forms of procedure which, together, constitute scientific method.

But of course, that philosophy shall acknowledge and heed as well as it can the obligation to conduct its search for knowledge in a manner scientific in the sense stated above does not mean that philosophy must or can use the same *specific* forms scientific method takes in this or that particular science. Just as the concrete methods of investigation in, say, biology, are different from those in mathematics, and yet the methods of each are nonetheless scientific in the generic sense described above, so must the methods of philosophy too be scientific in that generic sense, and at the same time take concrete forms specific to the nature of its own subject matter.

3. Defects of Method in Philosophical Inquiries

The defects of procedure which have rendered futile much of what philosophers have said appear traceable in the main to two sources.

One of these is the tacit assumption which has unfortunately been widespread, that in philosophy, even if in no other branch of systematic inquiry, it is possible to reach knowledge through thinking carried on in the vague terms of ordinary language, that is, without bothering to use a technical apparatus of thought. But the truth is that as soon as inquiry, whether in philosophy or elsewhere, comes to questions more difficult than those which everyday experience or casual reflection is able to answer, a technical terminology becomes a *sine qua non* of fruitful thinking. For a technical term is simply a term whose meaning is known exactly enough for scientific purposes; and hence, not to bother to use technical terms is simply not to bother to think exactly enough for such purposes. These make on the language employed to serve them two demands. One is that it be precise enough for *communication;* that is, precise enough to enable any person having the relevant mental or other equipment to identify the subjects of our assertions and to understand what it is we assert about these subjects, so that, by scrutinizing the subject of any one of them, he may test for himself the truth or probability of what we are asserting about it. The other demand is that the language be precise enough to permit drawing remote yet definite *inferences* from the assertions it is employed to make. One can easily imagine how far chemistry or geometry would *not* have progressed if chemists had not bothered to use more exact conceptions of "alcohol," "acid," or "ether"; or mathematicians, of "points," "planes," or "circles," than the vague conceptions those words stand for in ordinary language. The situation of philosophy is no different. Unpopular as a plea for technical language in philosophy is sure to be today, the fact must be faced that at the point where one ceases to be superficial, there technical language, far from making for unintelligibility, is on the contrary the only means of being intelligible and of making dependable inferences.

Technical terms, however, must not be confused with jargon terms. A jargon term is not necessarily precise. It is merely one which is not understood by most persons because it designates things with which only a comparatively few persons occupy themselves. Thus, every trade, art, and craft, as well as every science, has its own jargon. But the jargon terms of the sciences — unlike most of those of the trades or the crafts — get defined exactly; and therefore, in addition to being esoteric like the latter, they become technical. On the other hand, even terms in common use — such as *alcohol, acid,* and *circle;* or in philosophy, *property, truth, substance, proposition,* and so on — become technical terms as soon as their meaning is stated exactly.

4. Need for Empirical Verification of Philosophical Hypotheses

Philosophers, it is true, have sometimes defined their terms, and sometimes, although more rarely, have defined them with some precision. This brings us to the second of the two sources of defective method in philosophy alluded to above. It is that to specify exactly the meaning of a term is not enough to insure that it will be an effective implement for the winning of knowledge. For this, what is needed besides is that its meaning shall not be assigned arbitrarily, but shall represent characters which there is reason to believe are possessed by the things the term is used to think about. Such definitions — called "real" as contrasted with "nominal" or "shorthand" definitions — are actually inductions, more or less probable. Their validity can be tested by comparing the implications they are discovered to have with the characters which the things they are used to think about can be discovered empirically to have or lack.

Unfortunately, the definitions offered by philosophers have often failed to satisfy this capital requirement. Then they have in truth been arbitrary and have represented only new ways of using familiar words, not new hypotheses as to the nature of familiar things. Being responsible to no empirical roots, they have not been capable of empirical testing, but only of testing in respect to internal consistency and to consistency with other equally arbitrary definitions — the whole conceptual system so created, however, no matter how thoroughly coherent internally, hanging yet in the air for lack of empirical verifiability. The chief reason for this state of affairs, I believe, is that philosophers have often not realized clearly enough the nature of the facts their definitions were obligated to fit. For although these facts were no less empirical and accessible to observation than those of the natural sciences, they were nevertheless of a different kind, easy to overlook. Their nature will be described farther on, and illustrated in some detail in the next chapter.

5.   Two Maxims of Scientific Method in Philosophy

The point of central importance in this connection is that every genuine problem has data, that is, facts not themselves then questioned, about which the problem is, and by reference to which any proposed solution of it can be empirically tested. And since in philosophy what these facts are is often not very obvious, one of the basic maxims of knowledge-yielding method in philosophy is that, when a question is to be investigated, one should not only *ask oneself just which then unquestioned facts the question is about,* but also *state them explicitly.* Actually, however, they are too often merely alluded to, as if oneself and everybody else already understood quite well what they are.

The procedure just suggested will not only make clear the way to test empirically any hypothesis made about those facts, but will also greatly facilitate compliance with a second, equally important methodological maxim. It is that one should again not be content merely to name or allude to the question which is to be answered about the facts one has listed, but that *the question too should be stated as explicitly and unambiguously as possible.* Observance of these two maxims will automatically lead one to distinguish, and to treat separately, each of the several questions one's initial vague statement of a problem may unawares have been propounding all at once. This will not only clear away such difficulties as vagueness breeds, but will also be of positive help in solving the questions one isolates; for sharp formulation of a question is one of the most fertile sources of ideas as to possible answers.

These two maxims, however, are not so easy to comply with in philosophy that they need for this only to have been accepted. The concrete nature of the method they define, as well as the power this method may possess to solve the philosophical problems to which it is applied, can be made fully clear only by examples. Throughout the chapters which follow I shall therefore strive not only to meet as well as I can the demands of scientific method for precision of statement and logical cogency in argument, but also to obey where they are relevant — and thus illustrate the use of — the maxims that, as I see it, define the particular form which the empirical testing of hypotheses takes in philosophy.

Chapter 2

THE PROBLEMS OF ANY SCIENCE

It was premised earlier that philosophy is a search for knowledge, properly so called, as to certain questions, and that the knowledge it seeks is no less capable of attainment by man than is the knowledge sought by the natural or the formal sciences. This implies that philosophy attempts to be, and can become, itself genuinely a science. Before we ask what then specifically differentiates it from the natural, the formal, and the social sciences, it will be well for us to consider the logical movement and the terminal structure which appear to characterize any science, and which, therefore, we may expect to be also those of philosophy.

1. The Logical Movement and Structure of a Science

A science begins with the empirical scrutiny of its initial — or, as we may call them, primitive — data, and with the search, among their relations to one another, for functional relations, *i.e.*, relations of dependence. The specific nature of the dependence differs in different sciences. It may be mechanical, physiological, mathematical, psychological, semantical, or of some other kind. Such relations are discovered by observations made under conditions that are controlled or otherwise known; that is by *observation under experimental conditions*. Observation so made reveals what follows from what — what follows, as the case may be, mechanically, or physiologically, or mathematically, or psychologically, or logically, or in some other manner. This means, of course, that there are such things as mathematical experiments, thought experiments, psychological experiments, and so on, as well as physical, chemical, biological, and other material experiments.

Next, or rather together with observation and experimentation and indeed throughout, goes *formulation* of what is observed, discovered or supposed, in language unambiguous enough and otherwise appropriate for the two purposes mentioned earlier, *viz.,* communication and inference. Mathematical language, where it can be used, is adequate to these two purposes; and the particular manner of translating observations into it, which insures that it will actually serve them, is *measurement.* But even in the natural or the formal sciences, scientific language does not consist exclusively of mathematical symbols. It includes also "technical" terms — a technical term, let us repeat, being a term whose meaning has been stated with enough precision for those same two purposes. Thus, mathematical language, although of vast importance wherever measurement is possible and relevant, constitutes only one region of scientific language. Hence, that measurement is not possible or not relevant where facts of certain kinds are concerned does not in itself entail that those facts are incapable of being formulated in a manner adequate for scientific purposes.

The next stage, after observation and experiment, is *empirical generalization* of what has been observed. This yields empirical laws. Then comes *speculation,* that is, the making of explanatory hypotheses — empirical ones to explain particular facts observed, and especially theoretical ones making it possible to account for the empirical laws already discovered, to correct them, to define the limits of their validity, and to predict other empirically verifiable laws not yet discovered. At this stage, concrete observations enter again, but now for the purpose of testing the predictions deduced from the theories, and of thus checking the validity of the theories. In proportion as a science develops, the theoretical part of it becomes more prominent and the empirical part less — concrete observations serving more and more to test theories and less to provide material for empirical generalizations.

There is another process, however — seldom mentioned in discussions of scientific inquiry — which is the converse of generalization of particulars. It is *particularization of the general* — application of general knowledge, which is knowledge of laws, in such manner as to reach concerning some particular matter knowledge that could not have been reached by direct observation. An example from the field of natural science would be the knowledge as to the shape of the earth which the laws of physics, together with certain direct observations of the earth, give us. This, let it be noted, constitutes *heuristic* application — application of laws already discovered to the *gaining of new knowledge,* not to the guidance of action that aims at bending nature to our purposes or at protecting us from its ruthlessness.

Application of knowledge to the guidance of action is what ordinarily is meant by "practical" application. Knowledge as to the means effective to a given end or as to the results achievable with given means is practical or engineering knowledge. It acts as liaison between concrete tasks that we do not already know how to perform, and "fundamental" or theoretical knowledge, which may in a recondite manner be very relevant to the question as to how such tasks can be performed, but which usually was sought and gained quite without reference to any practical applications it might turn out to have. The word "engineering," however, must in the present connection be taken in the broad sense, which would enable us to speak of medicine, for example, as a branch of engineering, and to say that for any main field of scientific inquiry there can be a corresponding body of engineering knowledge resting upon it.

The preceding remarks as to the stages in the development of a science mean that the knowledge it wins tends eventually to take on the form of what logicians call a deductive system. But the postulates of the system are not there arbitrary, as they can be in a logical exercise. They are not the data of the system, but on the contrary are so selected, and if need be so modified, as to fit the data to be systematized. Systematic inquiry thus turns out to have both a theoretical and an empirical part, no matter whether the primitive facts of the field studied happen to be material, or psychical, or, as in mathematics, conceptual facts created by stipulations, or, as in philosophy, facts of the kind to be described farther on.

The appearance of anarchy which often exists in philosophy is due in no small measure, I believe, to a failure to realize that the over-all structure just described will also be that of scientifically mature and developed philosophy. Hence the specific place occupied and role played, in the philosophical enterprise as a whole, by the particular inquiries which engross this or that individual philosopher, often are not discerned. Instrumentalists, for example, are so deeply interested in philosophical engineering that they are prone to mistake it for philosophy itself. Again, ethical theorists seldom betray much awareness of the nature and function of theory in ethics.[1] But the perspective provided by an adequate view of the subject matter, the functions, the over-all structure, and the parts, of the philosophical enterprise is capable of removing many misunderstandings. It suggests, for instance, that some of the things some sociologists nowadays have to say about ethics — and would substitute as "scientific" for the "barren theorizing" of moral philosophers — are relevant to certain of the problems of philosophy and belong to the empirical region of its over-all undertaking; and yet that these things do not in any way dispose of the need for theoretical interpretation, which

---

[1] Cf. the writer's "The Nature and Function of Theory in Ethics," *Ethics*, Vol. LI, No. 1, October, 1940.

those sociologists ignore. On the other hand, a broad perspective also suggests that, in the performance of this interpretive task, ethical theorists have too much limited their material to the empirical generalizations reached long ago in their own social group — which generalizations, perhaps, are valid only under circumstances such as existed there in the past but do not now, and perhaps did not or do not exist in other groups.

2. What Constitutes the Subject Matter of a Science?

If the method of inquiry must be as genuinely scientific in philosophy as in the other sciences, what differentiates philosophy from them can only be a subject matter specifically its own. As we face the difficult task of defining it, the second of the two maxims of method stated above — which are relevant to the philosophy of philosophy no less than to other branches of philosophy — directs us at the outset to ask what, in general, is to be understood by the "subject matter" of a science.

We could say, of course, that it consists of the problems which that science alone proposes to investigate. But a complete list of them would be endless, and no partial list would enable us to decide in all cases whether a given problem does or does not belong to that science. What we need is therefore some general feature that defines directly or by implication the whole class of problems with which that science and no other occupies itself.

It may be objected, of course, that the line between one science and another is, at least in some cases, arbitrary — for example, between physics and chemistry. Yet there are some problems one would unhesitatingly call problems of physics not of chemistry, and others problems of chemistry not of physics. A line is therefore actually drawn between them somewhere, and, no matter where, the question remains before us, in what kind of terms is it drawn, or redrawn when this is desired.

To discern the answer several things have to be kept in mind.

The first is that every genuine problem has both a datum and a dubitatum, and that no problem is adequately stated unless both are explicitly mentioned. The datum consists of something *about which* the problem is, and which is "given" in the sense that its factuality is not in question at the moment but is either known, supposed, or postulated. The dubitatum, on the other hand, consists of *what is in question* about the datum. The dubitatum may be whether a *stated conjecture* about the datum is true; or it may be which one, out of all possible conjectures of a certain range, is the one true of the datum; (for instance *where* in particular a given kind of thing exists, or *what weight* a given thing has, etc.).

In the first case, the problem is one of *proof-disproof* and its dubitatum is more specifically a *probandum* (*probare*: to test, to try). In the second case, the problem is one of *discovery*, and its dubitatum more specifically a *quaesitum* (*quaere*: to seek, search for). In empirical investigations, however, problems of discovery are solved by trial and error, *i.e.*, by testing in turn a number of conjectures, until one is found that turns out true. Problems of proof-disproof are therefore the ones methodologically basic there.

Now, what differentiates the problems of one science from those of other sciences cannot be the general form of their dubitata, for in all sciences the questions asked about the facts concerned are of the same general forms we described earlier and proposed to call Epistemic or Scientific Questions. Evidently, therefore, the "subject matter" which differentiates one science from another must consist ultimately of facts of some particular kind, as to the epistemic relations of which to one another the given science and no other proposes to occupy itself.

But when we try to state what kind of facts these are for a given science, we are likely to find the question extraordinarily difficult to answer — indeed, impossible until we awake to the necessity of making two distinctions: One, between the problems *for* and the problems *of* a science; and the other, between the primitive and the derivative facts of the science.

3. Problems "for" and Problems "of" a Science

The problems *for* a given science are practical problems that happen not to be soluble without knowledge more recondite, exact, and systematic than ordinary experience or "on the job" reflection provide. We may call such problems the *practical* or the *technological* (*i.e.,* the engineering) or *casuistical* problems pertaining to a given science. They comprise not only problems of this kind that have actually arisen, but also any other practical problems that would be problems for that particular science, no matter whether or not they ever actually arise.

The problems *of* a science, on the other hand, are problems that are implicit in the practical problems for it, in the sense that the possibility of solving the latter depends on prior solution of the former. The problems *of* a science may be contrasted with the problems *for* it as *technical* (vs. technological or engineering problems), or as *theoretical* or *epistemic* or *scientific* (vs. practical or casuistical). They are of the kinds formulated in questions of the kind we proposed to call Epistemic or Scientific Questions. But the term "practical" currently has several meanings, seldom clearly distinguished, and we must therefore state next which of them is the one intended here.

4. What Is a "Practical" Problem?

There appear to be four principal senses in which the adjective "practical" is commonly used.

(*a*) Sometimes it is applied to something considered qua means to some specified end. It is then synonymous with "effective," "efficacious," *i.e.,* "capable of causing." Thus, to speak of some mode of procedure as practical is to say that in the existing circumstances employment of it is capable of causing the effects one desires to cause. A means — whether it be a recipe, a form of action, or an instrument — is therefore never practical or impractical *simpliciter,* but always practical or impractical *in given circumstances* and *to some specific end* (which may be of any kind).

(*b*) Sometimes the adjective "practical" is applied to something considered as an end or task which one might attempt *with given means.* The adjective then signifies that, with the given means, attainment of that end — performance of that task — is *practicable.* In loose, not strictly correct usage, "practical" is occasionally employed in this sense.

(*c*) When, on the other hand, one speaks of practical affairs, "practical" then commonly means *important,* directly or indirectly, for *biological purposes* — important for safety, life, health, reproduction, animal comfort, and the like. The persons called practical are then those motivated or assumed to be motivated directly or indirectly by such purposes; whereas unpractical or non-practical persons are those who disregard such biological utility or disutility as their pursuits may have. Thus, it would be called unpractical, or non-practical, to seek, *for their own sakes, i.e.,* irrespective of their possible direct or indirect bearings on health, welfare, safety, life, and the like, such things as sensuous enjoyment, esthetic pleasure, romantic adventures, religious experiences, or the satisfaction of curiosity, pride, greed, envy, ambition, loyalty, love, hatred, or other passions. The pursuing of such things for their own sakes would be termed *sentimental* as opposed to practical.

(*d*) There is, however, another and very common sense of "practical," which cuts across the distinctions just analyzed. It is the sense in which "practical" is opposed to "theoretical," "academic," "speculative," and the like. A problem is practical in this sense if it is a problem *as to means or ends, viz.,* a problem as to means to a given end ("how to do it"), or as to results attainable with given means ("what can be done with it"). One not practical in this sense, *viz.,* any problem as to something *other than* means or ends, we shall call a *mathetic* problem (μάθεσις learning, information, the act of learning, desire to learn) ; or more specifically, a *scientific, i.e.,* a science-making, problem, if the information sought is more technical than ordinary observation would yield.

It is true that the problems "of" a science — even the most abstrusely theoretical of them — have practical import actually or potentially, since they are implicit in the problems "for" it, which are practical, and which, let us here repeat and emphasize, include not only those which actually arise but also any that might conceivably arise. That is, there is no theoretical difference that could not make some kind of practical difference — that would not have bearing on some kind of problem, perhaps outlandish, as to means or ends. But even when this is fully granted, it does not follow that a person's *motive* for inquiring into a given theoretical question is desire to answer some practical question in which the former happens to be implicit. The logical relation between the two questions does not entail a parallel psychological relation between motives. To believe that it does would be as naive as to believe that a stout woman's motive for eating candy is desire to gain weight!

The fact is that the practical bearings of many of the problems to which scientific investigators address themselves are at the time and often remain quite unknown. The motivation for inquiry into those problems is therefore not that some practical problem is calling for solution of them, nor, as a matter of psychological fact, is it usually even the hope or belief that solution of them will somehow have practical value. The truth is that sheer curiosity — *philomathy,* the passion to know — is the typical scientific motive, even if it is not the only motive that actuates scientists. It is, moreover, probably the only motive capable of accounting for the enormous labor often devoted to scientific and scholarly problems extremely remote, or *prima facie* totally divorced, from any then existing practical problems. How strong a motive in itself is curiosity or challenge to ingenuity is shown by the widespread fascination of riddles, cross-word puzzles, conundrums, enigmas, and other equally gratuitous brain teasers. That curiosity exists and is often free — idle, without practical aim — and yet great, is a fact; and this, irrespective of the possible other fact that it is nonetheless so useful a trait in the long run that animals lacking it at certain stages of evolution disappeared, and that this is why man still possesses it today.

But the actual or potential practical utility of scientific research is nowise diminished by the fact that, in probably most cases, this utility is not what motivates the research. From the standpoint of practical utility of its results any other motive that actually gets the research done is just as good, or, if more powerful, better — whether it be sheer curiosity, scientific utility as distinguished from practical, desire for professional advancement, ambition for fame, or anything else. The mathematician, G. H. Hardy, in his discussion of the motives that actually lead men to prosecute scientific research, puts first "intellectual curiosity, desire to know the truth," adding that without it the others must come to nothing. Next, he puts "professional pride, anxiety to be satisfied with one's performance, the shame that overcomes any self-respecting craftsman when his work is unworthy of his talent." In the third place, he lists "ambition, desire for reputation, and the position, even the power or the money, which it brings."[2]

It is probable that in some men the altruistic desire to benefit humanity is no less real and potent, or is more so, than the egoistic motives Hardy lists in the third place. Also, the fact is not to be denied that engineering problems often initiate fundamental research. But, in putting intellectual curiosity first, Hardy is surely right both because without it other motives would as he says be

---

[2] Hardy, *A Mathematician's Apology,* Cambridge University Press, 1940, p. 19.

barren, and because, no matter what personal or humanistic practical motive may initiate a piece of research, it is above all curiosity — the sheer desire to know and understand — which then carries it forward.

Now, we embarked on the preceding analysis of the various senses of "practical" in order to make clear what exactly was meant when it was stated earlier that the problems *for* a science were practical problems that could not be solved without the aid of the special and recondite sort of knowledge that the science alone provides. We can now say that the problems that are problems *for* a science are practical in the twofold sense that: (1) they are problems *as to means or as to ends* (sense *d*) ; and (2) *the end concerned is itself practical in the sense of not scientific, i.e.,* it is not to solve any of the technical problems of the science concerned.[3]

Within a science, however, some problems arise which are both practical in that they concern means or ends, and scientific in that the end concerned is not as above a practical end, but is scientific, *i.e.,* is to solve some one of the technical problems of the science. The differences we have pointed out between the several senses of "practical" thus enable us to distinguish between *scientific utility* and *practical utility;* for example, between knowledge the gaining of which is sought as a means to the gaining of more knowledge, and which therefore has scientific utility; and knowledge the gaining of which is sought as a means to things quite other than increase of knowledge. The utility of such knowledge is practical, not scientific. To keep in mind the distinctions between the various senses of "practical" unfortunately requires

---

[3] Some problems are *questions* and others are simply *tasks.* A problem is a question when it is a call for knowledge, to replace an existing doubt — whether the knowledge called for be practical or mathetic. A problem is simply a task, on the other hand, when the knowledge necessary to solve it is already possessed, and what is called for is only *exertion, work.* Since the function of the engineer, as such, is not to perform the work — say of building a bridge — but to plan it and direct the workmen who perform it, the "practical problems" referred to in these pages are practical *questions* — *doubts* as to "how to do it" or "what it can do."

a certain effort. But to make it is the only way of avoiding the confusions which too often have infested discussions of pragmatism and the practical. As D. C. Williams has pointed out, the notion "that whereas it is right and salutary for a little subject, like the genetics of the fruitfly, to be technical and difficult, the biggest subject, philosophy, must fit loosely and easily the tastes of the tyro" is "a disastrous misconception."[4]

5. Two Possible Confusions

Two confusions, which seem to have often haunted discussions of pragmatism, need to be guarded against in the present connection.

One of them is between the *process* itself of inquiry and the *problem* inquiry attempts to solve. The process called inquiry or investigation is of course always engaged in as a means to an end — to the end, namely, of solving some problem. Inquiry is, indeed, a problem-solving process. But the problem inquiry is the means to solve need not in the least be itself a problem as to means to a given end or as to ends attainable with given means. It is therefore essential always to distinguish between the *problem to be solved,* for example, "how many satellites has Jupiter," and the *problem of solving it,* namely, "how one finds out." The distinction remains, irrespective of whether one proposes to employ the knowledge sought (as to the number of satellites) as a means to some ulterior end, or of whether one seeks it out of mere curiosity.

The second confusion to be guarded against is that between the possible utility of the fruits of an inquiry and the motivation for engaging in the inquiry. The latter need not in the least consist of the potential or foreseen utility of those fruits.

Of course, since the problems "for" a given science are prac-

---

4 D. C. Williams, "Mr. John Dewey on Problems and Men," *Harvard Educational Review,* Vol. 16, No. 4, Fall, 1946.

tical problems that cannot be solved without specialized and more or less recondite knowledge, their occurrence calls for an attempt to gain such knowledge, *i.e.*, for an attempt to create the relevant science if it does not already exist. Such practical problems thus are the motivators of scientific research in so far as it is practically motivated. Geometry, I believe, did arise in this way. (But the science of electricity did not.) Moreover, that scientific research makes possible the solving of certain practical problems is the justification of that research in so far as its justification is of the practical sort. We can say, then, that the practical function of a science is to *provide* the theoretical knowledge which alone makes it possible to solve the practical problems that are problems "for" that science. On the other hand, to *apply* this knowledge is the function of the particular branch of *engineering* based on the given science — to "apply" that knowledge meaning to reveal by means of it in concrete cases of given kinds the course of action that will be effective to a given end, or the results that will follow from a given course of action.

But to say that scientific research provides knowledge without which certain practical problems cannot be solved does not at all imply that to make solution of these possible is the purpose which actually motivates a scientific investigator. Neither the motivation nor the justification of a piece of research need be only, or at all, of a practical kind — whether practical in the narrow biological sense (*c*), or in the broader sense (*d*), which excludes from practical aims only that of merely satisfying curiosity.

6. "Subject Matter" Ultimately Defined in Terms of the Primitive Facts of a Science

We come now to the second of the two distinctions mentioned earlier as necessary for discernment of what constitutes the "subject matter" distinctive of a given science. It is the distinction between the *primitive* and the *derivative* facts of a science.

Among the facts of a given science, some are directly observable, whereas others are discoverable only by means of inferences, sometimes very recondite, from those directly observed. Those which are directly observable may be called the *primitive* or *initial* or *empirically basic* facts of the given science; and those facts of it arrived at by inferences from these may be called its *derivative* facts. The latter are more technical, abstract, and therefore esoteric than the primitive facts; and, as the science concerned develops, they become more and more prominent and, because of their explanatory and predictive power, more and more important. It is therefore easy to come to think that these abstract theoretical facts constitute the real subject matter of the science. But it is essential to remember that they represent inductions from or theoretical interpretations of the homelier, directly observed, initial and differentiating facts of the science. Its derivative facts therefore belong to it and are facts at all, only because they are implicit analytically or synthetically in the homely, directly observable, primitive facts of the given science.

Accordingly, although most of the statements formulating the discoveries of a developed science do not explicitly mention those directly observable facts at all, nevertheless *the latter are what constitute the "subject matter" which ultimately differentiates a given science from all others.*

Chapter 3

THE PRACTICAL PROBLEMS OF PHILOSOPHY

Let us now return to philosophy and, in the light of the distinctions we have made, see whether we can discern what exactly differentiates it from the other sciences.

1. What Kind of Practical Problems Are Problems for Philosophy?

The distinction between practical and theoretical problems applies in the case of philosophy as in any other, and the question with which we must begin is that of the kind of practical problems for the solving of which philosophical reflection is required.

They are problems that have three characteristics. First, like all other practical problems, they are as to means or as to ends; but whereas the practical problems to which the natural sciences are relevant are simply as to what means would be adequate to a given end, or as to what ends would be attainable with given means, the practical problems for which philosophical reflection is needed are as to the *value* — the goodness or badness of one kind or another — of a means sufficient to a given end or of an end attainable with given means; or of such a means or end as compared with alternative ones. These problems thus are, or involve the question, as to whether a proposed sufficient means ought to be employed or whether a proposed attainable end ought to be pursued — either at all or in preference to other likewise sufficient means or attainable ends.

The second characteristic is that in these problems the doubt does not arise from ignorance or misinformation as to the nature

of a proposed means or of a proposed end, but is doubt directly
and solely as to value; and the third characteristic of those problems is that common wisdom — wisdom already possessed — is
not sufficient to solve them.

But differentiation, thus in terms of "ought" or of what is
"good" or "best," of the practical problems to which philosophy
is relevant must not be understood to mean that they concern
only, or especially, matters of moral obligation or moral value.
The kind of obligation and of value concerned in a given case
may instead be esthetic, or logical, or sentimental, or economic,
or any other.

Further, the appraisals as good or bad or better or worse in
some sense, between which one hesitates in a given case, may be
appraisals of one's own; or one of them may be one's own and
its rival that made by another person; or both appraisals may be
by other persons, with oneself only as interested spectator. And
one's doubt may be more specifically as to whether what is
appraised has value of a stated kind V, or the opposite (*e.g.,* as
to whether a given act is moral or immoral, or perhaps a given
inference cogent or fallacious, etc.) ; or the doubt may be as to
the relevance — the congruousness — of a given type of appraisal
to the kind of thing of which an instance is being appraised (*e.g.,*
as to whether a murder can congruously be appraised as expedient) ; or the doubt may concern the relative importance of the
several types of value possessed or lacked by the thing appraised
(*e.g.,* whether the esthetic value of a church ceremony is more
important, or less, than its religious value).

2. Spontaneous Resort to Philosophical Reflection

The point to notice, however, is that if a person, even one not
otherwise curious about philosophical issues, is faced with a
conflict of appraisals and he proposes to deal with it rationally,
then philosophical reflection, whether he recognizes it as being

such or not, is the process by which he spontaneously attempts to settle the conflict. It is philosophical reflection, at least, in all cases where, as specified above, the doubt is not due to factual misinformation or ignorance about the concrete, individual means or end appraised. For if the doubt is due to this, it is then not philosophical and is to be settled not by philosophical reflection, but by informing oneself as to the true characters of what, under a misapprehension of its actual nature, was being appraised. If, for example, one comes to doubt that a certain law recently enacted is good, and one's doubt is due to ignorance or misinformation as to the provisions of that law, then what the doubt calls for is not philosophical reflection (as to what constitutes goodness or badness in a law) but information as to what the provisions of the law in fact are.

Philosophical reflection, evidently, is not engaged in only by philosophers, but is something almost every person spontaneously resorts to on certain occasions, even if he usually is unaware that his reflections at those times are philosophical in nature. But evidently also, the philosophy which brief and unsystematic reflection improvises on the spur of those occasions is unavoidably fragmentary, and more or less vague, superficial, uncritical, and therefore precarious.

3. Examples of Practical Problems "for" Philosophy

That there exist problems as to how one ought or ought not to proceed or as to what one ought or ought not to aim at that cannot be dealt with rationally without the kind of light philosophical reflection provides may be made evident by citation of a few concrete examples.

Recently in the writer's hearing a parent expressed doubt as to whether he ought to keep sending his child to a certain public school of the so-called "progressive" type, or ought to send him instead to a certain other school run by a religious denomination different from his own — these two schools being the only ones whose locations made it practicable for the child to attend. Evidently, the doubt could have been *de facto* removed in any one of several ways. For example, *emotionally,* as a result of hearing that at one of the two schools a certain procedure is followed of a kind the parent finds particularly offensive, or, as the case might be, particularly admirable. Or again, the doubt could have been removed *experimentally* by sending the child to one of the two schools chosen at hazard and observing the eventual results. This is the method of trial and blunder, which yields wisdom only after the occasion that called for it has passed, and thus, unless one made a lucky guess, only after one has already paid the price of lack of wisdom.

But if, as actually was the case, the parent knew what went on in each school his doubt might instead have been removed *rationally;* that is, by reflection on questions such as: What is education? What are the chief values of education? What manner of conducting it is most likely to attain best those values? What is religion? What positive and negative values does it have? How do these compare in importance with those of secular education? How important are denominational differences? and so on. Evidently, a set of coherent answers to these and allied questions would constitute a philosophy of education and a philosophy of religion.

Another example of a practical problem for the rational solution of which philosophical reflection is necessary would be that of a group of starving shipwrecked persons, one of whom gets killed in an accident. The practical question then arises for the survivors as to whether they ought or ought not to eat his body. Evidently, any *reasons* advanced on either side of the question are fragments, or embryos, of a philosophy of ethical or perhaps of religious conduct.

Again, let us suppose that a conflict of opinion arises between

John and James as to whether a certain means M ought or ought not to be employed to bring about a certain reform which both of them desire. And let us suppose further that John opposes employment of the means M — which both he and James agree would be effective — on the ground that this would be immoral, whereas James denies that it would be so. The problem in such a case is to resolve the conflict in a rational rather than an arbitrary manner; that is, by appeal to reasons both will acknowledge as relevant and sufficient. On such an occasion, each will spontaneously offer whatever reasons occur to him as supporting his opinion; and, let it be noticed again, any such reason automatically constitutes the embryo, or a fragment, of a philosophical theory — here, specifically, of an ethical theory. But, as already pointed out, any theory thus pulled out of the air under the spur of practical conflict is bound to be more or less partial, superficial, and uncritical, and therefore open to the criticisms which John and James at once each make of the other's improvised reasons.

Obviously, the need is for a philosophy — in this case, a philosophy of morality — that shall already have considered those reasons and taken into account the criticisms to which they are open, and that shall therefore be not only coherent internally, but coherent also with the relevant facts John and James both accept; coherent, namely, with whatever *other* concrete judgments of morality and immorality both of them agree in. Such a theory cannot be extemporized at the moment's need. To construct it, what is required is the long, painstaking, and critical sort of reflection which technical philosophy gives to the attempt.

4. The Major and Minor Branches of Philosophy

These examples show how the philosophy of education, the philosophy of religion, and the philosophy of morality, are related each to the solving in a rational manner of certain practical problems. Also, they furnish occasion to remark that there is no

such thing as philosophy *in vacuo,* but only the philosophy of this
or that subject, which subject may be of any degree of generality
or specificity.   Thus besides the philosophy of education, of
religion, and of morality, there is also the philosophy of art, the
philosophy of science, the philosophy of play, and so on.   But
there is also the philosophy of shoe-making, of the cosmetic art,
of tennis-playing, etc., since in each of these activities, there occur
questions of "ought" — of what in one sense or another is "right"
or "wrong."   At the pole of greatest generality, on the other hand,
we have such disciplines as the philosophy of reality, the philosophy of knowledge, the philosophy of language, the philosophy
of value — metaphysics, epistemology, semeiology, axiology —
and also the philosophy of philosophy, *i.e.,* metaphilosophy, which
is what in this chapter we are engaged in.   The problems pertaining to these branches of philosophy are the most general
philosophical problems, hence universal; that is, they are implicit,
however subtly, in the problems of the philosophies of even the
most highly specific subjects, and therefore have some bearing on
those problems.

5.   The Practical Function of Theory Essentially the Same in Philosophy as Elsewhere

The theories that constitute a philosophy — whether a philosophy of religion, of art, of morality, or of anything else — are
of course speculative inventions; but they are inventions that
purport to be, or to be capable of providing, *true* answers to
certain questions, and whose claim to be therefore *discoveries* is
to be tested, like other claims of truth, not only in respect to
internal coherence, but also by reference to the relevant sort
of facts.

But in this respect the case of philosophical theories, and that
of physical, or biological, or mathematical or other scientific
theories, is exactly alike.   And in all fields *theory* — empirically

confirmed theory, of course, not irresponsible speculation — is the only thing that furnishes a basis for rational solution of practical problems not rationally soluble on the basis of everyday experience or "on the job" ingenuity.

It is true that, theoretically, theories are only probable in various degrees; and therefore that, theoretically, they are always at the mercy of future experience. This fact, however, is no justification for the dogma that all problems, or even all practical problems, are to be solved "experimentally" as opposed to "rationalistically." For if "experimentally" or "empirically" mean anything as opposed to "rationalistically" or "deductively from theory," what they then mean is by the process of blind trial and error. But the occasions where this costly process is our only recourse are, alas, numerous enough without our allowing partial truths erected into catchwords to mislead us into using it where we need not. There is nothing to be gained by ignoring the solid difference between, on the one hand, the *testing* empirically of a new theory; and on the other, the *applying* deductively of an already tested theory to the solving of new particular problems that are of old kinds which the theory has already been shown capable of dealing with. Unfortunately, the maxim "learn by doing" seems too often interpreted in practice by those who voice it as implying that there is no difference between the two, and as meaning that the best way or the only possible way to learn how to solve one's practical problems is by trial and error on the job. As Franklin remarked long ago, "experience keeps a dear school."

6. Philosophy and Wisdom

It may be pointed out here that the preceding account of the relation of philosophy to practical problems of the kind described and illustrated accords exactly with the etymological meaning of the word "philosophy" as love of or search for wisdom. For to know what ought to be done or aimed at — that is, what would be best — when one faces given alternatives, is precisely what constitutes *wisdom*. Thus, philosophical reflection, considered in respect to its practical applications, has for its function to make clear which decision would be the wise one in any case where wisdom of the home-grown, limited kind finds itself in doubt and where the doubt is due not to ignorance of objective facts but to conflict of evaluations.

The task of philosophical reflection as distinguished from philosophical counsel is therefore to *obtain* the kind of knowledge which, in addition to knowledge of causes and effects, is necessary as basis for wise counsel in situations of unfamiliar kinds. Such knowledge is *philosophical knowledge*. It consists of the solutions, so far as attained, of the theoretical problems of philosophy. And *philosophical research* is the methodical search for such knowledge. On the other hand, *philosophical engineering*, or as we may also call it, *philosophical casuistics*, has for its task the practical interpretation of that knowledge — the *application* of it to the relevant practical problems.[1] This consists in the formulation of counsels based on that knowledge (as well as on general knowledge of causes and effects) — counsels as to what ought or ought not to be done or aimed at in given cases. Concrete *action* under the guidance of such counsels is yet another thing. It is the analogue of the action of the workman who builds according to the directions of the engineer. In either case, of course, the person who as engineer dictates what ought to be done may be also the person that actually does it or attempts to do it; and he may conceivably also have been the person who as pure researcher discovered the fundamental theoretical facts, knowledge of which enabled him as engineer to decide what procedures would be

---

[1] I use the word "casuistics" rather than "casuistry" because of the depreciatory connotation the latter has acquired. Philosophical casuistics, although not to be confused with philosophical inquiry, and dependent upon its results, has great practical importance. Indeed, without casuistics, as practical interpretation of the results of theoretical inquiry, the latter would have no *practical* importance.

effective to the results desired. Usually, however, these several functions are performed each by a different person.

7. "Problems of Men" and "Problems of Philosophers"

The problems which in the sense we stated are problems "for" philosophy, and which we contrasted with the problems "of" philosophy, are apparently those called "problems of men" by Professor Dewey and contrasted by him with "problems of philosophers" — these being the technical problems of "vain metaphysics and idle epistemology."[2] He asserts, it may be recalled, that philosophy "recovers itself when it ceases to be a device for dealing with the problems of philosophers and becomes a method, cultivated by philosophers, for dealing with the problems of men."[3] But if, as I have argued, the relation between the latter and the former is the very relation which I have described as obtaining between the problems "for" and the problems "of" any science, then it becomes evident not only that Dewey's distinction is invidious as implying that somehow philosophers are not men, since otherwise their problems would be some of the problems of men, but also that the dictum quoted is quite unsound. For it is then on a par with one that would assert, for instance, that biology recovers itself when it ceases to be a device for dealing with the problems of biologists, and becomes a method, cultivated by biologists, for dealing with the problems of sick men. This, obviously, would be to identify biology with medicine, whereas medicine is not biology itself but is (a branch of) biological engineering.

---

2 Dewey, *Reconstruction in Philosophy*, p. 124.
3 Dewey, *Creative Intelligence*, p. 65.

Chapter 4

THE THEORETICAL PROBLEMS OF PHILOSOPHY

In the preceding chapter we have seen in a general way how, even in the absence of independent philosophical curiosity, the attempt to solve rationally practical problems of a certain sort leads one automatically to engage in theoretical philosophical reflection. We now turn to an examination of the chief kinds of problems such reflection has to solve.

1. The Primitive Problems of Philosophy

The distinction made earlier between primitive and derivative problems applies in philosophy as in any other science; and what we now need to determine is *the nature of the data of the primitive problems of philosophy,* for their data are the initial and basic facts of philosophy and constitute the "subject matter" which ultimately differentiates it from the other systematic knowledge-seeking enterprises.

As with the primitive problems of such other enterprises, so with those of philosophy, their data consist of certain *directly observable facts* which, through inductive distillation, yield the kind of knowledge needed to solve rationally the practical problems. These, in the case of philosophy, are of the general form: *Does this (given thing) of kind K have value V, or not?* For example: Is this (given) syllogism fallacious, or not? Is this (given) act immoral, or not? Is this (given) consideration important, or not? etc.

Evidently, then, the theoretical problem which has to be solved if we are to be in position to solve rationally a practical problem of this form will be of the general form: *What exactly does it mean, to say of something that it has value V?* For example, that it is "fallacious," or "immoral," or "important," etc. And the answer to such a question will be of the general form: To say that something has value *V* means that it *has the generic character G (a, b, c, . . .); and in addition the differential character D (m, n, o, . . .) which marks off the species V of value from its opposite W.* Hence, to ask for the nature of the data of that initial theoretical problem is to ask: *From what kind of observable facts can one obtain inductively an account of what "having value V" means as predicated by a given person or group P?*

2. The Subject Matter Ultimately Distinctive of Philosophy

The answer, I now submit, is that those observable facts can consist only of *other evaluative statements by P, but ones that are beyond question.* And an evaluative statement by P is beyond question if and only if it constitutes a "definition-by-type," *i.e.,* a standard example, of what P means by "having value *V*," as distinguished from what he means by "having value *W*" opposite of *V*.

If, for instance, we take *V* = moral and *W* = immoral, then standard statements of moral evaluation by P might be such as: "This act, which is one of matricide, is a sample of what I call an immoral act"; "That act, which is one of alleviating sorrow, is a sample of what I call a moral act"; etc. A collection of such statements, constituting a representative sample of *P*'s standard applicative usage of "moral" and "immoral," is the kind of datum, and the only kind, from which it will be possible to obtain inductively a definition of what "to be moral" means as applied by *P*. Such statements, then, are the data of the primitive theoretical problems of philosophy. *They are the primitive, initial, empirically basic facts of philosophy,* which it is the task of philosophical reflection to construe. Hence *they constitute the subject matter which ultimately differentiates philosophy from the other systematic knowledge-seeking enterprises.*

The person P may be oneself; or P may be a group of persons that includes oneself; or P may be some other person or group, which one merely observes. But those standard statements of P are anyway *public* in the sense that they can be heard or read by others;[1] and they are beyond question. Hence, if doubt arises in P's mind, or dispute within the P group, as to the validity of some *other* statement predicating the same value V, then such standard statements by P will be the kind of facts by reference to which the validity or invalidity of the dubious predication of V will be rationally decidable by P, or authoritatively demonstrable to P by some other person Q. For, P's standard statements being public, other persons are in as good a position as himself to judge whether his dubious predication of V is consistent or inconsistent with his standard predications of V.

3. Conditions Under Which Conflicts of Evaluation Can Be Settled Rationally

It might be objected that validity or invalidity established in the way just described will have been established only *ex concessis,* but not really or in reality. This objection, however, can mean only that the *objector's own standard statements* predicating value V are not the same or not all the same as those of P; for "really" or "in reality" is here itself a value-term. This becomes evident if we notice first that after all, proof or disproof of anything is

---

[1] By "a statement," I do not mean the string of vocables, merely as such, which one employs as verbal symbol of an opinion; but the string *together with* the opinion it means. Hence a statement is *perceptually* public only so far as its vocable constituent goes. Its other constituent, *viz.,* the *meaning* of the string, is not perceived, but *understood* or not understood; and, if understood, then public too, in consequence of having been *published* by means of the string of vocables.

always and necessarily *ex concessis* — that is, from *conceded* premises and according to conceded principles of inference; so that, to speak of something as proved "in reality" rather than *ex concessis* can only mean, proved from premises and principles that *everybody* concedes.   But, secondly, "everybody" cannot here be taken to include infants, idiots, fools, or other "incompetents," for if it were so taken, then *nothing* ever could be proved "really" or "in reality."   Thus, "everybody" includes here only persons *conceded* by the person who speaks of "proof in reality" to be *competent, i.e.,* persons whose judgment as to what premises and principles to concede coincides with his own and is in this sense evaluated by him as *good*.

As regards principles of inference and of verbal expression, however, a peculiar situation exists, which guarantees that all parties to a disagreement accept the same ones.   If two persons who speak together disagree, or agree, then to this extent each *understands* what the other says; and this implies that both of them are in fact expressing themselves conformably to a common set of principles, namely, *the principles of intelligibility of verbal expression*.   Again, if evidence offered by either manages to convince the other of what it was intended to show, then to this extent both are in fact employing a common set of principles of inference.

In both these instances the status of the principles employed is similar to that of the rules of, for example, the game of chess, except that, unlike the latter, they can be obeyed without being known, and except also that they are natural (in the sense in which the "laws of nature" are so) whereas those of chess are artificial.   The similarity is this: Just as one does not have to play chess, but if chess is what one is playing then necessarily one moves the king only one step at a time, so likewise one does not have to play the game called verbal communication, but if one is actually communicating, then necessarily one's statements are to

this extent conforming to the conditions of intelligibility of
verbal expression. Of course, one's utterances need not conform
to those conditions, but in so far as they do not one is in fact
playing the different game called "employing words unintel-
ligibly." Similarly, the conditions of the game of coercive argument are binding on nobody, but in so far as one does not respect
them one is playing the different game called "proving nothing."

That two persons understand each other's statements and both
of them think logically does not by itself insure that a conflict of
evaluations between them can be settled rationally. For this it
is necessary in addition that both reason from common data. It
should be noted that in this respect there is no essential difference
between the case where the two value-predications in conflict are
entertained by one person, who is in doubt as to which one is
valid, and the case where they are made each by a different person.
In either case the ultimate data, by inductive reflection upon which
the kind of knowledge needed for rational settlement of the conflict can alone be obtained, consist of *other* predications of the
same value-term V by the same person or persons P, but predications of it that are *standard* in the sense stated in the preceding
section, *i.e.,* that are definitions-by-sample. Hence, that there
should *be* some predications of V that are standard for P is the
indispensable condition of rational solvability of the doubt or
dispute; for all that reflection can do is to make manifest the
until then non-manifest coherence or incoherence of the dubious
or disputed predication of V with those which, being on the
contrary standard for P, are for him beyond doubt or dispute.
"Rational" solution here means the solution logically coherent
with the predications of V that are standard ones for P. That P
will regard that solution as authoritative assumes that P is a person
or group of persons governed by reason.

Where no rational solution of a conflict of appraisals is possible
what other kind of solution may there be? Let us examine first

the case of a rational person who doubts the validity of one of his own appraisals, *e.g.,* of his appraisal of a certain act *A* as immoral. We assume here, as throughout, that the *nature* of the act appraised is fully known to him, and that he is in doubt only about its morality or immorality. Such doubt is then possible only because he has no clear, *i.e.,* no analytical, conception of what "to be immoral" means; for if he did have such a conception, *viz.,* that "to be immoral" means to have characteristics *a, b, m, n,* then, since *ex hypothesi* he has full information about the characteristics actually possessed by the given act, he could immediately decide deductively whether or not it is an immoral act.

Let us, however, suppose that, besides absence in him of any clear conception of what "to be immoral" means, there are also *no* acts which he finds himself able to declare *typical* of what he means by "an immoral act," and thus certainly immoral. Then he has *no data* out of which he could inductively extract a definite conception of the difference between morality and immorality. This means that, when he asks himself whether the given act is immoral, he *neither knows definitely what it is he wants to know about act A, nor is even in position to discover what it is he wants to know about it.* His doubt thus poses to him no problem into which to inquire, for inquiry presupposes data, and under our supposition he has none, either intensional or extensional. His doubt is then only a psychological quandary, and is "resolvable" only in a psychological, not in an epistemic sense; that is, it is only *terminable* by psychological events of some kind; such, for example, as those resulting from suggestion, or perhaps from alcohol or some other drug, or from meeting certain novel situations, etc.

Let us now consider instead the case where two persons are involved, one asserting that something, say an act *A*, has value *V* (*e.g.,* is moral) and the other asserting that it has the opposite value *W* (*viz.,* is immoral). We assume also that both are rational persons and are fully informed and agreed as to the actual nature of the act A; also that no conception of the difference between morality and immorality, which either is at the moment ready to offer, is accepted by the other. Let us further assume that there turn out to be *no* instances of acts which both these persons regard as typical of what they mean by being moral or being immoral. Then no *rational* way exists of settling the conflict between them, for they have no common intensional major premise from which to reach a solution deductively, nor any common extensional data from which to obtain inductively such a major premise. Under the circumstances, reflection may clarify and introduce coherence in the opinions of each, but this will not settle the conflict. It will only make more pointedly clear where essentially it lies.

In such a case, it can be "settled" only in some non-rational way; for instance, by *force* which — as regards action to be taken but not as regards opinions held — gives either victory for one and defeat for the other or compromise on the part of each. Or by *psychological craft* (whether it employ hypnosis, rhetoric, drugging, appeal to the passions, or other such means) that somehow manages so to alter the nature of one of the two persons that he then definitely approves (and calls "moral") some acts which before he definitely disapproved (and called "immoral"). Or again (if no action need be taken by both jointly) the conflict may possibly be disposed of by each going his own way and within his own territory living according to his own opinion.

One additional and important observation remains to be made. It is that, where the value-predicate V used by a person P is one not of mediate but of immediate value, then what it predicates is purely *de facto* approval or disapproval, by the person employing it, of that to which he applies it. The phrase *"purely de facto"* means here without reason or ground other than the directly experienced nature (as distinguished from the possible instrumentality) of that itself which excites the approval or disapproval. If, for example, a person who tastes orange juice approves the *taste itself* which he finds it has, and declares it "good," then the word "good" *in such a case* predicates of the taste simply his approval of *it* (*vs.* of the possible consequences of having tasted that taste). That he does approve the taste he experiences is then an ultimate fact. That fact itself (as distinguished from its consequences) is not capable of being good or bad, but only of being *reported* or *unreported;* and in English the statement that reports it is that *that taste* (not the approval of it) is "good." Such a statement may be *mendacious;* or, if the maker of it does not know well the language in which he is attempting to express his approval of the taste, his statement may be *worded* in a manner which in that language does *not correctly* express his approval. But his approval itself, of the taste itself which he tastes, cannot possibly be either *mistaken* or *well-taken.* It is purely a fact — the empirical fact that he happens to value that taste, *i.e.,* that he likes it, that he finds it pleasing, and this remains a fact irrespective of whether or not other persons also happen to value that taste, and irrespective also of what value, positive or negative, the consequences of his valuing it may have for him or for others.

4. The Two Directions in Which Philosophical Reflection Proceeds

When doubt exists as to whether or not a given thing of kind *A* has value of kind *V*, the doubt may be due to a lack either of historical or of philosophical knowledge relevant to the case. If the doubt can be settled by examining thoroughly enough the given thing or its relations to its spatial or temporal environment, then the knowledge that settles it is not philosophical but is of the kind which in a broad sense we may call historical.

On the other hand, if all the historical information we desire about the given thing is possessed and the doubt yet remains, then the knowledge needed to settle it is essentially philosophical; it is knowledge as to *what exactly* it means to say of something that it has *value of kind V*. This question is semantical, and, as pointed out in Section 1, the answer to it will have to mention, on the one hand, the *generic* character *G*, (*a, b, c* . . .) which anything must have in order to be congruously appraisable at all in terms of value *V* or of its opposite *W*; and to mention, on the other hand, the specific character *D* (*m, n, o* . . .) which differentiates the species *V* of value from its congruous opposite *W*.

The two directions in which philosophical reflection proceeds in its attempt to settle such a doubt thus are (*a*) search for that generic character, and (*b*) search for that differential character. The generic character determines the *predicament* of the given value-predicate; and the differential character determines whether that value-predicate or its contrary is the one true in any particular case that falls under that value-predicament. Analysis of a given value-predicate consists in discovery of those two characters *G* and *D*.

On a given occasion, one may confine oneself to the analysis of value predicates of a particular kind — for example, to predicates of esthetic appraisal, or moral appraisal, or logical appraisal, and so on; or, on the contrary, one may abstract from the various species or subspecies of goodness and badness such predicates respectively designate, and one may occupy oneself instead with the nature of goodness and badness taken most comprehensively; that is, with the nature of value in general, positive and negative. One is then attempting to formulate a general theory of value, as distinguished from a theory specifically of esthetic value, of moral value, etc.

It may be remarked in passing, however, that the custom, which has often prevailed in discussions of value, of speaking of "true, good, and beautiful" as if all predicates of appraisal could be subsumed under these three is deplorable for several reasons. One of these has to do with the inclusion of "true" in the list:

To say that the proposition $2 + 2 = 5$ is *not true, i.e.,* is false, is not to apply to it a predicate of value at all — it is not to say that it is a bad or blameworthy or defective proposition. What is bad is to *believe* that false proposition, or, equally, to *disbelieve* the true proposition that $2 + 2 = 4$, for in either case one's *opinion* is erroneous. Thus it is *erroneousness, not falsity,* which is a species of (negative) value. "True" — which, unfortunately, has two senses — is an adjective of value when it is used as opposite of "erroneous" and is thus being applied to beliefs or opinions. But it is not an adjective of value when it is used as opposite of "false," for it is then properly applied only to the propositions themselves, which may be believed or disbelieved.

But the "true, good, beautiful" trilogy has other defects. For example, beauty is a *species* of goodness; if taken in the broad sense common among estheticians, it is *esthetic* goodness, and is then a value-category not logically coordinate with goodness, but only with certain other species of goodness, such as moral goodness, logical goodness, etc. If, on the other hand, beauty is taken in the narrower, ordinary sense which it has when, for instance, one judges: "Not beautiful, yet pretty," beauty is then coordinate again not with goodness, nor now with moral goodness or logical goodness, but only with other species of esthetic goodness such as prettiness, sublimity, charm, etc.

Again, there are many adjectives used to express appraisals, which it would seem impossible without much violence to the common meaning of terms to class as adjectives of either esthetic, moral, or epistemic appraisal. For example, when I condemn a book as *tedious,* I am not asserting or implying that what it says is true, or moral or beautiful; nor even that it is false, or immoral or ugly. Other examples of terms which, beyond question, are used on many occasions as adjectives of appraisal, and yet do not plausibly fit under the headings of the traditional trilogy, would be holy, sacred, practical, expedient, important, exciting, real, irrelevant, interesting, uncomfortable, entertaining, likeable, etc., and their opposites.

Moreover, whereas certain predicates — such as right and wrong, beautiful and ugly, cogent and fallacious, good and bad — are explicitly and definitely predicates of appraisal, certain other predicates, which on many occasions describe without appraising, nevertheless on certain other occasions function definitely, even if tacitly, as evaluative. Take, for example, the statement that the style of a certain book is *repetitious.* This, ordinarily, would be meant and understood as expressing a judgment of appraisal, but it would express appraisal because both utterer and hearer then tacitly assume that in a literary style repetitiousness is a *bad* feature. If this assumption is not made, the statement is not evaluative at all but only descriptive of an objective characteristic of the given writer's style. If, on the other hand, that assumption *is* made, then the statement means that his style is *bad in a certain respect,* which is specified. The judgment, that is to say, is then evaluative analytically — discriminatingly — instead of in an ingenuously sweeping way, as would have been the judgment simply that the given writer's style is *bad.* That many predicates *prima facie* merely descriptive are nonetheless really evaluative on certain occasions is important to keep in mind, because adjectives that explicitly predicate value are employed relatively seldom, and this invites the erroneous belief that judgments of value are rather rare.

The character that determines the *predicament* of a given value-predicate is the character anything must have in order to be appraisable *without incongruity* in terms of either that value-predicate or its opposite; for example, appraisable as either moral or immoral. A question such as whether it is moral or immoral to scratch one's chin if it itches would be regarded as ordinarily quite incongruous. One would say that such an act is congruously appraisable, not in moral terms at all, but only in terms of decorum, or perhaps of hygiene. And if one's doubt of an assertion that a given thing of kind A is moral is due not to doubt as to the character which differentiates morality from immorality, but to doubt as to whether things of kind A are congruously appraisable in moral terms at all, then the task reflection has to perform here (and in all analogous cases) is that of identifying a certain value-predicament, *i.e.,* of ascertaining the predicament of a given value-predicate. In the instance we are considering, reflection might lead one to conclude, for example, that for something to be congruously appraisable in moral terms (1) it must be an act; (2) it must be a voluntary act; (3) the probable consequences of it must be known to the doer; (4) some of these consequences must be effects on the welfare of other sentient beings. The kind of things satisfying these four conditions, would then be the predicament of the value-predicates "moral" and "immoral." Another and simpler example would be *opinions.* If (1) anything that is an opinion, and (2) nothing that is not an opinion, is either erroneous or the opposite (say, "sound"), then "opinion," *when thus taken as name of whatever satisfies evaluability-conditions (1) and (2),* is the name of a value-predicament. Again, if (1) anything that is an inference, and (2) nothing that is not an inference, is either fallacious or cogent, then "inference," *when thus taken as name of whatever satisfies evaluability-conditions (1) and (2),* is the name of a value-predicament.

Every predicate and therefore every value-predicate, when unambiguous, has a specific realm of relevance — a category of subjects to which alone it is applicable congruously, whether affirmatively, negatively, interrogatively, hortatorily, or in any other of what C. W. Morris calls "moods." Thus "congruously applicable to" does not mean "true of," but only applicable *without absurdity, without irrelevance.* Hence it may be *false* that suicide, for example, is morally right, but the supposition, or the assertion, that it is morally right is *not incongruous;* that is, it is not absurd in the sense in which it would be so to suppose or assert that suicide is soluble in acetone, or is divisible by 346. The predicate "morally right" is therefore *congruously* applicable to suicide, no matter whether it be true or false that suicide is morally right. The answer to the latter question, on the other hand, depends on the nature of the *specific difference* between moral rightness and moral wrongness.

5. The Derivative Problems of Philosophy

The derivative problems of philosophy are all the semantical problems which have to be solved in the course of the attempt to perform the two kinds of philosophical tasks distinguished in the preceding section. As in the natural sciences, so in philosophy, the derivative problems are more abstract, recondite, and technical than are the primitive problems in which they are implicit, and in philosophy too they may seem quite divorced from practical problems. But the truth in both cases is that the derivative problems, no matter how highly technical some of them are, have vital implications for practice even if these are not obvious to superficial observation; and that, even when such technical problems seem to deal with topics quite other than those of the primitive problems, and are investigated by a given person perhaps only because of their intrinsic interest to him, nevertheless they are natural-scientific or, as the case may be, philosophical, if and only if they are implicit in the primitive problems in the sense that solutions of those recondite technical problems are prerequisite to solution of the primitive.

An example of derivative problems implicit in the problem of analysis of a value-predicate would be the following. Let us assume that what is to be analyzed is the difference between morality and immorality; and let us assume that someone has offered the answer that morality is essentially obedience to the will of God, and immorality disobedience to it. Then questions semantically derivative from the proposed analysis (and *eo ipso* philosophical) would be, for example: What kind of being is meant by the term "God"? Of what kind would be evidence that a being of the kind meant exists, and what in general is it "to exist"? If such a being should exist, how would his will be ascertainable? Would matters as to which he had not expressed his will be *ipso facto* out of the sphere of morality or immorality? Would what he commands be moral purely in virtue of his commanding it, or would he command it because it is moral? etc.

If the analysis offered of the meaning of "morality" should be not in terms of the will of a god, but, for instance, in terms of the good or evil consequences of acts, then philosophical questions derivative from that analysis would be, for example, as to what exactly it means to speak of something as being a consequence, or not a consequence, of a given act; what exactly it means, to be "good" or "evil"; whether there are degrees or quantities of each; if so how these are to be measured; what measurement consists in generally; what mathematical operations upon these measures of "goodness" or "badness" shall be regarded as significant for determining the morality or immorality of a given act; what the criterion of significance is in such cases; etc.

Thus, no matter what particular analysis is offered of the difference between a value V and its opposite W, the need to explicate some of the terms of the analysis gives rise to additional problems, which are "derivative" philosophical problems. In some cases the answers to these will, as in other sciences, necessarily be in speculative rather than in empirical terms; that is, in terms of entities whose properties are stipulated rather than observed and whose existence is postulated rather than observed. But here as elsewhere, the postulation of such entities has to be justified by observation that what it entails conforms also with facts other than the particular ones it was intended to explain. In philosophy these will be other semantical facts of the kind that are philosophical. In ultimate analysis, they will be those which are *primitive facts* of philosophy.

That various more or less reconditely technical problems are implicit also in that of analysis of a value-predicament becomes evident if we return to one of the examples given at the end of the preceding section. The question in that example was as to what characters something must have if it is to be appraisable, without incongruity, as either moral or immoral. And, as example of an answer someone might offer, we took the statement that to be congruously appraisable in moral terms something must be a voluntary act having probable consequences known to the doer, that affect the welfare of other sentient beings. Evidently, the need to make thoroughly clear the meaning of this answer gives rise to questions as to what exactly is meant by "welfare"; by speaking of an act as "voluntary," of its consequences as "probable," and of these as "known" to the doer. Again, are acts only, or also perhaps persons, states of affairs, desires, or feelings, congruously appraisable as moral or immoral? And additional such questions will arise concerning some of the terms employed in the answers that may be offered to the questions just listed. How far this process will need to be pushed will, on practical occasions, depend on how soon it has shed enough light to solve the particular practical problem that called for philosophical reflection on the given occasion. When, on the other hand, one's concern is more general, and what one seeks is philosophical knowledge sufficient to deal rationally with any practical problem of, let us say, ethics, then the process described above has to be carried as far as needed to obtain a complete ethical theory and indeed also a metaphysics.

Chapter 5

THE METHOD OF KNOWLEDGE IN PHILOSOPHY

What has now been said concerning the practical function, the subject matter, and the theoretical problems of philosophy has implications as to the form scientific method takes when applied to the investigation of these problems, and as to the kind of facts it can establish. We shall now consider those implications.

1. The Theoretical Problems of Philosophy Essentially Semantical

The account given in the preceding chapter of the theoretical problems of philosophy, primitive and derivative, entails that all of them are essentially semantical, although not all semantical problems are philosophical. By a semantical problem is meant here a problem as to the meaning of terms; but if, as will be maintained in a later chapter, a concept is essentially a complex consisting of *an abstract idea and of a word symbolizing it,* then a semantical problem may also be described as one of analysis or synthesis of concepts (whether intensional or extensional).

A semantical problem is philosophical if and only if the term whose meaning it concerns is (*a*) a term functioning as value-predicate, or (*b*) one functioning as value-predicament, or (*c*) one in terms of which a term of kind (*a*) or (*b*) is defined. Any term of one of these three kinds is "philosophical" as distinguished from "historical." As pointed out earlier, a given term, *e.g.,* "repetitious," sometimes does and sometimes does not function as value-term. When it does not, it is then not a philosophical but a historical term.

That semantical inquiry is not *eo ipso* philosophical is shown by the fact that one may inquire into the meaning of such terms as logarithm, iron, mass, acid, typhoid fever, schizophrenia, heredity, etc., and that the answers are furnished not by the philosopher but by the mathematician, the physicist, the chemist, the pathologist, the psychiatrist, the biologist.

On the other hand, inquiry concerning value-statements, if it were non-semantical, would also not be philosophical inquiry. If, for example, a man has declared that a certain act was morally right, one may, concerning that appraisal of his, ask and investigate such questions as whether, at the time he made it, he was under the influence of alcohol or some other drug, or of frustration, or of hunger, etc. Or one may ask of what kind was the social occasion on which he voiced that appraisal; or what kind of upbringing he has had, and so on. And these inquiries, although concerned with an appraisal, would not be philosophical but in a broad sense historical, or more particularly biographical. The facts they would yield would be relevant, not to the philosophy of moral appraisals, but to the physiology, the psychology, or the sociology of such appraisals. That is, they would answer, not the question as to what characters *of a given act* are *criterial* of its morality or immorality, but the very different question as to what characters *of a man's own situation* are *causative* of his pronouncing a given act "moral" or "immoral." The *causes* of the *utterance* of a particular judgment *J* are one thing; and the *evidences* or *criteria* of the *truth or erroneousness* of that judgment are quite another thing.[1]

---

[1] In a critical study of my book, *Philosophy as a Science*, Professor Mieczyslaw Choynowski comments at one point on a passage of that book which implies that the primitive facts of philosophy are not appraisals but statements of appraisal. He argues that any theory which explains given statements of appraisal by a person *P* and predicts additional ones by *P* (or by persons who resemble *P* in specifiable respects) is necessarily not a philosophical theory but a psychological or sociological one ("Czy Filosofia Jest Nauka?" *Przeglad Filozoficzny* rocznik XLIV, zeszyt 1-3, Warsaw-Krakow, 1948). But the task of philosophical theory as I conceive it is not to predict *events*, such for example as *utterances* of statements of appraisal by

As regards the concrete act appraised, scrutiny of it is not in itself a philosophical activity, but it may become relevant to a *casuistical* philosophical problem, that is, to a *practical* problem of the sort that are problems "for" philosophy. Scrutiny of the given act will acquire casuistical philosophical relevance in so far as the questions it attempts to answer are ones which the results of prior theoretical philosophical inquiry dictate as being the relevant ones to ask for the purpose of solving the given casuistical problem.

As indicated earlier, these questions would be of the forms: Does the given concrete act have characteristics *a, b, c,* requisite to any act's being congruously appraisable at all in *V-W* terms — say, in moral terms; and if so, does the given act have in addition characteristics *m, n, o,* which mark as morally right, instead of as morally wrong, any act congruously so appraisable? The task of philosophical *theory or research* — or more specifically in this example, of ethical theory or research — is and terminates with *discovery of which characteristics these are.* The task of philosophical *engineering or casuistics,* on the other hand, is and terminates with *dictation* (based on knowledge of those characteristics) *of questions of the above two forms about the given concrete act; i.e.,* its task terminates with the *counsel* that, for solution of the given casuistical problem, those particular questions are the relevant ones to answer. And the casuistical problem itself is solved when *scrutiny of the given concrete act* has answered them.

---

a person P. Its task, as stated above, is (by semantical analysis of the value-predicate V employed by P in a representative set of "standard" predications of V by P) to formulate *the criterion of truth and falsity* of dubious predications of V by P that is semantically implicit in the set of P's standard predications of V. That criterion has not only to account semantically (not psychologically or sociologically) for those standard statements of P, but also to be "predictive" — this, however, in the sense that it will also account semantically for such *other standard predications* of V by P as were not actually included in the given representative set, but are regarded by P when the question is raised as equally constituting samples of his standard predicative usage of V.

2. Philosophical Problems Solved When Purged of Semantical Obscurity

The fact that all the theoretical problems of philosophy are essentially semantical has the important consequence that, when all semantical obscurity has been removed from a philosophical problem, then either the problem is thereby automatically solved, *i.e.,* its solution made obvious; or else such problem as may then remain is not philosophical but is one to be solved by inquiry into facts of the kind we have proposed to call historical.

It may be further remarked that the semantical character of the theoretical problems of philosophy remains, irrespective of whether one's attempt to solve them be motivated simply by their intrinsic interest, or by the fact that certain urgent practical problems cannot be solved without prior solution of those theoretical problems. Also to be noticed is that many of the theoretical problems of philosophy, as they are ordinarily formulated, are not *obviously* semantical. But that they are nonetheless essentially so immediately appears when one notices the kind of questions on which turns the validity or invalidity of any proposed solution. For example, in so far as the question whether a God exists is philosophical, the validity or invalidity of any proposed answer to it obviously turns on the meaning of the term "God," on what exactly "to exist" means, and on what exactly is meant by "ascertaining" whether the kind of being meant by "God" does or does not have the kind of "existence" meant.

3. Scientific Method in Semantical Inquiry

The essentially semantical character of the theoretical problems of philosophy entails that the method of inquiry appropriate to them will be that which scientific — that is, knowledge-yielding — inquiry employs when its object is discovery of the meaning of a term.

The fact to be stressed here is one that has already been men-

tioned, *viz.,* that without data no problem is genuine and no inquiry possible.   Hence inquiry into the meaning of a term is
hopeless if the term is taken out of all context, for no data are
then supplied by which to test the validity of any definition of it
offered.   The problem becomes genuine and capable of scientific
solution only when one takes as datum a list of statements employing the term and constituting a representative sample of the
particular usage of it to be analyzed.   For then the question is no
longer, barely and insolubly, "What does the term mean?" but
has become "What does it mean *as employed in the statements
listed?"*   Then, the validity of any definition offered as answering
this question can be tested by observing whether the definition is
substitutable for the term in those statements without altering any
of their standard implications.   If it is so substitutable, then its
validity is empirically confirmed in proportion as the given list of
statements is longer and is a random sample of the usage to be
analyzed, and in proportion as the variety of standard implications
of them is greater.   If, on the other hand, the substitution is not
possible, then the definition offered is erroneous and has to be
rejected or amended.   This test, let it be noted, is objective in
that it can be performed by persons other than the maker of the
listed statements.   His own possible declaration of what he means
by the term concerned is a declaration only of the sense in which
he *intends* to use it or *believes* he has used it, and does not guarantee that his actual usage of it will or did conform to his declared
intention.

The method just outlined is the method of *empirical inquiry*
into the meaning of terms.   Like scientific empirical inquiry into
matters other than this — such, for instance, as those physics or
biology deals with — its findings are only *probable,* in greater or
smaller degree.   This, however, is no more a defect in philosophy
than elsewhere.   It means, on the contrary, that philosophical
findings obtained by that method will constitute knowledge **as**

genuinely probable as do the findings of the natural sciences concerning the questions — different from those philosophy asks — which they study. Assertions for whose claims to be probably true evidence is offered are better than assertions for whose claim to be absolutely true no evidence is given.

The method of empirical inquiry in philosophy, as described, of course does not in any way preclude, but on the contrary must be supplemented by, application of the formal tests of validity to its results, *viz.,* that of internal consistency of each of the definitions empirically reached, and that of consistency of these with one another.

4. Do Semantical Discoveries Have Extralinguistic Import?

Insistence that all the theoretical problems of philosophy ultimately are about the meaning of certain terms may provoke the question whether philosophy is then occupied merely with words, and if so, how it differs from lexicography.

The answer depends on what exactly the lexicographer's task is held to include and not include. I submit that it is essentially *historical* in nature, to wit, that it is the task of *recording* the usages in fact made of the words comprised in the lexicon; and hence that it is no part of the task of the lexicographer as such to introduce new usages, or to engage in theoretical analysis of the implications of the usages he records. The meanings of the technical and of the jargon terms he lists are not assigned to those terms by him, but are obtained by him from the specialists who use and sometimes coined those terms, as needed to represent physical, biological, or other discoveries they made. For instance, it is the physicist who tells the lexicographer what to put in his dictionary when he comes to such terms as molecule, electron, mass, etc. Again, the task of discovering the extension implicitly entailed by the intension which usage in fact attaches to a given term, or the intension implicit in the extensional usage in fact made of a given term, is not a lexicographical task — not even when (as in the instance of the Philosophical Lexicon which constitutes Book V of Aristotle's *Metaphysics*) the person who records the meaning semantical analysis presumably discovered happens to be also the person who performed the analysis. For even then, his task qua lexicographer is only to record the meaning which, qua semantical analyst, he supposedly discovered in as genuine a sense as that in which the prospector discovers gold or the chemist the properties of a substance. When the lexicographer comes to a philosophical term, the philosopher is the semantical analyst to whom the former applies if he wishes to give of the term concerned a technical, *i.e.,* a precise, nonarbitrary, objectively informative definition, instead of merely approximate synonyms or unilluminating phrases such as, for "beautiful," handsome, fair, beauteous, full of beauty.

Physics and chemistry, being the easiest and therefore the most advanced of the natural sciences, have reached a stage where they now have a fair number of technical terms defined substantially in the same manner by most physicists. A dictionary of them is therefore to that extent a dictionary of the authoritative, standard usage of those terms, instead of a dictionary of the various usages they have had in the history of their subject. Philosophy, on the other hand, being as I believe at a stage of its potential development corresponding perhaps only to that of physics at the time of Galileo, possesses as yet only a much smaller number of such terms. Hence dictionaries of philosophy still have to be mainly of the latter sort, *viz.,* dictionaries of the several usages of those terms which various philosophers have originated or followed, instead of dictionaries of authoritative philosophical usage. This state of affairs will necessarily continue so long as no set of evaluative statements exists, that, in the sense specified earlier, are "standard" alike for all or most philosophers; and so long also as the inductive distillation of the theoretical implications of the statements of such a set has not been carried forward as far and as rigorously as that of the standard statements of the natural sciences.

I believe, however, that the greater diversity of opinion, which exists in philosophy as compared with the natural sciences, is not due chiefly to lack of common sets of "standard" evaluative statements, for, as regards many such statements, there is I think very wide unanimity. Rather, it is due to inadequate realization of the relation of those standard statements to the task of theory in philosophy; and to consequent failure to check the empirical validity of the constructions of theoretical philosophy by reference to those standard statements — which, as we have seen, are the kind of observable facts the theoretical constructions ultimately have to explicate.

This brings up the second remark to be made in reply to the question whether philosophy is concerned merely with words, and hence whether the semantical discoveries which result from semantical analysis or synthesis can have extralinguistic import.

That they can have such import has recently been maintained by Everett Hall,[2] somewhat earlier by C. I. Lewis in his book *Mind and the World Order,* and by others. Indeed, Whewell had essentially the same insight when, in his *Novum Organon Renovatum,*[3] he remarked that controversies about the right definitions of terms are not questions of insulated and arbitrary definitions, but that "In all cases there is a tacit assumption of some Proposition which is to be expressed by means of the Definition and which gives it its importance"; so that "the dispute concerning the Definition . . . acquires a real value, and becomes a question concerning true and false."

The fact that semantical analysis or synthesis — whether of philosophical or of other terms — can have extralinguistic import,

---

[2] Hall, "A Categorial Analysis of Value," *Philosophy of Science,* Vol. 14, No. 4, Oct. 1947, p. 333.
[3] Book II, Ch. ii, Sec. ii, art. 7.

and does have it when its data consist, as I have insisted they must, of "standard" statements predicating the term concerned, is nowise paradoxical. Rather it is a corollary of the fact that those statements, as defining-by-sample the term they predicate, constitute necessarily correct linguistic formulations of certain extralinguistic facts. For it then follows that a correct inductive account of the *meaning* of any such statement — that is, an account of the semantical relation between the term it predicates and the terms figuring in the *definiens* of a correct inductive definition of that term — will constitute not only a semantical discovery but automatically discovery also of an extralinguistic fact. This is no more paradoxical than that solution of a mathematical problem should be capable of being automatically solution also of a problem about nature. Such a result necessarily follows in both cases if the semantical properties, possessed in the language used by the particular words or mathematical symbols employed to represent the extralinguistic entities and operations concerned, are *formally parallel* to the real properties of those extralinguistic entities and operations themselves. That the parallelism obtains, however, cannot be assumed but has to be ascertained.

This may be made clear by considering the very simple example of addition. To say that the numerals 30 and 50 respectively represent correctly the lengths in inches of two sticks means that the collection of numerals up to and including 30 or 50 is *formally parallel* to the collection of inches in the stick, and, in turn, that these two collections are formally parallel means here that their members can be put in one-to-one correspondence.

Again, to say that the semantical property of numerals which makes it possible to substitute "80" for "30 + 50" is formally parallel to the physical property of the lengths of the sticks to generate a certain greater length by laying one at the end of the other, means that that semantical operation with numerals and that physical operation with lengths are both of them "addition," in the sense that both equally satisfy the familiar defining postulates of addition-in-general, *viz.,* commutativeness, associativeness, etc. But had the numerals 30 and 50 represented instead degrees of temperature in two adjacent rooms, and the physical operation contemplated been that effected by opening the door between the two rooms, then, although linguistic addition of the numerals would still have yielded 80, this numeral would *not* then have had extralinguistic import. It would not have been the measure of the temperature obtained by opening the door; for the operation which opening it effects on the physical temperatures does not satisfy those postulates, is therefore not addition, and hence is not formally parallel to the addition of numerals.

In connection with the question whether philosophy occupies itself with "mere words," it is crucial to notice, finally, that the extralinguistic facts which its "standard" statements necessarily formulate correctly consist in part of impulses to action. This entails that when the value-terms those statements predicate are employed in other than standard evaluative statements, those terms there not only describe a particular kind of value, but also *incite to action,* whether *pro* or *contra* the thing to which they are applied. Moreover, they do so *independently of whether they are analytically understood or not.* Their push, like that of a command, depends only on knowledge of their practical import — that is, on knowledge of what they call upon one to do.

Because evaluative terms, whether applied fitly or unfitly, do impel to action, and if applied unfitly the action they prompt stultifies the agent, it follows that to speak of "mere" words is like speaking of "mere" dynamite. Words are "mere" words only when considered apart from their meaning. By virtue of the meaning words have, the speaking of a sentence can imprison a man, level a metropolis, or make fools of those who hear it; or can on the contrary give freedom, build a city, or bring wisdom. And it is not "mere words" philosophy studies, but the meanings of words of a certain kind, called evaluative, and of the words in terms of which these are defined. But evaluative words do not, like those of the natural sciences, simply describe the world man faces. They move him to interfere in it — in a manner likely to be wise or foolish according as he does or does not adequately understand their meaning. The word "democracy" is today a patent example in point. In society, words, and evaluative words in particular, are just about the most important things there are. For whereas man determines changes in extrahuman things chiefly by means of his hands, it is on the contrary by means chiefly of evaluative words that he determines both other men and himself to act or to refrain from acting.

Chapter 6

PHILOSOPHICAL METHOD, REALITY, AND THE MIND-BODY PROBLEM

Two philosophical problems — that of the relation between Mind and Matter, and that of the relation between a given mind and the particular material object called its body — were mentioned at the beginning of Chapter 1 as being among the principal of those with which this book is to deal. The classical hypotheses as to the nature of these two relations, however, have been aspects or corollaries of proposed solutions of the problem traditionally central in metaphysics — the so-called ontological problem or problem of the nature of Reality; and although vast amounts of thought have for centuries been given to this problem, no solution of it commanding general acceptance among philosophers has been reached. This suggests that it must have been somehow badly formulated and that, because of this, the manner in which it has generally been attacked must be unsuited to its true nature.

The conception of philosophy outlined in the preceding chapters implies that, like all other philosophical problems, the ontological problem and those of the Mind-Matter and Mind-Body relations are essentially semantical, and therefore that the scientific method of dealing with them is the method described in Chapter 5. This method, however, was described there too briefly and abstractly to give an adequate idea of its *modus operandi* and of its power. In the present chapter two things will therefore be attempted: one, to make clear what the problem as to the nature of reality turns out to be when conceived as an empirical semantical problem; and the other, to apply to this problem the method mentioned, and thereby make clear both how it works in practice and what it can accomplish. The performing of these tasks will aid us to define rightly, and to attack eventually in a manner appropriate to their philosophical character, the Mind-Matter and Mind-Body problems.

1. Some Formulations of the Problem as to the Nature of Reality

On the first page of the introduction to his *Appearance and Reality*, F. H. Bradley wrote: "We may agree, perhaps, to understand by metaphysics an attempt to know reality as against mere appearance, or the study of first principles or ultimate truths, or again the effort to comprehend the universe, not simply piecemeal or by fragments, but somehow as a whole." That the three characterizations of metaphysics proposed in this statement are mutually equivalent is anything but immediately obvious; but each is so ambiguous that any attempt to prove their equivalence or nonequivalence has to be based mostly on arbitrary or *ad hoc* interpretations of a number of the terms used in the statement. The ambiguity of these terms, however, does not mean only that we cannot tell whether or not the three characterizations of metaphysics offered are equivalent; it means also that each of them is too vague to enable us to identify exactly the subject "metaphysics" which it purports to describe. But this, notoriously, is true also of most of the other characterizations of metaphysics to be found in books that claim to deal with the subject. "An unusually resolute effort to think consistently" would be another example; and yet another, quoted also by A. E. Taylor, describes metaphysics as "an attempt to become aware of and to doubt all preconceptions."

There can be no doubt, however, that the characterizations of metaphysics which are most nearly traditional and are most commonly encountered are those framed in terms of the distinction between "reality" and "appearance." About as clear an account of the nature of the subject in these terms as may be found proposed anywhere is that of A. E. Taylor. In his *Elements of Metaphysics*[1] he describes metaphysics as "a systematic and impartial inquiry as to what we really mean by the familiar distinction between 'seems' and 'is,' that is to say, a scientific inquiry into the general characteristic by which reality or real being is distinguished from mere appearance, not in some one special sphere of study, but universally."

2. Need to Specify the Data of the Problem

But even this formulation fails to specify the data of the problem. Moreover, it tends to suggest that these are of the same logical type as would be, for instance, the data of a problem as to the nature of chalk, or of rubber; and therefore that, to solve it, we must compare concrete samples of real being with concrete samples of merely apparent or unreal being, and observe what characteristics differentiate the former from the latter. But that the problem is not of this logical type is perhaps sufficiently shown by the fact that since some philosophers are idealists, some materialists, and others adherents of still other doctrines, samples of real being could not be picked without begging in the very act what the contending philosophers would regard as the question at issue.

To avoid this, the data to which we look as starting point must be of quite a different kind. I submit that they can consist only of concrete examples of the manner or manners in which the word "real" or its cognates "really" and "reality" are used predicatively. That is, our data will have to consist of *statements* such as that a certain substance, which seems to be paper, is really asbestos; or

---

[1] p. 4.

that mermaids do not really exist; or that trees far away appear blue but in reality are green; and so on. Such concrete instances of the predicative use of the word "real" or its cognates constitute the factual data which a hypothesis as to the meaning of those words must fit and by reference to which its tenability can be empirically tested; for the problem then is as to what those words mean — connote, intend — *as predicated in the given examples.*

Of course, I take it that what we are interested to analyze are examples which, like those just given, illustrate common usage; but it is worth noting that if examples of some freak usage of those same words were given instead, then, if it interested us to do so, we could analyze equally well the meaning those words had there. The essential point is that either no applications of a word are given us, and then we can make it mean anything we please; or else concrete examples of *some* applicative usage of it are furnished, and then we have data by which to test empirically the validity of any proposed definition of what it means in that particular sort of context. A definition of it so reached will be a so-called real or objective definition, as distinguished from an arbitrary and merely verbal definition.

The second of the two maxims of method mentioned at the end of Chapter 1, enjoins us, it will be recalled, to state explicitly what we are seeking to discover about the data the first maxim requires us to list. In the present case, then, what we wish to discover is the meaning which the word "real" or its cognates have *in the sample statements we take as data.* Any hypothesis as to this will therefore have the form of a definition of the word concerned; and since a definition is good if and only if it is exactly equivalent to the term defined, the test of the adequacy of any definition that occurs to us will consist in the possibility of replacing the term defined by the definition proposed, in any of the sample statements taken as data.

But what will be the test of that possibility itself? It will be,

I submit, that after this replacement the given statements shall have the same implications and shall themselves be implied by the same statements as before the replacement.

3. Some Technical Senses of "Real"

As soon as we begin listing statements in which the word "real" or one of its cognates is used predicatively, the suspicion forces itself upon us that the word means one thing in some of them and something else in certain others. We are therefore led to divide our sample statements into several groups and to scrutinize each group separately.

The first may well consist of examples in which the adjective "real" is evidently used in some special and purely technical sense. In law, for instance, real property is contrasted with personal or portable property, and "real" therefore means nonpersonal or immovable. In mathematics certain numbers are called real numbers and contrasted with imaginary numbers, although both kinds are real enough, in an ordinary sense of the term, to be accurately described and fruitfully employed by mathematicians. Again, in logic real definitions are contrasted with verbal or nominal definitions, although words are just as real, in an ordinary sense, as are things other than words. It is clear that no problem involving the distinction between reality and appearance arises in connection with these or possible other more or less arbitrary uses of the word "real" in the idiom of some particular art, science, or profession. We may therefore dismiss them from consideration.

4. What It Means To Be "Really" of a Kind K

The group we come to next is much more significant. It consists of statements such as that a certain dog looks or seems or appears ferocious, but is not so really or in reality; or that a certain seemingly valid argument is really fallacious; or that the stone in a certain ring, although it appears to be glass, is a real diamond; or that a certain substance seems to be paper but is in reality asbestos; and so on. All these, let it be noted, are descriptive statements. That is, in each some entity, for example a substance, is given, and the hypothesis is offered that it is of a certain kind, for example, of the kind called paper. For the sake of generality, let us call *E* the entity given in any of them and call *K* the kind to which it is claimed to belong; and let us note that, whatever the kind *K* may be, there is always some set of characters, *a, b, c, d,* such that, if and only if a given entity possesses all of them, it is of kind *K*. This simple analysis puts us in position to describe exactly the occasions which give rise to the question as to whether a given entity *E* really is, or only appears to be, of a kind *K*.

They are occasions on which *only some* of the characters of *E* are manifest to observation, and on which these manifest characters — which constitute the *appearance* of *E* at the time — happen to be the same characters as would be manifest in the existing circumstances if *E* should happen to be of kind *K*.

For example, under present circumstances, the color, shape, texture, and flexibility of the sheet I hold are manifest to observation; they are its present appearance; whereas the combustibility of it, if it be combustible, is not now manifest. But further, the color, flexibility, and other now manifest characters of the sheet are the same characters as would be manifest under present circumstances if the sheet were of the kind called paper.

Now, if the things which in our past experience manifested this same color, flexibility, and so on, did later turn out in most cases to possess also combustibility and the remaining characters of paper, then what we naturally say in the present case is that this sheet *seems* or *appears* to be paper; that is, its present appearance is the same as that of paper.

Furthermore, if, on applying the proper tests, we find that this sheet does have also those remaining characters of paper, then we express this by saying that it not only appears to be paper, but *really* is paper; whereas, if it turns out to lack some of them, what we say is that, although it appears to be paper, it is *not really* so, or is not real paper.

Thus, in terms of an entity *E,* and of a set of characters *a, b, c, d — all* of which must be possessed by it if it is to be of kind *K,* but *only some* of which are at the time manifest in it — we have defined exactly the type of situation which governs the use of the notions of appearance and reality in cases where the nature of the thing a descriptive statement describes consists of a complex of characters. When on the contrary a single character is concerned, as when we say that the trees on a distant hillside appear blue but really are green, the analysis of "really" is very different. We shall consider it farther on at the appropriate place.

What now can we conclude is the qualification introduced by the words "real" or "really" in statements of the kind we have been examining? A moment's reflection makes evident that in our example what is qualified as "real" is not in fact the paper itself at all, for paper does not have two species — one called real paper and the other unreal or seeming paper. What is not really paper is not paper at all. Rather, what is qualified is the descriptive proposition "This is paper," and the effect of inserting the qualification "really" into it is to assert, not simply that proposition, but also *that it is true.* To say "this is really paper" is exactly the same as to say, "truly, this is paper," or to say, "that this is paper, is true."

Accordingly, the occasions on which we say "this is *really* paper," instead of simply "this is paper," are occasions on which we wish to assert that, notwithstanding some assertion or item of evidence to the contrary, it is *true* that this is paper. On the other hand, the occasions on which we say simply "this is paper" are those on which we are answering the question "What is this?" without anything having suggested that it is not paper.

Of the same type in essentials as the example we have examined, and analyzable in the same manner, would be examples where some additional connotation, relevant only to some specific sort of situation, is given to the adjective real. Thus, for instance, real is sometimes used as opposite of artificial and then means being really made by nature, not by man. Again, real is occasionally used as opposite of counterfeit, spurious, intended to deceive, and then means genuine or authentic, *i.e.,* really having been made by the person, or in the manner, or at the time, etc., alleged. Or the notion of intent to deceive might be absent, as when a person who owns a Rembrandt, and who has commissioned a painter to make as exact a copy of it as possible, eventually says to a visitor that the one at the left is merely a copy and the other a real, *i.e.,* really an original, Rembrandt. Again, we contrast a man's ostensible reason for doing a certain act with his real reason, *i.e.,* with the reason really operative; and so on.

5. "Really" as Qualifying "Exists"

These remarks complete the analysis of the notion of reality as it figures in statements of the type we have been examining. I turn now to examples of a different kind. They consist of existential assertions, that is, of assertions which, instead of answering as before the question "What is this?" answer the question "Are there any so and so's?"

Instances of existential assertions in which the notion of reality enters would be that, in reality, no mermaids exist; that the man called Hamlet by Shakespeare did not really exist; that Utopia is an imaginary country but that Spain is real; that there is really such a psychological state as hypnosis; or that black swans really exist but green swans do not.

In some of these statements, "is real" apparently means simply "exists," but in others the notion of reality clearly is additional to that of existence. The examples which are of the latter sort may be dealt with first and briefly, since in them the import of the word "really" or of either of its cognates is essentially the same as in the descriptive statements we have considered. That is, in existential statements too, its import is to assert that the statement in which the word enters is *true* notwithstanding some doubt or item of evidence to the contrary.

For example, the sort of occasion on which one would naturally say "mermaids do not really exist," or "mermaids are not real," instead of simply "no mermaids exist," would be one on which, perhaps, a child had been reading a story about mermaids or had seen a moving picture representing some. The simplest explanation of such a story or picture would naturally be that there are mermaids, and the story or picture therefore constitutes an item of circumstantial evidence that mermaids exist. The import of the statement that mermaids do not *really* exist would thus be that the evidence is misleading — that, in spite of it, the truth is that mermaids do not exist.

In such examples, realness is thus not a character differentiating one species of existence from another and inferior species called unreal or seeming existence; any more than, in our earlier example, realness differentiated one species of paper from an inferior one called seeming or unreal paper. In both groups of examples alike, what the word "really" or either of its cognates qualifies is the statement itself in which it occurs, and its force is the same as that of the adverbs "truly" or "certainly."

6. What It Means "To Exist"

Let us now return to the sort of assertions in which "is real" is used simply as synonymous with "exists." Our task is then to analyze the meaning of "to exist." This will not only make explicit the meaning of these assertions, but also clarify by contrast that of assertions — such as those just discussed and certain others yet to be considered — in which the notion of reality is added to that of existence.

The question as to what exactly it means to say that something of a given kind K exists is best approached by limiting attention at first to cases where what is in view is specifically physical existence, as distinguished from, for example, mathematical or psychological existence.

In all such cases the assertion that there exists something of a kind K is, I submit, exactly synonymous with the assertion that something of that kind *is somewhere;* that is, occupies some place in space at some time. It is important to notice, however, that an assertion of existence may be more or less determinate.

For example, least determinately, one might assert that there are black swans, or, which is the same thing, that black swans exist; that is, they are at *some* place, not specified.

But, somewhat more determinately, the assertion made might be instead that there are black swans *somewhere within a specified region* — for instance, in Australia.

Or thirdly and now quite determinately, the assertion made might be that there is a black swan *here now;* that is, at the specific place to which one is pointing at the time.

These examples make evident that in the phrases "there is" or "there are" one is using the word "there" not in some idiomatic sense but literally, that is, as indicative of spatial location whether completely indeterminate or partially or wholly determinate. In these phrases, moreover, temporal location also is indicated, likewise more or less determinately, at least by the past, present, or future tense of the verb, and often through specification by date of some period or particular moment also.

Physical existence, thus, is essentially spatiotemporal ubiety; and that which has or lacks ubiety, that is, is or is not present at some place in space at some time, is always some *what* or *kind* — which may be a kind of substance, or of property, or of relation, or of activity, or of change, or of state, and so on.

When existence other than physical is in view — for instance, mathematical existence — the meaning of existence is closely analogous. The difference is only that the place concerned is a place in some order other than the space-time order.

Thus, for example, the assertion that a square root of 9 exists, but no square root of 3, means that the character "being square root of 9" characterizes a certain place in the order of whole numbers, namely, the determinate place called 3; whereas the character "being square root of 3" characterizes none of the places in the series of whole numbers.

In any assertion of existence, thus, no matter whether it be more particularly one of physical existence, or of mathematical, or psychological, or other existence, two components always are essentially involved, namely, a *what* and a *where*. And generically a *where* or place is the sort of thing specifiable in terms of *ordinal* relations; that is, of relations such as between, next to, beyond, among, outside of, and so on, which, logically, are not specifically either spatial or temporal, since there is such a thing, for instance, as *qualitative* betweenness. The color Orange is *qualitatively* between Red and Yellow, even when it is not placed spatially between them.

This analysis, it should be noted, incidentally results in making explicit also the meaning possessed by the word "reality" when it is used not as an abstract term synonymous with "realness," but as a concrete, *denotative* term; as, for example, in such statements as that reality is exclusively material, or exclusively mental, or of both these kinds, or of the nature of will, and so on. When the word "reality" is so used it means "everything that exists." It is obvious that reality in this sense is not the opposite of appearance, but of nonexistence, or nothing.

At this point it may be remarked also that when the word "reality" is used thus denotatively, then that, *if anything,* which it denotes is known to us, that is, known to us to exist, only if our existential judgments are *true.* Hence, if their truth (or erroneousness) is to be something ascertainable at all, it cannot possibly be defined as correspondence (or noncorrespondence) to the allegedly denoted reality, that is, to something known at all to exist only if those very judgments of existence happen to be true.

7. The Question as to What Water "Really" Is

We shall now examine a use of the word "really" or its cognates, radically different from any we have so far considered. An example of it would be the statement that the wood of the table is really a cloud of minute particles at relatively vast distances from one another; and another example, that water is really a compound of oxygen and hydrogen.

When this is asserted about water, the word "really" cannot have the same meaning as when we say that the liquid in a given glass is really water. For the statement that water is really H_2O evidently does not mean that water only seems to be water but in truth is something else; nor does it mean that it only seems to have the familiar properties of liquidity, tastelessness, capacity to quench thirst and fire, and so on, but has *instead* of these the property of being analyzable into oxygen and hydrogen; nor does it mean simply that it is true that the composition of water is H_2O.

What it means, I submit, is that *for certain purposes,* such as some of those of chemists, the property of being analyzable into and synthesizable out of hydrogen and oxygen is *the important or relevant* property, whereas for such purposes the other, more familiar properties of water are irrelevant. And analogous remarks apply to the statement that the wood of the table is not "really" hard and solid. If it is intended to mean — as, indeed, it sometimes is — that the hardness and solidity are illusory, *i.e.,* that wood only seems to have these properties but does not really have them, then the statement is simply false. For when a person asserts that the wood of the table is hard and solid, what he means is that it is such that if, for instance, one attempts to press the hand or another piece of wood through it, the attempt fails; and this, beyond question, is true. The fact that the wood has this property, however, is perfectly compatible with its having also the different property that if what one attempts to pass through the wood is something vastly smaller, *viz.*, subatomic particles of some kind, this attempt succeeds.

Therefore, if the statement that the wood is not "really" hard and solid is to be the statement of something true, it can mean only that in so far as a person's purposes are such as certain of the purposes of physicists, the second property but not the first is *important*.

In statements of this type, then, the definition of realness which, at the time they are made, tacitly governs the use in them of the word "really" is that *to be real is to be relevant to the purposes or interests which rule at the time.* In such cases, the opposite of "to be real" is thus not, as before, to be a deceptive appearance, nor to be nonexistent; but to be irrelevant, unimportant, insignificant, negligible, of no interest or value for the purposes ruling at the time.

Additional examples belonging to this group would be such statements as that the real way to talk to a mob is such and such; that you really must do this or that; that such and such a proposal is not realistic; that nothing is more real than an idea; that such and such a consideration is very real; and so on. The example mentioned earlier, in which we say that the trees on the distant hillside seem blue but really are green, analyzes in a manner slightly different from that which applies to the statement that water is really H_2O; but there, too, realness consists in relevance to interests or purposes postulated as for the time ruling. For, evidently, that the trees display the color blue when they are observed from far away is exactly as true as that they display the color green when they are observed from a distance of a few feet.

The two properties are perfectly compatible, and the trees truly possess both. Which color we say the trees "really" have is therefore a matter only of whether only the near point of observation is relevant to the purposes which rule us at the time (as when they are the ordinary practical or scientific purposes), or of whether on the contrary any point of observation we have chosen is relevant to our then ruling purposes (as when we are landscape painters).

8. Ontological "Positions" Distinguished from Ontological Hypotheses

We have studied so far four main types of statements in which the word "really" or one of its cognates figured. The four types differed markedly in certain respects, but they were nevertheless alike in a respect to which attention must now be called, namely, all of them were statements of something or other that had the status of *hypothesis*. That is, what they formulated by means of the word "real" or its cognates was in each case something that was either true or false, and was therefore susceptible of being more or less fully verified or confuted. Since the predicate "real" is "the ontological predicate," those hypotheses may be termed *ontological hypotheses*.

But now we must notice yet another group of statements in which the word "real" enters, but which express not hypotheses at all, but something else altogether, to which the categories of truth, falsity, probability, confirmation, proof, or disproof do not apply at all. What those statements express I shall call *ontological positions*.

Just what an ontological position is, as distinguished from a hypothesis in which the notion of reality figures, will become clear if we return to the tacit major premise which, as we saw, was assumed by the assertion that water really is H_2O. That tacit premise, it will be recalled, was that to be real is to be relevant to certain of the purposes of chemists. Now, to adopt this or any similar major premise for one's activities through a given time is to *take a position* as to what, for the time, one will mean by "being real." And to be governed, even if unawares, by such a major premise at a given time is to be then *occupying a position* as to what it is to be real. That is, the statement of such a major premise is the statement of an ontological position. It is always of the form "to be real is to have such and such a character."

An ontological position, thus, is essentially of the nature of an exclusive or basic interest in the things which have a certain character; it is a rule one adopts, or tacitly proceeds under, as to what things one will regard as alone of interest, or will rank as basic or primary. For example, the ontological position that to be real is to have a certain character *C* would consist in interest exclusively or basically in things having this character; it would be the rule of admitting to consideration only the things having character *C*, or at least of positing them as fundamental and absolutely prior in interest or importance.

Now, an ontological position may be consciously embraced, or it may be occupied unawares. It may be occupied by many persons, or by few. It may be congenial to one person, and repugnant to another. It may be occupied at a certain moment, and relinquished the next in favor of a different one. But just because an ontological position is not a contention at all but essentially a being ruled at the time by some particular sort of interest, an ontological position cannot be true or be false; nor therefore can it be shown more or less probably true than another, or be refuted, or be proved. These possibilities exist only in the case of hypotheses.

The ontological position, for example, which natural scientists, while functioning as such, occupy, is that to be real is to be perceptually public or implicit in what is so. But it is evident that these words do not formulate a hypothesis as to properties empirically discoverable in some concretely given entity called reality; for no empirical facts one might adduce could prove or disprove what those words express, or render it probable, doubtful, or improbable. Plainly, they describe no hypothesis at all, but simply the criterion by which the things in which the natural sciences interest themselves are distinguished from the things these sciences ignore. Truth, falsity, and probability are thus categories logically incongruous to ontological positions — as inapplicable to them as would be the predicates thirsty or bitter to logarithms or to algebraic equations. Ontological positions may only be occupied or not occupied, be embraced or abandoned.[2]

9. Some Objections Considered

Ontological positions, it should be noticed, are formulated either descriptively or functionally. Descriptive formulation is *in terms of a stated character,* in which the person concerned is for the time being interested exclusively or supremely, and presence or absence of which in any given thing thus determines whether he calls it real or not. An example of descriptive formulation would be that of the ontological position occupied by natural scientists as such, *viz.,* that to be real is to be perceptually public or implicit in what is so. Others would be that to be real is to be introspectively observable or implicit in what is so; that to be real is to be individual; that to be real is to be unique and changeless; that to be real is to be free from contradictions; that to be real is to be a coherent whole; and so on.

Functional formulation, on the other hand, is of the form: To be real (for a given person) is to be anything (no matter what its intrinsic nature may happen more particularly to be) that is *relevant (i.e.,* instrumental whether positively or negatively and

---

[2] Cf. the writer's "A Defense of Ontological Liberalism," *Journal of Philosophy,* Vol. XXI, No. 13, June 19, 1924. The above analysis of the nature and epistemic status of ontological positions is, I believe, in essential harmony with conclusions reached by J. Loewenberg in a penetrating article entitled "The Question of Priority," *University of California Publications in Philosophy,* Vol. 13, pp. 37-69.

whether directly or indirectly) *to the attainment of the purposes
ruling at the time in the person concerned.* These may be specified either by particular description of them, or else, only broadly,
as, for example, the purposes of theoretical physicists as such, or
of playboys, or Christians, or esthetes, or voluptuaries, or adven-
turers, or patriots, etc., as such.

Now, what must be noticed is that the things which, because
they are thus *interesting qua instruments* to the given person,
qualify as then real for him may nevertheless be *intrinsically* of
no interest to him at all. This is the answer to the possible
objection that one may find some things uninteresting, and yet
call them real.

On the other hand, if a person remarks about something:
"That's interesting," this does *not* mean that the thing is "real"
in the sense of not illusory or not nonexistent. It means that the
thing is not only of the general kind in which he is taking interest
at the time (and is thus holding as real in the sense of important),
but is an *especially interesting* one among such things — one
which particularly attracts attention because, perhaps, it rewards
or promises to reward it more than others of its kind.

Another possible objection, plausible at first sight, to the account given of the nature of an ontological position would be
that "the world of appearance has always been and will always
be an object of interest for the metaphysician, and it does not
become real by virtue of that fact."[3] It is quite true, of course,
that the metaphysician's interest in the world of appearance does
not obliterate the difference between a thing's really being of kind
K, and its only seeming to be of that kind; nor between saying
that there really exists something of kind *K*, and saying that there
only seems to exist something of that kind. But that this is true
does not in any way invalidate the account given above of the
nature of ontological positions, *for any proposed analysis of that*

---

[3] Cornelius Benjamin in *Ethics,* Vol. LII, No. 3, April 1942.

difference is an ontological hypothesis, not an ontological position.

On the other hand, the sense in which it is true that the metaphysician's interest in appearances confers reality upon them becomes evident if one notices that any metaphysician — or, more specifically, any ontologist — at the time he is functioning as such, is occupying the ontological position that *to be real is to be relevant to the question as to the nature of reality, appearance, and unreality.* By virtue of his interest, this question, and hence also the subject of any of its parts, including appearance, become for him a *real* question, and a *real* subject of inquiry; that is, a question and a subject that count, that are important, to which thought should be given. But that the ontologist's interest in appearance does in this sense make appearance real for him obviously does not entail that his interest makes really a ruby something which has only the appearance of being a ruby!

10. Is There Still Another "Problem of Reality"?

But, it might now be argued, the account so far given of the problem, or rather problems, as to the nature of reality is *Hamlet* without the Prince of Denmark; for the doctrines called Idealism, Materialism, Voluntarism, and so on, purport to be, not "positions" in the sense defined above, but rival hypotheses, any one of which, therefore, is theoretically susceptible either ultimately of disproof, or else of greater confirmation than its rivals. And, it might be contended, the problem about reality, which they concern, is different from all those we have distinguished and is the great problem of metaphysics. I believe, however, that this contention, although plausible at first view, is mistaken.

If an answer to that allegedly different question could be proved to be true, this would be sufficient to show that the proposed answer had genuinely the status of a hypothesis, not of a "position." And A. E. Taylor, for instance, has maintained that a certain answer *can* be proved true — the answer, namely, that reality is free from contradictions and thus is self-consistent. This is known to be true, the argument runs, because it follows from the logical Law of Contradiction. This law says that if anyone thinks that something A has a certain character B, and also that it does not have character B, then what he thinks cannot be true. But "to think truly about things is to think in accord with their real nature, to think of them as they really are, not as they merely appear to an imperfect apprehension to be; hence to say that non-contradiction is a fundamental condition of true thinking is as much as to say that it is a fundamental characteristic of real existence."[4]

"Reality," or "real existence," is evidently used here by Taylor not in the sense of real-ness, but in the denotative sense, in which it means whatever exists, whatever is a fact; and one may well grant that all existing facts are mutually consistent and each existing fact self-consistent, *i.e.,* that all of them, and the components of each of them, are capable of existing together, since they do exist together. But, let it be well noted, this does not entail that whatever is self-consistent and consistent with other facts is itself a fact. That some swans are green, for example, and that no swans are green, are of course mutually inconsistent; one or the other is false. But that some swans are green is not a self-contradictory assertion, nor is it one incompatible with any known law of nature; yet this does not guarantee that things "as they really are" include green swans. That anything which is a fact is consistent with itself and with other facts tells us *by itself* exactly nothing as to whether or not some swans are green, nor, more generally, as to the truth or falsity of any other equally consistent assertion of particular fact.

Freedom from contradiction, then, is not, as Taylor claims, a "universal and certain criterion of reality," or indeed a criterion of reality at all. For to say that something C is a criterion of

---

[4] A. E. Taylor, *Elements of Metaphysics,* pp. 18-20, 22.

something R means that C is an infallible sign of R — that wherever C is present, R also is present; and, as just pointed out, that an assertion is free from contradiction is no sign that it is the assertion of a fact. What can be justly claimed is only that presence of contradiction in any assertion is a criterion of error, and thus of the unreality or non-factuality of what is asserted. This, however, is something very different.

Nevertheless, the principle Taylor seems actually to employ at most places in his book is the *equation* "to be real is to be self-consistent"; *i.e.,* the principle that not only is being self-contradictory being unreal, but also that being self-consistent is being real. The latter, obviously, does not follow from the logical Law of Contradiction and, as shown by the example of the green swans, is not known to be true. Rather — if "being real" is taken in the sense of "to exist" — it is known to be false unless, perhaps, restricted to the realm of pure logical and mathematical entities. But I believe that although the metaphysicians who employ the equation generally assume it to be a hypothesis (and one known to be true) about the nature of reality, nevertheless that equation, as employed by them, has actually the status of an ontological "position" in the sense already described, and as such is tenable, but is not the sort of thing capable of being either true or false. That is, it represents only their own temperamentally rooted refusal to be satisfied with — to attach positive value or importance to — anything other than what is, as they say, "intelligible," that is, rational, consistent, orderly, and therefore at least theoretically capable of being anticipated.

But the irrational, the unexpected, the accidental and unpredictable, has likewise positive value for some persons. It, and not the systematically coherent, is the real for persons who by temperament are impulsive rather than rationally purposive, adventurous rather than prudent, romantic rather than scientifically reflective, and who value excitement and strong emotion more than peace and serenity. And most of us, at times, are such persons. This opposite ontological position is equally tenable.

Let us, however, now return to the contention that Materialism, Idealism, etc., are answers to a question about reality other than any of those we have examined. Let us consider, for example, the statement that ultimately reality is exclusively mental. It may be construed in either of two ways.

First, it may be taken as but another way of saying that to be real is to be either a mind or a mind's ideas. If so construed, it is the statement of what we have called an ontological position, not of a hypothesis; and, as pointed out, it is then not the sort of thing which either is true or is false. It only declares the primacy, for the idealist, of minds and their ideas, and his intent to define everything in terms of them.

On the other hand, the word "reality," in the statement that reality is exclusively mental, may be taken denotatively, that is, taken to mean "everything that exists." The statement then means that there is in the universe nothing else than minds and their ideas. In ordinary usage, however, the adjective "mental" is applied only to such things as feelings, thoughts, volitions, hopes, memory images, and so on, or to the minds comprising them; whereas such other things as the wood of the table — which, beyond question, also exists — are normally called "material." I submit, therefore, that the statement that reality is exclusively mental, as meaning that minds and ideas are everything there is — or similarly, that reality is exclusively material — cannot possibly be true unless some meaning at variance with the customary one is forced, *ad hoc,* by means of the qualification "really," either on the verb "to exist," or else on the adjectives "mental," or "material." Let us see how this would be done.

A materialist, for example, might say that what he contends is that nothing which is not material has *real* existence. This, however, would be but saying that the realm of material existence is the only one he chooses to acknowledge, the only one of interest to him. Thus, because he would be restricting his assertion to a particular realm of existence, which he elects to rank as alone or supremely important to him, he would in fact again not be stating a hypothesis as to the nature of everything that exists, but again only declaring the ontological position he chooses to take.

But instead of using the word "really" to limit arbitrarily the scope of "to exist," one might use it instead to stretch, equally arbitrarily, the denotation of the term "mental," or "material." An idealist, for example, might say that what he maintains is that everything which exists is *really* mental, that is, *really* consists of minds and their ideas, notwithstanding appearances to the contrary. It would follow from this, however, that since beyond question the wood of this table can be sawed, sandpapered, coated with paint, burned, etc., then minds, or their ideas, can in some cases be sandpapered, put into the fireplace and burned, and so on. Yet such properties, and the things which have them, are the very ones ordinary language *means* by "material" properties and things, and are also the very ones to which it *intends to poin*t when it mentions "non-mental" properties and things. And, let it be well noted, they are pronounced "material" not in virtue of something which scrutiny of them reveals, but in virtue simply of the conventions of language; just as persons of the black race are declared to be Negroes, not because scrutiny reveals negro-ness in them, but simply because "Negroes" is the name language employs to denote persons of that race; or again, as the inhabitants of Indiana are Hoosiers, not because careful observation of them discovers that they possess "hoosier-ness," but simply because "Hoosier" is the nickname by which it is customary to denote them.

It is thus impossible that wood should only seem to be material but really be mental. To suppose it, would be to suppose that wood lacks the properties the language denominates "material," and has instead those it denominates "mental"; whereas the fact is that properties such as those of wood are the very ones the word "material" is intended to denote. That wood is material is a "definition-by-type" of what we mean by "material."

Under the circumstances, to assert nonetheless that wood is really mental — a primitive sort of mind, perhaps — is not to voice a new insight into its nature. It is not to mention a hitherto undetected but observable character of wood. It is, I submit, only to elect *arbitrarily* to employ the word "mental" to denote not only the things it is customarily intended to denote, but also those customarily denoted by the word "material." *To do this, however, is exactly the same logically, and just as futile, or indeed, semantically perverse, as would be electing to say henceforth that members of the white race are really Negroes, or that Negroes are really white.* Obviously, this would not be revealing any hitherto unnoticed fact about the color of their skins. It would only be tampering wantonly with established language.

It is true, of course, that the idealist, who asserts that reality is mental, or the materialist, who asserts it to be material, usually *believes* himself to be discerning and revealing a generally un-recognized fact about such things as wood, or about such things as thoughts, and thus to be solving a genuine problem. But the preceding remarks, together with the earlier parts of this chapter, show that he is in fact doing no such thing but only stating, and mistaking for a hypothesis, the ontological "position" he proposes to take; or else that he is then dealing with only a pseudo prob-lem, which evaporates when one distinguishes and analyzes the different meanings the word "reality" or its cognates have in the several sorts of contexts in which they function in the language. Monistic "reduction," no matter whether idealistic, materialistic, voluntaristic, or of some other type, is *a priori* doomed to failure because it is a logical monstrosity. As a matter of logic, it is an attempt to show, not that a given *concrete thing* is really of a kind other than that to which it appears to belong (which sometimes is the fact and can be shown); nor to show that a given *kind* of thing is, in spite of appearances, really one of the *species of a certain genus* (which, again, sometimes is the fact and can be shown); but to show that a *given kind* of thing is really some *other kind* — which is an absurdity and hence cannot be a fact. As Paulsen (in criticizing materialism) pointed out, the attempt is logically of the same sort as would be that of proving that the kind of thing we mean by "wood" is not itself but is really the kind of thing we mean by "iron."[5]

11. The Mind-Matter and Mind-Body Problems

But there is a genuine and profoundly important philosophical problem as to mind and matter. It is not, we have now seen, as to whether everything is mental and nothing material, or everything material and nothing mental. For there is no doubt at all that some existing things have and others do not have the properties, such as those I have mentioned, which we mean when we speak of material properties; nor that some existing things have and others do not have the properties we mean to refer to when we speak of mental properties. The genuine problem as to mind and matter has for its datum that certain things — for example, wood — in fact are denominated "material" and not "mental," and others — for example thoughts — in fact are denominated "mental" and not "material." And the problem itself is as to what exactly the words "material" and "mental," *as respectively denotative of the ones and not of the others,* mean, imply, or connote. As already pointed out, any hypothesis offered as to what they mean has to be tested by observing whether or not it fits the things the words "material' and "mental" respectively

---

[5] Paulsen, *Introduction to Philosophy,* transl. F. Thilly; Henry Holt & Co., pp. 82–3.

denote; that is, by observing, in the case of the word "material," whether the (possibly complex) character the hypothesis supposes to constitute the meaning of "material" is in fact possessed by all the things the language *denominates* "material" and by none of those it *denominates* "mental"; and, in the case of the word "mental," by making the analogous observations.

Then, when one has in this way tested and more or less fully confirmed a hypothesis as to the intension which the words "material" and "mental," or "matter" and "mind," respectively have *as denoting certain things and not certain others,* the further problem arises as to how, in the light of that result, mind and matter are or can be related. As to this, the preceding discussion has shown only that their relation cannot be identity. The question as to the relation between the individual's mind, and the particular material object called his body, is another question still, closely related to the preceding one, but not identical with it.

Discussions of the relations between mind and matter, mind and nature, mind and the body, have in many cases been carried on without sufficiently precise analysis of the meaning of these terms; that is, with little more than the vague, ingenuous understanding of it which everyone has of all the words of ordinary language, and which is serviceable only for the immediately practical purposes of everyday human intercourse. Or else the meaning assigned to those terms has been more or less arbitrary and question-begging. A large part of our effort in this book will go to ascertaining in just what sense of "mental" and of "mind" the things commonly denoted by those words are mental and are minds. We shall also ask what exactly it is, to be "material" and to be "matter"; and what exactly characterizes as "his own" the human material body the individual so describes. These tasks are directly preliminary to that of analyzing the mind-body relation.

Before turning to them, however, we must first analyze certain basic categories — causality, substance, purposiveness, freedom — which we shall have to employ, and the analysis of which, I believe, remains essentially the same whether one be using them to talk about material or about mental things and events. To their analysis we now proceed.

PART II

Fundamental Categories

Chapter 7

CAUSALITY: CRITIQUE OF HUME'S ANALYSIS

The notion of causality will play an essential part at many places in the remaining chapters of this book; but a variety of opinions are current today as to the nature and the role of the causal relation. One finds accounts of what science now means by causal connection, but also statements that the notion of cause is not employed in science at its maturity, but only appears at the crude, early stages of its development. Again, many philosophers are dissatisfied with Hume's analysis of causality, upon which Mill's failed to improve. Yet, in default of some definite and more acceptable positive analysis, Hume's probably remains still the most influential. Inasmuch as the analysis of causality I shall offer in the next chapter diverges sharply from Hume's, I shall now first set forth the reasons I see for rejecting his account.

1. Hume's Skepticism

Hume's famous skepticism is not, like that of some of the ancients, a doctrine he propounds, but rather the acknowledgment by him of "a malady, which can never be radically cur'd, but must return upon us every moment, however we may chace it away, and sometimes may seem entirely free from it."[1] This malady, as Hume observes it in himself, consists in the fact that although reflection shows certain ones and certain others of our beliefs to be mutually incompatible, yet we cannot give up either the ones or

---

[1] Hume, *A Treatise of Human Nature,* Selby-Bigge ed., p. 218.

the others. The self-stultification which is noticeable at so many points in Hume's writings, and which so baffles the reader who would extract from them a consistent doctrine, is rooted in that malady. Again and again, especially in the *Treatise,* Hume disregards at one place conclusions he had reached earlier, and he could not without doing so proceed to say what he next wants to say. The *Treatise,* I believe, is thus to be regarded not as an attempt to set forth one consistent doctrine, but much rather only as an account of the philosophical sights to be seen from the road one travels under the guidance of certain principles which Hume accepts from the outset—one of the chief of these being that nothing exists or is known to us except "perceptions." Hume simply follows these principles remorselessly wherever they seem to him to lead; and when the conclusions to which they bring him are mutually incompatible or incompatible with firm natural beliefs, he just admits the fact as he would admit having gout or a cold in the head and similarly calls it a malady. His great service to philosophy thus is not that he solved, but much rather that he raised, important philosophical problems. There is perhaps no philosophical book more intellectually irritating—nor therefore more thought-provoking—than his *Treatise.* This is true in particular of what he has to say in it concerning causation.

2. Hume's Analysis of Causality

Hume's "official" view on this subject may perhaps be summarized as follows: To be is to be perceived. No connection is ever perceived between a cause and its effect. Therefore there is none. An "object" of kind *A* is called the cause of one of kind *B* if, in our experience, objects of kind *A* have always been followed each by an object of kind *B*. But such following of one object upon a certain other is not "necessary." In logic and mathematics, that is necessary the contradictory of which is self-contradictory. But no self-contradiction is ever involved in supposing an object we call a cause to exist without its effect following, or one we call an effect to exist without having been preceded by one such as we call its cause. Where objects are concerned, "necessity" is the name not of a relation among them, but only of the felt "propensity, which custom produces, to pass from an object to the idea of its usual attendant." Necessity, then, is "but an internal impression of the mind"; it is a relation between certain ideas, something "that exists in the mind, not in objects." Hume accordingly offers two definitions of cause. According to one, formulated in purely objective terms, "we may define a cause to be *an object, followed by another, and where all the objects similar to the first are followed by objects similar to the second."* According to the other we may say, in subjective terms, that a cause is *"an object followed by another, and whose appearance always conveys the thought to that other."*[2] The first of these is the basic one, since unless we had experience of causation as there described, the "conveying of the thought," in terms of which the second definition is worded, would not occur.

3. Hume's Analysis Fails To Fit Some of the Facts

As stated at the outset, I believe that this account of the nature of causation—simply as succession *de facto* regular—represents an incorrect analysis of the ordinary notion of cause—of the notion, that is to say, in the light of which our ordinary judgments of causation actually are made. To make evident the incorrectness of that analysis it will be sufficient to show, on the one hand, that there are cases which conform to Hume's definition but where we judge the events concerned not to be related as cause to effect; and on the other hand, that there are cases which do not conform to Hume's definition but which we nevertheless judge to be cases of causation.

As to the first, if a man were so situated as always to have heard

---

[2] Hume, *An Enquiry Concerning Human Understanding.* Open Court ed., p. 79.

two clocks striking the hours, one of which always struck immediately before the other, he would according to Hume's definition
of cause have to say that the strokes of the first cause the strokes
of the second; whereas in fact they do not. Of course, the relation he observes between the strokes of the two clocks is the effect
of a common remote cause of the strokes of the two clocks. But
although this is true, it is irrelevant; for to say that B is caused by
A is one thing, and to say that both B and A are caused by C is
quite another thing. The example thus shows that Hume's definition of the relation of cause and effect fits some cases where the
relation between the two events concerned is in fact not that of
cause to effect but a different one.

Other examples of sequences which are regular, and yet the
terms of which are not related as cause to effect, are not hard to
find. Thomas Reid mentioned the succession of day and night;
and we may add to the list the fact, for instance, that in infants
the growth of hair is regularly followed by the growth of teeth;
or that in human beings birth regularly follows the tenth return
of the moon since conception.[3]

In connection with such cases, it should be noted that what observation of *de facto* regular succession or correlation of two
events does is not to *answer* the question whether one of the two
events causes the other, but much rather to *raise* the question as to
whether one causes the other, or whether some antecedent third
causes both, or whether the conjunction of the two is simply accidental. For although causation of B by A entails constancy of
their conjunction (*i.e.,* recurrence of B as often as A recurs), the
converse does not hold: constancy of conjunction, far from itself

---

[3] A striking instance, in the case of which the relation between the events concerned is patently neither that of cause to effect nor that of joint effects of a common cause, is quoted by Morris Cohen (*Reason and Nature,* p. 92) from an
unpublished study by George Marshall at the Brookings Institute. It is that, for a
number of years, the membership in the International Association of Machinists
shows a very high correlation (86%) with the death rate in the Indian state of
Hyderabad.

being the relation of cause to effect, is not sure evidence even of indirect or of as yet hidden causal connection between the events concerned.

To show now, on the other hand, that there are cases which do not conform to Hume's definition, but which we nevertheless judge to be cases of causation, I shall mention a simple experiment I have sometimes performed with students. I bring into the room and place on the desk a paper-covered parcel tied with string in the ordinary way, and ask the students to observe closely what occurs. Then, proceeding slowly so that observation may be easy, I put my hand on the parcel. The end of the parcel the students face then at once glows. I then ask them what caused it to glow at that moment, and they naturally answer that the glowing was caused by what I did to the parcel immediately before.

In this case it is clear that what the spectators observed, and what they based their judgment of causation upon, was not repetition of a certain act of mine followed each time by the glow, but *one single case* of sequence of the latter upon the former. The case, that is to say, does not conform to Hume's definition of causation as constant conjunction but is nevertheless judged by unprejudiced observers to be a case of causation.

If I then further ask: What makes you think that my having done what I did caused the parcel to glow? they answer: Because nothing else happened to the parcel at the time. Thus, by the *cause* of the observed glowing they do not mean some event having repeatedly preceded it. They mean *the only change introduced into the situation immediately before the glowing occurred.*

It may be said truly, of course, that the change they observed was perhaps not the only change which actually occurred in that situation, and that their judgment as to the cause of the observed glowing was thus perhaps mistaken. To urge this, however, is to question not their conception of the meaning of "causation," but their claim that what they observed was a true case of what they meant and still mean by that word. For what indicates what they meant when they called what I did the cause of the observed glowing is not whether what I did *really* was the only change that occurred in the situation immediately before, but whether they *believed* it to have been the only change. So long as they do believe it to have been the only change, they continue to describe it as having been the cause of that glowing—even if a glowing should never again occur on repetition of my act.

4. Hume on Ascertainment of Causation by a Single Experiment

In this connection, it is interesting to note that Hume himself asserts that "we may attain the knowledge of a particular cause merely by one experiment, provided it be made with judgment, and after a careful removal of all foreign and superfluous circumstances." But how a *single* experiment, in which a case of B was observed to have followed a case of A, can assure us that *every* case of A is followed by a case of B is anything but obvious. One would expect, rather, that, once causation has been defined merely as *de facto* constant conjunction, the only way to observe its presence or absence would be to observe *many* cases of A and note whether or not a case of B follows constantly, *i.e.*, each time.

Hume perceives this difficulty, or rather the difficulty corresponding to it when his second definition of causation is the one considered—the difficulty, namely, how the customary expectation of B upon the occurrence of A, which he has stated before is the result of having *repeatedly* observed B following after A, can be present when the sequence, A,B has been observed not repeatedly but only once. He attempts to meet this difficulty by saying that even then we have had millions of experiments "to convince us of this principle, *that like objects placed in like circumstances, will always produce like effects*," and that this principle then "bestows an evidence and firmness on any opinion, to which it can be applied."[4]

By itself, however, this principle would support equally the generalizing of *any* sequence observed—of one which is accidental as well as of one which turns out to be causal. The possibility of its being useful therefore rests on the stipulated preliminary "careful removal of all foreign and superfluous circumstances." But the principle does not tell us how to discover by one experiment which these are; for obviously the "foreign and superfluous circumstances" are those which are not the cause, *i.e.,* on his view, those which are not *constantly* followed by *B.* Preliminary removal of the circumstances which are "foreign and superfluous" therefore amounts to preliminary discovery of the circumstance which *is* the cause! Thus, the principle is good not for discovering the cause in a single experiment, but *only for generalizing it* if we have already managed somehow to discover it by a single experiment. If, however, causation can be ascertained by a single experiment, then causation does not consist in constancy of conjunction even if it entails such constancy.

5. Hume's "Rules by Which To Judge of Causes and Effects"

Hume appears to have been obscurely conscious of this. For one thing, he introduces the two definitions of cause quoted above by the remark: "So imperfect are the ideas which we form concerning [the relation of cause and effect] that it is impossible to give any just definition of cause, except what is drawn from something extraneous and foreign to it." And, after the second definition, he repeats that both definitions are "drawn from circumstances foreign to the cause." Again, in his "Rules by which to judge of causes and effects," which are rules for discovering a cause by a single experiment and therefore, as pointed out above, really concern causation in a sense other than that of empirically

---

[4] Hume, *Treatise,* pp. 104–5.

constant conjunction, Hume at first refers to causation as "that constant conjunction, on which the relation of cause and effect *totally* depends"; but in the third rule, he no longer says "totally" but instead "chiefly"; and in the fourth rule he describes "constant repetition" only as that "from which the *first* idea of [the causal relation] is derived."[5]

Of the rules given by Hume for discovering a cause by a single experiment, the fifth, sixth, and seventh are the clearest statements not only up to Hume's time, but until the appearance of Herschel's *Discourse* nearly a hundred years later, of what Mill afterwards called the experimental methods of Agreement, Difference, and Concomitant Variations. Hume's fourth, fifth, and sixth rules, which are the most important theoretically, are as follows:

4. The same cause always produces the same effect, and the same effect never arises but from the same cause. This principle we derive from experience, and is the source of most of our philosophical reasonings. For when by any clear experiment we have discovered the causes or effects of any phenomenon, we immediately extend our observation to every phenomenon of the same kind, without waiting for that constant repetition, from which the first idea of this relation is derived.

5. There is another principle, which hangs upon this, *viz.* that where several different objects produce the same effect, it must be by means of some quality, which we discover to be common amongst them. For as like effects imply like causes, we must always ascribe the causation to the circumstance, wherein we discover the resemblance.

6. . . . The difference in the effects of two resembling objects must proceed from that particular, in which they differ. For as like causes always produce like effects, when in any instance we find our expectation to be disappointed, we must conclude that this irregularity proceeds from some difference in the causes.

---

[5] Hume, *Treatise,* pp. 173 ff. (Italics mine.)

It will be noticed that in the fourth rule the principle mentioned earlier (same cause, same effect) is supplemented by its converse (same effect, same cause), but is now presented explicitly as a principle not for discovering causal relations but only for generalizing them once we have managed to discover them somehow in a single case by a "clear experiment." But the fifth and sixth rules might be thought to give us just what we need for such discovery, viz., the criteria by which to decide which circumstances are "foreign and superfluous" to the cause.

Scrutiny of them, however, reveals that they do not do this, for they are presented by Hume as corollaries of the principle mentioned in the fourth rule (viz., same cause, same effect; same effect, same cause), and this principle is not as he there asserts derived from experience, nor is it derivable from it. As he himself has shown earlier with admirable clearness,[6] neither reason nor experience gives us anything which would warrant us in assuming (as the principle in his fourth rule does assume and has to assume if the fifth and sixth rules are to be corollaries of it) that those instances, of which we have had as yet no experience, resemble those of which we have had experience. A principle, which experience might conceivably have yielded, would be that like antecedents placed in like circumstances *have always been observed to have had* like sequents, and that like sequents have always been observed to have had like antecedents. But this principle not only does not yield his fifth and sixth rules as corollaries, but indeed is itself *invalidated by every situation to which Hume would apply these two rules.* For (to quote from rule 5) "where several different objects produce the same effect" what obviously follows is that, as a strict matter of experience, an *exception* to the principle "same effect, same cause" is then confronting us and the principle is thereby invalidated. Just this is what follows, and not, as Hume asserts, that these different objects must have some hidden

---

6 Hume, *Treatise,* pp. 87 ff.

common quality; for either such a common quality is itself observed, and then the objects are experienced as alike rather than, as supposed, different; or else a common quality is not observed, and then, to know that it exists nonetheless we should need to know that the same effect has the same cause in all cases, future as well as past; and, as recalled above, Hume himself has shown that neither experience nor reason can give us this knowledge.

Chapter 8

ANALYSIS OF THE CAUSAL RELATION

The chief findings of our examination of Hume's analysis of causality in the preceding chapter may be summarized as follows: (*a*) A sequence of phenomena may be recurrent and yet not causal, and a sequence occurring only once may nevertheless be causal. (*b*) This invalidates Hume's official doctrine that causality consists in *de facto* regularity of sequence. (*c*) Hume's common sense tacitly gets the better of his official doctrine when he declares that causation of a phenomenon B by a phenomenon A can be detected by a single experiment. (*d*) But the fact that causation can be so detected implies that causation does not consist in, even if it conditionally entails, regularity of sequence. (*e*) Hume seems vaguely aware of this when he declares that his characterization of the causal relation is drawn from circumstances extraneous and foreign to that relation, but he makes no attempt to say what then the relation does consist in.

1. The Principal Questions Concerning the Causal Relation

To analyze the causal relation and to offer answers to a number of questions which arise concerning it is the task to be attempted in the present chapter and the next. At the outset, however, it will be well to state as clearly as possible the principal of those questions, instead of only alluding to them without explicit mention. They are as follows:

What exactly does it mean, to say that the cause of something

B was *A?* What sorts of entities can, and what sorts cannot, be causes or effects? Are instances of causal connection observable? How is the notion of cause related to the notion of law? Is the notion of cause scientifically obsolete today? How are causes related to conditions, to agents, to forces, to properties, to powers? How is causality related to telism? Does a cause compel its effect? Does everything that occurs have a cause? Does the same cause always or necessarily have the same effect, and the same effect the same cause?

These questions are for the most part closely interrelated, and therefore cannot be discussed altogether separately; but this is all the more reason for stating them as distinctly as possible at the very start. The first on the list—that of the nature of the causal relation—is obviously the most fundamental.

2.   The Data of the Problem as to the Nature of Causality

The data of the problem as to the nature of causality do not consist of the opinions or theories as to this, which have been formulated by philosophers or scientists at various times. Such opinions or theories constitute attempted *solutions* of the same problem, or, some of them perhaps, of some slightly different problem. But whether they be correct or incorrect, or instructive or not, they are certainly not *data* for the problem as to the nature of causation. They could be data only for a *history of theories* of the nature of causation. It is thus a methodological mistake for Russell (if, as I believe, he is there really concerned with the problem of the nature of causation) to take as data, in his essay entitled "On the Notion of Cause"[1] the definitions of the term he finds in Baldwin's *Dictionary;* for a criticism of them is not a criticism of the notion of cause but of what the authors of these definitions thought were correct analyses of that notion.

The problem of the nature of causality is that of discovering the

---

[1] Russell, *Mysticism and Logic,* Ch. IX.

right or a right definition of the term "cause" as actually employed. And the data of this problem—the empirical facts the definition sought must fit — consist of *phrases that are actual instances of the employment of that term as predicate* (whether affirmatively, negatively, or interrogatively) ; that is, of its employment to designate the relation asserted, denied, or queried, as between the events the given phrase mentions.

I take it, however, that the usage of the term "cause" we are now interested to analyze is not any of the odd usages it may happen to have in the language of crude or careless speakers or of deliberate innovators, but is its ordinary, common usage when confident rather than hesitant and strict rather than loose. The phrases constituting data relevant to the analysis we are interested to undertake will then be such as that the 1938 New England hurricane caused the death of a number of persons; that its tidal wave caused a number of yachts to become lodged on the top of a bridge; that it caused to fly away numerous shingles from the roof of my house; that it broke, *i.e.*, caused to break, a large branch of an old tree in my garden; that my writing these words just now did not cause the ring of the door bell that followed it; that the starting of the furnace just now was caused by the closing of the electric contact in the thermostat; that the failure of the engine of my car to start as usual this morning was caused by the fact that the spark plugs had become covered with dew; and so on. Indeed, the data will include also phrases employing any of the innumerable verbs of physical or psychological operation, such as to push over, to blow off, to break, to kill, to uproot, to bend, to dissolve, to remind one of, to inhibit, to encourage, etc.—all of which signify causation of particular kinds of effects.

The question we seek to answer about these data is then, what definition of "cause" fits the employment of the term in these and similar phrases—the test of "fitting" or "not fitting" being whether the *definiens* of a proposed definition can or cannot, in such phrases, be substituted for the word "cause" without altering what is admittedly entailed by the propositions the given phrases formulate.

It is important in this connection to be clear that data statements employing the verb "to cause"—*e.g.*, that the wind caused a branch of my tree to break—are not given as being true rather than false, but only as being ones in which as a matter of English, the verb "to cause" was the proper one to describe the relation which the utterer of the statement had in mind, and which he presumably *believed* to have obtained between the wind and the breaking of the branch; whereas to have used for this (instead of "caused"), for instance the word "motivated," or "bribed," or "planned," would have been improper—not suitable to express in English what was meant.[2]

It will be noticed that the statements I listed as samples of the data of our problem do not include any such ordinary statement as that the swallowing of arsenic causes death. My reason for excluding this statement and others like it would be that it is elliptical, and that the literal statement of what it means, *viz.*, that ingestion of arsenic in some cases causes the death of the animal that ingested it, does not specify either by general description or by individual mention the cases it summarizes and therefore does not enable us to decide whether a proposed definition of cause does or does not fit them.

---

[2] Bertrand Russell states that although it is customary to give the name "effect" only to an event which is later than the cause, there is no kind of reason for this restriction. "We shall do better," he writes, "to allow the effect to be before the cause or simultaneous with it, because nothing of any scientific importance depends on its being after the cause." (*Scientific Method in Philosophy*, p. 226). It may well be granted that, on the basis of knowledge of the relevant causal law and of minutely detailed observation of a given event, the cause of that event could be inferred no less well than its effect. But the fact that *inference* can be from effect to cause as well as from cause to effect does not warrant the assertion that a cause may be after its effect. To assert it is either to confuse cause with premise and effect with conclusion, or else deliberately and needlessly to rob the words "cause" and "effect" of a part of the meaning they certainly have as employed in ordinary usage.

3. Definition of Causality in Terms of the Factors of Experiments

The methodological nature of our first and fundamental problem being now clear, let us turn to the problem itself. The general character of the account of the causal relation which I would submit may already have been surmised from my criticisms of Hume's views, and in particular from the described classroom experiment with the paper parcel. Broadly stated, my contention is that the relation of cause and effect is rightly defined not, for the reasons stated, as by Hume in statistical terms (*viz.,* as sequence empirically 100 percent regular), but in terms of what is called an experiment; and that an experiment is the sort of thing we observe when we observe a state of affairs S in which only two changes occur: one, a change C introduced in S at a time T_1, and the other, a change E spontaneously following in S at a time T_2. The first change may be introduced by ourselves, or by someone else, or by the natural course of events as for example in an eclipse; and of course a change in the given state of affairs at a given time cannot be the only change in it at that time unless it is the total change in it at that time.

If it should be objected that "introduced" is itself a causal verb, and therefore cannot legitimately be employed in a definition of causality, the reply would be that what is being defined is, specifically, causation *of a change E in S by an earlier change C in S.* This is defined by the specification that C and E are the only two changes in S. In the face of this definition of causation within S, it is perfectly legitimate (although not obligatory) to suppose an earlier, partially overlapping, state of affairs Z in which C was the *second* of two only changes, B and C, and in which C was therefore caused by B in the same generic sense of "to cause." We could then say that C was introduced into S by change B in Z; for C figures *both in Z and in S,* but in Z as effect (of B) and in S as cause (of E).

But as stated above, even the supposition just described is not obligatory, for the word "introduced" can be left out of the definition altogether.   It then reads that causality is the relation which obtains between an event C at a time T_1, and another event E at a later time T_2 if C and E are two changes in a given state of affairs S and are the only two changes in it.

If, however, it should now be objected that change E in S might not be the effect of change C in S at all, but might have been introduced into S by some cause outside of S, the reply would then be, first, that to suppose this is simply to reject outright, but not to criticize or invalidate, the proposed definition of causation in S of E by C.   For if C and E do, as supposed, meet the conditions that definition lays down, then C *was, by definition,* the cause of E.   Secondly, however, the statement of the above objection itself employs the verb "introducing" or "causing," but without defining it.   That statement therefore leaves us wholly in the dark as to *what the supposition is,* which it purports to formulate and the possibility of the truth of which is alleged by the objector to invalidate the definition proposed.

Let us now return to what occurs when we perform or witness an experiment.   If we believe that the first change we observe supervening in the state of affairs constituted by the setup of the experiment is the only change at the time in it, then we declare that it was the proximate cause of the change which followed it in that state of affairs, and that the latter change was the proximate effect of the former.   We are aware, of course, that we might be mistaken in believing that the first change we observed was the only change that occurred in the given state of affairs at that time; but we are quite sure that *if* it was the only change, then it was what caused the change which followed it; *for just this is what it means, to say that it "caused" the latter.*   That is, the sort of relation described is not a *sign* that a causal relation (in some other sense of the term) hiddenly exists between the two changes concerned.   Rather, the relation described is *the causal relation itself*.

The canon of what Mill called the method of difference is thus a description of the very sort of relation which is called causation of a sequent event by an immediately antecedent one.   Accordingly, that canon is not, as Mill thought, the description of a *method* for discovery or proof of the existence, as between the two events, of some relation *other* than the one that canon actually describes, such perhaps as the relation of invariable regularity of sequence.   What that canon furnishes can be called a "method" for the ascertainment of causal connections only in the sense in which the police description of some fugitive from justice can be said to be or to provide a method for identifying him; that is, that canon furnishes us with a description of the specific sort of relation we are to look for when cases of the relation called "causality" are what we look for.

As more than one critic has pointed out, Mill's formulation of the canons of Difference and of Agreement—to say nothing of the others—is, for a variety of reasons, hardly felicitous.   Before attempting to improve on them, however, I must point out that although discussions of causality are generally worded as if the term covered nothing but the relation of cause to effect, it covers in fact also another relation, *viz.*, that of a *condition* to what is dependent, but only in part, upon it—fulfilment of the condition thus permitting, or contributing to the possibility of, the dependent event, but not necessitating the event.   Mill notwithstanding, common sense is right in distinguishing between cause and condition; and we must therefore also distinguish between the effect of an event and the contingencies—the possibilities—to which the event gives rise.[3]   The distinctions are as follows:

---

[3] There seems to be no unambiguous or special term in common use to designate an event *B* qua made possible or contributed to by another event *A*; that is, no definite term for the relational status of *B* when the relation between *B* and *A* is "unless *A*, not *B*."   To say that this is the relation between *A* and *B* is to say, about

The *cause* of an event B was an event A which, in the then existing circumstances, was *sufficient to* the occurrence of B; and therefore, conversely,

The *effect* of an event A was an event B which, in the then existing circumstances, was *necessitated by* the occurrence of A. Again:

A *condition* of an event B was an event A which, in the then existing circumstances, was *necessary to* the occurrence of B; and therefore, conversely,

A *resultant* of an event A was an event B which, in the then existing circumstances, was *contingent upon* the occurrence of A.

An "event," let it be noted, may be either a *change* of some feature of a state of affairs, or (to use Dr. Charles Mercier's term), an *unchange, i.e.,* the *persistence unchanged* during some time, of such a feature. For example, the question "What occurred then?" could, with equal propriety, be answered by mention of a change, *e.g.,* "He got up," or of an unchange, *e.g.,* "He remained motionless." Either answer reports the occurrence of an event. But a cause is always a *difference* occurring in a state of affairs S in which the effect is another and later *difference.* If the event is a change, then its cause is a change in a state of affairs other-wise unchanging at the time; whereas if the event is an unchange, then its cause is an unchange in a state of affairs otherwise consisting of changes. Thus, should a state of affairs be contemplated in or about which no change was occurring or had ever occurred,

---

A, that it is *necessary to* (but not that it is sufficient to) occurrence of B; and, about B, that it is *contingent upon* (but not that it is necessitated by) occurrence of A. The common name of the relational status of A in such a case is "condition of"; A is said to be a condition of B. To designate the then corresponding relational status of B, the best term available would seem to be "resultant of" (in a sense analogous to that which this term has when used in connection with the composition of forces) ; or "dependant of" (employing, for this usage, the optional spelling "dependant" instead of the more common "dependent"). Let us therefore agree that when B is contingent upon A, we shall call B a resultant or a dependant of A. For a pointed criticism of Mill's criticism of the common distinction between cause and condition, see Dr. Charles Mercier's *Causation and Belief,* pp. 49, 50.

then questions of cause or effect concerning it would be incongruous. To avoid expanding our discussion unnecessarily, we shall at most places word it hereafter, as up to this point, in terms of examples where the cause-event and the effect-event are changes, rather than unchanges.

In defining above the distinction between cause and condition, and between effect and resultant, use was made of the notions of sufficiency and necessity. Reasons will be given farther on to show that it is legitimate to speak not only of *logical* but also of physical, of psychological, or more generally of what we shall call *etiological* necessity and sufficiency; that is, of necessity and sufficiency *as between events,* instead of as between logical entities. At this point, I wish to emphasize only two things. One is that "necessitated by" is the converse of "sufficient to," and "contingent upon" the converse of "necessary to," irrespective of whether the necessity concerned be logical or etiological. The other thing is that causal relations are not, as often assumed, two-term relations, but that, as indicated in what precedes, some *set of circumstances*—some *state of affairs*—always enters in as a third term. This point too will be more fully considered later.

I shall now submit definitions of the basic relations which experiments can exhibit, and I shall then add a number of necessary remarks. In framing the definitions, I shall employ not only the term *change* (which will be symbolized by C) but also Mercier's term *unchange* (which will be symbolized by U) to mean as stated above persistence unchanged for some time of some feature of some state of affairs. It should be kept in mind in this connection that change and unchange alike *take time,* however short or long; that is, at a strictly durationless instant, no event whatever occurs—nothing either changes or persists.

The various features of a state of affairs S will be symbolized by the letters, a, b, d, e, g, h. Thus, an expression of the form

C (a, b) will read: Change of features a, b (of a contemplated state of affairs S); and an expression of the form U (d, e) will read: Unchange of features d, e, (of S). The definitions of etiological sufficiency and necessity, of their negatives, and of the converses, are as follows:

Let us assume a state of affairs S (a, b, d, e, g, h) in which only the following events occur: at a time T_1, a change C (a, b) and therefore automatically, also an unchange U (d, e, g, h); and at a later time T_2, a change C (g, h) and therefore automatically, also an unchange U (d, e); then:

I. C (a, b) in S was *both sufficient and necessary to, i.e.,* was *both cause and condition of,* C (g, h) in S; and conversely, C (g, h) in S was *both necessitated by and contingent upon, i.e.,* was *both effect and resultant of,* C (a, b) in S.

II. C (a, b) in S was *not sufficient* to C (d, e) in S, since C (a, b) occurred, and yet C (d, e) did not then occur; and conversely, C (d, e), since it did not occur, was *not necessitated* to occur in S by C (a, b).

III. C (d, e) was *not necessary* to C (g, h) in S, since C (d, e) did not occur and yet C (g, h) did occur; and conversely, C (g, h) was *not contingent upon* C (d, e) since C (g, h) occurred in S although C (d, e) did not.

Often, however, what we assert about a given event is that it was sufficient *but not necessary* to a certain other; or again, that it was necessary *but not sufficient* to it; or sometimes, of course, that it was *neither sufficient nor necessary* to another, *i.e.,* that the two were etiologically independent. The question then arises how in such cases we are able to divorce sufficiency and necessity.

As regards the part of such assertions that consists of *affirmation* of sufficiency or of necessity, definition I provides adequate basis; for if, in S, C (a, b) was sufficient to C (g, h), *i.e.,* to *both* C (g) and C (h), then automatically it was sufficient to *each,* for example to C (g); and if C (a, b), *i.e.,* both C (a) and C (b) was

necessary in S to C (g, h) then automatically *each*, for example
C (a), was necessary to C (g, h).

But definitions I, II, and III do not enable us to answer theoretically by a single experiment also the question whether C (a) was *not sufficient,* or was *not necessary,* in S to C (g); for this question concerns not the whole but *only a part* of the change at time T_1, and of the change at time T_2, in S.

To answer it, we need theoretically at least *two* experiments — one of them, the experiment already described, in which C (a, b) and C (g, h) are the only two changes in S; and the other experiment, one in *another* state of affairs Z (a, b, d, e, g, h) theoretically exactly similar to S, but in which C (a) is the only and therefore the total change at time T_1 of Z; so that we may then observe what total change follows in Z.[4]

Let us suppose that the only change in Z that follows C (a) is C (g); and, for convenience in comparing S and Z, let us here represent schematically the events both in S and in Z, as follows:

	At time T_1	*At time T_2*
S (a, b, d, e, g, h)	$\begin{cases} U\ (\quad d, e, g, h) \\ C\ (a, b, \quad) \end{cases}$	$\begin{cases} U\ (\quad d, e, \quad) \\ C\ (\quad g, h) \end{cases}$
Z (a, b, d, e, g, h)	$\begin{cases} U\ (\ b, d, e, g, h) \\ C\ (a, \quad) \end{cases}$	$\begin{cases} U\ (\ b, d, e, \ h) \\ C\ (\quad g, \ ) \end{cases}$

Then, that C (g) is the only change that follows C (a) in Z tells us (according to Def. I) that C (a) was sufficient, and also necessary, to C (g) in Z; and also (according to Defs. II and III) that C (b) was *not necessary* to C (g) in Z since C (b) did not occur in Z yet C (g) did; and that C (a) was *not sufficient* to C (h) in Z since C (a) occurred in Z and yet C (h) did not.

Now, finally, to decide whether *in S,* C (a) was or was not sufficient, or necessary, to C (g), what we must do is to consider the implications which the above findings *regarding Z* have *for*

---

[4] Note that "time T_1" and "time T_2" mean only an earlier and a later time, whether in S or in Z; *i. e.,* the time T_1 of S may or may not be the same time as time T_1 of Z; and likewise with the time T_2 of S and of Z.

S, when these findings are *taken together with the assumption that S and Z are exactly similar.* It must be realized, however, that when we do this we are automatically taking C (a) no longer as the name of one individual, *i.e.,* uniquely dated, event; but as the name of a *kind* of event, of which one instance occurred in *S,* and another instance theoretically exactly similar yet other as to date, occurred in Z. And it must be stressed that it is only when one is thus considering, not individual events as such, but only *instances of a kind, as such,* that one can ever say (as we shall presently be able to say concerning certain events in *S*) "sufficient *but not necessary,*" or "necessary *but not sufficient.*" (On the other hand, when one considers an individual, *i.e.,* a uniquely dated, event, one can still by means of Def. I say "sufficient," but *then* "necessary" goes with it automatically; and one can still say "necessary," but then "sufficient" automatically goes with it.)

Keeping these remarks in mind, we may now state the implications, as regards C (a) and C (g) *in S,* of the assumed exact similarity of *S* and Z, taken with what we now know about *S* and about Z. They are:

1. C (a) in *S* was *both sufficient and necessary* to, *i.e.,* was *both the cause and the condition of,* C (g) in *S*; and conversely, C (g) in *S* was *both necessitated by and contingent upon, i.e.,* was *both the effect and the resultant of,* C (a) in *S*.

2. C (a) in *S* was *not sufficient to, i.e., did not cause,* C (h) in *S*; and conversely, C (h) in *S* was *not necessitated by, i.e.,* was *not the effect of,* C (a) in *S*.

3. C (b) in *S* was *not necessary to, i.e.,* was *not the condition of,* C (g) in *S*; and conversely, C (g) in *S* was *not contingent upon, i.e.,* was *not the resultant of,* C (g) in *S*.[5]

---

[5] Because, for brevity, our notation contemplated in *S* at each of the given times a complex change involving only two features of *S,* we have, in the statements of these implications had to say *the* cause, *the* effect, *the* condition, *the* resultant. But if the complex change in *S* at each of the given times had involved three or more features of *S,* then, in the eight definitions, we should have had to say instead *a part of* the cause, *a part of* the effect, *a* condition, *a* resultant.

On this basis, we are then able to say that, in S, C (a, b) was *sufficient but not necessary* to C (g) ; and conversely, that C (g) *was necessitated by but not contingent upon,* C (a, b). That is, C (a, b) was sufficient indeed, but more than sufficient, *i.e.,* not all of it necessary, to C (g) ; and conversely, that C (g) was necessitated indeed by C (a, b), but not contingent upon the whole of C (a, b).

On that same basis, we are able to say also that, in S, C (a) was *necessary but not sufficient* to C (g, h) ; and conversely, that C (g, h) was *contingent upon, but not all of it necessitated by,* C (a). A concrete example of the divorce of sufficiency and necessity will be given and discussed in Section 7.

Lastly, the definition of what it means to say that a given change C (m) in a given state of affairs V was *neither necessary nor sufficient* to a certain later change that occurred in V, has to be framed in terms of the supposition of not two only but *three* theoretically exactly similar states of affairs. The three, which together define that relationship, are: (1) V as described; (2) W, in which C (m) occurred but C (n) did not follow; and (3) X, in which C (n) occurred but C (m) did not precede.

In the present discussion, the events whose various etiological relationships were being defined were specifically *changes*. When instead they are *unchanges* the definitions, *mutatis mutandis,* remain the same.

4. Etiological Necessity Distinguished from Logical

It is true that sometimes one meets the contention that "necessity" is something found only among logical entities, not among physical or psychical entities. But this contention is rooted only in a tacit and arbitrary decision to restrict "necessity" to what is only *logical* necessity; for common sense and common language recognize types of necessity other than logical. When, for instance, we speak of "the necessities of life" we mean certain physical things — food, water, etc. — without which life ceases; and the impossibility of its being maintained without them is not logical — not a matter of contradiction in terms — but physiological.   Again, it would commonly be said that cutting off the head of a living man suffices to kill him (or, synonymously, that his dying is rendered inevitable, or is necessitated, by it) ; or that explosion of a certain specifiable quantity of dynamite is sufficient to blow up a given tree stump; or that the sound of finger nails grating on a blackboard is sufficient to give some persons the shivers, etc.; and the sufficiency and necessitation meant in these cases are similarly not logical but (respectively) physiological, physical, psychological.   It is in each case *causal* sufficiency — sufficiency of the occurrence of a phenomenon *A* to occurrence of another phenomenon *B*, and therefore necessitation of occurrence of *B* by *A*.   It is a relation between *events,* not between timeless logical entities.   To designate necessity as between events — whether physical, physiological, psychical, or other — I shall, as stated earlier, use the inclusive term "etiological necessity."   The adjective "etiological" is chosen for this purpose in preference to certain others, *e.g.,* "ontological," "real," "natural," "eventual," which also suggest themselves, but each of which seems more liable to misconstruction in certain contexts.

In this general connection, mention must be made of a paper by R. B. Braithwaite, in which he argues for a theory of causation of the same general type as Hume's and criticizes, among others, the theory I maintain.[6]   He seems to assume, however, that only logical necessity is "genuine" necessity.   I say "seems" because he defines "genuine," as used in such contexts, only as "not to be analyzed in a Pickwickian sense" (p. 468, note) ; and the question might thus well reduce to whether a given analysis — for example,

---

[6] R. B. Braithwaite, "The Idea of Necessary Connection," *Mind,* Oct. 1927 and Jan. 1928.

mine, or his — is or is not Pickwickian. Like him, I agree with G. E. Moore "in thinking that the task of philosophy is to analyze propositions which are universally accepted, not to reject the propositions of common sense because they cannot be analyzed in a particular way" (p. 469). But it seems to me that common sense, in all the statements I have given as examples, does mean to assert necessity as between certain events. Common sense would say, for instance, that, to kill Charles I, it was *enough* — i.e., it was *sufficient* — to cut off his head. And the converse of "sufficient to" is "necessitated by"; that is, cutting off his head necessitated his dying. But, apparently because this necessitation cannot be analyzed as *logical* necessitation, Braithwaite denies that it is "genuine"; asserting that "if causal propositions are taken as asserting a genuine necessary connexion between events then . . . there are no true causal propositions" (p. 468). And he then offers an analysis of causation in terms of two universal propositions of fact (*vs.* "of law") which — just because it leaves out the very necessitation common sense means to assert when it asserts causation — seems to me to be an analysis of causation only in a Pickwickian (or Humean) sense. Moreover, the force of Braithwaite's discussion is weakened throughout by the fact that his examples are for the most part *general* causal propositions, whereas the causal propositions of the truth of which common sense is most confident are singular propositions. In such a causal proposition as that swallowing a pound of arsenic always causes death, physical or physiological necessitation is of course not to be found; but this is because the proposition is simply false. If the man's stomach is immediately pumped out, he may not die; or, if someone immediately shoots him through the heart, his death is caused by this not by the arsenic. Any general causal proposition which, like this one about arsenic, omits to specify what the circumstances at the time are assumed to be (and thus presents the causal relation erroneously as dyadic instead of triadic) is almost certain to be false. Even in the much stronger example of cutting off a man's head it is conceivable that the science of the future might discover some way of preventing this from killing him. But when we pick as examples singular instead of general propositions of causation, the circumstances are thereby automatically given. The supposition, for instance, that some way exists by which Charles I's head could have been stuck on again and his life preserved is then irrelevant; for what common sense asserts about his death is no universal proposition, but is only that, in the circumstances *that were present at the time* (which included the fact that no such surgical feat occurred), the beheading did suffice to cause his death.

Braithwaite's reference to the possibility that a definition may be Pickwickian raises the important methodological question as to how one can find out whether or not a proposed definition of what a term means is really what it means. For after all, one might attack skeptically even Hume's own contention as to the nature of *logical* necessity. One might ask him how he knows, for instance, that from "This man is tall and handsome" it necessarily follows that "This man is tall." For, conceivably, this might not be really, but only seemingly, an example of logical necessitation. And, if the reply were that to suppose the first true and the second false is to suppose a contradiction, one might still ask whether this very sort of relationship between two propositions is *really* what logical necessitation of the second by the first consists in.

The answer, of course, is that, ultimately, this is a matter of the meaning which the words "contradiction" and "logical necessitation" *in fact* have in the language. And it seems to me, similarly, that when the question is instead as to whether the definition I proposed, of "causation" or "necessitation among events," is what these terms really mean, the answer is ultimately again a matter of whether the proposed definition fits the use the language does in fact make of those terms.

To show that it does fit, and thus that it is not Pickwickian, I now ask what in fact one would do if one wished to discover, for instance, whether or not, in order to bring a certain chair from the other side of the room, it is enough, *i.e.*, is sufficient, to say "Chair, come here!" Evidently, one would not proceed by asking whether the supposition that the chair does not come implies a contradiction. Rather, one would simply make the experiment, *i.e.*, one would utter the command. Then, if the chair did not come, this single experiment would have proved that, under the circumstances which existed, uttering that command was not enough, was not sufficient; *i.e.*, that it did not cause, did not necessitate, movement of the chair.

On the other hand, if the chair had then immediately come (and one's command really was, as it is assumed to have been, the single change then in the circumstances), then I submit that one would likewise have proved, and again by a single experiment, that the command was enough, sufficed; *i.e.*, that under the circumstances then existing, it caused, necessitated, the coming of the chair.

The evidence that the definition of causation I have proposed is what causation, *i.e.*, event-necessitation, really means is thus that when we desire to find out whether a given event will, under the circumstances existing at the moment, suffice to cause, *i.e.*, necessitate, the occurrence of a certain other, we actually proceed as the definition proposed would require us to proceed, and the definition does not call for repetition of the experiment. In practice, it is true, one would repeat the experiment a few times, but this would be done only to minimize the chance that the change introduced, *e.g.*, the command, was not really the only change that occurred at the time in the given state of affairs; and evidently, to do this would not be to proceed on a different definition of causation, but on the contrary to increase the probability that one really complied with the requirements of the given definition.

In the case of terms such as sufficiency and necessity, which are in common use, the philosopher's business is not to restrict or to expand arbitrarily either their application or their implication, but first to classify the variety of instances in which they are actually employed, and then to discover analytically the intension which corresponds to each class of employments. Occasion for ruling instead of analyzing arises only at the "edges" of such classes, where ordinary language hesitates and where ruling therefore does not violate any established usage. That is, the philosopher's business, where such terms are concerned, is not to make over existing language, but only to perfect it — to purge it of defects, such as vagueness, ambiguity, or inconsistency, which it happens still to contain.

5. Is Causation Observable?

The analysis we have now made of the nature of the causal relation shows that this relation is not, as sometimes assumed, a mysterious one, hidden behind what we are able to observe in any instance of it. The truth is only that it is hard and often impossible to attain certainty that the relation we actually observe in given cases really conforms to the definition; that is, in the main, that the change we observe in the state of affairs constituted by the setup of a given experiment is the *only* observable change in that setup at the time.[7]

The difficulty of making sure of this, however, is of a type not at all peculiar to causality, for it is of the same type as, and theoretically neither greater nor less than, in any other case where

---

[7] Changes of kinds or magnitudes not amenable to observation are of course never observed but only postulated; and the need to postulate them arises only if no cause, or no effect, of a given event is observable, and if we assume that one nevertheless exists.

we are called upon to establish through observation the truth of a *universal negative* proposition. The proposition in the case of causality is that no observable change other than a certain observed one occurred at a given time in a given set of circumstances. It is difficult to make sure that no other occurred; but it is likewise difficult to make sure by observation that there is at a given time no mosquito in a given room, or no flea on a given dog. All we really know in any such case is that we have searched and not found any; that our method of search was one capable of revealing cases of the sort of thing we were looking for; and that the more thorough and careful was our search with such a method, the less likely it is that a case of what we look for would have escaped our observation. Thus, theoretically, all that observation can yield is probability, in higher or lower degree, that the universal negative proposition we are concerned with is true; but actually, there are cases where the thing searched for, and the method of search used, are such that the supposition that the thing might have eluded our search retains no plausibility whatever. If, for example, the statement had been that there is no horse or, more specifically, no horse of ordinary size in a given room, then, if the room were well lighted, not too large and not encumbered with large objects, and our eyesight reasonably good, the probability that we should not have found a horse if one had been in the room would, it may fairly be claimed, be zero.

The bearing of these remarks on the question of the observability of the causal relation is that this relation is not in principle, or even in practice, unobservable, but that in many cases it is difficult or impossible to attain certainty that what we observe really conforms to the definition of the relation. However, if any specific doubt as to its conformity arises, additional observation often can dispose of the doubt and thus increase the probability that the given case conforms to the definition. That the conditions under which experimentation is carried on are in many cases so favorable that a causal connection is conclusively established by it is the harder to deny when one remembers that experiments performed under laboratory conditions are the very foundation of the imposing achievements of which natural science can boast today. But, for instances where causation is really observed, we need not go outside common experience: I submit that, when Charles I lost his head, it would have been mere silly perversity on the part of the executioner or of other close spectators to maintain that the blow of the axe was not certainly but only probably what caused the head to come off.

Upon analysis, Hume's contention that causation, in the sense of necessitation of an event by another, is never observable among events, ultimately reduces to two propositions, one true and the other false. One is:

(*a*) That *logical* necessitation is not observable among events. This is true, for events themselves are not logical entities, but physical or psychological entities. The other proposition is:

(*b*) That "necessitation" always means logical necessitation. This is simply false; for it is a proposition about language as it actually is — a proposition as to what the word "necessitation" or its cognates are in fact used to mean in ordinary language. And physical or psychological necessitation is undeniably what common usage means in innumerable instances — whenever, for example, such expressions as "physically impossible," "psychologically inevitable," "physiologically necessary," etc., occur; and in all verbs of physical or psychological causation, such as to break, to bend, to cure, to kill, to drag, to annoy, to induce, etc. — all of which in fact are used in the sense of "to make occur" an event of this or that specific sort. Moreover, it would be only by using "to observe" in a Pickwickian sense that it would be possible to deny that we ever observe one thing breaking, or bending, or killing, or dragging, etc. another thing.

What the correct analysis of *physical* or *psychological* necessitation is, is of course a distinct question; but that a given analysis does not reduce it to *logical* necessitation is not the least evidence that it is an incorrect analysis. Rather, if it did so reduce it, this would be evidence that the analysis is Pickwickian.

6. Causality a Relation Between Concrete Individual Events

The relation which an experiment seeks to exhibit is, as we have analyzed it, a relation between two concrete, individual events and a set of concrete circumstances: the definition of the relation does not employ the notion of collections or kinds of events.

Accordingly, if the requirements specified in the definition are really met by the relation between two concrete events in a given case, then the two events concerned really are cause and effect even if each of them should happen to be completely unique in the history of the universe. Just because the definition does not employ the notion of recurrence of the sequence, the observing of such recurrence is theoretically unnecessary to the identification of cases of causation. There is need to repeat an experiment only in order to make certain or more probable that the requirements of the definition were actually met. Moreover, as pointed out earlier, regularity of sequence does not at all guarantee that the earlier of the two events concerned causes the other, but only suggests that perhaps it does; and we can be said to have observed that indeed it does, only when we have succeeded in testing that suggestion by means of an experiment, as described in what precedes.

It was to avoid having to say, as Hume's definition would require, that day was the cause of night and night was the cause of day, that Mill added, in his own definition of causation, the requirement of "unconditionality" to that of invariability of sequence — without perceiving, however, that as soon as "unconditionality" was introduced, the requirement of invariability became superfluous. For if an event B "unconditionally" followed from an antecedent event A, *i.e.*, if the event A was indeed *sufficient* without additional conditions to the event B, then obviously as often as A might recur identically, B would necessarily recur also. But this "unconditionality" is the very thing which Mill had declared was not revealed by mere regularity of sequence. Hence it has to be ascertained experimentally, and therefore in some individual case, by the "method of difference." Mill, however, never seems to see that this means that the canon of difference is then the very definition of the relation called causation, not the description of a sign of that relation; and that it defines this relation in terms of *one* experiment.

His failure to see this is perhaps due mainly to the fact that he never clearly perceived the difference between experimentation itself and comparison of two (or more) experiments for purposes of generalization by abstraction.[8] He never was adequately conscious that it is one thing to introduce an only change into the set of concrete circumstances of a given concrete entity and note what change, if any, this entity then undergoes; and a very different thing to compare two more or less similar such experiments which yielded an effect of the same kind, and to note in what respects alone the change introduced in each case, and also the circumstances in each case, agreed, *i.e.*, were alike, in the two experiments. To compare in this way the two experiments is indeed to use the "method of agreement," but as so used it is a method of *abstraction* for purposes of generalization of the results of experiments, not at all itself a method of experimentation. Discrimination of the *concrete event* which caused a given event in a given case is one thing, and discrimination of a *common kind,* to which the cause event in each of several cases belonged, is quite another thing.

---

[8] This has been noted by W. S. Jevons, *Pure Logic and Other Minor Works,* p. 251; and is apparent even in Mill's formulation of the canon of difference.

The *experimental* use of the method of agreement, on the other hand, would consist in taking a concrete set of circumstances, under which a certain phenomenon P continues, and *altering* the circumstances, one by one, without this causing the phenomenon to cease, until a single one remains unaltered; which, one concludes, must be the cause. It is perhaps needless to say that causation is not often discovered in this way. What this procedure actually is good for is to eliminate wrong hypotheses as to what is the cause.

7. Ambiguity of "The Cause of an Event"

To the definition I have given of the term "cause" it might be objected that we cannot, without violation of it, refuse to regard as part of the cause of a given change in a given state of affairs any part of the change antecedent to it in that state of affairs; but that on the contrary we very frequently in ordinary language seem to use the word cause in such a way as to do just that. For example, at the instant a brick strikes a window pane, the pane is also struck perhaps by the air waves due to the song of a canary near by. Yet we usually would say that the cause of the breakage was the impact of the brick, and that the impact of the air waves, although it was part of the prior total change in the given state of affairs, was no part of the cause. This being the way in which the word "cause" actually is sometimes used, how then can a definition which forbids us to call the cause anything less than *the whole* of the prior change in the given state of affairs be regarded as a correct analysis of the meaning which the term "cause" actually possesses?

But the incompatibility of this use of "cause" with the definition is only apparent, and the appearance of it depends on a confusion between two different questions, due in turn to the fact that the phrase "the cause of an event" is used in one case in the sense of "the *concrete* event which caused a given *concrete* event," and in the other in the sense of "the *kind* of event an instance of which caused a given event *of a stated kind*."

Explicitly stated, the first of the two questions is then, *What did cause the whole of the completely determinate change which occurred at the given time T_2 in the given state of affairs?* The second question, on the other hand, assumes the answer to the first as already obtained by observation, and goes on to ask, *What part of what caused it is left if we subtract from that cause such portions and specificities as were unnecessary to causation of the part, described not more determinately than as "breakage of window pane," of what occurred at time T_2?*[9]

When the question faced is the first, then the song of the canary, the precise mass, shape, position and speed of the brick, and every other part and specificity of what occurred at time T_1 is causally relevant to one or another part or feature of what occurred at time T_2. Hence, when events and states of affairs are taken thus in their full determinateness and entirety, the earlier of the two only changes in the given state of affairs is not only sufficient but also necessary to the later change, and the later not only necessitated by but also contingent upon the earlier.

On the other hand, consider the situation when the question faced is the second one. Since the whole of the earlier event is sufficient to the whole of the later, it is sufficient to all its parts and all their features, — in particular, to the part described abstractly only as "breakage of window pane." But not the whole of the earlier event is necessary to this part of the later. The canary's singing, for example, is not necessary to it, although the singing too had effects, and these too were parts, but *other* parts, of the whole later event.

---

[9] The words "determinate," and "determinable," or "indeterminate," are used here and throughout in W. E. Johnson's sense (*Logic,* Vol. I, Ch. XI). For example, the description "breakage of window pane" specifies a less determinate kind of event than would the description "breakage of window pane into five pieces," and the latter description in turn a less determinate kind than would be specified by "breakage of window pane into three large and two small pieces"; and so on.

Thus, whenever that of which we ask for the cause is an event not taken in its full determinateness and entirety, but only described, (*i.e.,* taken only in so far as it has the features needed to make it an instance of the abstract kind the description names), then, in every such case, what is asked is identification of its cause *similarly by abstract description only, i.e.,* identification of it *only as instance of a certain kind of event,* namely, a kind such that any instance of it, in any circumstances of a certain kind, causes an event of the given kind (*e.g.,* of the kind "breakage of window pane").

Moreover, since in the great majority of cases we *put a name* on the event whose cause we ask for, the second of the two questions distinguished above is the one we are asking in such cases. The question we ask is then a call not literally for the cause of the event occurring, but a call to *abstract, i.e.,* to *extract,* from its cause such parts of it as alone are causally relevant to those parts which we select and abstract out of the occurring event by the mere act of *putting a name* on that of which we seek the cause. It is to be noted that the abstractive problem so set concerns not solely the one event occurring, but essentially also at least one other occurrence. For it is the problem of discovering the respects in which the concrete cause of the concrete event occurring resembles the concrete causes of one or more certain other concrete events that resemble the given concrete event in the respects implied by the name we put on this event.

8. Pragmatic Interest in Causal Connections

Throughout a discussion of causality it is well to bear in mind that although man's interest in certain kinds of events rather than others does not determine what causal connections consists of, nor what causal connections subsist in nature, that interest nevertheless determines the kinds of events into the causal connections of which man will inquire and therefore the connections he will discover.

Man's interest in causal connections is at the outset, and throughout largely remains, interest in controlling or in foreknowing the occurrence of events of kinds important, whether favorably or unfavorably, for his purposes. Moreover, the only kinds of events he is able to cause or present "at will" and directly, *i.e.,* those immediately caused to occur by his merely willing them, are certain changes in his own body, the most important of which (so far as he is dealing with things other than men) are the movements of his limbs, especially his hands. Hence any events voluntarily caused by man in parts of nature other than his own body have to be caused ultimately through some movement in his own body, directly itself caused by the mere volition.[10] Thus, man's search for causal connections in nature is in large part prompted by one or the other of the two practical interests respectively described by the following two questions:

(*a*) How, *i.e.,* through what intermediary causal steps, can some movement of mine that I can cause by merely willing it cause (or as the case may be, prevent) in the extra-somatic world an event of a certain kind K important to me.

(*b*) What kind(s) of event(s) important to me would be caused (or as the case may be, prevented) by an event of kind K, which I can directly or mediately cause at will.

The first question is as to the kind of means by which I can at will cause (or prevent) an effect of a particular kind K important to me. The second question is as to the kinds of *aims* which the kinds of events causable (or preventable) at will by me directly or indirectly would enable me to achieve.

Now it is obvious that for practical purposes, whether of the one or the other of these two sorts, causal knowledge is of direct

---

[10] The experimental investigations in recent years of the possibility of affecting material events other than bodily ones directly by volition—the so-called "psychokinetic," or "PK" effect—suggest that the statement above may have to be qualified somewhat. See in this connection J. B. Rhine's recent book *The Reach of the Mind.*

value only so far as it has been generalized.   Hence, whenever our purposes at the time are practical ones — and this means ordinarily — then the interest to us of strictly concrete individual facts of causation is chiefly the indirect one of constituting raw material for generalizations, *i.e.,* for causal laws.   This explains why we so naturally and so persistently confuse the question, what did cause one given concrete event, with the very different question, in what respects does that cause resemble the causes of certain other events of the same sort previously observed taking place under similar circumstances.   For it is from the answer to this second question that we learn what in such environments we need do to cause the occurrence of another event of the given kind.   And evidently just this is, in many cases, the practically very valuable information we desire ultimately to obtain.   But although it is true that, in so far as we are practical beings, we are not directly interested in concrete individual facts of causation, it is not true that there are no such facts.

9. Causality Distinct from Legality

To say that causation is basically a relation between concrete individual events is not to deny that there are such things as causal laws, nor to deny that laws, and therefore causal laws too, concern events qua cases of the kinds the particular laws specifically mention.   For, as already pointed out, if in a number of individual cases of causation, the causes, the effects, and the circumstances, respectively, are alike in describable respects, then an empirical generalization becomes possible, which covers these cases and all others resembling them in the described respects; and such a generalization (whether in the instance it turn out to be valid or invalid) is of the nature of a causal law.   But the notion of cause nevertheless remains distinct from the notion of law; for a law is simply a proposition concerning some percentage — usually 100 per cent, *i.e.,* all — of the cases of some specified kind; and they need not be cases of causation. They may be cases of coexistence of certain properties in certain substances; or the law may express only a statistical correlation between facts not standing one to the other as cause to effect; or a law may be a mathematical or a logical law; and none of these laws concern causes. And, conversely, the notion of cause can be defined, as we have done, without introducing the notion of law.[11]

D. H. Parker, in his *Experience and Substance*,[12] declares it to be a mistake (and one with which he charges the present writer) to believe that "causality between unique events is primary, and that cause in the sense of causal law is secondary." The reason he gives is that "the unique happening is always capable of generalization." He illustrates what this means by reference to the unique fact that Brutus killed Caesar: It "can be generalized, as, first, that Brutus would kill any tyrant, generalizing Caesar, and, secondly that any brave patriot would kill any tyrant, generalizing Brutus."

These two generalizations, one might remark, are highly dubious; yet their dubiousness does not in the least render dubious that Brutus's act was what caused Caesar's death. But even if they were valid, I am at a loss to understand why Parker regards them as showing that my contention as to the analysis of the causal relation is mistaken; for my contention is not that there are no causal laws, nor is it that there are cases of causation not theoretically capable of being generalized. My contention, so far as Parker's example is concerned, would have to do only with the

---

[11] Reference to Meyerson's insistence on the distinctness of causality from legality would be appropriate here were it not that by "cause" he does not mean what ordinarily is meant and is here under discussion, but he means the hidden respect of identity between the antecedent and consequent in a causal law, which hidden identity explains the law, and which identity a *theory* of the phenomenon supposes. "Cause" in this peculiar sense thus means the theoretical *explicans* of a *law*. But the relation between a law and the *explicans* of it is very different from that between a given concrete event and another concrete event by which it was caused, and also from the relation between a kind of event and the kind of effect a case of it regularly causes.

[12] P. 230.

meaning of "killed," *i.e.,* of "caused to die," in the statement that Brutus killed Caesar. What I would contend as to this is that to say that a certain action which Brutus performed with his dagger in his hand "caused" Caesar's death means that this action of Brutus's was the only change in Caesar's immediate environment immediately before the beginning of the event called Caesar's dying. Parker's remarks do not show this contention to be mistaken, for they do not concern it. Nor does the possibility of the generalization that, under circumstances such as those that were Caesar's, such stabbing through the heart as Caesar underwent would cause any man to die, have any bearing on that contention. Furthermore, Parker's perfectly true statement that the possibility of generalization is necessary to the practical value of causality is also irrelevant to my contention; for the question as to what it means to say that a certain individual event caused a certain other, and the question as to whether causality would have practical value for us if causal generalizations were not possible, are distinct questions. I do not recall whether I have anywhere said that causal laws are "secondary," but if I did what I meant was that a causal law is not causal because general (since even non-causal laws are that), but only because each of the facts that are the material generalized is a causal fact in its own individual right (instead of, as Hume would have it, only by right of its co-membership with others in a certain class of pairs of successive events). For any one of them to be a causal fact, it is irrelevant whether or not it is unique, *i.e.,* whether or not there ever exist others resembling it. Hence, no contradiction is entailed in the supposition that there might exist individual causal facts but that none of them ever recurred.

10. Causality Not a Two-Term Relation

Causality is often assumed to be a relation involving only two terms, cause and effect. But, as pointed out earlier, the circumstances constitute a third term, which cannot be included in the cause since the latter is always a single change or single unchange in the circumstances. A causal law is therefore not of the form: "An event of kind *A* always causes an event of kind *B*," but always of the form: "An event of kind *A within circumstances of kind C* always causes an event of kind *B*."

Mill, it will be recalled, would have it that causality was a dyadic relation, for he wrote: "The cause, then, philosophically speaking, is the sum total of the conditions, positive and negative taken together; the whole of the contingencies of every description, which being realized, the consequent invariably follows."[13] This definition does away with the familiar distinction between cause and conditions, and to justify this Mill writes[14]: "Nothing can better show the absence of any scientific ground for the distinction between the cause of a phenomenon and its conditions, than the capricious manner in which we select from among the conditions that which we choose to denominate the cause." He takes as an example the fact that a stone thrown into water falls to the bottom, and points out that sometimes one and sometimes another of the conditions of it is called the cause.

Such plausibility as this gives to his contention, however, is due only to the fact that the statement he uses as example is simply false if taken, as he makes it, without such qualifications as that the stone is not pumice, and that it is within the gravitational field of the earth. Mill afterwards mentions such qualifications as conditions any one of which would sometimes be — correctly, he says, in common parlance — spoken of as "the cause" of the fall of the stone to the bottom.

But it would *not* be correct, even in common parlance, to speak of any of these as the cause unless it constituted *a difference being*

---

[13] *System of Logic,* 8th ed., p. 241.   Mill later adds the requirement of unconditionality to that of invariability.
[14] P. 238.

introduced in contemplated circumstances, in which until then the stone was not falling to the bottom. That there is nothing capricious about the common use of the distinction between cause and condition becomes obvious as soon as we make the given statement unambiguous either by mentioning the kind of stone meant and the circumstances in which the stone is assumed to be, or, still better, by considering an individual case. Suppose for example that the stone concerned was a certain granite pebble which had been on the bank of, say, the Ten Mile River in Rhode Island. Then, that the stone was at or near the surface of the earth is a circumstance given as present. Moreover, it is one which is a *condition* of the stone's falling to the bottom; but it cannot possibly be spoken of as what *caused* its fall since no difference as to this circumstance occurs; *i.e.,* there was a time during which it was already present and yet the stone did not fall. On the other hand, that the bank on which it rested was washed away by the current at the time in view would be a possible answer to the question as to what caused the stone to fall when it did, for it would constitute an immediately antecedent only difference occurring in the circumstances that existed.

11. Causes Distinguished from Agents and from Forces

Causes and effects are always events, never "substances," if by the latter be meant such entities as gold, oil, trees, mountains, dogs, men, which are commonly also called "things" or "objects" as distinguished from the properties they have and from the states or the relations in which they are at given times. But substances, in this sense, and only substances, can be agents and patients. A substance is an *agent,* and "operates" or "acts upon" another, in so far as some change in it or of it causes a change in or of that other substance. The latter substance, on the other hand, then "undergoes" or "responds with" a change, and is in so far a *patient.* Consider, for instance, the statement that a certain man made a chair. Analysis of the meaning of this statement reveals three different relations: (1) The relation between the man and the *lumber* out of which he makes the chair is that of *agent* to *patient*. It is a relation between two substances, and so is (2) the relation, *viz.*, that of *creator* to *created*, between the man and the *chair* he has made. (3) The relation of *cause* to *effect*, on the other hand, is present in the example only between the *volitions or the movements* of the man, and the *changes of shape and of relations* of the pieces of lumber; and both of these are events, not substances, although obviously these events are changes in the states and relations of the two substances concerned, *viz.*, the carpenter and the lumber. The three relations mentioned are of course here intimately associated, but this is no reason for confusing them with one another.

There are some relations other than those of agent to patient and of creator to created, which must likewise be distinguished from the relation of cause to effect; namely, the relation of *part* to *whole* and that of *component* to *compound*. A wheel, for example, or an engine, although necessary to the existence of an automobile, is not a cause of it but a part of it. Similarly, oxygen is not a cause of water but a component of it. If, however, an electric spark were occurring in a vessel containing hydrogen, and then oxygen were introduced, the introduction of it (which is an event) would properly be said to be the cause of the synthesis of water (which is also an event) immediately ensuing in such a case.

It is important also to notice that *forces* are never properly spoken of as causes. If, when the string by which a weight was suspended is cut and the weight falls, one asks what caused it to fall, many persons would answer that the force of gravitation did so. But obviously the right answer would be that, in the given circumstances (*viz.*, neighborhood to the earth and absence of any support other than the string and the air), the *event* consisting of severance of the string was what caused the weight to fall at that time. For "gravitation" is simply the name for the general fact, *i.e.,* for the law, that if at any time in such circumstances a body is left unsupported it falls. This law was just as much a fact before the string was cut as after; yet it caused nothing either before or after because it is not itself an event but only a relation between certain kinds of events and of situations. This, which is true of the "force of gravitation," is equally true of the other "forces of nature." On analysis they all turn out to be causal laws; that is, the description of a "force" is always a statement that in situations of a given kind, an event of a certain kind always causes an event of a certain other kind. And no law — not even a causal law — ever can itself function as a cause.

In such an expression as "the force of the explosion was not enough to lift the stump," the meaning of the word "force" is not the same as in the expression "a force of nature." In the former, it designates the *magnitude* of a given case of the sort of event concerned, *viz.,* explosion; and the assertion is that although the given event was of a kind some cases of which do cause such an effect as was desired, yet this case, having only the magnitude it did have, had not that effect.

12.   The Relations of Events to "Times"

It is essential to realize that every event has some duration, *i.e.,* takes some time, occupies some segment of time. If we agree to mean by an "instant" a *point* in time, *i.e.,* a wholly durationless cut of time, then we can say that at an instant nothing occurs, *i.e.,* nothing either changes or lasts; but that whatever occurs takes place *from* a certain instant *to* a certain other. No instant is next to any other instant, and therefore between any two instants there is an infinite number of other instants. But a segment of time, *i.e.,* a duration, and whatever event occupies it, can be next to another, and is so if and only if the terminal instant of one is also the initial instant of the other; just as a segment of a line is strictly next to another segment of it if and only if the last point of one and the first point of the other are the very same point. "A time," in the sense of a segment of time, is theoretically infinitely divisible into smaller and smaller segments, but each of the segments resulting at any given stage of the division has an initial and a terminal instant, has some duration, and is next to every other segment, whether long or short, of which the last instant is the given segment's first, or of which the first instant is the given segment's last. On the other hand, "a time," in the sense of an instant, has no duration at all, is indivisible, and has no next predecessor or successor. In proximate as distinguished from remote causation, the last instant of the cause and the first instant of the effect are identically the same instant, and it is therefore not possible that some other event should occur after the cause-event and before the effect-event and "thwart the action of the cause."[15]

13. Contiguity, or Action at a Distance?

Contiguity in time and space is commonly regarded as essential to proximate causation; that is, to causation in any instance where no intermediary chain of effects and causes is involved. Hume, for example, when endeavoring to discover the characteristics of the relation between objects — he should have said events — that are considered causes and effects, writes: "Nothing can operate in a time or place, which is ever so little remov'd from those of its existence. Tho' distant objects may sometimes seem productive of each other, they are commonly found upon examination to be link'd by a chain of causes, which are contiguous among themselves, and to the distant objects; and when in any particular

---

[15] That the beginnings and ends of events are not sharp—not objectively marked by one specific instant or point—is true in many if not all cases. Yet two events— say a falling and a landing—are conceptually distinct; and although one's specification of a particular instant, as marking the end of what in the particular case one meant by the "falling," will unavoidably be more or less arbitrary, it will nonetheless automatically mark the beginning of what in the particular case one correspondingly meant by the "landing."

instance we cannot discover this connexion, we still presume it to exist."[16]

But there are instances where observation, as distinguished from theoretical interpretation of what is observed, testifies that causation sometimes occurs at a distance in space, or in time. For example, the approach of a magnet causes pieces of iron at a distance to move towards it. Another example, but one where the effect follows the cause not immediately but only at a distance in time during which no observable changes occur, is provided by an experiment in which two colorless liquids—potassium iodate and sulphurous acid—are mixed together without any observable immediate effect. But after a lapse of time the mixture suddenly acquires vivid color. This example has the appearance of being one where an event (the mixing) causes another event (the advent of color) *at a temporal distance empty of changes.*

The interpretation which chemical theory puts on the observed fact is here that although the mixing apparently has no effect during the intervening time, nor the eventual emergence of the color apparently any cause immediately preceding, nevertheless the time interval is really occupied by two chemical reactions, *i.e.,* by certain molecular changes — one of the reactions having to be completed before the other can begin, and the second having as perceptible immediate effect the vivid color. In the instance of the magnet and the iron filings, on the other hand, the theoretical interpretation of the observed fact is that the filings were in contact with something called the "field" of the magnet. In both examples, the need to interpret the fact observed, instead of taking it at its face value, arises ultimately from the tacit assumption that contiguity is an essential character of direct causation.

Nevertheless, in the definition of direct causation we offered, we did not stipulate contiguity of cause and effect. The reason was that the notion of *boundaries* of a thing, and therefore the

---

16 Hume, *A Treatise of Human Nature,* Selby-Bigge ed., Part III, Sect. II, p. 75.

notion of contiguity or contact which logically depends on that of boundaries, is in final analysis definable itself only in terms of "action," *i.e.,* of causation of one or another kind of effect at some locus; and thus that a given thing has not just one kind of boundary but several, which do not all coincide. This entails that one identical instance of causation can be causation at a distance in terms of one kind of boundary of the things concerned; but also causation in contact in terms of another kind of boundary of the same things.

Doubtless, our first notions of the boundary of a thing are tactual and visual: the boundary is at the point in space where light is reflected by the thing, and where presence also of the light-reflecting and tactual boundary of one's own body would then cause a tactual sensation. But in the instance of, say, a fog, or a mass of gas, or a magnetic or electrical field, such a notion of boundaries has little or no applicability. Instances of this kind lead us to say, more generally, that *the boundaries of a thing are the points at which approach to the thing first is capable of causing directly effects of specified kinds and magnitudes.* More briefly, a thing extends to wherever it can act directly, *i.e.,* act without needing therefor to act on some intermediary other thing.

This entails that we cannot speak simply of "the" boundary of a thing, but must distinguish between its light-reflecting boundary, its tactual boundary, its gravitational boundary, its magnetic boundary, and so on; and indeed that we should have to specify, for instance, the minimum magnetic effect which for our purposes on a given occasion has any relevance. A thing, thus, has boundaries of various kinds, some of which lie beyond certain others; and no one of them is more truly "the" boundary of the thing than is any of the others.

The light-reflecting and tangible boundary of a thing (the two happen to coincide in space) could be described equally properly as the "field" of light-reflection, and of tangibility or mechanical action, of the thing. It is a surface, whereas the magnetic, or the electrical, or the gravitational field of a thing is a volume.

The habit of regarding in most cases the light-reflecting-tactual boundary as "the" boundary of a thing, and of conceiving contact or contiguity in terms of it, might therefore be considered an instance of intellectual provincialism. It has, however, the pragmatic sanction of being the kind of boundary relevant to the dealings we most commonly have with things. Also, some one of the various kinds of boundaries of a thing has to be chosen as origin, in terms of relation to which the loci of the other kinds of boundaries can be described; and the light-reflecting-tactual boundary is the most convenient one to employ as origin.

It is thus evident that the action of the magnet on the iron filings is "action at a distance" only in the sense that magnetic contiguity or contact between them occurs at a point which lies beyond that to which the filings would have to be brought in order to make their light-reflecting-tactual boundary contiguous with the light-reflecting-tactual boundary of the magnet.

Because our definition of direct action defines it without employing the notion of contiguity, we are able to say that a thing extends to wherever it can act directly, i.e., act without acting on some intermediary thing. But this definition of a boundary of a thing automatically provides a definition of "contiguity" in whichever one of the senses of this term corresponds to the kind of boundary being considered. Moreover, with contiguity thus defined in terms of causation, contiguity of the relevant kind is analytically guaranteed wherever there is causation.

It is worth noting that if contiguity had been stipulated in the definition of causation, and had been there defined as contact of the light-reflection and tactual boundary of one thing with that of another, then such a definition of causation would have failed to fit instances of causation where contact in *this* sense is not present — for example, the instance of the magnet and iron filings. Moreover, in cases of causation such as this, where what we perceive is distance, instead of contact in the sense we just assumed to have been stipulated, we could not restore theoretically contact *in that sense* by postulating it between postulated intermediary entities *individually non-light-reflecting and intangible,* such as molecules or atoms or lines of magnetic force. For contact *in that sense* between entities that do not reflect light and are not tangible is a contradiction.

14. Causation and Transfer of Energy

It is sometimes asserted that, for natural science, causation means transfer of energy. The truth, however, is only that natural science well may, and perhaps does, choose to concern itself only with those cases of causation in which transfer of energy occurs. That "transfer of energy" is not, for natural scientists any more than for anyone else, the definition of causation by means of which they identify cases of causation empirically is shown by the fact that cases of causation were identified by them long before anything was known about energy, and still today are identified in numberless cases without making the measurements needed to find out that energy has been transferred. "Transfer of energy" is thus only an account, although no doubt a true one, of what hiddenly occurs in certain cases which are previously, and therefore in some other manner, known to be cases of physical causation.

If there is a meaning of causality peculiar to natural science, or more particularly to physics, it is rather that causality is the relation which subsists between the state of a physical system at one time and at another time, if specification of the values of the quantities which define the state of the system at (any) one instant makes it possible to ascertain through laws of physics the values of these quantities at all other times — these quantities being, for instance, the position and velocity of a particle as defining its mechanical state; or the volume and temperature of a gas as defining its thermodynamic state, etc.[17]

With further reference, however, to the relation between causality in the ordinary experimental sense and energy, the question may be raised whether energy is not itself ultimately defined in terms involving such causality, rather than causality defined in terms of energy. To discern the true state of affairs in this matter is not easy — chiefly, perhaps, because of the difficulty of ascertaining just what the physicist is speaking of when he speaks of "energy."

To avoid confusion we need first to distinguish between the concrete, existing physical world itself, and the conceptions, mathematical and logical, which the physicist constructs and uses in his investigations of it — conceptions, for example, such as those of a "particle" having position but no extension, and of the "mass," "acceleration," etc., of it. These conceptions are all "symbolic" in the sense that, although suggested by our experience, they represent "an idealization of that experience";[18] and the laws of physics concern *directly* only such idealizations. That is, they directly concern only entities, conditions, and situations that never actually occur. These symbolic or ideal conceptions, nevertheless, "apply" to the concrete, observable physical world in the sense that, by means (in part) of them, the physicist is able to make concerning it predictions which observation verifies. This is possible because, in addition to formulating the laws of physics in terms of idealized entities, he also stipulates certain laboratory operations (which include experimental procedures and the taking of measurements of various sorts) as rules for trans-

---

17 H. Margenau, "Metaphysical Elements in Physics," *Reviews of Modern Physics,* vol. 13, no. 3, July 1941, p. 187. In this sense, "causality . . . has meaning only when applied to constructs of explanation, *i.e.,* to theories. A theory is causal if a set of quantities can be found whose propagation is self-regulatory through laws which remain unchanged in time."

18 R. B. Lindsay and H. Margenau, *The Foundations of Physics,* p. 80.

lating observed physical facts into terms of the idealized entities, and conversely, for translating into terms of empirically verifiable predictions the outcome of mathematical operations upon the idealized entities. By virtue of this, the words which are the names of the idealized entities and of their various properties — words such as "particle," "mass," "force," "energy," etc. — can come to be also names for certain observable phenomena and their observable properties. But it is essential not to forget that they come to be names for these only in so far as the definitions of those words in terms of ideal conceptions are supplemented by descriptions of certain laboratory operations. It is *these operations* which make, and alone make, those same words stand for something more than ideal conceptions, *viz.,* for really existing, observable physical entities and their properties.

This means that if the word "mass," for example, is to be regarded as the name of something which exists not just in the world of the physicist's idealized conceptions, but actually in the observable physical world, then the definition of "mass" in this sense cannot consist merely of a certain mathematical function of the mutual acceleration of two "particles,"[19] but must include also, as an intrinsic part, a statement of the laboratory *operation* that shall be used in ascertaining the property of actually existing objects (such as a given billiard ball) which shall be called their mass. This laboratory operation will consist, for instance, in comparison by means of some specified apparatus of the billiard ball with some other existing physical object chosen as unit of "mass." Such comparison, however, constitutes an *experiment* — a procedure consisting in this, that one introduces into a given situation some only change, *e.g.,* the placing of a body of unit "mass" on one pan of a balance which bears the billiard ball on its other pan; and that one then observes the change of position of the pointer caused thereby. And, let it be emphasized, the

---

[19] This function is specified by Lindsay and Margenau, *op. cit.* pp. 92–3.

description of the experiment is *not* the description of a way of ascertaining the presence and quantity of something called "mass" defined *independently* of it, but is on the contrary *an intrinsic part of the definition itself* of what is being ascertained, *viz.,* the mass of the ball. For to say that the "mass" of the given ball can be defined independently of this procedure only means (if it happens to be true) that there is some alternative procedure, *also experimental,* which always yields the same figures as the procedure just referred to, for any given object.

The notion of cause and effect (as I have defined it in experimental terms) thus implicitly but inescapably enters into the notion of mass when by mass is meant a measurable property of observable physical objects. Mass, however, is one of the variables of which mechanical energy is a function; and, although the concept of energy can be extended beyond mechanics, energy is primarily a mechanical concept.[20] It is extended to thermodynamics through the mechanical theory of heat, and "has meaning for electricity only to the extent to which electrical theory can be developed along mechanical lines." Therefore the notion of cause and effect (in the experimental sense I have specified) is implicit also in that of energy whenever by energy is meant not merely a function of certain ideal conceptions, but a measurable property of observable, actually existing physical systems. The notion of causality is thus epistemically prior to that of energy, and therefore cannot itself be defined in terms of energy.

This fact, it should be noted, is sufficient to dispose of the contention occasionally met with[21] that the notion of causality belongs only to the infancy of science and is obsolete in the case of a science so advanced as physics. Those who so contend are usually not considering causality itself — *viz.,* the relation actually present in standard cases of the applicative use of the term "cause" such

---

20 *Op. cit.,* p. 127.
21 Cf. B. Russell's *Scientific Method in Philosophy,* p. 220.

as those listed in Section 3 above — but instead have in mind one
or another of the many unsatisfactory analyses of that relation
put forward by philosophers at various times.   Thus, if anything
gets proved, it is only that physics makes no use of this or that
defective notion, which some philosopher mistakenly thought constituted the right analysis of causality.   Aside from this, however,
the fact usually emphasized — that the term "cause" just does
not occur in the statements which formulate the discoveries of
modern physics — leaves untouched the contention of the present
section, *viz.*, that, in the manner described, the notion of causality
(as defined in terms of experimentation) actually is *used*, even
if for the most part tacitly, throughout physics as well as the other
natural sciences, and cannot be eliminated from them.

15.   Causation, Volition, and Compulsion

Many contemporary writers allege that the common-sense belief
that a cause compels, or produces, or necessitates its effect represents only a gratuitous transference to nature of the fact that in
us an effort of will occurs when, for example, we are causing some
heavy object to move or are attempting to resist the push or pull
of a spring.

It is true that even distinguished scientific minds have been
guilty of such anthropomorphization of natural causes.   Sir John
F. W. Herschel, for example, writes that when "we press our two
hands violently together, so as just to oppose each other's effort,
we . . . perceive, by the fatigue and exhaustion, and by the impossibility of maintaining the effort long, that something is going
on within us, of which the mind is the agent, and the will the
determining cause."   This, he believes, gives us "a complete idea
of *force*"; and we come to know that force is the cause of motion,
and that motion can therefore be considered the signal of the
exertion of force, when we perceive that the same action of the
mind, which, when our limbs are encased in plaster, enables us

to fatigue and exhaust ourselves, puts it in our power, when our limbs are free, to move ourselves and other bodies.[22]   Herschel, moreover, does not shrink from extending the notion of cause as act of will to nature outside of man, for he writes: "Of force, as counterbalanced by opposing force, we have . . . an internal consciousness; and though it may seem strange to us that matter should be capable of exerting on matter the same kind of effort, which, judging alone from this consciousness, we might be led to regard as a mental one; yet we cannot refuse the direct evidence of our senses, which shows us that when we keep a spring stretched with one hand, we feel our effort opposed exactly in the same way as if we had ourselves opposed it with the other hand."[23]

In these remarks, Herschel evidently fails to distinguish between the nature of the *relation* "cause of," and the nature of the *event* which, in the particular case of voluntary movement, happens to serve as first term of that relation.   The reply to Herschel's remarks is thus that we judge that volition to raise our arm causes it to go up, not because we discern a peculiar causal virtue in volition as such, but simply because the volition was the only change we observed in the state of affairs immediately antecedent to the upward motion of the arm.   Had the observed immediately antecedent only change been of any other sort — *e.g.,* had it been the sight of a baseball approaching our eye — we would have judged *it* — and rightly so — to be in this case the cause of the motion of our arm.   Cases of psycho-physical, or of psycho-psychical causation are detected in exactly the same way as cases of physico-physical causation, *viz.,* by observing whether the relation between the events concerned conforms to the definition of the causal relation, already given in experimental terms.   The intrinsic nature of the events themselves is never what origi-

---

22 Herschel, *Preliminary Discourse on the Study of Natural Philosophy,* Sec. 77.
23 *Op. cit.,* Sec. 81.

nally reveals to us that one of them was the cause of the other.[24]

We may now ask, however, whether refusal to anthropomorphize the causes of events in nature entails that these events then cannot be said to be produced, or necessitated, or compelled by their causes. I submit that it entails nothing of the sort. "Produces" is substantially synonymous with "causes," and has no more anthropomorphic implication than has the latter term. Again, as already pointed out, "necessitation," as between events, is essentially the same thing as "causation." As regards "compulsion," however, it is alleged that it has an essential reference to will — that to be compelled to do something is to be caused to do it *against one's will*. But that this analysis of compulsion is incorrect is shown by the existence of cases where what we are compelled to do is something we wish to do anyway. For example, if, when I am hungry and impatiently waiting for the dinner bell, someone comes, and by threats or promises that would move me to obey him even if I felt averse to eating, compels me to go and eat, he is then compelling me to do the very thing I wish to do. Again, when I am on a train traveling to New York, I am at the time compelled to move through space in the direction of New York, although presumably, since I boarded the train, that is also what I want to do.

The right analysis of compulsion is thus that, for a human being to be compelled or forced to do something is for him to be caused to will to do it no matter whether he also likes to do it

---

[24] Almost all philosophers who discuss causation today reject the contention, as by Herschel, that we gain true insight into the "inner nature" of causation in the cases where a volition of ours is what causes our body to move. Substantially the same contention, however, although expressed in terms more sophisticated than Herschel's, has recently reappeared in Parker's book already cited (pp. 235 ff., especially p. 243). But Parker, like Herschel, seems to me to mistake insight into the nature of the *event* (viz. volition) which functions as cause in certain cases, for insight into the nature of the *relation* (called causation) between this event and the event which functions as effect. We do have insight also into this relation, but we do not have it exclusively nor peculiarly in the cases where one of the terms of the causal relation happens to be a volition or a persisting intention, or, for that matter, a feeling of strain.

or dislikes to do it. And, for nonhuman objects, presumably not capable of desire or reluctance, to be compelled or forced is to be caused to do something even if there are, in the object's state, factors which, were they the only ones, would prevent that thing from occurring. For example, a ship can be said to be *forced* by a hurricane to drift in a certain direction if it is caused to do so by the hurricane even if all its anchors are out and its engine is pushing with all its power in the opposite direction. Again, a piece of trailing ivy can be said to be *forced* from its position by a given pull if the pull is such as to cause it to move even if it is attached to the ground by rootlets.

16.   Causation, Mechanism, and Telism

A case of telism no less than a case of mechanism is a case of causation. Causation of an event E by an act A is *telic* whenever the cause of the act A performed at time T_2 consisted in the performer's *desire* at time T_1 for the occurrence at time T_3 of the event E, and he believed that the act A would or might cause E. For example, my pulling the switch chain on my lamp just now was a case of telism. My desire for light caused the pulling motion of my hand, and this in turn caused occurrence of the light which I had desired should occur, and which I had believed would be caused by such an act. The analysis may be represented schematically as follows: Belief that an act A would cause occurrence of E, plus occurrence of desire for occurrence of $E \rightarrow$ occurrence of Act $A \rightarrow$ occurrence of E.[25]

The reference in the statement above to successive times T_1, T_2, T_3 does not exclude the possibility that the segment T_1 of time,

---

[25] The word "desire," in the statements above, is meant in the broad sense for which the seldom used word "conation" would be more appropriate. That is, "desire" is meant in this connection to include volition, although, of course, for some purposes volition needs to be distinguished from desire in the narrow and ordinary sense the term has when we say, for instance, that we desire to do many things which we nevertheless do not will to do.

which the desire occupies, may in part overlap the segment T_2 which the act A occupies, and one or both of these segments overlap also the segment T_3 which E occupies. That is, the temporal relation of the three events can be as follows:

Time T_1 of the desire: _____

Time T_2 of the act A: _____

Time T_3 of the event E: _____

But even in such a case the three segments of time concerned, and the three events which respectively occupy them, are successive at least in the sense that the *initial instant* of the time of the desire is earlier than the initial instant of the time of the act, and the initial instant of the time of the act earlier than that of the initial instant of the time of the event E.

This order of succession is emphasized here to make evident the erroneousness of the opinion sometimes expressed that telism is causation of an earlier event by a later. This opinion rests on confusion of the desired later event E itself with the earlier desire for this event E. It is not *the event* E that causes the act A which brings it about, but the *desire for* the event E; and this desire begins earlier than the act A which it causes, and earlier still than the event E which A in turn causes.

What differentiates telism from mechanism is that in telism the cause-event is, whereas in mechanism it is not, *desire* (for the eventual occurrence of something which has not yet occurred). It should be noted that this analysis of telic causation holds equally whether the term "desire" be, as ordinarily, taken to stand for a certain sort of psychical state, or be on the contrary assigned some purely physiological or behavioral meaning. In either case, desire as cause has to figure in the account of the nature of telism. If a physiological or behavioral meaning is assigned to the term "desire," causation is telic when and only when the cause is a physiological or behavioral event of the particular kind specified as being the kind which the word "desire" designates.

17. Summary

It may be well now to review briefly the main conclusions reached in this and the preceding chapter. To begin with, we examined Hume's contention that causality is nothing but sequence that has in fact been regular in our experience; and we pointed out in criticism of it that there are examples of regularity of sequence which we judge not to be examples of causation, and examples we do judge to be so without observing such regularity. Attention was then called to the fact that Hume himself gives rules for ascertaining a causal connection by means of a single experiment, *i.e.,* without repetition of sequence, but that this conflicts with his definition of cause as regularity of sequence; so that the rules he gives, which are sound, are really based on a very different conception of causation — one, namely, which conceives it in terms of the advent of a single difference in a given state of affairs. The latter conception, I contended, is the correct one — the so-called Method of Difference thus being in truth the description of the causal relation, and not a method for discovering a relation other than the one it describes.

It was then argued that the distinction between "cause of" and "condition of" is perfectly valid, corresponding as it does to that between "sufficient to" and "necessary to." Also, that "effect of" similarly corresponds to "necessitated by," and "resultant of" to "contingent upon." Considerations were adduced to vindicate the legitimacy of speaking not only of logical necessity, but also of physical and psychological necessity, or, more generally, etiological necessity, *i.e.,* of necessity as between events. Detailed definitions, phrased in terms of experimentation, were given of the four relations just mentioned, and of their negatives.

Attention was then called to a number of important features of the causal relation. In particular, it was emphasized that its terms are always events, never substances or forces, and that it is thus distinct from, although closely connected with, the relation of agent to patient, which is a relation between substances; again, that the causal relation is not a dyadic but an essentially triadic relation, the indispensable third term of it being some given state of affairs in which only two changes occur — the earlier one being then called the cause of the later and the later the effect of the earlier. Again, it was argued that causation is basically a relation between concrete, individual events; but that it is capable of being generalized whenever, in several instances of causation, the causes, the effects, and the circumstances, respectively, are of the same kinds — such generalization of particular facts individually causal yielding causal laws.

Again, it was maintained that the causal tie between a cause and its effect is empirically observable, since it consists in the very relation which the so-called method of single difference specifically describes; but that it is difficult to be certain that what one observes in a given case really conforms to the description, and therefore that empirical observation of causal connection is as subject to error as, in general, is empirical observation of what a universal negative statement asserts. Again, it was pointed out that the vocabulary of causation differs from that of developed science because man's original and most common interest in causal connections is directly related to his practical purposes — the import of the question: "What causes A?" usually being: "What sort of human act, or what sort of event causable by a human act, would suffice to cause (or prevent) a desired (or dreaded) event A?" Thus, although causation is essentially a relation between two concrete only changes in a given concrete state of affairs, man's interest in the causes of concrete individual events is in many or perhaps most cases only the indirect one that they constitute the raw material for the discovery of causal laws, and that only laws furnish any basis for empirical prediction or control of events.

It was pointed out that any event occupies a segment of time, and that, at a strictly durationless instant, nothing either changes or lasts, *i.e.,* no event at all occurs. As regards the possibility of "action at a distance," attention was called to the fact that the term "contiguity" or "contact" has several senses, and that two things may, for example, be magnetically in contact and yet be at a distance mechanically.

It was then argued that, whether causation does or does not always involve transfer of energy, causation is definable independently of the notion of such transfer, and moreover that energy, in so far as it is something detectable and measurable, is ultimately not definable without recourse to the notion of causality.

Further, it was argued that — contrary to what often is alleged — the belief that a cause compels or necessitates its effect is correct, and is not derived from the feeling of muscular strain in causation of motion by human effort. And it was pointed out at the last that telism is but a special instance of causality, and is therefore in no way incompatible with causal determinism.

Chapter 9

THE UNIVERSALITY AND UNIFORMITY OF CAUSATION

The analysis of causality in the preceding chapter has included
no discussion of two widely accepted propositions. One is that the
same cause always has the same effect, and the same effect the same
cause; *i.e.,* that causation is always *uniform*. The other is that
nothing exists or occurs without some cause; *i.e.,* that causation
is *universal*. We must now consider these two propositions.

That causation is universal and is uniform is generally regarded
as something we only postulate; that is, as something for the truth
of which we have no sufficient evidence or even any evidence at
all, but which we nevertheless believe naturally. Our "animal
faith" in it is regarded as reflectively justifiable by the pragmatic
consideration that we have nothing to lose but might possibly
gain something by believing it. For in so far as causation were
not uniform, past experience would furnish us no guide for the
future; and if there are causeless events, knowledge of such
causal uniformities as there happen to be would not enable us to
anticipate those events. Hence, if it is false that causation is
always uniform, or that it is universal, we are in so far helpless
and badly off; *yet not more so if we believe it to be true than if
we believe it to be false.* Whereas, if it is true, then to believe
it true and conduct ourselves accordingly is the only course giving
us a chance of becoming able to predict or control events. Having
thus nothing to lose but perhaps something to gain by proceeding

on the assumption that causation is universal and always uniform, we are pragmatically justified in so proceeding notwithstanding the absence of evidence that the assumption is true.

I believe, however, that something more than this can be said concerning both the universality and the uniformity of causation.

1. The Universality of Causation

The definition of "cause" which in the preceding chapter we found reason to regard as representing the meaning that term has in standard instances of its common use did, it will be remembered, emphasize that causality is not a dyadic relation — involving only a cause-event C and an effect-event E — but is essentially triadic, the third term of it being some state of affairs S in which only two changes occur: one, a change C at a time T_1, which is then called the cause-event; and the other, a change E at a later time T_2, which is called the effect-event. Now, on the basis of this definition, I think it can be shown that the supposition that some events have no cause implies a contradiction.

To perceive this, however, it must be kept in mind that the events of which it is true are events taken each in its full concrete determinateness and entirety. That is, they are not selected *parts* merely of what is occurring at a given time and place, nor are they occurrences considered only in so far as exemplifying some more or less abstract kind. This entails that they are specifiable only in terms of their time and place, *i.e.,* only by means of some such phrase as "what is occurring here now," or "what occurred at place P at time T." Hence the symbol E, which we shall employ to represent the event we consider, will not be a name for an instance, susceptible to always more particular description, of some more or less abstract kind of event. It will be simply a tag or proper name which, for the sake of brevity of reference, we assign to the whole completely determinate event actually occurring at the determinately given time and place; and the referents of the symbols C and S will similarly be a whole completely determinate event and state of affairs, respectively.

This is important to keep in mind here since ordinarily we employ such letter symbols not themselves as proper names, *i.e.*, not as symbols of full concrete events and states of affairs, but as *symbols of names,* to wit, of *class names,* which we apply to given events and states of affairs. As pointed out in the preceding chapter, however, as soon as we *classify* an event, *i.e.*, refer it to some abstract kind — which is what we automatically do as soon as we apply to it a descriptive name instead of merely tagging it with a proper name — we are leaving out some part or character of what is actually occurring. And it follows, of course, that when an event is thus considered only as an instance of a named kind E, *i.e.*, considered only more or less abstractly and partially, then a question as to the cause of it is a question not as to the cause of it in its full concreteness and entirety, but is really a question as to what *kind C* of events cause events of *kind E* in circumstances of a stated *kind S*, there and then exemplified. And this implies that, even if the characters or parts of the actual occurrence that are more determinate than or additional to those which make it an instance of the kind E had been different from what they actually were, the answer to the question as to what caused occurrence then and there of an event of kind E would have remained the same, to wit, antecedent occurrence in the given state of affairs of kind S of an occurrence of kind C. That is, those more determinate characters or additional parts are *accidental, not essential,* constituents of the event whose occurrence is to be explained, since it is being considered only qua instance of kind E. The parts or characters of the antecedent event, additional to or more determinate than those which make it an instance of kind C, are therefore correspondingly accidental

not essential to causation of an event considered only qua of kind
E. But the question as to the universality of causation concerns
*events as they actually occur, each in its full concreteness and
entirety; and therefore no need or possibility remains of discard-
ing there as causally accidental any part or aspect of the antecedent
change in the given concrete state of affairs.*

If we keep these considerations clearly in mind, and employ
the symbols C, E, and S as proper names of entire fully concrete
events and states of affairs, the reason why no event can be causeless then becomes discernible. We shall consider two cases,
which are the only possible ones.

The first is that in which the event E at the time T is the whole
of the change occurring at that time in the state of affairs — call
it S — then existing in the entire universe. In this case, if S
*changed at all preceding E, then the whole of that change C auto-
matically qualifies as cause of E under the definition.* But the
question then at once arises whether any change at all prior to E
need have occurred in the universe. May not E have been the
very first change, and the state of affairs S thus have endured
without change during all time prior to the time T of E?

That this is impossible appears from the following considerations. The supposition that S endured changeless for any time,
long or short, prior to E, implies that prior to E time was "passing"; and the "passing of time" means that some "clock" is
"beating," *i.e.*, that some succession of changes is occurring.[1] Let
"C" be the name of the last of them preceding E, or, if we prefer,
of the entire succession of them prior to E. The "enduring" of
S thus means that while C is occurring no change in S is occurring.
But the case we are considering is that where S is the state of
affairs existing in the *entire universe* at the time E occurs. Hence

---

[1] The nature of time as essentially the relation between "successive" events is
discussed in some detail in Chapter 15.

the change C — the beat or beats of the "clock" — has to be itself a part of S; so that at most only the remainder of S, *viz.*, the part of S other than C, can without contradiction be supposed to have endured changeless. But then, even if no other change than C occurred in S prior to E, even then E had a cause, for then C itself qualifies as cause under the definition.

Let us now examine the second possible case, that where E is the whole of the change occurring at a time T in an indicatively given state of affairs that is *only a part* of the state of affairs existing in the entire universe at that time.

To suppose that this S endured unchanged for some time whether long or short prior to E, is again to suppose tacitly that some series of changes C was occurring prior to E; but in the present case C need not have been itself a part of S. It can have been occurring outside of S, since the S we are now considering is only a part of the state of affairs in the universe at the time T. But even if C is thus outside S, even then E necessarily has a cause. This results from the following facts:

1. At the time T of E, there is another state of affairs Su, consisting of S plus the then state of affairs in the rest of the universe.

2. Under the supposition that S endured for some time prior to T, there necessarily was some change in Su prior to T. Let C denote the whole of it.

3. Then C was the only change in Su at its time R.

4. At time T, there was a total and therefore only change in Su, namely, E plus some additional change F; for, *ex hypothesi*, E is only a part of the change in the state of the universe, *i.e.*, in Su, at time T.

5. Hence C qualifies under the definition as cause of E plus F.

6. But that E plus F has a cause implies that E has a cause.

Conformably to the definition, this cause consists of some part of C that was the total change prior to E in a limited state of affairs Sk consisting of S plus some part of Su adjacent to S.

2. The Uniformity of Causation

Still considering events each in its full determinateness and totality, the question as to whether causation is not only as just shown universal, but also uniform, takes the following shape when stated in terms of the conception of causality reached in the preceding chapter:

Given that in a certain concrete state of affairs S_1 only one change C_1, likewise concrete, is introduced, and that, automatically, *i.e.*, without introduction into S_1 of any other change, C_1 is followed by only one other change E_1 in S_1 (C_1 and E_1 being then respectively "cause" and "effect" as earlier defined); and given further that, in another precisely and completely similar state of affairs S_2, only one change C_2, precisely and completely similar to C_1, is introduced; is it then possible without contradiction to suppose that C_2 should not cause, *i.e.*, should not be automatically followed by, an only other change E_2 in S_2, precisely and completely similar to E_1?

That a contradiction *is* involved, *i.e.*, that the supposition is necessarily false, *i.e.*, that causation is necessarily uniform, becomes evident if we advert to the following considerations:

(*a*) Where logical entities are concerned, "necessitation" means implication; but where concrete events are concerned, "necessitation" means causation, and "causation" means the triadic relation we have described. Wherever there might be doubt as to which of these two meanings the word "necessary" is being employed in (or the related expressions "sufficient to," "contingent upon," "possible," "impossible"), we shall, as proposed in the preceding chapter, avoid ambiguity by speaking respectively of *logical* and of *etiological* necessity (or sufficiency, possibility, etc.).

(*b*) That the triadic relation constituting causality obtained between S_1 and changes C_1 and E_1 in S_1 means that C_1 caused, *i.e.*, etiologically sufficed to, *i.e.*, etiologically necessitated, occurrence of event E_1; and our supposition is that S_2 and C_2 are precisely and completely similar to S_1 and C_1.

(c) Etiological sufficiency to the occurring of a later event having the same nature as E_1 was defined (faithfully to the meaning of experimental sufficiency) *solely* as antecedent occurrence in the state of affairs considered of an only change having the very nature we are supposing both C_1 and C_2 to possess; and, that etiological sufficiency was defined *solely* in this way means in particular that it was defined *wholly without specification of any particular date for either event.* The specification contained in the definition as regards time was only that the event it defines as effect, *i.e.,* as etiologically necessitated, be later than the one it defines as cause of it, *i.e.,* as etiologically sufficient to it. Thus, by the very definition of causation in terms of experimentation with concrete changes in concrete states of affairs, the difference between the two instances we are considering, which *ex hypothesi* is solely a difference of absolute dates, is wholly irrelevant to causal necessitation.[2] Causal necessitation is a matter wholly of the triadic relation described, and causal necessitation of an event having a given determinate nature is wholly a matter of the determinate nature of the other two terms of the triadic relation in the given case.

(d) Hence it would be a contradiction to suppose (*i.e.,* it is logically impossible) that change C_2 in S_2 would not similarly cause occurrence of E_2 in S_2, for this would be to suppose that a change having identically the same nature in each case, in a state of affairs also having identically the same nature, *at one time is and at another time is not etiologically sufficient* to occurrence of a later change having identically the same nature as E_1, *not-*

---

[2] As regards this point, see W. E. Johnson, *Logic,* Vol. III, p. 70; L. Silberstein, *Causality,* p. 53; A. P. Ushenko, "The Problem of Causal Inference," *Philos. of Science,* Vol. 9, No. 2. April 1942; and the references he gives there to D'Abro's *The Decline of Mechanism* (p. 179) and to Lindsay and Margenau's *Foundations of Physics* (p. 522).

*withstanding that etiological sufficiency was defined in a manner
wholly independent of times.* Differences of absolute times, *i.e.,*
of absolute dates, have any relevance at all to causation only in
so far as differences in the state of affairs at the two dates go with
the difference of dates.

(*e*) Hence the supposition that C_2 in S_2 might not cause E_2
can escape contradiction only if its reference is, not in fact merely
to different absolute times, but tacitly in addition to differences of
nature between C_1 and C_2, or between S_1 and S_2. But the question at issue was as to the necessity of an event E_2 if there are no
differences of nature between C_1 and C_2 nor between S_1 and S_2;
and under this supposition it is logically impossible that E_2 should
not then occur.

(*f*) To these remarks, however, we must now add that, as
pointed out in Section 1, there is no such thing as a "passing" of
time, nor therefore as differences of date, without some changes
going on — be they only the ticking of a watch, the revolutions
of the earth, one's own breathing or heart beat, or even the
changes of one's mental states. Time, being essentially the relation between, as we may say, a "tick" and a "tock" of one sort
or another, there cannot logically be such a thing as time wholly
empty of changes, but only time empty of changes of some particular kind; or, to put it the other way around, it is logically
possible not that time should be wholly empty, but that it should
be *empty of all except changes of some particular kind;* for
instance, of all changes except the ticktock of some clock. This,
I believe, is actually what we imagine when we think we imagine
empty time — the clock then being our own physiological rhythms
of breathing or heart beats. These, or the beats of any other
kind of clock, can constitute "mere times" or "mere dates," as
distinguished from "events occurring at those times," only in the
sense that although their "ticks" and "tocks" are themselves
events, they are, or are assumed to be, ones that "do not count";

i.e., that do not make any (relevant) difference; *i.e.,* that do not cause or affect events of the kinds one proposes to date by means of them. And they are suitable for this purpose because they are rhythmical, because their rhythm is constant, and because they constitute a linear order.

Now, in what preceded, we had argued that causation is necessarily uniform because differences merely of absolute date are irrelevant to causation. But it turns out that "differences merely of absolute date" means differences that (in addition to having the other characteristics just mentioned) *happen to be* causally irrelevant to the events we date by means of them. Hence the causal irrelevance of the ticktocks of the clock we use to those events has to be empirically ascertained. The evidence of it consists in the fact that the ticktocks are uniform, *i.e.,* present no novelty of individual nature, and that (within certain limits) they keep occurring irrespective of whether the other events which we propose to date by means of them occur or not.

However, as pointed out in the preceding section, it is logically possible for the ticktocks to be causally independent of a given concrete event E only if, or only because, prior to E there occurred some change in S other than the ticktocks; for if none such should have occurred, then necessarily the ticktocks themselves would have been what had caused E, and, of course, the ticktocks do cause *something*.

What has been said in this and the preceding section of course leaves quite untouched the fact that not every case of sequence is a case of consequence. That a certain event was followed by a certain other on a certain occasion does not in the least guarantee that it will be so followed the next time it occurs. What we have contended is not that *history* is uniform, but that *causation* is uniform — not that if an event A was once followed by an event B, B will recur as often as A does, but that if an event A *caused* an event B which followed it, *i.e.,* if A was the only change antecedent to B in a then existing state of affairs S, then if A recurs at any time *and the state of affairs is again the same, B* will necessarily recur. This, evidently, is a very different contention.

3. The Principle of "Uniformity of Nature" as Employed in Prediction

Although as a matter of conceptual analysis it is true irrespective of particular dates that under the same circumstances the same event has the same effect and the same cause, this proposition is useless for the task usually assigned to the "principle of the uniformity of nature," namely, that of guaranteeing inferences from observed cause to unobserved effect, or from observed effect to unobserved cause. For we can hardly claim that actually we ever observe that two events, or sets of circumstances, or things, are strict duplicates in every qualitative and quantitative respect. That is, although the proposition "same cause, same effect" is true, we never really meet cases to which it would be applicable.

What we do meet are events or things that are *similar* in greater or less degree to certain others previously observed by us; and, if we are to make any causal inferences at all from observed to unobserved events, it is thus on similarity not on strict sameness that they have to be based. The principle we use in these inferences therefore is: similar causes, under similar circumstances, have similar effects. But whether this is a safe principle of inference in a given case depends on whether, in the given case, the similarity is in relevant respects and is great enough in such respects.

Which respects and degrees of similarity are relevant, *i.e.,* count, and which respects and degrees of dissimilarity make no difference for causation of an effect of the kind and degree we seek to predict in a given case — this we can know only if we have discovered it through prior abstractive and eliminative experimentation. The principle which actually governs our causal inferences when they are cautious is therefore very much less simple than even the amended one above, or than any of the usual formulations of the principle of the "uniformity of nature." It is, so far as I can see, substantially as follows:

Given that a thing, its state, its circumstances, and the change which now occurs in them, are similar to the things, their states, their circumstances, and the change in these circumstances in each case which were observed on a number of previous occasions, then the probability that the behavior of the thing in the present case will be similar in a specified respect and degree to the behavior of the similar things observed on the similar previous occasions will be the greater as

(*a*) the similarities we are able to observe between the present case and the earlier ones are similarities in the same respects as, and in degrees not inferior to, the respects and degrees of similarity that existed among those of the earlier observed cases themselves in which the behavior of the things concerned was of the kind and degree we are now seeking to predict; and as

(*b*) the dissimilarities we are able to observe between the present case and the earlier ones are dissimilarities in the same respects as, and in degrees no greater than, the respects and degrees of dissimilarity that existed among those of the earlier observed cases themselves in which the behavior of the things concerned was nevertheless uniformly of the kind and degree we are now seeking to predict.

Chapter 10

Causality, Substances, Properties, and Events

The remarks made in the last section of the preceding chapter suggest that the notion of Substance and that of Causality are intimately related. Indeed, if we should ask what exactly is to be understood by the expression "a state of affairs" which entered in our analysis of the notion of Causality, the answer would be that a state of affairs consists of some substances, each in some state and in some relations to one another; so that changes in the given state of affairs are additions to or subtractions from the set of substances considered, or changes in their properties, or in their states, or in their external relations to one another.

Moreover, the need to analyze the notion of Substance is thrust upon us by the fact that when later we come to ask what exactly is a mind, one of the hypotheses we shall have to examine will be whether, as traditionally has been held, a mind is a substance — though an immaterial one; or whether, as a view fashionable today would have it, a mind rather is only a "function" of a human body — a way of operating peculiar to the body of a man and perhaps of a dog, an ape, and some others of the higher animals. To decide this, one of the things we shall have to know will be what exactly is a "substance." Analysis of the notion of Substance and of the related notions of Properties and of States of a substance is the task we now therefore undertake.

1. Data of the Problem of the Nature of Substance

Although a number of philosophers since Aristotle have offered definitions of Substance, and we might conceivably find ourselves eventually led to accept one of them, we cannot start with any of them; for, as in the case of Causality, those definitions represent purported solutions, but not data, of the very problem we propose to investigate. To obtain a non-arbitrary, empirically confirmable or infirmable, analytical account of the meaning of the term Substance, we have to employ the method of semantical inquiry described in Chapter 5, which takes as data statements that are "standard" in the sense defined earlier and that predicate the term whose meaning is in question — here, the term Substance.

Our data will therefore consist of such statements as that copper is a substance, water is a substance, education is not a substance, and so on; and our problem is to discover a definition of the term Substance that will explicate the meaning it has when applied to and denied of things of the kinds those standard predications of it exemplify. As previously noted, a definition that does this will be neither arbitrary nor necessarily final. Its epistemic status will be that of an explanatory hypothesis — one purporting to account for the listed standard positive and negative linguistic applications of the term, and to predict other such standard applications of it not explicitly listed.

2.   An Implication of the Data of the Problem

As soon as the problem of the nature of substance is stated in the manner just described, it becomes evident that a correct account of the meaning of the term cannot imply that causal interaction of two different substances is impossible; for both copper and nitric acid, or both wood and a chisel, are some of the things called substances in our data statements, and although each is different from and existentially independent of the other, they nevertheless sometimes interact. This, together with the fact pointed out by Hume, that theoretically anything might cause anything and that only observation tells us what in fact can cause what, makes evident that the difficulty which Descartes, the Occasionalists, and the Parallelists found in the supposition that Mind and Matter, conceived each as being a substance, interact, was quite gratuitous. It arose only from an arbitrary initial definition of Substance. Our own inquiry into the meaning of "Substance," on the contrary is inductive.

3. Substances, Properties, and Qualities

Two questions face us: One is as to what exactly it means to call something a "substance"; the other is as to what it means to assert that substance of a specified kind does or does not exist, and how one finds out whether or not it does.

As to the first, the hypothesis I offer is that the nature of a substance, irrespective of whether instances of it exist or not, analyzes into properties and relations of properties; and that in substances that have parts, the properties of the substance depend on the properties and relations of its parts.

To make the meaning of this hypothesis clear, it is necessary first to distinguish the sense in which the term "property" is used in it from certain others of its senses.

The term "property" has been employed, for instance, in connection with *events* rather than substances, and by R. B. Braithwaite so employed in a rather peculiar manner.[1] He speaks of "being the fall of a hundred-pound rock" as a property of an event, notwithstanding that these words would seem to be a description of a certain *kind of event,* rather than of a property of events of that kind. Indeed, he also calls "being a rock weighing more than (perhaps) one pound" a property of an event, notwithstanding that in this case no event, but only a substance, would seem capable of having the character those words describe. Again, some writers use "property" to designate anything predicable of a substance, even including, for example, the substance's being at a certain place at a certain time.

---

1 "The Idea of Necessary Connexion," *Mind,* Vol. XXXVII, No. 145, Jan. 1928, p. 66. This article, which appeared in two instalments, begins in the preceding issue of *Mind* (Oct. 1927).

Such usages of the term seem needlessly arbitrary, and the sense of "property" with which alone we shall be concerned here is narrower, and in close accord with the sense it has in the natural sciences. It is that in which, for instance, ductility is said to be a property of silver, combustibility a property of paper, hardness a property of diamond, bitterness a property of quinine, and so on.

Even in such instances, however, many persons do not discriminate between "property" and "quality," and would therefore say indifferently that bitterness is a property or a quality of quinine. But it is crucial here (and generally in epistemology) to realize that such a term as "bitter" means something very different when one speaks of some *substance, e.g.* quinine, as bitter, and when one speaks of a *taste* as bitter; for "bitter" is the name of *the taste itself* said to be bitter, but is *not* the name of *the substance itself* said to be bitter. The name of the latter is "quinine"; and "bitter," as predicated of quinine, is the name of a *property,* in the sense of a *capacity,* of quinine. But as predicated of a taste one is tasting, "bitter" is *not* the name of a capacity of it. It is the name of the very species of taste-quality one is experiencing.

More particularly, to say of a substance that it has the property, being bitter, is to say that contact of that substance with the tongue normally causes the person concerned to experience the taste-quality called "bitter." To be this quality, and to be the capacity to cause the experiencing of it, are obviously two very different things. Substances have *properties,* that is, causal capacities; and some causal capacities are capacities to cause the experiencing of certain qualities. But no substances, or at least no material substances, are known to us to have any qualities as just distinguished from properties. This is a point of cardinal importance.

Examples of properties of certain substances would be malleability, fusibility, solubility, brittleness, solidity, plasticity, corrosiveness, combustibility, abrasiveness, poisonousness, dangerousness, irritability, irritatingness, and so on. These, and all other properties of substances, are statable in the form of laws of causation or of coexistence — in the form of laws of the behavior or of the state or of the action of the substance concerned, in circumstances of specifiable kinds. For example, to say that paper not at the moment burning nonetheless has the property called *combustibility* is to say that, in circumstances of certain kinds (which include, for instance presence of oxygen) application of fire to a sheet of paper regularly causes it to burn. Again, to say of carborundum that it is *abrasive* means that, under certain conditions, friction of it against certain other solids causes them to wear away. And again, to say that under certain conditions water is *liquid* means, for instance, that it is then such that tipping its container regularly causes the water to flow.[2] More generally, to say that a substance S has a property or capacity P means that S is such that, in circumstances of kind K, an event of kind C, occurring in S or about S, regularly causes an event of kind E to occur in S or about S.

If a property of a substance analyzes as a connection between a change in one and in another of its own states, that property may be called an *internal* property of it. For example, it is an internal property of certain substances that if their temperature increases, their viscosity decreases. On the other hand if a property of a substance analyzes as a connection between a change in it and a change in another substance standing in some external relation to it, that property may be called *external*. Thus, for example, that if a diamond's edge is drawn against glass, the glass gets scratched, is an external property of diamond, and also of course an external property of glass.

---

[2] To define liquidity in terms of free movement of the constituent molecules though without tendency for them to separate would be to offer a *theoretical explanation* of the behavior of liquids; it would not be to offer an account of the properties by which liquidity is perceptually identifiable.

4. The Parts of a Substance

Let us consider next the parts of a substance. They are themselves substances, which, however, may be either of the same kind as, or different in kind from, the given substance. Relatively to a mode of partition that yields parts of the same kind as the substance partitioned, that substance may be called *divisive* or homeomerous, and is commonly referred to as a "stuff" or a "material." In so far, on the other hand, as a mode of partition yields parts different in kind from the substance partitioned, the latter may be called *indivisive* or heteromerous, and is commonly referred to not as stuff, but rather as a "structure" or an "organization of parts," or more commonly by the ambiguous term "a thing." The parts of a piece of chalk, for instance, are themselves pieces of chalk; but the parts of a typewriter are not themselves typewriters. In either case, however, the properties of the whole are dependent on the properties and relations of its parts.

5. Existence of Instances of a Substance

If we now turn to the second of our two questions regarding substances, namely, what it means to say that a substance does or does not exist, we notice at once that the expression "a substance" is used sometimes in the sense of a *kind* of substance, and sometimes on the contrary in the sense of an *existing instance* of some specified kind of substance. There may or may not exist instances of a given kind of substance; but whether any do or not, the kind concerned remains definable. "Gold," "horses," "water," are the names of kinds of substances, and instances of each of these kinds exist. On the other hand, "phlogiston," "centaurs," "the elixir of life," are likewise the names of certain kinds of substances, but no instances of any of them exist. Yet, in both cases equally, it remains possible to define, in terms of certain properties systematically connected, the kinds of substances meant by those words.

The question we now face, however, is as to just what it means to say that an instance of a given kind of substance exists.[3]   It means, I submit, that the properties or capacities, in terms of which is defined the kind of substance one mentions, *obtain somewhere*.

But to say that those capacities "obtain" somewhere does not mean that the adjectives — such as "fusible," "ductile," "malleable," etc. — which correspond to those capacities, are predicable of that place itself.   They are predicable only of an instance, existing there, of the given kind of substance.   What can be predicated of that place is only that it is occupied by an instance of the defined kind of substance.   And to say this — or, equivalently, that an instance of that kind of substance *exists* there, or that the capacities definitive of that kind *obtain* there — means both that one or more of those capacities is being exercised there, and that any one of the others, but none precluded by them, would be exercised there instead or in addition, if the circumstances were different in certain respects.[4]

Further, to say of anyone of those capacities that it is *being exercised there,* or is manifest there, means that events of certain kinds are occurring there and are being caused to occur by events of certain other kinds — these kinds of cause-events and of effect-events being those in terms of which the particular capacity concerned is defined.

---

[3] The term "instance" is ambiguous.   Sometimes "an instance" is used to mean an *existent* of a given kind, so that "to exist" means to have instances, to be instantiated.   This furnishes no analysis, but only a synonym, of "to exist."   Sometimes, on the other hand, as in these pages and in the most common usage, it is about *instances* of a given kind of thing that one asks whether any exist.   An instance, in this usage, is then itself a species, but an "infima species," *i.e.,* a completely determinate (*vs.* determinable) species, of some genus.   I have discussed this important point more fully in the course of an article, "C. I. Lewis' Analysis of Knowledge and Valuation," *Philos. Review,* Vol. LVII, No. 3, May 1948.   See pp. 262-5.   My discussion there concerns the term "member" (of a class) rather than "instance" (of a kind or a class), but the point is the same.

[4] However, properties of a certain kind, which we shall consider in detail in Chapter 15, are predicable of places as such: we speak, for instance, of a smelly place, a dark place, a warm place.

Finally, we come to the question, What are the *states* of an existent instance of a given kind of substance? I submit that they too analyze as "properties" in the sense described, *i.e.,* capacities; but the capacities more specifically called states are the capacities an existent instance of a substance *actually possesses at a given time,* as distinguished from the different capacities which, at that time, it only has *the capacity of acquiring.*

To say, for example, of a given instance of the kind of substance called "lead," that it is at the time in the *state* called *liquid* means that it actually has at that time the capacity of flowing, *i.e.,* that it would flow if the container were tipped. But to say of it at that same time that it has also the property or capacity called *solidifiability* means that at that time it does not have the capacity called *solidity,* but only the *capacity of acquiring this capacity; i.e.,* that under certain conditions it would relinquish its present capacity to flow (liquidity) and would acquire solidity in its stead. Further, there are capacities which it neither has at the moment nor has the capacity of acquiring; they are the capacities foreign to the nature of lead.

The states of an existent instance of a kind of substance have each a specific date, and the series of them constitutes the *internal history* of the given instance. Its *external history,* on the other hand, is the series of its *adventures, i.e.,* of those events external to it which caused, and those which were caused by, changes in its states.

It is to be particularly noted that *kinds* of substances, as such, have no states and no history. Indeed, they do not even "have" properties, except in the sense in which any logical complex "has" its logical constituents. This is the sense in which a year has days, a choice has alternatives, or a list has the items it lists. Of a given piece of lead one can say that, at a given time, it is solid, that it is cold, and so on. But of the *kind* of substance called "lead" one cannot say that it ever *is* liquid, or solid, or hot, or cold; but only that it is such that if at any time and in certain circumstances a then existing instance of it has a certain temperature, then that instance has also solidity; that if it has instead a certain other temperature, then it has also liquidity; and so on. Thus, if we are asked what differentiates that *kind* of substance from other kinds, we cannot answer in historical terms, *i.e.,* in terms of dated states; but only, abstractly, in terms of relations of dependence among kinds of states or of changes of state of hypothetically existent instances of the given kind of substance. This is to say that the kind analyzes exhaustively as a system of properties.

In connection with the conception of the states of an existent instance of a species of substance as themselves consisting of capacities, and changes of state therefore as consisting of changes of capacities, the question obviously arises as to whether *all events* consist only of changes of capacities — capacities having themselves been defined in terms of causal connections between events of specified kinds.

This question cannot be satisfactorily answered without reference to what will be said in Chapter 15 concerning the relation of physical events to our perception of them; but in the light of that relation, the answer will have to be that the events called "sensations" — which we shall argue are psychical not physical and are caused in us by certain physical events — are events which do *not* consist of changes of capacities. If, however, we leave out of our conception of a physical event the conception of the sensations which, in perception of that event, it causes in us, then all that remains in our conception of the physical event is some change of capacity to cause some change of capacity to cause. . . . This is to say that the infinite regress implied is avoided by, and only by, the fact that our conception of a physical event includes that of its capacity to cause (directly or indirectly) certain events which are *not* themselves changes of capacity, namely the psychical events called sensations.

6. Uniformity of Causation and the Nature of Substances

In the light of the preceding analysis of the notions of Substance, and of Properties and States of substances, we may now return to the question of the uniformity of causation. A property, we have seen, is essentially a relation of etiological necessity, *i.e.,* of causation, among changes of states of instances of a given kind of substance; or as between a certain change of state of an instance of a given kind of substance and a change of state of another, when the two stand in some particular external relation, such, perhaps, as "in contact with," or "immersed in," etc. And because the relation a property constitutes is one of etiological necessity, it automatically follows that it is uniform: If *A* necessitates *B*, then of necessity *B* accompanies *A* always, *i.e.,* irrespective of *A*'s particular date.

Moreover, a particular *kind* of substance is, and is nothing but, a particular system of properties; and an existing instance of the system is an existing instance of that kind of substance. This entails that an expression such as "a piece of lead," or "a horse," or "a piece of bread" *means* "some existent which, in situations of certain kinds, behaves or operates on others uniformly in certain manners."

Hence, it is a contradiction to suppose that although a piece of bread nourished me today, another piece of precisely the same kind of bread, eaten by me tomorrow under circumstances (including my own state) of the same determinate kinds might not nourish but perhaps poison me tomorrow. For so to suppose is to suppose that, in respect of at least one property, the bread I eat tomorrow is of a different kind from that I ate today. Just because our sole conception of any particular kind of substance is, analytically, nothing else than the conception of some particular system of properties, and properties are nothing else than causally necessary uniformities of behavior or of action under uniform circumstances, it is contradictory to suppose — and therefore is *a priori* impossible — that two existing things might be precisely and completely of the same kind, and yet that in circumstances of precisely the same kind one of them might not behave in the manner specified in the definition of the kind of substance of which both are supposed to be instances.

Indeed, even to suppose about something existent merely that it is a substance is, analytically, to suppose that it behaves uniformly under uniform circumstances; for this is the very nature of the kind of thing meant by the word "substance."

Of course, two instances of one determinable kind of substance may, without contradiction, be supposed as different as one pleases in such of their properties as are additional to and independent of those which define the determinable kind both exemplify. But it is a contradiction to suppose them different in any of the properties that enter in the definition of that kind. If being nourishing, not poisonous, is one of the properties that figure in the definition of what it means to be "bread," then to eat any existing substance that is bread cannot cause poisoning. But if that property is no part of what it means to be "bread," then no contradiction is involved in supposing that one species of bread is nourishing, and another species poisonous, any more than in the fact that although two substances are both metals they melt at different temperatures.

Again, the fact that causation is necessarily uniform does not in the least preclude the possibility, for example, that the thing I am now holding, which until now has consistently behaved in the ways that together define the kind of substance meant by "fountain pen," should on a given occasion begin behaving instead in the ways that together define the kind of substance meant by "snake." *A priori,* this is just as possible as that the thing I am holding should become broken and *eo ipso* cease to be a fountain pen, or that the thing on which I am now writing should catch on fire and therefore cease to be paper and become instead ashes, smoke, and gases. If, however, my pen should turn into a snake, we would then say that it had been not an ordinary but a very special kind of fountain pen, since those of the ordinary kind — however much otherwise they may be like mine — differ from it at least in lacking the capacity to become snakes under circumstances such as those under which my pen did (supposedly) become one.

The essential point of the preceding remarks is that whenever we speak of some existing thing and call it "bread," or "a metal," or even "a substance" — *i.e.,* do not merely say that it *looks like* or *seems to be* that — we are *eo ipso* supposing that its behavior is uniform at all times in some respects. Therefore we cannot without contradiction suppose also that its behavior might not be uniform at all times in those respects, or in no respect at all. The contradiction between the two suppositions remains, quite irrespective of whether it is true or false that the concrete thing we speak about *is* bread, or a metal, or a substance. It should be noticed, moreover, that if we were to assert that nothing need behave uniformly at all times in any respect, we should in so doing be cutting out of the language that we then could use without contradiction all such words as "bread," "metal," "water," "pencil," "tree," etc., which are substance names, and also the word "substance" itself, and the word "things" in the sense of indivisive substances. That assertion, thus, would so tie our tongues that hardly anything would remain that we could say; for we then could not employ any of those words *even in formulating our doubts or negations.*[5]

---

[5] In a work written many years ago, *Causation and the Types of Necessity,* I had taken the position that, although inapplicable in practice because we never observe strict sameness, the proposition that the same cause has uniformly the same effect under the same circumstances is known to be true, as H.W.B. Joseph has contended (*Introduction to Logic,* pp. 406–9), simply as a corollary of the Law of Identity. For to suppose that something *A,* which is in strictly the same state and in strictly the same circumstances as on an earlier occasion, does not behave in also

The analyses in this chapter of the notions of Substance and of Properties and States of a substance have throughout taken physical substances as standard examples. Our treatment, however, has ignored certain crucial questions concerning these because it was not possible to answer them without first having an account of the manner in which physical events, properties, and substances get known. The bases for an account of this will be laid in Chapters 12, 13, and 14. The account itself, which will be offered in Chapter 15, will, it is hoped, remove such difficulties as remain in the analysis of the notion of Substance given in the present chapter.

NOTE: The views of Dr. Broad on the nature of Substance as a continuant (*Examination of McTaggart's Philosophy,* Vol. I, pp. 264–278) somehow escaped my notice until after the present work was completed. My confidence in the essential soundness of my analysis of the concept of Substance is increased by the fact that it turns out to resemble Broad's analysis of it in a number of important respects.

---

strictly the same way is to suppose that the nature of that thing has changed in at least one of the properties that constitute it. The need to argue the matter in detail was made evident to me by the criticisms of R. B. Braithwaite in his article in *Mind* on "The Idea of Necessary Connexion," already cited; by those of Prof. J. W. Robson and Dr. Dickinson S. Miller in personal correspondence; and by the latter's article, "An Event in Modern Philosophy" (*Philos. Review,* Nov. 1945).

Chapter 11

CAUSALITY, DETERMINISM, AND FREEDOM

The category of Substance is but one of several that are intimately related to that of Causality. Prominent among the others are the category of Chance and that of Freedom. The last in particular has been discussed so often as to make evident that the questions connected with it are widely felt to be of great practical importance.

Among the principal of these are whether man's will is free; whether freedom of will would be compatible with determinism; whether determinism is equivalent to fatalism; whether freedom of will is a prerequisite of moral responsibility; whether there is such a thing as acting against one's will; whether, even if one is free to act as one chooses, one's choosing of a certain course of action rather than another is not itself determined. In the light of our analysis of causality, we shall now attempt to purge these and a number of related questions of the ambiguity which has infected them, and which has so largely prevented the reaching of definitive answers to them.

1. Determinism as Universality of Causation

The word determinism is commonly used in a variety of senses. In one of them, it refers to the contention that causation is universal — that every event has some cause and some effect. Indeterminism, or — to use Charles Peirce's term — tychism, is then the doctrine that some events are wholly fortuitous — that they are matters of pure chance; chance being then conceived as having an *objective* status in the universe, instead of the merely subjective status ascribed to it when by "chance" events one means, as ordinarily one does, events which indeed have a cause, or which conform to some law, but which we cannot explain or predict for lack of sufficient knowledge.[1]   In Chapter 9 reasons, which need not be repeated here, were presented to show that causeless events are an impossibility, and hence that determinism in the sense of universality of causation is necessarily true, and indeterminism in the sense that some events are matters of objective chance necessarily false.

2. Fatalism

Fatalism, or inevitabilism, differs from determinism conceived as universality of causation in holding, apparently, that although everything which occurs has some cause — thought of traditionally as divine preordination, or, currently, in human affairs as subsurface psychological or physiological urges, or as economic, cultural, or other more or less hidden social determinants[2] — nevertheless human volitions have no genuine effect; and that "fate," as conceived in one way or another, predetermines whether or not a volition will have any efficacy in a given case.   At least, something like this seems to be what is implied by the fatalism of persons who draw from it the counsel, presumably intended to be practical, that "there is no use struggling against fate."

If, however, everything is fated, then it may be fated on a given occasion that one shall struggle.   And, since we do not know

---

[1] As to the several meanings of "chance" in Peirce's writings, see "A Comment on Peirce's Tychism," by F. M. Hamblin, *Journal of Philosophy*, Vol. XLII, No. 14, July 5, 1945.

[2] See for example: "Man's Control over Civilization; an Anthropological Illusion," by Leslie A. White, *Scientific Monthly*, Vol. LXVI, No. 3, March 1948.   Although its author argues on the basis of a supposedly thoroughgoing determinism, he nevertheless writes that man's behavior "is *merely* the function of his culture, *not its determinant*" (p. 242, italics mine).   Also, that "understanding culture will not . . . change the 'fate' that it has in store for us" (247).   Yet he admits that man's behavior too has effects.   The use made in this mystagogical article of the terms "culture" and "cultural forces" affords as clear-cut an instance as could be found of the fallacy logicians describe as "hypostatization of abstractions."

what is fated, the statement that there is no use struggling against fate really contains no counsel for any given present case, but is at most a counsel to take philosophically whatever occurs.

The assumption that human volitions, although caused, do not themselves really have any effect, is completely arbitrary since it flies in the face of everyday evidence. What is true is only that human volitions are not omnipotent. For instance, they cannot prevent earthquakes or volcanic eruptions or the tides, but there are other things which we know they can prevent or cause. And it is experimentation, the growth of knowledge, and the exertion of effort — and not assumptions *a priori* as to what is fated — that reveal which things human volitions ultimately can or cannot cause. Fatalism and inevitabilism, thus, appear to be chiefly names for a peculiar instance of confused thought.[3]

3. Determinism as Theoretically Universal Predictability

The proposition that every event has some cause and some effect is commonly taken to imply that every event which occurs was theoretically predictable, *i.e.,* could have been predicted by a mind that had in the past observed all that there had been to observe and had distilled from it inductively all the laws implicit in it. Such theoretically universal predictability constitutes a second and more frequent meaning of "determinism."

---

[3] The article last cited is typical in this respect. As a sample of its logic may be cited a footnote (p. 242) in which one reads that "whether a man—an average man, typical of his group—'believes in' . . . Determinism or Free Will, is not a matter of his own choosing. His philosophy is merely the response of his neuro-sensory-muscular-glandular system to the streams of cultural stimuli impinging upon him from the outside." But if so, then obviously White's own belief in determinism too must be merely such a response. And then, of course, the question whether all events *are* determined is left open as completely by the fact that he believes and says they are, as it would be by the fact that a phonograph would say they are if the words had been impressed on the record. The author writes as if beliefs were neither true nor erroneous, but only accepted or rejected; and as if there were no such thing as *evidence* of the truth or erroneousness of a belief, but only *causes,* none of them connected with its truth or erroneousness, for its being accepted or rejected. Or does he mean to imply that he himself is not "typical of his group," *viz.,* anthropologists, and that although *their* belief in determinism has merely such causes and therefore is as likely to be erroneous as true, *his* belief in it is on the contrary determined by evidences of its truth?

The logical apparatus of prediction, however, always consists of two pieces of knowledge — one, of the form "Whenever an event of kind C occurs in a situation of kind S, then an event of kind E occurs"; and the other, of the form "This event and situation (from which a prediction is to be made) are respectively of kinds C and S." But if C or S should happen to be kinds *never exemplified before* in the history of the universe, then past observation and induction could not possibly have yielded the first of the two pieces of knowledge indispensable for prediction that in the given case the effect-event will be of kind E. Hence the nature of the effect-event in the case of the given sequence would be completely unpredictable notwithstanding the universality of causation; notwithstanding that one knew all that anterior observation and induction could possibly have yielded; and notwithstanding that the individually given sequence is a causal one since, as we have emphasized, its causal character does not consist in or require that it should have occurred before repeatedly or at all, but is a matter solely of its being of the "single difference" pattern.

It is worth noting in this connection that every experiment performed in the course of a piece of research constitutes a set-up which, in one respect or another, is novel in kind, at least so far as the individual experimenter is concerned, and indeed, in a great many cases, novel also in the history of the world. For obviously, were not the experiment in some respect novel, it would then be actually or theoretically superfluous; its outcome would be actually or theoretically predictable on the basis of what had been or could have been observed in earlier instances of its kind.

There are a number of different ways in which the situation one confronts at a given time may be of a novel kind. For example, the entity one faces might be a chemical compound now brought into existence for the first time in the history of the world. Although it might then be possible to predict some of its properties on the basis of the fact that it belongs to a certain class of substances, yet it has, in addition to such generic properties, also some specific ones, which cannot possibly be predicted but must be discovered by experiment. Or again, even if we have already experimented with a given entity a number of times and observed how it behaved, it may be that the very treatment the entity has undergone in these experiments has finally resulted in altering some property of it (as, for example, in cases of fatigue of materials); and our experimentation with it may be the first time in the history of the world that such an entity has been subjected to that kind of treatment. If so, the alteration that treatment brought about in it could not possibly have been predicted. Or again, the change occurring in the circumstances of an entity of a familiar kind may be novel in the history of the universe, as probably was the accidental addition of sulphur to rubber by Goodyear. Or the change in the circumstances of the entity, although it is a change of a familiar kind, may occur at a time when the entity is in a state — e.g., at a temperature or a pressure — very different from any in which it ever was before when a change of that kind occurred in its environment. And so on.

If "determinism" is taken to mean universal predictability, then to assert determinism amounts to asserting that *no* event ever has been or will be novel in the history of the universe; and indeterminism, in the corresponding sense, would be the contention that *some* events are "new under the sun," *i.e.,* that they, or at least some features of them, are genuinely unprecedented, and therefore were unpredictable. I submit that indeterminism, as so conceived, is true.

4. Predictive Inference, Prescription, and Prevision

To the considerations marshalled in the preceding section, it might be objected that in all the cases considered the behavior of the entity concerned did conform to some law even before it became possible to discover empirically what that law is, and therefore that God, at least, could have predicted what the outcome of the experiments would be.

If, however, we ask *how* God could have known it, we find ourselves forced to distinguish between three things: predictive inference, prescription, and prevision.

(*a*) Predictive inference is knowledge of a future event, *arrived at by inference from observations of past events.* Let us agree, somewhat arbitrarily but usefully for present purposes, to limit the use of the word "prediction" to this sense, thus distinguishing knowledge of the future by prediction from knowledge of it by either prescription or prevision. Then we can say that even God could not *predict* in cases such as those we have considered, where, *ex hypothesi,* the event from which prediction would have to be made is one of which no instances ever have occurred in the past, so that material for a generalization as to the nature of its effect was wholly lacking.

(*b*) If, however, we say that God knows what the outcome of the experiment will be because he himself *prescribes* what it will be, the question then becomes how God knows that when the time comes he will not change his mind and make the outcome different from what he had earlier prescribed it would be. For even if we should postulate that ultimately God causes everything that occurs, and that he can by fiat cause anything he pleases whenever he pleases, this would not entail, but rather preclude, that God's future course *must* be consistent with his past prescriptions. It entails only that, if he will, he can make it so. This brings us to the third possibility, *viz., prevision;* for if God knows in a given case that, when the time comes, he will make his course conform to his past prescription, only genuine prevision can be the source of this knowledge.

(*c*) Prevision (or, to use a broader term, preperception), as distinguished from predictive inference, would simply be present *observation* of future events, in a manner as direct as that of our present observation of present events. And we may add that retrovision (or, again more broadly, retroperception), as distinguished from memory and from inference as to the past, would be observation, similarly direct, of past events not observed at the time they occurred.

On the basis of our ordinary assumptions concerning the relations of observation to time it is not easy to conceive how such faculties could exist. But modern psychical research has brought forth evidence, very difficult to dismiss, that certain persons occasionally are capable of some preperception or retroperception, and thus that our usual assumption that the time of observation of an event and the time of the event must be the same is valid only with some exceptions, even if these are rare.[4] But the point of importance in the present connection is that those faculties — whether possessed by God or by man — would not presuppose determinism rather than indeterminism in the universe. Since they are conceived as faculties not of inference but of observation, they would operate equally well in a chaos and in a cosmos. They would presuppose only that the events, which today are as yet future, will be such as they will have been when, eventually, they have occurred. But this, being a tautology, is true no matter whether the universe is deterministic or indeterministic in any of the several senses of these terms.

5. "Indeterminacy" and Freedom

In connection with determinism conceived as essential predictability, something should be said as to the implications of the Heisenberg "principle of indeterminacy." It asserts, it will be

---

[4] References to reports of evidence for veridical preperception are given in footnote No. 10 farther on in the present chapter.

remembered, that the position and the velocity of a particle cannot both be measured exactly. Precision in measurement of position, for instance, automatically entails sacrifice of precision in measurement of velocity. But since exact knowledge of both would be needed for exact prediction of future positions of the particle, exact prediction of this is impossible. This fact concerning particles has been hailed by some believers in "free will" as meaning that causality is not universal and that "free will" is therefore consistent with modern science.

But, as we have now seen, unpredictability of some events does not imply that they have no cause nor that causality is not universal. Moreover, in the instance of the particle, the unpredictability referred to is not due to the particle's behavior being causeless, but on the contrary to the fact that the very process of observing the particle would *cause* a disturbance in its behavior. Again, even if the behavior of a particle were sometimes causeless, it would not in the least follow that human volitions also are causeless, *i.e.*, are purely fortuitous events. And finally, even if it did follow, it may be doubted whether persons who regard "free will" as something to be prized really mean, by speaking of the human will as "free," that human volitions are matters of pure chance. Yet "objective" chance, pure fortuity, is the only strict opposite of determination. This is true whether the events concerned be motions of subatomic particles, or be human volitions.

6. Determinism as Denial of Free Will

If every event that occurs has some cause, then even human choices between alternative courses of action are the necessary effects of some antecedent events. Determinism as thus inclusive has been widely regarded as precluding freedom of the will. Indeed, Webster's dictionary makes this the very definition of determinism when it states that determinism is "the doctrine that the will is not free, but is inevitably and invincibly determined by psychical and physical conditions." When determinism is conceived in this way, then indeterminism means specifically that, even if every event of other sorts is an effect necessitated by some antecedent event, human volitions, or at least some of them, are not in the same case, but are in some sense "free."

Plain men, moralists, and theologians for the most part share and alike treasure a firm belief that man possesses free will. The plain man, because of the eulogistic connotation of the word "free," considers free will important perhaps chiefly as a matter of pride; the moralist, because he believes it to be the indispensable basis of moral responsibility; and the theologian, because he believes that it enables him to conceive the Creator as guiltless of the evil his creatures do. But for whatever reason free will may be held precious, those who so hold it seem often to have only a very unclear idea of what exactly it is that, under this familiar label, they are so certain man possesses. The disputes which frequently arise between determinists and libertarians are due in no little measure to the ambiguities which infest the notion of free will. These we shall now attempt to remove, for only after this has been done may we hope to perceive clearly whether or not man has free will and whether free will and determinism are incompatible.

7. Freedom To Act as One Wills

By the statement that a man is free, common sense means that he can do what he wills; hence the range of his freedom is the range of acts which he can do if he wills to do them. Even when the expression used is not "freedom of action" but specifically "free will," cross-questioning or a call for examples brings out that in most cases what is really being referred to is freedom to act as one wills, i.e., freedom of action.

The acts concerned, of course, need not be physical but may

equally well be mental. For example, if a person has willed to give his thought for ten minutes to a certain problem in mental arithmetic but in three minutes finds himself thinking instead about a fishing trip, he cannot be said to have been free to do what he had willed to do since it turned out that in fact he could not do it.

That freedom, in the sense of freedom to do what he wills, is possessed by man but is limited in extent is obvious. I am at this moment free to stand up if I will but not to float up to the ceiling if I will.

8. Meaning of "I Can"

Not only in common-sense statements of what is meant by freedom but also in the attempts of philosophically disciplined persons to describe this with exactness, the expressions "I can," "I could," "I could have," or, synonymously, "I have the power to," etc., usually play a prominent part. Analysis of their meaning, however, is seldom offered, but in lieu of it, only italics or emphasis of vocal utterance. Indeed, the need for and possibility of analysis of their meaning seems usually not to be even realized. Yet so long as, in our discussions of freedom or free will, we go on using these expressions uncritically — that is, using them only on the basis of our ordinary merely intuitive understanding of their meaning, instead of on the basis of an exact analytical understanding of it — just so long do we fail really to get to the bottom of the topic.

I therefore begin with the fundamentally important question, What does it mean to say that a man *can* do what he wills? and I submit that the acts a man "can" do if he wills are *the acts which his merely willing them to occur causes to occur*. More specifically, the statement, for example, that "I now can stand up if I will" means that, of the various conditions upon which occurrence of my standing up now depends, all happen to be now in fact met except only volition by me to stand up. In other words, "I now can stand up if I will" means that the present state of affairs is such that addition to it of merely volition by me to stand up would cause the standing up to occur.[5]

Thus, three expressions turn out to be synonymous. They are:

I can do A (if I will)

I am free to do A (if I will)

Volition by me to do A would now suffice to cause occurrence of A.

The synonymy of these three expressions is here the absolutely basic fact. Unless it is discerned at the outset and kept clearly in mind throughout, no possibility exists of dispelling the obscurity which generally envelops discussions of "free will." Freedom in the sense they define I shall call *freedom of efficacy, i.e.,* freedom such as efficacy of one's volitions constitutes and confers.

The first noteworthy consequence of that synonymy is that freedom to do what one wills *requires* causal efficacy of one's volitions: It requires that one's volition to do A should *determine* occurrence of A; hence, that determinism to this extent should be a fact is far from being incompatible with freedom to act as one wills. *In a completely indeterministic universe — a universe where nothing caused anything and all occurrences were therefore "objectively fortuitous" — there would be no freedom at all to do anything;* indeed, no event would then constitute a *doing*. It is even a question whether the notion of "events" would retain any applicability in such a universe.

To what was said above concerning the meaning of freedom of efficacy, *i.e.,* freedom to do what one wills, something must now be added, namely, that to have such freedom means not only that one can do something A if one but wills, but *also that one*

---

[5] Cf. the writer's "A Neglected Meaning of Probability," *Proceedings of the Sixth International Congress of Philosophy,* 1926, p. 347. Also S. S. S. Browne's "Paralogisms of the Free-Will Problem," *Jour. of Philos.,* Vol. XXXIX, No. 19, Sept. 10, 1942, pp. 518–9.

need not do it unless one wills; i.e., that, in the circumstances existing at the time, abstention from willing to do *A* would prevent one's doing *A*. As to this, the fact is that, just as one fails to do some things one willed to do, so one does do some things one did not will to do. Hence, although freedom not to do something unless one wills does exist, it too, like freedom to do something if one but wills, exists only in some cases.

9. Activities, Volitions, Acts, and Deeds

However, the expression "to do something" is ambiguous, and removal of its ambiguity is necessary if the meaning of freedom of efficacy is to be completely clear. To remove it we need to distinguish between processes, responses, activities, acts, and deeds, and to decide what "to do something voluntarily" or "involuntarily" means. The definitions about to be submitted respect, I believe, the ordinary usage of the words they define, so far as it is firm; but where it is not firm and stipulations are therefore permissible and necessary, the definitions will make clear the sense in which those words are intended to be used in these pages.

A *process* in the body or mind of a person *P* is any event, *i.e., any change or unchange,* occurring in it. The word process connotes the fact emphasized already that any event takes some time, whether long or short, *i.e.,* is not strictly instantaneous but occupies a segment of time.

An *activity* is a process considered qua cause.

A *response* is a process considered qua effect.

Volition is desire (or, as the case may be, fear, *i.e.,* aversion) that is preferential, and therefore decisive among desires (or aversions) competing for expression in action. More explicitly, to *will* that an event *E* should occur is to desire occurrence of it *more* (or, as the case may be, to fear occurrence of it *less*) than occurrence of any of its envisaged alternatives. By an "envisaged alternative" of *E* is meant some event *F* different from *E*, that one thinks of and that one tacitly or explicitly believes would, in the circumstances existing at the time, tend to result directly or indirectly instead of E if one desired occurrence of F most (or, respectively, feared it least). F may consist merely in non-occurrence of E.

Desire or aversion that is not preferential will be called *impulsive,* or *impulse.*

An *act* A of a person P is an event in P, bodily or mental, whose cause was a desire by P, whether preferential or not, that A should occur. *Action* is performance of an act.

A *voluntary act* of a person P is one which, under the circumstances existing at the time, would occur if and only if P willed it to occur.

An *involuntary act* of a person P is one which, under the circumstances then existing, *occurs impulsively, i.e.,* without volition of it by P.

An act A of P is *purposive* if and only if it is performed by P as a means to an end; *i.e.,* if and only if the cause of A in the existing circumstances was, jointly:

(a) desire by P (or aversion), whether preferential or impulsive, for (or to) eventual occurrence of an event E, and

(b) belief by P that, in those circumstances, his acting in manner A probably would cause or contribute to cause (or, respectively, to prevent) occurrence of E. The belief may be either explicit or tacit. A tacit such belief would consist in an instinct or habit to act in manner A in such circumstances whenever P desires (or, respectively, fears) occurrence of E.

Causation (or prevention) of E is then called the *end, aim,* or *purpose* of the act, and the act is called a *means* thereto. The desire for (or aversion to) occurrence of E is called the *motive* of the act.

A purposive act A is *skilled* if the doer's belief that A would cause or contribute to cause (or prevent) E is based on good evidence that acting in manner A in circumstances such as then existing would or probably would cause (or prevent) E.

A purposive act is *successful* if the effect of it F turns out to conform to its aim E; *i.e.,* to be or to include E.

An act that is not purposive is called *mechanical.*

A *deed* is an event whose cause was an act.

A deed D was *intentional* if its cause was an act purposive of D.

A deed D was *unintentional (accidental)* if the doer of the act which caused D did not believe it would cause D.

A deed D is *incidental* if the doer of the act A which caused D believed it would or might cause D, but his motive for doing A was not desire for D.

Operation is causation in a substance Z of an event (a response) E by an event (an activity) C in a substance S, which may or may not be the substance Z itself.

S is in so far *agent, active, operating, affecting;* and Z in so far *patient, responsive, operated on, affected.*

If S and Z are the same substance, the operation is *internal;* but if S and Z are different substances, the operation is *external.*

10. Freedom To Will

What was said in Sections 7 and 8 concerned man's freedom to do what he wills. It is often asserted, however, that he has not only some freedom of action, but also freedom "of will." Let us therefore now consider freedom to will, as distinguished from freedom to act as one wills. To make freedom, at least, mean the same thing in both cases, willing has to be regarded as itself a species of act, and more particularly, of mental act. Then, to say that I am free *to will* to stand up (or, synonymously, that I can *will* to stand up) means that mere volition by me *to will* to stand up would cause me *to will* to stand up. (The question as to whether the bodily act of standing up would then result is not relevant here, and may be ignored.)   Freedom to will, then, like freedom to perform a bodily act or an external deed, would come under the general heading of freedom of efficacy.

But now, is there really such a thing as willing to will?   Do the words "to will to will" describe a psychological event that actually occurs and is different from that described by the simple verb "to will"?   Or, on the contrary, is the psychological operation described as willing to will as mythical as the physical operation of climbing upon one's own shoulders?

It seems clear at least that the additional, endlessly numerous expressions "to will to will to will," "to will to will to will to will," etc., describe nothing that ever actually occurs; but it does not follow from this that "willing to will" never occurs.   Indeed, it might be contended that just this is what occurs whenever we make a choice between alternative plans of eventual action rather than as between alternative immediate acts — for example, that to decide to spend the morrow's evening making out one's income tax report, instead of to spend it perhaps reading or at the theater, is to will now *to will tomorrow evening* the event consisting of making out one's tax report.

But this is not a correct analysis of the example; for what is willed now is not to *will* tomorrow to perform that act, but simply to *perform* it when tomorrow evening comes.   Once volition to perform it tomorrow has taken place, what causes it to occur (if it does) on the morrow evening is not the occurrence at that time of an additional volition planned the day before, but simply and automatically the coming of the morrow's evening, that is, the coming of the time and circumstances envisaged in the previous day's volition as those under which the act of making out the tax report shall occur.   For the very effect of present volition to perform an act of a certain kind when certain circumstances present themselves is to set up in oneself a psychological mechanism which is such that, when the circumstances envisaged do present themselves, their presence then normally causes in oneself action of that particular kind automatically.

Accordingly, the only sort of case where willing to will actually occurs is that where the act now willed to be later performed is itself specifically an act of willing. For example, a person who had become convinced that he was "weak willed" might, in order to "strengthen his will," will today to do on the morrow some deliberate willing. He might, for instance, will now to will strongly on arising the next morning to perform the duties of the day notwithstanding obstacles, instead of, as hitherto, allowing them to be pushed off to another day by the slightest interference.

Now, in such a genuine case of willing to will, what about freedom? The case is one where what one wills has three features:

(*a*) What one wills is that a certain act shall be done *when a certain time comes.*

(*b*) The act willed to be then done is not — like that of floating up to the ceiling — of a kind impossible to man, but on the contrary — like that of standing up — an act which is *possible* in the sense that men sometimes do perform it.

(*c*) The act willed to be done when the time envisaged comes is itself an *act of willing.*

In the first and second of these respects, the case of willing today to do on the morrow a certain *act of willing* is exactly parallel to that of willing today to do on the morrow a certain *physical act.* Moreover, that the act willed to be done on the morrow is in this case specifically itself an act of willing has no bearing one way or the other on the question of freedom, which, for *all* cases having peculiarities (*a*) and (*b*), is the question: *Can* one do when a set time comes whatever act one has earlier willed to do when that time comes? And (to put it in terms of today and tomorrow) this means, as we have seen: **Is one's** *volition today* to perform tomorrow an act *A*, *e.g.*, an act of willing, sufficient to cause one tomorrow to perform that act?

The answer, I submit, is that sometimes it is sufficient, and sometimes it is not. Whether or not it is sufficient depends on whether or not the circumstances otherwise happening to exist between today and tomorrow are of certain kinds; for, in view of the essentially triadic nature of the causal relation, an event *A* can never be said *simpliciter* to be sufficient to cause a certain event *B*, but only to be sufficient to cause it *under circumstances C*. For example, my willing today to prepare my tax report tomorrow evening will, under normal circumstances, be sufficient to cause me to do so; but will not be sufficient if, perhaps, the house catches on fire tomorrow evening, or if visitors come then unexpectedly, or if I am reminded that I already two weeks before prepared and sent in the report. Similarly, my willing today to spend, on arising tomorrow, five minutes willing strongly to cease procrastinating would ordinarily suffice to cause me so to spend those five minutes on the morrow; but it will not cause me to do it if, on arising tomorrow, I find the house on fire, or if I wake up with migraine, etc. Freedom to will, then, like freedom to perform acts other than acts of will, exists, but has limits. Whether we have it on a given occasion depends on what the circumstances happen to be then and subsequently. If they happen to be such that, in order that the volition planned to be done tomorrow (say, volition to do *A*) should occur tomorrow, nothing additional is needed other than that we should now will that volition of act *A* shall occur tomorrow, then we now *can,* *i.e.*, are now free to, *will tomorrow* to do *A*. Otherwise not.

11. Freedom, and Determination of a Volition by an Anterior Volition

The preceding remarks make plain that in the very cases where we are free *to will*, determination of a later volition by an earlier one not only is compatible with freedom to will but is required for such freedom. For to say that we are free to, *i.e.*, that we can, will tomorrow what today we will to will tomorrow means, as we have just seen, that, in the circumstances that happen to exist in the case, today's volition *determines, i.e.,* suffices to cause, occurrence tomorrow of the volition willed today to occur tomorrow. This alone would suffice to show that *freedom to will a certain act, and determination of the willing of that act by an antecedent event, are not always (if they are ever) mutually exclusive.*

Subsequent volitions are determined by an antecedent one also in cases of another kind,[6] namely, the much more common ones where an antecedent and latently enduring volition to attain some distant objective determines the numerous and more specific volitions that eventually turn out to be required for attainment of that objective. An obvious example would be a student's resolve to obtain an A.B. degree. The process of obtaining it consists of a long series of particular voluntary acts, some of which are performed automatically without additional volition when occasion arrives, but many of which, on the other hand, do require specific volition at the time the need to perform them arises. The determinant of these subordinate, particular volitions obviously is the enduring will to obtain the degree.

12. Free Will as Undetermined Volition

There is one sense often assigned to the term "free will" which we have not yet specifically examined, and which is in a way the inverse of fatalism. It is that although our volitions, or some of them, are efficacious, *i.e.,* determine occurrence of the effects they were intended to cause; yet some at least of our volitions are themselves wholly or partly undetermined, *i.e.,* uncaused, and in this sense wholly or partly "free."

---

[6] I am indebted to Professor F. C. Dommeyer for having called my attention to them.

Apparently, the sort of situation thought of as exemplifying volition "determined only in part" is one where a factor or set of factors F is indeed necessary to (and its presence therefore a partial determinant of) the occurrence of a volition V, but is *not* '*sufficient to cause V*. That is, absence of F determines nonoccurrence of V, but presence of F does not suffice to determine occurrence of V; so that, it is concluded, when F is present V is *then* wholly free.

Let us now consider this contention. Let us assume, as it requires, that in a given case *all* the factors F acknowledged to be necessary to occurrence of V, yet together not sufficient to cause it, are present. I submit that, in these circumstances, one or the other of two things is necessarily true concerning the occurrence or nonoccurrence of V: Either it is then *wholly determined* by the presence or absence of some other factor or factors D, for to suppose it only partly determined by them would be to suppose (contrary to the assumption made) that they really were parts of F; or else the occurrence or nonoccurrence of V is then *wholly fortuitous* — wholly a matter of "objective chance." For, as already pointed out, pure fortuity — absolute chance — is the only strict contradictory of complete determination. "Free" volition then would mean pure fortuity of volition — purely chance volition.

We have given reasons (in Chapter 9) for believing that objective fortuity, *i.e.,* causelessness, of an event is an internally contradictory conception; but in any case, that purely fortuitous volition is what man's supposedly precious "free will" consists in, is a conclusion obviously incompatible with that preciousness. Hence, it is rejected by any one committed *a priori* to the position that, whatever "free will" turns out to be, it is something precious. And, when a person committed to this has also committed himself to the gratuitous proposition that universal determinism and freedom are incompatible, nothing remains for him but to say that in the circumstances contemplated, the volition V is neither determined nor fortuitous, but is "free." To say this, however, is to say exactly nothing unless some *positive* account of what "free" then means is furnished. But none is furnished, and "free" therefore turns out to be but a fancy name for the "excluded middle" between the contradictories "determined" and "not determined."[7]

13. Responsibility; and Determination of Volitions by Circumstances

The fact is that what we will in given circumstances depends on, *i.e.,* is determined by, the nature of those circumstances, as well as (in some cases) by some earlier volition of ours; and as we shall see in all cases also by, or rather in accordance with, the particular kind of volitional nature which happens to be our own. It is obvious that if, at the time at which in historical fact I willed to spend the morrow's evening preparing my tax report, I had been not in my usual surroundings but instead, say, shipwrecked on a raft in the middle of the ocean, I would at that time of course *not* have willed to spend the morrow's evening making out the report, unless I happened at the time to have been irrational and irresponsible. But it will hardly be claimed that "free" volition means irrational and irresponsible volition, *i.e.,* that it occurs without regard to the situation one believes one confronts. Willing that were thus uninfluenced by the situation being faced — so that if, for instance, on being asked at dinner whether one will have apple or mince pie, one would be as likely to will to stand on one's head, or to will to recite the multiplication table, as to will to answer the question — such willing, I say, would not illustrate volition free in any significant sense. It would illustrate only erratic, random volition.

---

[7] If, in the contention that free will means undetermined volition, some one of the other senses of "undetermined" which we distinguished were substituted for that of "causeless," *e.g.,* "unpredictable," or "anomic," etc., several variants of that contention would be obtained. But a critique of each, analogous to that just offered, would apply.

It might be said, however, that although if I had been on a raft in the middle of the ocean and had been responsible at the time I *would* not have willed to spend the morrow's evening making out the tax report, nevertheless I *could* even under those circumstances have willed to do so, and that this is what it means to say that I was free so to will. But, as we have seen, to say that I *could* then (*i.e.,* at time T_1) have so willed, means that *volition at time T_1* by me *to will at time T_2* to prepare the report at time T_3 would have sufficed to cause me *to will at time T_2* to prepare it at time T_3. In fact, it might or might not have sufficed. But in any case such volition at time T_1 in the abnormal circumstances supposed would have been irresponsible. For once more, to say that a given act of will is responsible means that if one knows the sort of situation one is facing and knows the consequences of responding to it in this or that particular manner, then the manner in which one wills to respond to it is determined at least in part by this knowledge. As often has been pointed out, to praise or blame, or otherwise reward or punish a person for his voluntary acts — that is, to hold him responsible for them — is a rationally defensible practice not because his volitions are "free" in the sense of not determined, but on the contrary only because the very fact of his now being rewarded or penalized for what his volitions have been is one of the factors that determine what his volitions will be henceforth.

14.   Freedom of "Self-Determination"

It might, however, be urged that although what one wills or does not will at a given time is indeed contingent upon the circumstances, nevertheless it depends also in part on the sort of person one is, or, more specifically, on the particular sort of "volitional nature" one has, *i.e.,* on the particular instincts, volitional dispositions, habits, and tastes, which are characteristic of one's particular self. To have any given one of these traits means to be such that, in the presence of a certain situation, or in the presence of any situation of a certain sort, one's volition is such and such. Thus, although presence of a given situation does cause one to will a specific sort of act, it would not cause one to will it if one were a different enough sort of person. And, in the light of these facts, it might be contended that to have "free will" means that one's volitional acts are at least in part determined by, or better determined in accordance with, one's own volitional nature, and not solely by the external circumstances present at the time.

Now, it is a question whether the use of the words "free will" to mean this is felicitous, but they are sometimes in fact so used; and there is no doubt that, if this is what one means by "free will," then man possesses it. This is the "freedom" which is sometimes called freedom of self-determination. It should be emphasized in connection with it, however, that if, as can hardly be questioned, some animals have a "volitional nature" as defined above and perform voluntary movements, then these animals too have "freedom of self-determination" in that very same sense.

15. Freedom of Choice

We turn next to the question as to what freedom of choice or freedom to choose means, as distinguished from freedom to act as one has chosen to act. The answer, I submit, is that one has freedom of choice whenever one has a choice at all. That is, freedom of choice consists in having a choice; and having a choice consists in being aware of alternatives — aware of alternative possible courses of action, instead of aware of only one possible course.

To speak of a course as "possible" means here that, in the existing circumstances, merely willing to embark on it would suffice to cause one to do so; it does not mean that the intended result of embarking on it would certainly be obtained. Many persons have had the choice between attempting to swim across the English Channel and not attempting it; but most of those who chose to attempt it failed to do it.   Alternative possible courses of action towards a given aim thus are alternative possible ways of attempting to reach it; and to have a choice of such possible ways is simply to be aware of several.   The more numerous they are in a given case, the greater is one's freedom of choice of courses of action, even if it should be true that none of them would cause the result one intended, and therefore that in fact one could not have caused it, *i.e.,* was not free to cause it.

But even if in a given case one has freedom to cause the result one intends, in addition to freedom of choice of ways of attempting to cause it, the question remains as to whether his *choosing* the particular way he does choose is itself determined or free. The answer is that it is determined — determined by the fact that one of the several possible ways of proceeding (or, for that matter, one of the several sorts of result he can cause) is preferred by him, *i.e.,* is more satisfactory to him, or less repugnant than its alternatives.   But a choice determined *by this* — by his *preference* — is precisely what is meant, if anything, by speaking of a person's choice as "free."   Hence the disjunction commonly taken for granted to exist between determinism and freedom is illusory.

16.   Is Freedom Ever Compatible with Compulsion?

One sometimes speaks, however, of "acting against one's will," or of being "compelled to do something against one's will." We must therefore inquire more particularly what the state of affairs really is in such cases.

It will be recalled that to say that one is "free to," or "can," perform an act A means that, under the circumstances existing at the time, one's volition to do A suffices to cause A to occur.   But doing A may happen to be repugnant to our desires; and yet we may be caused *to will* to do A by the fact that the alternative to doing *A* happens to be something still more repugnant to us. This seems to be the sort of situation commonly in view when one speaks of being compelled to do some voluntary act "against one's will."

To free this phrase of its paradoxical character it is necessary to distinguish between what we deliberately will, *i.e.,* decide, choose; and what we positively or negatively desire. Our desires and aversions relevant to a given situation are usually many. Some of them are mutually compatible, and some on the contrary mutually incompatible and therefore competitive. The one which wins the competition is called our *will* (in the narrow sense, *i.e.,* deliberate will), our *decision,* or our *choice;* and its defeated competitors simply *desires,* or *aversions.* That is, what we (deliberately) *will* is what we *prefer* — what we *desire most,* or are *least averse to* — among the alternatives open to us in the situation we face.

In the light of these remarks, it appears that the sort of situation where we are said, loosely speaking, to be "compelled to act against our will" is one in which the alternative we choose among those open to us is repugnant to us, but less so than the others. In such a case, what we do is, as always, what we *will* to do, but what we will to do is not anything we *like* to do. It is, on the contrary, something that frustrates some desire of ours, but that we are caused nonetheless to *will* by the fact that the alternative to willing it would be even more frustrating.

It is to be noticed, however, that since even then we are aware of alternative possible ways of acting, or of alternative effects we can cause, and our preference among them determines which one we choose, our choice of it is even then free; for as already pointed out, determination of our volition *by our own preferences* among alternatives open to us is what freedom of choice consists in. Such determination, of course, is equally the fact when the alternatives we face happen to be attractive instead of repugnant and we choose the most attractive. In such a case, however, we do not speak of the determination as compulsion, or of the act as "against our will."

17. Does Antecedent External Determination of One's Volitional Nature Negate Freedom?

We may now consider a question, connected with the determination of volitions discussed in preceding sections, but not specifically examined there. It may be put as follows:

It is true enough, we may be told, that although one's particular volitions are determined by the circumstances one confronts at a given time, yet they are so determined only in accordance with the specific sort of volitional nature one happens to have. But this volitional nature is itself the resultant of a variety of causal factors, such as one's heredity, the sort of family training one has received, and the psychological pressure over many years of the evaluations, customs, and laws prevalent in the social groups to which one has belonged. Thus, the argument goes on, what a man wills in any given situation is, in ultimate analysis, completely determined by his circumstances, antecedent and present. And the conclusion is then drawn that, just because a man's future volitions are determined by his nature and his circumstances at the time as strictly as the behavior of a stone is determined by its nature and its circumstances, the man has no more freedom than the stone; and therefore is ultimately no more responsible, and no more to be blamed or praised for what he does, than is the stone.

Two comments on this contention suggest themselves. First, the fact that the sort of volitional nature a given person happens to have is the effect of causes outside itself does not entail that that volitional nature is any less truly his than, for instance, is a black eye or a broken leg caused in him by somebody else, similarly without opportunity for him either to accept or reject it; or again, than are his own the white, black, or yellow skin, or the color of eyes or hair, or the vigorous or weak constitution, or the musical or other aptitudes with which birth from his particular parents endowed him. For to contend that such things, and similarly one's volitional nature, cannot truly be called one's own is to assume that only what one has chosen, *i.e.,* only what one had opportunity to accept or reject, is genuinely one's own. But this would be to violate ordinary usage and force upon the words "one's own" a definition *ad hoc,* and one, moreover, which would entail a paradox; for since one's choices depend not only on the alternatives one is aware of, but *also in part on the particular sort of volitional nature one possesses, i.e.,* on one's tastes, desires, aversions, etc., possession of a volitional nature of one sort or another is *prerequisite* to the making of any choice whatever, and thus cannot possibly itself be originally a matter of choice.

Moreover, it is quite gratuitous to assume, as sometimes is done, that, unless one's volitional nature was ultimately a matter of one's own choice, one is not morally responsible for one's acts, and that blame or praise for them is not justified. For praise and blame are essentially forms of reward and punishment, and a sufficient justification for applying them is their capacity to cause the volitional nature of the person concerned to become different from, and presumably better than, what it was. If the person is, like most of us, one whose eventual volitional nature can to some extent be shaped by means of praise and blame, then praising or blaming him for his acts is justified, no matter whether the volitional nature he now has was "wished on him" from outside, like a black eye, or was generated by himself. And, if his future acts are capable of being determined by memory of the satisfactory or unsatisfactory consequences of his past acts, or by promises or threats of eventual such consequences, then he is morally responsible for his acts; for just this is what it means to be "morally responsible" for them. Moral responsibility thus refers essentially to the future; whereas legal, or more generally historical, responsibility refers to the past — to what one has done.

In connection with moral responsibility, however, it is necessary to distinguish between responsibility for what one *does,* and responsibility for what one *is.* The need of the distinction is made evident when one considers volitional dispositions implanted in a person by posthypnotic suggestion, or generated in him by the surreptitious administration of some drug, *e.g.,* of an aphrodisiac. For the question then arises as to whether he is morally responsible for his resulting voluntary acts. The answer is still the one given in the preceding paragraph; namely, that if praise or blame for them, and promises or threats as to future similar acts, are capable of shaping his future acts, then he is morally responsible for what he does, and reward or punishment for it is justified. But he is not morally responsible for being the sort of person which the posthypnotic suggestion, or the surreptitious administration of a drug, has made him become. These operations caused alterations in his volitional self in a manner analogous to that in which an automobile accident, or mayhem, or surgical interference with his nervous or his muscular system, or infantile paralysis, could cause alterations in the mechanisms of his body. The moral responsibility for the psychological alterations caused by hypnosis, drugging, or the like, belongs to the person who caused those alterations in him, unless that person did so with his knowledge and consent. If, on the other hand, the alterations caused in his volitional nature by those operations — or indeed in any other way — left it incapable of being reshaped by means of rewards or punishment, promises or threats, then the reshaping process, if one exists at all, is no longer to be called *moral reform* but *psychiatric treatment;* and he belongs not in a "reformatory" but in a mental hospital. A reshaping process is moral reform, or on the contrary psychiatric treatment, in so far as it employs respectively "appeals to reason" such as reward and punishment or promises and threats, or on the contrary "psychological" means such as psychoanalysis, hypnosis, electric shock, etc.

The second comment on the contention that if external forces contributed to determine the shape of a man's volitional nature he is then ultimately not free, is that man, but no other animal, has at moments some choice as to the sort of volitional nature he will have henceforth. For man is unique among the animals in that he alone is interested in and capable of self-observation and self-appraisal. He is not, like them, either fated or content to live his life unaware of what sort of person he happens to be. He is curious to reflect on his own acts, thoughts, feelings, tastes, impulses, desires, habits, dispositions, interests, and purposes. He insists on beholding himself in the mental mirror called reflection. This mirror, it is true, mercifully shows him but a subconsciously edited image of himself; yet there are but few men who, in their more sober private moments, wholly like every feature of even that tempered image of themselves.

Among the things a man beholds in the mirror of reflection are various aspects of what we have called his volitional nature; and, once he has beheld them, he is then in position, as he was not before, to choose between attempting to purge them of what he dislikes in them and not attempting it. To this extent, and from that moment, he has freedom of choice as to what sort of volitional nature he will strive to have. And although, as we have seen, one is not always free to achieve or to obtain what one has chosen, nevertheless there are many occasions on which one has some of this freedom — occasions, namely, where the willing is sufficient to the achieving or the getting of what one chose to strive for.

It might be objected that, when a man beholds his own volitional nature and thus gains freedom of choice between attempting and not attempting to alter it, the choice he then makes as to this is even then determined — dependent on the very sort of volitional nature which is now his and from which he is thus not free even when he beholds it. But this, translated into more concrete terms, means that *his own liking or disliking* of certain traits of the nature he perceives to be his is the very thing that determines him either to let these traits remain, or to strive to eliminate or reshape them. And it is hard to see what more than this could reasonably be meant by the demand for freedom of choice as to the kind of volitional nature one will have. For obviously, it cannot mean that a being, as yet of no particular nature and as yet nonexistent, shall have opportunity to choose his own nature. The most which can significantly be demanded is therefore opportunity to make oneself over if one does not like what one is; and this opportunity — this freedom — man does have to some degree in consequence of his unique capacity to observe, appraise, and alter to some extent what he happens to be at a given time. Here too, then, we find that man really has freedom, but that it is limited. Freedom of the particular kind just considered is, like all others, freedom inside some jail, sometimes a narrow and sometimes a roomy one.

18. Does the Possibility of Inference Predictive of Human Acts Negate Freedom?

We saw earlier that the possibility of prediction as distinguished from prevision, *i.e.,* the possibility of discovery of future events *by inference,* requires a universe deterministic in the sense that at least the events we seek to predict occur not haphazard but according to laws. That some events do occur according to laws is shown by the fact that, when the relevant empirical facts are available to us, we are able to predict with considerable success not only such events as eclipses of the sun or moon, but also the approximate number of suicides in a city during the next year, the times of departure and arrival of trains, and even the behavior of individuals whose dispositions, habits, tastes, and circumstances we happen to know well. This fact lends an interest more than merely theoretical to the question whether predictability of a person's behavior implies that he is not free.

As regards, first, what we have described as freedom of self-determination, it is obvious that predictability of a person's acts (of will or of body) does not negate this freedom, but on the contrary depends upon it. For as we have seen, it means that what a person wills to do in circumstances of a given kind depends on himself; *i.e.*, on the particular sort of volitional nature which is his — on the dispositions, habits, tastes, or other native or acquired regularities of volitional response to circumstances of given kinds, which together constitute his volitional self. These traits, although not as immutable as the laws of physics, constitute the laws of his individual nature at given periods of his life; and, like the law of gravitation and other laws of extrahuman nature, are when known the very things which make prediction possible.

As regards, secondly, freedom in the sense of freedom to act as one wills, it too is consistent with predictability. For, as we have also seen, freedom to perform a certain act (whether of body or of will) means that, in the circumstances existing at the time, mere volition that the act shall occur is sufficient to cause it to occur. We have this freedom as regards some acts, and do not have it as regards some others; but possession of it is perfectly compatible with the supposition that our volition at the time, which determines occurrence of the act, was itself determined and was theoretically predictable.

Thirdly, as regards freedom of choice, we have seen that it consists in being aware of alternative courses of action, each of them such that it would actually be embraced if we should but will to embrace it. Obviously, such freedom of choice as we do have is quite compatible with antecedent determination and pre-dictability of the volitional act which on a given occasion constitutes the choosing of one of the alternatives and the rejecting of the others.

19. Does the Possibility of Veridical Preperception of Human Acts Negate Freedom?

Were prevision, as distinguished from predictive inference, only a postulated faculty of a hypothetical omniscient being, there would be little reason for discussion of it outside theological works which take as known the existence of such a being. But there is considerable empirical evidence that some human beings at times have experiences which depict future or past events veridically, and yet do not come under the heading of predictive inference or of memory.

For these experiences, the names Precognition and Retrocognition are generally used rather than Prevision and Retrovision, because the experiences do not always consist of visual images. But in relation to our present problem, Precognition and Retrocognition are terms even more unsatisfactory because they categorize the experiences concerned as *cognitive,* whereas the truth is that, even when the experiences are veridical, they are not themselves cognitive at all. This assertion may seem paradoxical, but is not really so because (*a*) "cognition" means knowledge — here, knowledge that something is (or was, or will be) a fact; and (*b*) knowledge does not consist simply in belief of something which truly is (or was, or will be) a fact, but in belief of it *based on evidence sufficient to show* that it is (or was, or will be) a fact. For example, I might now believe — whether or not as result of a vision or dream — that the Pope has died; and it might be a fact that he has died. But this would not mean that I *know* he has died. I could be said to know it only if my belief, in addition to its happening to be true, were *based on adequate evidence* that he has died. Precognition or Retrocognition are bad terms for the kind of experience they are used to designate because they tacitly postulate not only (*a*) that the experience is veridical, but also (*b*) that it includes evidence of its own veridicality; whereas the fact is that experiences of the kind referred to are sometimes erroneous, and that, even when they are veridical, their veridicality does not become evident until afterwards. Hence, even when veridical, the experiences called Precognition and Retrocognition are not in themselves really cognitions at all.

The best names for them would seem to be Preperception and Retroperception; for the general process of interpretation of sensory images, called Perception, is as we know fallible; and we therefore customarily distinguish between *veridical* perception and *erroneous* perception (the latter being technically called illusion, or hallucination, according as the sensory images interpreted are caused normally or abnormally). Moreover, a veridical perception does not contain evidence of its own veridicality, nor does an illusion or hallucination contain evidence that it is only this. The evidence either way comes only afterwards, consisting as it does of the coherence or incoherence of the given perception with the rest of our experience. And it is because these features of perception are also features of the kind of experience now in view that I propose for it the names Preperception and Retroperception.[8]

The instances where preperception and freedom at first sight seem incompatible are those presenting together the three following features:

(*a*) the preperception turns out to have been veridical;

(*b*) the person whose freedom is in question is the prepercipient himself;

(*c*) the event preperceived is either an act of the preper-

---

[8] The only objection—and it seems minor—which I can see to these names is that sometimes the sort of experience concerned takes the form of an insistent hunch, or of a spoken warning, rather than of a visual or other percept.

cipient, or an external event of a kind capable of being caused or prevented at will by human beings in circumstances such as those in which the prepercipient is between the time of his pre-perception and the time of the event's occurrence.

The apparent incompatibility arises from the fact that the event E preperceived eventually occurs; and yet that if this event is of a kind which, in the circumstances, the prepercipient would pre-vent if he could, and which he could prevent if he would, then preperception of it would motivate him so to act as to prevent it.

Let us consider the logic of the situation in terms of a concrete instance — one which has often been referred to in discussions of veridical preperception. It was reported by the late F. W. H. Myers in the *Proceedings of the Society for Psychical Research for 1895,* Vol. XI, pp. 487–8. The person concerned was Mrs. Atlay, wife of the Bishop of Hereford. In March 1893 she wrote Myers as follows:

"I dreamt that the Bishop being from home, we were unable to have family prayers as usual in the chapel, but that I read them in the large hall of the Palace, out of which, on one side, a door opens into the dining room. In my dream, prayers being ended, I left the hall, opened the dining room door, and there saw, to my horror, standing between the table and the sideboard, an enormous pig. The dream was very vivid, and amused me much.

"The Bishop being from home, when dressed I went down into the hall to read prayers. The servants had not come in, so I told my governess and children, who were already there, about my dream, which amused them as much as it had done me. The servants came in and I read prayers, after which the party dispersed. I opened the dining room door, where, to my amaze-ment, stood the pig in the very spot in which I had seen him in my dream."

The governess, Emily Nimmo, appended her own written state-ment that Mrs. Atlay had related the dream when she came into the hall before prayers. And inquiries by Myers brought out the fact that the pig escaped from its sty while prayers were being read; its escape having been due to the fact that the gardener, who was at that time cleaning the sty, left it imperfectly secured, so that, the servants "having left every door open, the pig met with no obstacle on his voyage of discovery."

Since there can be no doubt that the presence of a pig between the table and sideboard of the dining room of an episcopal palace is an exceedingly rare if not unique event, chance coincidence is not a plausible explanation of the dream. The fact that the dream was recounted to other persons before its fulfillment excludes the possibility of explaining it away as an instance of the familiar illusion of *deja vu;* and the fact that the pig did not escape until after the dream had ended and been reported to the governess excludes the possibility that noise made by the pig in the dining room should have caused the dream. The episode thus is about as clear-cut a case as one could have, in terms of which to consider the theoretical bearing of veridical prepercep-tion on freedom; although for this purpose the case would of course be just as good if, instead of real, it were imaginary.

Obviously, if recollection of the dream had caused Mrs. Atlay to have had the entrances to the dining room, or the gate of the sty, securely fastened and kept so until she went into the dining room, the pig would not have been there. But if the dream had caused her to take these precautions, *it would not have constituted veridical preperception* since the event preperceived would then not have occurred. The fact, however, was that the dream was regarded by Mrs. Atlay as a ridiculous mere dream and therefore did not cause her to take the precautions which would have pre-vented its fulfillment; so that the dream did turn out to be veridical. The situation is then this: for the dream to have caused her to take these precautions, it would have been necessary *that she should have considered the dreamed event a real con-tingency* — something that would or might happen unless she acted to prevent it. But this very belief would have resulted in non-veridicality of the dream.[9]

On the other hand, for the dream to have been *veridical* (as in fact it was), one or the other of two things were necessary: either (*a*) that the event preperceived should *not have been believed a risk* and those precautions therefore not taken; or else (*b*) that, although believed a risk and those precautions taken, *they should have turned out insufficient* through some accident too extraordinary to have been thought of or guarded against, and the dream therefore fulfilled. This, however, would have meant, not that Mrs. Atlay had no freedom of efficacy, but only that — as we pointed out earlier is the case — there are limits to such human freedom, especially when what a person wills is not merely an *act* but is a *deed, i.e.,* some event external to the act, and which he intends the act to cause (or as the case may be to prevent) either directly or mediately. Man's freedom to do what he would is limited sometimes by his ignorance of means; and sometimes by lack of means, for example, by his lack of the necessary bodily strength or dexterity, or of the necessary tools, or helpers, etc. Obviously, no plausible conception of man's freedom can imply that his volition suffices to cause or prevent every event he wills to cause or prevent, for we know perfectly well that it fails to do it in many cases; and this quite irrespective of whether the eventual outcome of the volition was or was not veridically pre-perceived or susceptible of being so.

Aside, then, from events over which man, through ignorance

---

[9] To consider occurrence of an event *E* a contingency is to believe that *E* will or may occur if (or as the case may be, unless) some other event *A* occurs. In the present connection, *A* would be a certain act of the prepercipient: if *E* is objectionable, an act which would prevent *E* or make it improbable; or, if *E* is desirable, an act which would cause or facilitate *E*. An event which is a contingency and is *objectionable* is called a *risk, danger,* or *peril*. On the other hand, for an event which is a contingency and is *desirable,* the most nearly specific term would seem to be "opportunity": one speaks, for instance, of the *risk* of losing, but of the *opportunity* of winning.

or lack of means, has no control, and limiting ourselves to those he can — *i.e.,* is free to — cause or prevent at will, the essential point is that, *at the time he preperceives an event E, he cannot know whether his preperception is, or is not, veridical;* and that its turning out eventually to have been the one or the other *depends in part on whether he did not, or did, consider E a contingency,* and therefore, respectively, did *not* so act as to prevent occurrence of *E* and thereby made his preperception veridical; or on the contrary *did* so act as to prevent *E* and thereby made his preperception non-veridical. It is true that, even in cases where *E* does occur, he could have prevented it, *i.e.,* he was free to prevent it if he would. But as we have seen, this means only that volition by him to prevent *E* would have sufficed to prevent *E*. But *E* occurs because he believed there was no risk it would occur and he therefore did not will to prevent it. The fact that his not having willed to prevent it was determined — determined by his belief that there was no risk *E* would occur, and this belief itself determined by the rarity of *E* — that fact is perfectly consistent with the other fact that he was free to prevent *E*, *i.e.,* once more, that volition by him to prevent *E* would have prevented *E*.

The appearance of incompatibility in the cases we are considering, between veridical preperception and "free will," is thus due only to failure to analyze the several senses of this ambiguous and emotion-laden term, or to failure to realize that although man has some freedom in each of the several legitimate senses of this term his freedom always has limits.

To conclude our discussion of the relation between preperception and freedom, it will be interesting to consider briefly another recorded instance. It is one peculiar in that although the preperception was veridical in the broad sense that it was preperception of a danger which eventually did occur, nevertheless some features of the preperception were non-veridical; and, because the preperception was remembered at the time of that danger, the accident preperceived was averted, and the preperception was therefore to this extent erroneous.

The case is that of the dream of a lady, whom Myers states he knows but to whom he refers only as Lady Z. Her letter to him, which appears on p. 497 of the volume of the *S. P. R. Proceedings* already cited, is rather long, so I shall quote only portions, and summarize the rest.

On a certain day, Lady Z resolved to have her coachman drive her the next day, with her child and the nurse, to visit a relative. "During the night," she says, "I had a painfully clear dream in vision of the brougham turning up one of the streets from Piccadilly; and then of myself standing on the pavement and holding my child, our old coachman falling on his head on the road, — his hat smashed in." This dream so distressed her that she almost decided to go by train instead of driving; but she finally decided to drive. On the return journey, at about the place visioned, she saw other coachmen looking at hers, and then noticed that he was leaning back in his seat as if the horses had been pulling violently, which, however, they were not doing. Then "my dream flashed back upon me. I called to him to stop, jumped out, caught hold of my child, and called to a policeman to catch the coachman. Just as he did so the coachman swayed and fell off the box. If I had been in the least less prompt, he would have fallen just as I saw him in my dream." It turned out that he had fainted because of illness, of which he had said nothing. The dream proved to have differed from the reality in only two points: "In my dream we approached Down-street from the west; in reality we came from the east. In my dream the coachman actually fell on his head; . . . in reality this was just averted by the prompt action which my anxious memory of the dream inspired."

It is obvious that no incompatibility exists either between those features of the preperception which were veridical, or those which were not, and the prepercipient's freedom to act as she chose at the time.

How the possibility of veridical preperception is to be explained is of course a separate question, and one which we are not called upon to speculate about in the present connection. But that veridical preperception, not explicable as imaged expectation or as chance coincidence, sometimes occurs is something which cannot be left out of account when the nature of time and the notions of pastness, presentness, and futureness are the subject of inquiry.[10]

20. Summary of Conclusions

Complying in essentials with the method recommended in the first chapter, we have in this one considered in turn a number of common expressions in which enter the terms "freedom," "free will," "being free," "being undetermined," and others with which these are often contrasted; and we have attempted to analyze in each case the meaning of the term as employed in the given expressions. We may now summarize the chief results that have emerged.

We considered first "determinism" in the sense of universality of causation, and pointed out that "indeterminism," in the corresponding sense, asserts the occurrence of wholly causeless events — chance being thus conceived as having *objective* status. On the basis of arguments set forth in Chapter nine, we concluded that indeterminism as so conceived is false. Attention was drawn to the fact that, if the account of the causal relation given in

---

[10] The two cases of veridical preperception quoted are selected from the many reported by F. W. H. Myers in the *Proceedings of the* (English) *Society for Psychical Research,* Vol. XI, pp. 485–585. For a critical survey of the evidence for spontaneous precognition, see H. F. Saltmarsh, "Report on Cases of Apparent Precognition," *ditto,* Vol. XLII, 1934–5, pp. 49–103. As regards experimental evidence for precognition, see S. G. Soal and K. M. Goldney, "Experiments in Precognitive Telepathy," *Proceedings S.P.R.,* Vol. XLVII, 1943, pp. 21–150. Also, J. B. Rhine's "Precognition Reconsidered," *Journal of Parapsychology,* Vol. 9, Dec. 1945, pp. 264–277. See also, Gardner Murphy, "An Approach to Precognition," *Journal of the American Society for Psychical Research,* Vol. XLII, Jan. 1948, pp. 3–14.

Chapter eight is correct, universality of causation does not of itself entail that there are any causal regularities, nor, therefore, that every event which occurs was theoretically predictable.

We turned, therefore, to determinism conceived as asserting or implying that every event could have been predicted if one had previously observed everything there had been to observe and had performed adequately all the inductive generalizations for which those observations would have furnished materials. We pointed out that, even with such exhaustive knowledge of the past and of the laws implicit in it, prediction of the effect of an event novel in kind would not be possible; and therefore that determinism, conceived as asserting the possibility of universal prediction, postulates that no event has ever been or ever will be novel in kind. But there seems to be good reason to believe on the contrary that many events, or even perhaps all events, are to some extent novel — different in some respect from any that ever have occurred before. We therefore concluded that determinism, in the sense of theoretically universal predictability, is false.

We then distinguished between prediction in the specific sense of *inference* as to the future based on knowledge of the past, and prevision in the sense of present *observation* of the future. Strange as it may appear, there is evidence that such observation is sometimes possible to some extent. We pointed out, however, that the possibility of prevision in this sense would not postulate either determinism or indeterminism. Some remarks were then made concerning the Heisenberg "principle of indeterminacy" to the effect that it is not incompatible with universality of causation, and moreover implies nothing one way or the other as to man's possession of "free will."

We then mentioned a third sense in which "determinism" is often used, *viz.*, that the human will is not free; and we then turned to an examination of the meaning of the ambiguous and vague term "free will." We pointed out first that ordinarily, when a man is said to be "free," what is meant is that he is free to, *i.e.*, can, do what he wills. Freedom in this sense we proposed to call freedom of efficacy. The meaning of "I can" or "I am free to" was then analyzed, and found to be that my simple volition (to do, say, *A*) is, under the circumstances existing at the moment, sufficient to cause *A* to occur. It was then concluded that man in some cases does, and in some cases does not, have freedom to act as he has willed.

Freedom to will, as distinguished from freedom to act as one wills, was next considered. It was pointed out that willing is itself an act — a mental act — and therefore that the analysis of "I am free to will" or "I can will" is in essentials exactly parallel to that of "I am free to do *A*" or "I can do *A*"; and that the conclusion is therefore similar: man in some cases is, and in some cases is not, free to *will,* that is, free to do eventually the willing which he now wills to do eventually. Freedom to will thus comes under the general heading of freedom of efficacy. At that point, an inquiry was made into the nature of voluntary and involuntary acts and deeds.

We then examined the contention that free volition is volition undetermined, wholly or partly; and we found that, once the conditions admitted to be necessary but not sufficient to a volition *V* are present, the alternatives are that either *V* is then wholly determined by some other factor, or else *V* is wholly undetermined. "Wholly undetermined," however, has no strict sense other than "purely fortuitous," and purely fortuitous volition would not be the precious thing free will is assumed to be. And to say then that, under the conditions stated, *V* is neither determined nor fortuitous but "free," is but to make this word denote in this context violation of the logical Law of Excluded Middle.

We next considered the fact that volitions are determined not only sometimes by antecedent volitions to will, but also, and much more extensively, by the nature of the circumstances a man believes himself to be facing at the time, and by the nature of the consequences he believes this or that volition would have. Volition not so determined would be irrational, irresponsible volition. Therefore, what moral responsibility presupposes is not a "free will" in the sense of an irrational, erratic will, but on the contrary a will determined by the factors just mentioned. Were the human will not so determined, rewards and punishments would be nugatory and therefore senseless.

Attention was then called to the fact that a person's volition in a given situation depends not only on what he believes the situation and probable consequences of his volition to be, but also on the particular sort of volitional nature which happens to be his — *i.e.,* on his habits, dispositions, tastes, interests, desires, and so on. The fact that this too is a factor in determining what his volition shall be on a given occasion is what appears to be meant when it is said that he possesses "freedom of self-determination." It was pointed out that although man does have freedom in this sense, so does any animal that has habits, dispositions, tastes, etc.

Freedom "of choice" was next considered, and found to consist in awareness of alternative possible courses of action — the choice, or volition, of a particular one among them being determined by one's preference, *i.e.,* by the fact that it is the one liked most, or disliked least, among the alternatives open on the given occasion. The greater the number of such alternatives one is aware of, the more "freedom of choice" one has; but one always has at least the choice between willing and not willing to act in a given possible manner.

We then argued that there is really no such thing as "acting against one's will." It was shown that the situations in which one is compelled to act, supposedly, against one's will are really situations where — although one still has freedom of choice — the choice is between alternatives to all of which one is averse; so that one's choice of the least repugnant among them, although not against one's *will,* nevertheless frustrates one's *positive desires.* Compulsion in this sense and freedom of choice sometimes coexist.

Notice was taken of the fact that although what a person wills in a given situation depends on his volitional nature, still what this volitional nature happens to be itself depends ultimately on determinants — such as heredity, upbringing, and other social factors in his earlier environment — that are external to him. It was pointed out that, although it is true that he did not choose these factors, nor therefore the particular volitional nature they generated, this volitional nature is not on this account any the less his own; and moreover, that a paradox would be involved in asking that he should make any choices, and, in particular, choice of it, antecedently to possession of any volitional nature. But it was also pointed out that a person's volitional nature is not completely fixed forever; that man, unlike the animals, is capable of self-observation and self-appraisal; and that, if he dislikes any aspect of the volitional nature he finds to be his, he can take steps to cause it to become different henceforth. That is, he has, to some extent, opportunity to choose what his future volitional nature shall be.

We then discussed the notion of moral responsibility, and the question as to when praise or blame, reward or punishment, promises or threats, are appropriate. We found that a man is morally responsible for what he *does,* as distinguished from what he now *is,* in so far as those means are capable of reshaping his volitional nature; and this, irrespective of how his present volitional nature came to be what it now is — whether as a result of his own past attempts to shape it, or as a result of external events that were beyond his control.

Lastly, we considered, and answered in the affirmative, the question whether the possibility of veridical predictive inference, or of veridical preperception, of a person's future acts is compatible with possession by that person of the kinds and degrees of freedom which we had found reasons to believe men do possess.

The results we have reached in this chapter, particularly as to whether or not man has free will, do, I believe, vindicate as far as they go, and concretely illustrate the meaning of, the contention in Chapter 5 that the answer to a philosophical question — such as that of free will and determinism — becomes obvious in the light of ordinary empirical knowledge (or else becomes one for investigation by some one of the empirical sciences) as soon as the analysis of the concepts explicitly or implicitly involved in formulating the question has been successfully completed.

PART III

Nature, Matter, and Minds

Chapter 12

NATURE, MATTER, AND MIND AS BEHAVIOR

With benefit of the analyses of fundamental categories in Part II of our study, we shall in this third part consider first the contention of contemporary naturalistic philosophy that mind is a part of nature. In this connection, we shall ask what exactly is to be understood by "the material world" and how it is related to "nature"; and we shall then examine critically the modern attempt, which radical behaviorism constitutes, to conceive minds in materialistic terms. The subsequent chapters of Part III will be devoted first to a number of basic questions which arise when one tries to define with precision what ultimately differentiates the things or events we call mental from those we call material. Of especial importance among those questions will be that of the status of so-called sense data, and that of the nature of the "objective reference" said to be an essential feature of perception of the material world, and also of memory and of some other forms of cognitive activity. The remaining chapters of Part III will be given to an account of the nature and the typical operations of minds.

1. Naturalism, Materialism, and Behaviorism

The sciences commonly called natural, that is, the physical and the biological sciences, are today adult. The practitioners of them — so long at least as they remain within their own technical fields — display in the form of firmly established habits of procedure a mastery of the essential principles of knowledge-yielding method, and in consequence the achievements to their credit are both many and great. The demonstration of men's power to win knowledge, which their success in the investigation of nature provides, is impressive and has been the inspiration for the philosophies which in the last few decades have called themselves naturalistic.

According to these philosophies the traditional antithesis of mind and matter or psychical and physical is invalid. Mind, they assert, is to be conceived fundamentally in biological terms. "Mind" is the name of the manner in which the bodily organism behaves when it is functioning cognitively or intelligently in adapting itself to its environment and especially in adapting its environment to itself. Mind is "a distinctive way of operating"[1] — a way not manifested by any objects other than the human body or at times the bodies of some of the higher animals. Mind is not something distinct from nature. It is a part of nature. Mind, then, should be studied by the same methods as other parts of nature, and that it can be so studied is shown by the successes of physiological and behavioristic psychology. Such, in broad outline, is the so-called functional view of mind taken by the contemporary naturalism which believes itself to have transcended, and thereby disposed of, the classical problem of the relation between mind and body.

We must ask, however, what exactly is this "nature," to which naturalistic philosophers constantly refer. Just how, if not omnivorously and therefore nugaciously as a mere synonym of "everything," is the term nature to be understood? Some naturalistic philosophers explicitly identify naturalism and materialism. Others disavow the equating of nature with the material world.

---

[1] J. H. Randall, Jr. in "A Note on Mr. Sheldon's Mind," *Journal of Philosophy*, Vol. XLIII, p. 210. Cf. W. H. Sheldon's "Are Naturalists Materialists?" *ibid.*, Vol. XLIII, 1946, pp. 196 ff., and his "Critique of Naturalism," *ibid.*, Vol. XLII, 1945, pp. 253 ff.; replies to it by Dewey, Hook, and Nagel in *Journal of Philosophy*, Vol. XLII, 1945, pp. 515–530.

All of them, however, lay stress on "scientific method," and seem most nearly agreed that nature is whatever is at least theoretically susceptible of investigation in a scientific manner.

But, as pointed out earlier, a scientific manner is strictly speaking any manner capable of producing knowledge, and scientific method therefore cannot be identified with the specific forms it takes in the physical and the biological sciences. Most naturalistic philosophers, I believe, would agree that to limit it to these forms would be to conceive it too narrowly. Whether, in practice, they refrain from doing so is another question. But if scientific method is essentially any method capable of yielding knowledge — knowledge that the proposition investigated is true, or is false, or is more probably so than certain others — then it follows that investigation, in so far as not scientific in method, is not really investigation at all, but is guessing, snap-judgment, wishful thinking, or the jumping to conclusions outranging evidence. Hence there is no subject that is not susceptible, at least theoretically, of investigation in a scientific manner; and "nature," defined as whatever can be so investigated when we have the relevant equipment or opportunity, is but a synonym for "everything." Naturalism would then be opposed only to self-confessedly irresponsible dogmatism — only to the making of assertions without any claim that they are based on evidence. But even the assertions put forward as "divine revelations," which naturalists scorn, are not in this case; for divine revelation, if there should be such a thing, would be but a particular instance of testimonial evidence, and when the testifying witness is known to be expert in the matters as to which he testifies and to be truthful, then acceptance of his testimony, as establishing at least a probability, is good scientific procedure in cases where verification otherwise is not practicable. But the persons who accept certain propositions as being divine revelations claim to have good evidence that the witness exists, is expert, and is truthful. One may well ask, indeed, whether their evidence for this *is* good, and I would myself deny that it is. But their mere act of offering it is tacit acknowledgment by them of the obligation not to be irresponsibly dogmatic — of the obligation to base assertions on evidence adequate to support them. They too, then, would be naturalists *in intent* if naturalism is essentially allegiance to scientific method, even if, in point of actual procedure, they fail to live up to its requirements. In such failure, however, they are not alone, for the writings of professed naturalistic philosophers themselves, although abounding in praises of scientific method, are often far from constituting shining examples of its practice.

If, however, we mean by "nature" everything there is, then of course mind is a part of nature. But the assertion that mind is a part of nature then contradicts nothing that anybody maintains, and does not either solve or transcend the problem really in view when one asks how mind is related to nature. For that problem, even if in slightly different words, then reappears within omnivorous nature as the problem of the relation between mind and the material world, and between mind and body.

It follows that if the term nature is to mean anything not wholly nugacious, then what it means is the material world and its processes. This is what the sciences called "natural" study; and it includes, of course, human and animal bodies, their anatomy and physiology, and their behavior. Some of the more consistent naturalistic philosophers apparently mean by "nature" precisely that. At all events, precisely that, *viz.,* the material world, its events, things, processes, and laws, is what the term nature denotes in the present work.

This immediately brings up the question as to what exactly in turn is meant by "the material world." The answer is that the material world comprises, first and basically, such things, events and relations as are or can be perceptually public — public in the sense in which the process commonly called external or sensory perception reveals the same fact (*e.g.,* that a cat is now curled up in my lap) to all normal persons who perform that process while sensorily oriented to the same place and time and with the same question in mind. And secondly and derivatively, the material world includes also such things, events, and relations as are existentially implicit in those which are perceptually public; for example, molecules, atoms, electrons, etc., their states and changes, and the laws of their relations. That these are "existentially implicit" in the perceptually public ones means that they are *constituents* of the latter: for example, that the molecules and the atoms are parts of the things perceived; that the event called expansion, perceived to occur in the perceived thing called a mass of gas, analyzes into change of a certain sort in the relations of the parts of the gas to one another; and that the laws of the expansion analyze into the laws which govern that sort of change of relations among those parts.

In connection with the definition of "the material world" as basically the perceptually public world plus, derivatively, whatever is existentially implicit therein, it is necessary to distinguish between being *public,* being *perceptually public,* and being *published.*

To be *public* is to be known by all qualified persons that have investigated, and to be knowable by any qualified person that investigates. Being "qualified" to investigate means possessing such capacities as are relevant to the topic of investigation and to the question raised about it. For example possession of the sense of smell if the comparative intensity of various odors is in question; or possession of arithmetical skill if the question concerns the sum of 1234 and 4321.

To be *perceptually public,* accordingly, is to be perceptually known, *i.e.,* to be perceived, by all qualified persons that have investigated perceptually, and to be perceivable by any qualified person that investigates perceptually. What exactly the process called "perceiving" consists in will be considered in detail in a later chapter. The only point relevant here is that the *same state of affairs* — *e.g.,* that it is now raining here — *can become known to all qualified persons* by means of the process called "perception." Such analysis of this process as may be offered does not alter, but only may explain, the fact that that state of affairs can become so known.

Thirdly, to be *published* is to be made public by means of perceptually public *signals; i.e.,* by means of formulation — whether vocal, graphic, gestural, or other — in some language. For example, my *feeling dubious* of something S is not perceptually public; but if I utter aloud the words "I feel dubious of S," my feeling dubious of S is thereby *published, i.e., made known by linguistic signals* to all persons who may perceive my words and are "qualified" in the sense that they understand English.

From the remarks made above concerning naturalism, nature, and the material world, we now turn to an examination of the account of mind proposed by radical behaviorism. I say *radical* behaviorism, because merely *methodological* behaviorism acknowledges the existence of events mental in the sense of directly observable only by introspection, and professes the study of behavior to be essentially a *method* for the study of the mind to which those events belong; although even writers whose behaviorism supposedly is only methodological speak at times as if the mind *consisted* of certain forms of behavior. The metaphysics of a behaviorism that really is only methodological is — whether its practitioners realize this or not — a *dualism,* either of the interactionistic or the epiphenomenalistic kind. Thus, not methodological but only radical behaviorism really contends that a mind is a part of nature in a sense of "nature" other than its nugatorily all-inclusive sense. The behaviorism of Professor Edgar Singer is a clear-cut instance of radical behaviorism. Let us see what he has to say.

2. Singer and Stevens on Mind Conceived as Behavior

Consciousness, Singer declares, "is not something inferred from behavior; it *is* behavior. Or, more accurately: Our belief in consciousness is an expectation of probable behavior based on an observation af actual behavior." He adds that "it is essential to my thesis that I regard my own mind as behavior, quite as frankly as I take my fellow's mind to be nothing else."[2]

Singer thus takes as his point of departure the fact that we perceive physical objects and physical events. He notes that among them are certain ones we call human bodies and their behavior. These bodies behave under certain circumstances in ways different in certain respects from those in which any other objects behave. Prominent among the modes of behavior peculiar to them is the mode speech constitutes. "Consciousness" or "mind" is then simply the name for these distinctive modes of behavior, just as, Singer would I suppose say, "goldness" is the name for the set of modes of behavior which distinguish a certain metal from all others. Among the human bodies we perceive there is for each of us one which is peculiar, in that, for example, he cannot walk around it and perceive it visually from all sides. Each of us calls the human body of which this is true for him, *his own* body. But although the angle from which we perceive our own body is peculiar, we are nevertheless able to observe its distinctive behavior almost as adequately as we can that of other human bodies; and the features which distinguish its behavior from that of all other human bodies we call "our own consciousness" or "our own mind." This, I take it, is the state of affairs Singer contemplates when he writes the words quoted above.

The attempt to define consciousness, mind, and mental events in terms solely of behavior is intimately connected with the persistent effort since the turn of the century to make psychology a

---

[2] Edgar Singer, *Mind as Behavior*, R. G. Adams & Co., Columbus, 1924, pp. 10, 12.

natural science. This aim has entailed that, as with Singer, the facts taken as primitive for psychology had to be facts of the perceptually public sort. The example in this respect of other natural sciences already sure of their ground has been followed in general automatically, but some psychologists are fully aware that ultimate appeal exclusively to facts of this kind is that on which depends the status of a natural science, desired for psychology. S. S. Stevens, for instance, writes on the matter with admirable discernment as follows:[3]

> An essential characteristic of all facts admitted to the body of scientific knowledge is that they are *public*. . . . "Objectivity" in science is attained only when facts can be regarded as independent of the observer; for science deals only with those aspects of nature which all normal men can observe alike. . . . Since the subject matter of science consists exclusively of "objective" occurrences, the relation of the psychologist to the object of his investigation is fundamentally not different from that of any other scientist to his subject matter. Sometimes the psychologist is supposed to be observing his own consciousness . . . psychology regards all observations, including those which a psychologist makes upon himself, as derived from "the other one," and proceeds on this basis to formulate operations which define consciousness in general. The psychology of "the other one" makes explicit for psychology the distinction which all science recognizes between the experimenter and the thing experimented upon or observed. The psychologist may fulfill the role both of experimenter and subject matter. He can observe a phenomenon and then, taking his observations as data, he can in the role of experimenter treat them as "objective," verifiable facts and draw conclusions from them. . . . The proof that the experimenter, while acting as observer or subject, is himself the object of study lies in the fact that at any moment another psychologist could step in and take over the task of experimenter without altering the results. In other words,

---

[3] S. S. Stevens, "The Operational Basis of Psychology," *American Journal of Psychology*, April 1935, Vol. XLVII, pp. 327–9.

the role of experimenter is distinct from that of subject. . . . The criterion of acceptability applied to an experimenter is that his discriminatory responses shall agree with those of other experimenters. . . . The body of psychological science as it now stands relates to verifiable responses obtained from organisms treated as objects of study by capable experimenters who may or may not have served in the role of investigated organism. It is obvious that in abnormal and animal psychology the experimenter maintains a position of observation external to the system under observation. The same relationship must obtain in all scientific psychology. The utility of this type of "objective" approach lies in the fact that all operations involved are essentially public and repeatable.

3. The Naturalistic "Meaning" of a Language Response

It is a question, however, whether psychologists always fully realize the obligations which the status of a natural science — desired by them for psychology — carries with it. These obligations, as described by Stevens in the passage quoted, seem perfectly clear and straightforward until one recalls that, where human beings rather than the other animals are concerned, stimuli and responses will consist largely of *words*. That this fact complicates the problem is something brought out by Stevens himself, who goes on to say:

> It is inevitable that much of the psychology of "the other one" should be derived from his language-responses. . . . However, these responses can be considered in two quite different ways. They can be studied purely as muscular reactions, comparable to any other muscular twitchings, or else they can be studied in their role of symbols. The first approach is straightforward and free of entanglements; but the second plunges us immediately into the problem of the meaning of words. . . . Difficulties arise most often when we accept words as data, for what we really want as data in most instances is the meaning of the words. We care more for what the words imply than for the words themselves.

If the experimenter assumes that the words used by the subject mean what they would mean if the experimenter used them, he is apt to be in error, for the meaning of a word depends upon the past history of the person acquiring the meaning, and no two personal histories are identical. However, the experimenter can be more certain of the meaning, for the "subject," of some words than of others. An operational test in which words are applied to concrete objects or situations would show the meaning of such words as *yes* and *no* to be more certain and predictable than the meaning of words like *brown* and *beautiful*. Only such words as the former can be accepted as data if maximal rigor is desired. . . . Complete rigor can be obtained only providing it can be demonstrated that the meaning is known, or else that the experimenter knows the complete history of the subject as regards the particular words in question, *i.e.*, how the subject acquired the words. The latter alternative is readily achieved in animal experimentation where the experimenter provides the animal with "words" (conditionings) whose history he knows, and which can therefore be accepted as reliable data.[4]

Let us, however, assume that an experimenter somehow has come to know that a word which has been uttered by the subject has the same meaning for both the subject and himself; and let us now ask what sort of thing this "meaning" can consist of if the experimenter *in his capacity as natural scientist* is to be warranted in taking that meaning, instead of the word itself which has it, as being the subject's response.

Light is thrown on this question if we note first that words uttered by a human subject are far from being the only examples of publicly perceptible events that have a meaning, and the meaning of which (instead of the event itself perceived at the moment) a natural-scientific experimenter can occasionally be warranted in taking as result of his experiment. For example, under certain conditions of pressure, etc., the fact that a thermometer is regis-

---

[4] *Loc. cit.*, pp. 329–30.

tering 212° F. means, to an experimenter who perceives it but is
perhaps at the time not in position to perceive the water in which
it is plunged, that the water is boiling.   In such a case, the meaning of what is actually perceived consists of something not at the
moment perceived but susceptible of being perceived and therefore
belonging to the physical world.

Again, under certain conditions, a curved line in a cloud
chamber means to an experimenter who perceives it that a corpuscle has been emitted by an atom; and, not the line itself but
this its meaning, is what he takes to be the fact observed by him.
In such a case the corpuscle emitted and the emission of it are
not actually perceived, and moreover are not capable of being
perceived; but the corpuscle and its motion are nevertheless regarded as parts of the physical world because the corpuscle is
regarded as existentially implicit in — as standing in the relation
of part-to-whole to — certain perceptually public entities.

These examples lead us to the general conclusion that, for any
natural science, the meaning of any perceptually public fact must
always consist of some other fact *in nature;* that is, it must consist
either of some fact itself capable of being perceptually public, or
else of some fact implicit in the sense stated in Section 1 in facts
capable of being perceptually public.

With this conclusion in mind, let us return to word utterances.
Our question, it will be recalled, was, of what kind the meaning
of a word uttered by a human subject can be if an experimenter
bound by the conditions definitive of all *natural* science is to be
warranted in taking that meaning (instead of the word that has
it) as result of his experiment.   Since the conclusion reached
above is completely general, the answer it provides is that he is
warranted in doing this *only if that meaning consists of some-*
thing which is itself a part of the material world, i.e., to repeat,
of something itself perceptually public or of something existentially implicit in something perceptually public.   This obviously

precludes a natural-scientific psychology from including in its terminology any terms of which the meaning would consist instead of something *psychical, i.e.,* of something only introspectable or of something implicit in introspectables. From the standpoint of a psychology which claims to be concerning itself with a part of nature, any such term would be just as devoid of meaning as it would be for chemistry, astronomy, or any other natural science. Thus, a natural-scientific psychologist can use at all a word that as commonly used means something psychical, *only if he redefines it to mean some material event or thing.* This is what the radically behavioristic and physiological psychology, which alone is psychology as a natural science, has done.

4. Mind vs. the Behavior of Bodies that Have Minds

It is easy, of course, so to define the word "mind" that what it is then made to mean shall be a part of nature, just as by defining black as a species of white it is easy to make Negroes a part of the white race. But, as pointed out earlier, such high-handed verbal procedures are futile. What they do is only to construct an arbitrary language which, by using familiar words in novel senses, makes it seem that one is talking about the things these words familiarly denote, whereas in fact one is talking about something wholly different. Thus, for example, what radical behaviorism chooses to call "mind" is something which in ordinary English would be called *"the behavior peculiar to bodies that have minds."*

Study of the behavior of such bodies and of its physiological basis is a perfectly legitimate and an important enterprise, and it is genuinely a department of natural science so long as it proceeds in the manner described by Stevens. It then neither clashes with, nor replaces, the study of what is ordinarily meant by "mind." Philosophers, thus, have no call to be irritated as they sometimes are at behavioristic psychology so long as the latter strictly attends to its "knitting" as defined by Stevens. Legitimate occasion for irritation arises only if the claim is made — whether explicitly or tacitly — that what a natural-scientific psychology thus studies is what the term "mind" commonly means or "really" means. For only confusion can result from using the word "mind" to mean the behavior peculiar to bodies that have minds. Such use leads to the belief that natural-scientific psychology has made important observations of that which we who speak ordinary English refer to when we speak of mind; whereas the truth is that any psychology which is genuinely a natural science does not really observe this mind at all, but only something else, which remains different from mind even when arbitrarily called by the same name.

5. Arbitrariness of the Behavioristic Definition of "Mind"

It may be objected, of course, that to define mind in such a way that it is then distinct from nature is just as arbitrary as to define it in such a way that it is then a part of nature. To judge of the merits of this objection, it is necessary to distinguish the sense in which any definition may be called arbitrary from that in which some definitions are and others are not arbitrary.

It is acknowledged that if a term is our own in the sense that we introduce it into the language, we are at full liberty to define it as we please. Indeed, we have this liberty under certain conditions even if the term is one already existing in the common language. If we state unambiguously our private definition of it and if in addition we state that on a given occasion we are using the term in the sense defined by us instead of in the ordinary sense, then anyone who acquaints himself with our definition will be in position to understand the statements we make, in which the term figures. That is, if we have stated the *connotation* we propose to attach to the term, other persons will then be able to understand what properties it is that we are asserting or denying when we use the term as predicate of a sentence. Or, if what we have done is to exhibit the concrete things we propose to *denote* by a term, then other persons will be able to understand which things we are speaking about when we use the term as subject of a sentence. The difference between the second situation and the first is only the difference between understanding which things are being talked about, and understanding what is being said about them.

A convention — either one specially made or one currently existing — as to the denotation or as to the connotation of a term is thus indispensable if the term is to be useful for purposes of identifying, respectively, the things about which someone who uses the term proposes to say something, or the properties which, by means of the term, he proposes to affirm or deny of something. Where terms in ordinary use are concerned, the convention relied upon is tacit — shared in automatically through imitation rather than deliberately entered into. Where novel terms are concerned, on the contrary, the convention needs to be stated and consciously accepted. But whether a convention as to the use of words be tacit or explicit it is always *arbitrary* in the sense that if a different word had been agreed upon wherewith to denote certain objects or to connote certain properties, it would have worked just as well.

But there is also another sense of "arbitrary." It is a condemnatory one, in which some conventions as to the use of words can and others cannot be called arbitrary. A given convention is in this sense arbitrary *when it clashes with a preexisting commonly accepted one.* A clash may be said to occur when a word in common use in certain contexts is made for instance to denote *in the same context* a kind of thing *different* from that which it has hitherto denoted. In some regions of the West, the word "branch" is used to denote not only as it commonly does certain parts of a tree, but also any small stream. The contexts for the two senses, however, are very different and therefore the two usages do not clash. But if a person should decide to use the word "branch" to denote the objects commonly called roots, then, since the context, *viz.* trees, is the same for the novel as for the accepted usage of the word, the novel one would clash with the preexisting common one and would be condemned as anarchical and vicious.

Now, I submit, arbitrariness vicious in this way is exactly what we have when the word "mind" is employed to denote part of the material world (specifically the part which preexisting ordinary usage calls the behavior distinctive of bodies that have minds) instead of what in preexisting ordinary usage is denoted by "mind."

Ordinary English, which has greater resources than the language of radical behaviorism, readily permits us to differentiate between consciousness or mind and the perceptually public evidences of it. If, for example, someone pricks my hand with a pin, he has reason to believe I am conscious of pain only if he perceives a bodily sign of it, *e.g.*, a jerking motion of my hand, or an exclamation. But I, in order to know whether or not I am conscious of pain, have no need at all to observe any such public facts; I know it at once and directly in the quite different manner called introspection — a mode of observation Singer seemed to ignore. Furthermore, in ordinary English, "pain" is the name of something one can directly observe only in this way; whereas "the bodily evidences of pain" is the name of something observable only otherwise, and by everybody, *viz.,* perceptually. Moreover, it would be relatively easy to build a dummy so contrived that it would jerk away its hand and say "ouch!" whenever a pin was stuck into it. Yet no one, other than a radical behaviorist, would call it conscious unless he believed that, in addition to moving its hand and uttering a cry, it was at the same time itself experiencing the introspectable sort of event commonly denoted by "pain."

Again, it is possible to act overtly as if one were angry, and yet not be angry; or, conversely, to be angry and not show it in one's behavior. Of course, we may be told that more searching observation of one's behavior by means of such instruments as perhaps the pneumograph, the plethysmograph, or the galvanometer would enable other persons to tell. But the significant fact is that I myself can tell without recourse to such instruments or to any other tests in terms of perceptually public behavior. I can tell simply by introspection. It may well be that certain bodily changes — of the kinds such instruments testify to — are indissolubly concomitant with the mental state called anger, but since I do not even know what these changes are, and in any case am not at the time harnessed with the instruments necessary to make them perceptible, these changes are not what I am reporting when I report that I am angry. What I directly report is on the contrary a certain unique sort of fact not public at all as are modes of behavior, but observable only by myself, introspectively.[5]

6. The Natural-Scientific Definition of "Mind" Dictated Only by a Certain Ontological Position

Definitions of "mind" that are naturalistic in the sense that the study of mind then has the status of a natural science do not transcend the issue between materialism and idealism nor the difference between mind and nature. Such definitions are materialistic — whether professedly or, in epiphenomenalistic naturalism, virtually. They only tamper with the usual denotation of the terms employed and thereby obscure the issue. They do not represent a *fact*, which naturalism has discovered, but only a deep-seated *resolution* to make every term of the language used by natural

[5] Singer believes that "consciousness" is in the same case as, *e.g.*, "life," which was once believed to be something other than the bodies that have it but is now acknowledged to be nothing other than certain specific modes of behavior of these bodies. But there is a crucial difference between the two cases. In that of "life" nothing constituting it is ever observable (in ourselves any more than in our fellows) other than modes of behavior; whereas in the case of "states of consciousness" — for instance, anger — something other than and additional to the modes of behavior perception reveals is observable (introspectively) by us in ourselves but not in our fellows. An admirable statement of the case against identification of mind with behavior is to be found in Chapter IX of Blanshard's *The Nature of Thought*.

science — and therefore the term "mind" too — denote at any cost something in the perceptually public world. This resolution, let it be well noted, is not demanded by any objective evidence to which everybody would have to bow. It represents only the initial perfectly free espousal of the ontological position which defines both the scope and the limits of all *natural* science. As pointed out already in what precedes, this seldom stated and seldom conscious ontological commitment is this: *To be real is to be either something susceptible of being perceptually public, or something existentially implicit therein.*

To commit oneself to this ontological position is of course to commit oneself to ignore either strictly or virtually the world of introspectively accessible facts, that is, the world of mind; but to have thus decided to ignore it is not in the least to have invalidated the contrast traditionally expressed by the words mind and nature, or mind and matter, or psychical and physical. This contrast is based on the existence of two modes of observation, namely those ordinarily called, respectively, introspection and external perception, which common sense readily discerns and rightly regards as making known to us facts of two different kinds. Exactly what each of these two modes of observation consists in, and how they are related, is one of the most fundamental and most taxing problems of philosophy. Inquiry into it is reserved for later chapters. Here I content myself with appealing simply to the testimony of common sense that introspection is one thing and perception of the kind called "external" another; that the one gives us access to mind and the other to nature, *i.e.,* to the material world; and that mind and nature are two different, although to a certain extent connected, realms of facts.

7. The Behavioristic Definition of "Introspection"

As we have seen, the meaning of a term in natural science can only be something in nature — something perceptually public or existentially implicit in what is so. This would appear to entail that the term introspection can have no naturalistic meaning, but some behaviorists are very subtle and have assigned even to "introspection" a meaning in terms of public behavior. W. S. Hunter, for example, defines introspection as a type of verbal response, one, namely, of the form "I am conscious of this," or of similar forms. He writes as follows:[6] "Consciousness as a scientific concept is to be identified with a certain kind of stimulus-response situation. This situation is constituted typically of a language response to sensory stimulation. We have termed this situation an irreversible SP-LR relationship, where SP stands for a sensory process and LR indicates a language response. Language responses, which we have called symbolic processes, are substitute processes which have not as yet become so automatic as to lose their associative relations with the original stimulus-response situation." And as regards introspection: "As one type of report, introspection must be seen in its place as a kind of stimulus-response situation." Hunter describes it more particularly in another article.[7] He there points out that it is difficult to determine whether a given substitute process is in addition a symbolic process, i.e., a language response properly so called (as distinguished from, for instance, the automatic word-utterances of a parrot); and he writes: "A symbol can only be positively and specifically identified where responses can be conditioned to the associative traces of the originally effective stimulus. . . . In human subjects the responses 'I am conscious of this,' 'I saw that,' etc., have been conditioned to these associative traces of stimulus response connections." An introspective report is then a language response conditioned to such traces.

In comment on these behavioristic definitions of the words "consciousness" and "introspection," it may be remarked first that

---

6 W. S. Hunter, "The Subject's Report," *Psych. Rev.*, Vol. 32, No. 2, March 1926, pp. 153–4.
7 Hunter, "The Symbolic Process," *Psych. Rev.*, 1924, Vol. 31, p. 486.

what these words denote in ordinary English is not a language response and is not necessarily (but only may be) accompanied by one. For instance, to be conscious that one did see the moon, it is not in the least necessary either to utter or to mutter the words "I saw the moon," or any other words. Again, to be conscious of pain at the moment one's hand is being stung by a bee, it is not at all necessary to utter the words "I am conscious of pain"; nor does introspective discovery of, for instance, the fact that at a certain time one is feeling slightly uncomfortable, require that one should report the fact verbally, or that one should give any other perceptually public evidence of discomfort. What is true is only that unless we do some such thing a psychologist who is observing our responses is unable in the given cases to find out whether or not we are uncomfortable, or are feeling pain, or remember that we did see the moon. But to find out these things, we ourselves need make no verbal responses whatever, nor do we need to wait for or attend to the non-verbal perceptual evidences, if any, which the psychologist who is watching our behavior might use in default of our uttering any words. What he observes when he observes what *he* calls our "being conscious" or our "introspecting" is thus something else altogether than what *we* refer to by these same words.

8. Observed Psychological Events vs. Postulated Brain Traces

In connection with the "associative traces" in terms of which "introspection" is defined by Hunter, it is interesting to ask what sort of fact they may be. It can be assumed that any natural-scientific psychologist who appeals to them takes them to be physical facts — specifically, brain modifications of some kind such perhaps as persistent chemical or structural alterations of the synapses between certain neurons. If they are brain facts, however, it should be noted that their existence, in any case where a given language response is alleged to be conditioned to them, is not known through perceptual examination of the brain; nor, *a fortiori,* is the specific nature of one particular brain trace, as distinguished from the specific nature of another, so known or indeed known at all.   For example, nobody who knows that I remember having seen the moon did or could have found it out by examining my brain, perhaps under the microscope, and identifying at some place there a "brain trace," to say nothing of one specifically different from the trace which would correspond to my remembering instead having seen Jupiter.   This means that these brain traces are only postulated, and this for the sake of explaining certain observed natural facts, *e.g.,* the observed language responses constituting the so-called introspective report.

That the status of brain traces is purely that of postulates is realized by some psychologists;[8] and of course postulation of unobserved brain traces for purposes of explaining *otherwise inexplicable* observed facts would be quite as legitimate, with appropriate precautions, as postulation of, for instance, electrons and protons for analogous purposes in physics.

But what I wish especially to point out in connection with the postulation of brain traces is that they are postulated not simply in order to explain certain facts for which no adequate cause is perceptually observable, but more particularly in order to explain them in terms of something of a *bodily* sort.   Underlying the postulation of these traces there is thus the assumption that all facts in the physical world, *including* those consisting of word utterances of the kind which would ordinarily be described as reports of facts introspectively observed, have ultimately and solely *physical* causes, *i.e.,* causes consisting of events in the material world.   But for the truth of this assumption, no evidence whatever is offered.   It is simply carried over by force of habit from the realm of extra-human objects (where theoretical parsimony perhaps requires it) to the part of the material world

---

[8] Cf. C. L. Hull, "Mind, Mechanism, and Adaptive Behavior," in *Psych. Rev.,* Vol. 44, No. 1, January 1937.

consisting of human bodies, where in certain cases theoretical parsimony would rather forbid it. More specifically, it is not required in order to explain the particular sort of word utterances called "introspective reports" because we are able to assign to them an *observable but non-physical cause, viz.,* certain antecedent mental facts introspectively observable — the very ones those utterances claim to report.

Hull, it is true,[9] calls a "logical absurdity" the supposition that an idea, *i.e.,* something non-physical, might cause something physical. To say that it is a logical absurdity, however, means (if anything more than that it clashes with Hull's own language habits or perhaps with his metaphysics) that the supposition is somehow self-contradictory. But he makes no attempt whatever to show that it is so. Nor does he even define the term "physical." I submit, however, that the question whether an event *A* can be what causes another event *B* under given circumstances *C* is not to be decided *a priori* by asking whether *A, B,* and *C* are all in some unspecified sense "physical," nor by asking oneself whether the supposition that a psychical event causes a physical event happens to titillate one's private sense of the ludicrous; but only by asking whether the *relation* observed to exist between *A, B,* and *C,* is *of the same form* which makes us anywhere else describe a given relation as a causal relation. I submit further that the relation observable by a given person between the psychical event introspectively observed by him, which his language response claims to report, and that language response itself, *is* of precisely the same form as the relation, not observed but only postulated by the behaviorist, between the again only postulated brain traces and the language response — this form being the very one which alone would enable him to describe these brain traces as *causing* or *conditioning* the language response.

---

[9] In a paper entitled "Goal Attraction and Directing Ideas Conceived as Phenomena," *Psych. Rev.,* 1931, Vol. 38, pp. 489–506.

Accordingly, no one of us, in his own individual case, needs to postulate brain traces, which are not observable, as causes of his utterances of so-called introspective reports; for *he,* even if not anyone else, is able to assign to them an *observed* cause, *viz.,* a certain introspectively observed mental event. The need to *postulate* a cause for such utterances of ours can arise only for a person other than ourselves, who can observe us only perceptually, *i.e.,* only in our public, physical aspect, and who finds in what he so perceives nothing sufficient to cause those utterances. But the need for him not merely to postulate a cause for them, but to postulate it specifically as *physical* (*e.g.,* as consisting of brain traces) arises only if either he assumes — gratuitously as just pointed out — that postulation by him of a mental event in us will not do; or if the *ontological position* which he has adopted — *viz.* materialism — requires him to limit himself to causes of the physical kind, for in the latter case, of course, appealing to a non-physical cause would amount to cheating at solitaire.

9. The Conservation of Energy

Here, however, it might be objected that the principle of the conservation of energy precludes psychophysical causation. But, as Keeton has made clear,[10] the "conservation of energy" is far from having the status of an established fact. For one thing, the expression is extremely ambiguous — the ambiguity inhering both in the term "conservation" (constancy of sum? identity of substance? convertibility? equivalence of manifestations? correlation of manifestations?) and in the term "energy" (a substance? a property of a substance? a property of a system? a relationship between phenomena?). And, Keeton further points out, "no possible experimental evidence could add one whit to the probability of the theory in any one of several of the forms in which it is generally used."[11]

---

[10] M. T. Keeton, "Some Ambiguities in the Theory of the Conservation of Energy," *Philosophy of Science,* Vol. 8, No. 3, July 1941.
[11] Cf. C. D. Broad, *The Mind and Its Place in Nature,* pp. 103 ff.

This indicates that the conservation of energy is simply a postulate, and more particularly a *defining postulate,* of the notion of "an isolated physical system" (irrespective of whether or not anything short of the whole physical universe could be an isolated physical system). That is, conservation of energy is something one *has to have, if* (as the materialistic ontology of physics and more generally of naturalism demands) *one is to be able to conceive the physical world as wholly self-contained, independent, "isolated."* Accordingly, when what observation reveals seems to be dissipation of energy instead of conservation, conservation is saved by postulations *ad hoc;* for example, by postulating that something else, which appears when the energy one observed disappears — but which was not until then conceived as energy — is energy too, in "another form";[12] or again, by postulating, as some physicists have proposed, the existence of "neutrinos," to save conservation in spite of the decay seemingly implied by the continuity of the beta ray spectrum.[13]

Conservation of energy, thus, would be an obstacle to the possibility of psychophysical (and of physicopsychical) causation only if it were known to be a *universal* fact; or, more particularly if it were known that, even in the case of an introspective report, the cause of not only the *occurrence* of the report, but also of the *particular content of the report,* is physical. But this is not known — only postulated, and postulated only to save the universality of the conservation of energy. And what need, other than a doctrinaire one, have we to *postulate* a physical cause, when *observation* reveals a psychical one? Whenever I put money in my pocket, I tacitly postulate that there is no hole in it. But have I, as a scientifically open-minded person, any business to postulate it even on the rare occasions when I find a hole there? On these occasions, the burden of proof that there is no hole even then is on those

---

12 Cf. Lindsay and Margenau, *Foundations of Physics,* pp. 125–7.
13 A. W. Stern, "The Neutrino Concept," *Philosophy of Science,* Vol. 8, No. 4, October 1941; Lindsay and Margenau, *op. cit.,* p. 514.

who would so assert; and appeal by them to the very universality postulated is obviously no proof whatever that the exception to it we observe is not genuine.

10.   Dewey on How Mind Is To Be Known

This chapter may well close with a few words of comment on the contention of the outstanding protagonist of philosophical naturalism, John Dewey, as to how mind is to be known.[14]   In substance, Dewey's contention is that mind is one among other perceptually public phenomena — more specifically it consists of certain forms of biological behavior, and of cultural behavior in a social environment.   Mind is therefore to be known through inquiry of the same sort as yields knowledge of other public phenomena, and the idea is fallacious that, to know mind, "the only method that is at all appropriate is that of *introspection*" (p. 29), this method being described by Dewey as one "of complete and indubitable immediate knowledge — a method that eliminates, once for all, the need of reflection and inquiry" (p. 34).

I doubt, however, whether any one who, like myself, believes that mind is directly observable only by introspection would acknowledge this conception of introspection as anything but a caricature of what he believes.   At all events, I, for one, hold that reflection, inquiry, experiment, inductive generalization, theoretical interpretation — in short, all the processes through which scientific knowledge is won about anything — are called for, no less than elsewhere, in the study of the sort of facts which introspection, and introspection only, directly exhibits to scrutiny.

Dewey's attack on introspection as a method for knowing mind rests on three bases.   The first is the misconception, just noticed, of what those who hold that mind is directly observable only by introspection mean by this.

The second of the bases of Dewey's attack is the contention that

---

[14] John Dewey, "How Is Mind To Be Known?" *Journal of Philosophy*, Vol. XXXIX, No. 2, January 15, 1942.

having e.g., a pain, is not a mode of *knowing* what pain is. The reply here is that if "knowing what pain is" is taken to mean knowing what is causing it on a particular occasion, or knowing the general conditions under which pain does or does not occur, etc., then, indeed, having a pain is not "knowing" what pain is in this sense of that verb.

But it is also true that some one might know perfectly in *this* sense what pain is, and yet, if he had never himself had a pain, he would not know what pain is in the *other* sense, where "knowing" it means feeling or having felt or had pain. Dewey, it is true, refuses to this other sense the name of "knowledge," and so would Parker, who holds that there is "knowledge" only in cases where a concept is applied to what is experienced.[15] In this refusal, however, both Dewey and Parker are disregarding arbitrarily the fact that when, in perfectly good English usage, it is said of a man that he has known sorrow, or pain, or terror, or doubt, etc. what is meant is precisely that he has himself *felt* them — "had" them — and *not* that he knew that what he felt was, in English, called "sorrow," or "pain," etc.; nor that he knows what the laws of their occurrence are. The assertion is simply that he knows *these feelings,* not that he knows anything about them.[16] Dewey's declaration that having a pain is not a "mode of knowing" what pain is must not, therefore, be accepted as if it were the report of a fact as to the nature of knowing. The only fact which that declaration really makes known is a fact about Dewey, namely, that he, personally, refuses to employ the verb "to know" to denote one of the things which in English it does denote.

The third of the bases of Dewey's attack on introspection con-

---

[15] D. H. Parker, "Knowledge by Acquaintance," *Phil. Rev.,* Vol. LIV, No. 1, January 1945.

[16] On the question as to whether these two senses of "to know" are heterogeneous, or on the contrary are two species of one generic sense, see *Philos. and Phenomenol. Research,* Vol. V, No. 3, March 1945, pp. 328, 334, 339, where, as against Nagel, I argued for the latter contention.

sists in disregard of the fact that, *before* one can attempt to gain scientific knowledge of the properties, structure, states, and relations of mind — or indeed, of matter (or of any more specific things of the mental or material kind, such as pain, sorrow, thoughts, or copper, oaks, sharks) — one must *know first* that the concrete entity one is about to scrutinize scientifically is in truth a specimen of a *mental* entity, or of a *material* one, or of a *thought,* or of an *oak,* etc. And knowledge of this — indispensable from the very start if one is to avoid *quid pro quo* — can, of course, be obtained only by *semantical* inquiry; that is, by asking what the concrete entities one is about to subject to scientific inquiry are *called,* or asking *which concrete entities* the words mind, or matter, or pain, or copper, etc. are, in English, employed to denote, *i.e.,* to direct attention to. For unless some concrete specimens of what they denote are, *to begin with,* known to be such, there is nothing for scientific inquiry *to begin on.*

Which concrete things, then, do the words mind, or mental events, denote? I submit that, as this question would ordinarily be meant, it is not the question as to what these words denote in the doctrinaire language of naturalistic philosophy, any more than the question as to what the words matter or material events denote is a question as to what they denote in the equally doctrinaire language of idealistic philosophy. It is simply the question as to what they denote *in ordinary English.*

It may be urged, of course, that ontological assumptions are imbedded in ordinary English too, which is therefore not metaphysically neutral but is infected with Cartesian dualism. The fact, however, is that ordinary English is neutral in the only sense relevant here, namely, in the sense that it does not beg the question as to whether, or how, mind and matter are related, just as it does not beg the question as to whether or how copper and gold, or chimpanzees and men, are related. Ordinary English merely uses these various different words to denote things which are so obviously different that, in most cases, they can easily be told apart prior to scientific inquiry into their properties, relations, etc. This is the case with, for example, "mental events" on the one hand, and on the other, "linguistic behavior" or any other modes of perceptually public behavior. The events to which the word mental, as used in ordinary English, turns the attention are those which only introspection presents directly.

But that mental events are not any kind of perceptually public behavior does not in any way imply that the kind of questions scientific inquiry asks about any events upon which it is directed need not be asked about the events introspection exhibits. Nor does it imply that knowledge *about* mental events may not be obtained, in considerable amounts, by *inference* from observation of the signs of them which bodily behavior concomitant with them may constitute. Yet observation of *mind itself directly,* by introspection, remains one thing; and observation of speech movements or of other bodily signs of mind, by what is called "external perception," remains altogether another thing.

I conclude, then, that nothing which either naturalistic philosophy or behavioristic or physiological psychology has to advance invalidates the traditional and common-sense contrast of mind and nature or psychical and physical. The thesis that mind is a part of nature either reduces to the innocuous statement that mind is a part of what there is, or else to the forcing of a Pickwickian sense upon the word "mind."

Chapter 13

THE RELATION OF SENSA TO SENSING

Mind, up to this point, has been defined merely as the realm of facts directly observable only through what is commonly called introspection. But the persons who, unlike radical behaviorists, acknowledge the availability of such a mode of observation and the existence of a realm of facts distinct from the physical and disclosed through introspective observation are not all agreed as to which observations exactly shall be called introspective. Attention to one's own sensations, in particular, has traditionally been called introspection, but nowadays some would distinguish it, as "inspection," both from introspection and from so-called external perception.[1] Some would distinguish between sensation and "sensa" or "sense data" and class the first perhaps as mental, but the second as nonmental; or perhaps as "neutral" and capable of entering both into mental contexts and into physical.

The ordinary, unanalytical understanding we all have of the meaning of the terms "introspection" and "mental" enables us confidently to apply them to certain things and to deny them to certain others. But there are yet other things which that ordinary understanding does not enable us to classify with assurance one way or the other. To decide in these cases it is necessary to inquire into the latent theoretical basis of the unhesitating com-

---

[1] For example, C. D. Broad in *The Mind and Its Place in Nature.* Also Ledger Wood, "Inspection and Introspection," in *Philos. of Science,* Vol. 7, No. 2, April 1940.

mon willingness to apply these terms to certain things and of the equally unhesitating common refusal to apply them to certain others. Only after we have done this can we hope to have an instrument for nonarbitrary classification of the disputed cases.

The two connected questions, as to exactly what is introspection and what is mental, and the question as to just what is physical, are basic both in the theory of knowledge and for metaphysics. But accounts of the relation between mind and body have too often been attempted on a basis consisting of little more than the ordinary unanalytical understanding of the terms "mental" and "physical," without preliminary performance of the laborious task of answering in a precise and nonarbitrary manner the three questions just mentioned. Yet it is only after these questions have been so answered that one really knows what one is speaking of when one speaks of psychical or of physical; and it is therefore also only then that one has the basis on which it may be possible to construe in a likewise precise and nonarbitrary manner the relation between mind and nature.

1. Moore's "Refutation of Idealism"

The psychical and the physical, as I have emphasized earlier, are ultimately definable each only in terms of the sort of facts which are its "primitives." How, in such terms, "nature" or "the physical" or "the material world" is to be defined has been stated in what precedes and need not be reiterated here. Some of the questions to which the definition offered gives rise, however, will be considered in a later chapter, where the nature of so-called external perception and of the objects it makes public is analyzed. In the present chapter and the next, which are crucial for the argument of the whole book, the question to be answered is as to the essential nature of the "mental" or "psychical." The issues on which the answer turns have, it seems to me, been brought into clearer focus than ever before by the contemporary discussions of the status of "sensa" or "sense data," of the relation of sensa to sensing, and of the relation between introspection and "inspection." These discussions themselves, however, stem chiefly from G. E. Moore's famous paper, "The Refutation of Idealism," published in *Mind* in 1903. Its acute and searching criticism of the proposition that *esse* is *percipi* has been widely held to have finally proved the latter's falsity and thus to have robbed of their basis the idealistic philosophies which in one way or another had been built upon it; and the distinctions there made by Moore have, to a large extent, been employed in subsequent discussions relating to sense data.

It is true that, in the preface to his *Philosophical Studies* — in which book the article was reprinted in 1922 — Moore writes that "this paper now appears to me to be very confused, as well as to embody a good many downright mistakes." And more recently, in commenting on a version of the contentions of the present chapter substantially identical with the one in the following pages,[2] Moore has indicated that he now agrees with the point I chiefly attempt to prove there although he does not think I have succeeded in proving it — the point, namely, that a sense datum cannot possibly exist except while it is being directly apprehended;[3] for example, that a toothache cannot exist without being felt, whereas the moon can exist without being perceived.[4]

But the acceptance by many persons of the argument of Moore's original article has so influenced the course of subsequent philosophical thought that the article is now a classic and is commensurate in importance with the celebrated proposition it attacks. This means that, irrespective of what Moore's views may have since come to be, the argument of the article has to be examined here. The point of central interest in it is the assumption it makes

---

[2] *Viz.*, the essay "Moore's Refutation of Idealism," contributed by the author to the book, *The Philosophy of G. E. Moore*. Library of Living Philosophers, Vol. IV, ed. by Paul Arthur Schilpp, Northwestern University, Evanston, 1942.

[3] *The Philosophy of G. E. Moore*, p. 660.

[4] *Loc. cit.*, p. 653. At this place Moore says that he "now agrees"; at the other place, that he is "inclined to think."

as to the relation between awareness and what one is aware of; for it is on this assumption that turns the answer to the question whether sensa may exist unexperienced and may therefore be nonmental; and it is principally this crucial question the present chapter attempts to settle.

As against Moore in that article,[5] I believe there is a certain class of cases of which it is true that *esse* is *percipi*. This class, moreover, is the very one in terms of an instance of which his discussion is worded. I think it can be definitely proved that, so far as this class is concerned, Moore's argument does not prove, as it claims to do — or even render more probable than not — that *esse* is *percipi* is false. I shall, however, try to show not only this but also that, for this class of cases, *esse* is *percipi* is true. The latter will be more difficult to demonstrate conclusively, but I believe I shall be able to show at least that the burden of proof definitely rests on those who would deny even in these cases that *esse* is *percipi*. When my argument has been set forth, I shall then point out why it seems to me that the only objection Moore brings against it in the recent book already cited fails to invalidate it.

The considerations I shall set forth in support of the proposition that in certain cases it is true that *esse* is *percipi,* will not constitute an argument for idealism, for I believe that there is also another class of cases concerning which it is false that *esse* is *percipi*. Accordingly, even if my argument is successful its effect will be only, on the one hand, to rob of its basis the kind of realism Moore's article has been used to support and, on the other and chiefly, to make clear that certain facts do belong to mind, which that realism tends to reject from mind.

The chief question we shall be attempting to decide, it should be remembered, is an extremely elusive and difficult one, for were

---

[5] In what follows, unless some other reference is given, the views of Moore to which I refer are throughout only the views set forth in his "Refutation of Idealism" as republished in the *Philosophical Studies* (Harcourt Brace & Co., 1922).

it not so it would have been settled long ago. Any hope of deciding it may therefore be entertained only if, as one inquires into it, one exercises the most meticulous care. Unfortunately, the cost of this to the reader must be that, to follow the argument and grasp such force as it has, close and prolonged attention on his part will be necessary. One wishes it were possible to write philosophy always so dramatically and entertainingly, or at least simply, that it would captivate instead of taxing the reader's attention. But in philosophy as in mathematics, physics, economics, and the other sciences some problems turn up which, although ultimately of the highest practical significance, are nevertheless highly technical; and there, in philosophy as in the other sciences, the literary values generally have to be slighted. They become of secondary importance at such points as compared with strictness of reasoning and the exactness of terminology it requires, for these alone make solution of such problems possible.

That the problem of the present chapter is of this kind must be my apology to the reader for the closer demands on his attention to be made in it. He may be assured, however, that no pains have been spared to achieve clarity, at least, throughout.

2. Moore's Argument

In what follows, familiarity with the text of Moore's article will be assumed, but it may be well to state here briefly what I understand to be the essence of its argument. Using the sensation of blue as example, Moore points out that the sensation of blue admittedly differs from the sensation of green, but that both are nevertheless sensations. Therefore they have (1) something in common, which he proposes to call "consciousness," and (2) something else, in respect of which one differs from the other, and he proposes to call this the "object" of each sensation. We have then, he says, "in every sensation two distinct elements"; and therefore assertion that one of them exists, assertion that the other exists, and assertion that both exist, are three different assertions. From this it follows that "if any one tells us that to say 'Blue exists' is the *same* thing as to say 'Both blue and consciousness exist,' he makes a mistake and a self-contradictory mistake."[6] Just because the *esse* of blue is something distinct from the *esse* of the *percipi* of blue, there is no logical difficulty in supposing blue to exist without consciousness of blue.

The point on which turns the validity or invalidity of this argument is of course what sort of distinctness is to be granted between the sensation or consciousness and the blue, for existential independence is not a corollary of every sort of distinctness. Existential independence is entailed by distinctness of the sort we admit when we say that for instance cat and dog or green and sweet are distinct, but not by the sort of distinctness we admit when we say that cat and spinal cord or blue and color are distinct.

Moore believes that blue and the *percipi* of blue are "as distinct as 'green' and 'sweet' ";[7] and if existential independence is to follow from this, "as distinct" must be taken to mean here that the distinctness is of the same logical sort as that of green from sweet. To show that it is of the same sort Moore advances both destructive and constructive considerations. The destructive consist of his criticism (which I do not pause here to summarize) of the hypothesis that blue is "content" of the sensation of blue; the constructive, of the positive account he himself offers of the relation of sensation to blue or, more generally, of awareness or experience to its "objects." This account is substantially as follows: A sensation is a case of "knowing" or "experiencing" or "being aware of" something; and this awareness is not merely "something distinct and unique, utterly different from blue; it also has a perfectly distinct and unique relation to blue. . . . This relation is just that which we mean in every case by 'knowing'[8]

---

[6] Moore, *Philosophical Studies*, pp. 17–18.
[7] P. 16.
[8] P. 26–7.

. . . the relation of a sensation to its object is certainly the same as that of any other instance of experience to its object[9] . . . the awareness is and must be in all cases of such a nature that its object, when we are aware of it, is precisely what it would be, if we were not aware."[10]

As against these contentions, I shall argue that if "knowing" is taken as the name of a unique relation, then this relation is a generic one and two species of it have to be distinguished; that one of these allows the object known to exist independently of the knowing of it, but the other forbids it; that in the case of the latter relation the known is "content" of the knowing in a sense not disposed of by Moore's criticism of that term; and that in this very sense blue is "content" of the sensation of blue and therefore cannot exist independently of it.

I shall lay the basis for my argument by adopting and exploiting a certain distinction which S. Alexander finds himself led to mention and to use in the course of his attempt to define the difference between the mental and nonmental, and, in terms of it, the nature of introspection.

3. Alexander's Proposed Criterion of the Mental

Alexander declares that "Any experience whatever may be analyzed into two distinct elements and their relation to one another. The two elements . . . are, on the one hand the act of mind or the awareness, and on the other the object of which it is aware."[11] An object is an appearance of a "thing," and a "thing" consists of a group "of objects within a certain spatio-temporal contour."[12] The object is said to be "contemplated" by the mental act which experiences it. Not objects only, however, but also mental acts themselves, are observed or experienced; and the observation or experience of them is called by Alexander not

---

9 P. 28.
10 P. 29.
11 S. Alexander, *Space, Time, and Deity,* Vol. I, p. 11.
12 *Op. cit.,* Vol. II, p. 92.

"contemplation" but "enjoyment."[13]   According to him, "Introspection *is in fact merely experiencing our mental state*,"[14]
although in general he distinguishes introspection from enjoyment
as being "enjoyment lived through with a scientific interest"[15] —
distinct enjoyment as contrasted with vague and blurred.[16]

That which leads Alexander to conceive the mental as essentially *act* is the difference between experiencing and experienced,
i.e., between the active and passive poles of experience.   "In each
case of experience," he tells us, "the *-ing* and the *-ed* are distinguishable, and the *-ed* is nonmental."[17]   But the distinguishing of
the nonmental from the mental in experience in terms of the
difference between *-ed* and *-ing*, if not supplemented by a certain
distinction, would be the source of a glaring contradiction.   For
note that Alexander declares (1) that any experience whatever
involves a mental act and an object; (2) that a mental act experiences itself, *i.e.*, is experienced as well as experiencing; and (3)
that in any experience the *-ed* is nonmental.   From these three
assertions it would immediately follow that a mental act, in being
experienced, is an *-ed* as well as an *-ing*, that is to say, is nonmental as well as mental.

4.   Cognate vs. Objective Accusatives

Alexander's way of avoiding this contradiction is by appeal to
the distinction between the cognate and the objective accusative.
He writes: "The difference between the two ways in which the
terms (*viz.*, the mental act and the object) are experienced is
expressed in language by the difference between the cognate and
the objective accusative.   I am aware of my awareness as I strike
a stroke or wave a farewell.   My awareness and my being aware

---

[13] "Introspection may be called observation but observation is not necessarily the
observation of external objects" (II, 90); also, "the enjoyed enjoys itself, or experiences itself as an enjoyment" (I, 13).
    [14] I, 18.
    [15] II, 89.
    [16] I, 18.
    [17] I, 23.

of it are identical. [On the other hand] I experience the tree as I strike a man or wave a flag."[18]

There is not, I believe, any word in the language to denote that in general (or perhaps that ambiguously) which has, to the process a verb names, the same relation that a noun in the accusative in general — i.e., in the accusative no matter whether cognate or objective — has to the verb. I shall, however, need a word for this and will therefore borrow for the purpose from grammar the word "accusative" itself — as W. E. Johnson, similarly, borrows from grammar the word "adjective" to refer to the sort of entity which any word grammar calls an adjective stands for.[19] Thus, for example, I would speak of a stroke struck as the cognate accusative, but of a man struck as an objective accusative, of the sort of process called "striking." But, for reasons of euphony which will appear later, I shall, instead of "cognate," use the synonymous form "connate." Also, since the relation of "objects" of awareness to the awareness thereof is what we shall ultimately be concerned with — and we must not allow our terminology to prejudge for us surreptitiously the nature of that relation — I shall use the term "alien accusative" for what would otherwise be called "objective accusative"; that is, I shall say that an accusative of a process may be connate with or alien to — homogeneous with or heterogeneous to — the process. For example, in what is expressed by the phrase "jumping a jump," the jump is connate accusative of the process called "jumping"; whereas in what is expressed by "jumping a ditch," the ditch is alien accusative of the jumping.

5. Accusatives Coordinate or Subordinate in Generality to a Given Process

Let us next notice that the relations "connate with" and "alien to" (as they concern a process and an accusative of it) may each

---

[18] I, 12.
[19] W. E. Johnson, *Logic*, Vol. I, p. 9.

be either symmetrical or unsymmetrical. Each is *symmetrical* when its terms are of strictly coordinate generality, as for instance "jumping" and "jump" (connate accusative), or "jumping" and "obstacle" (alien accusative). A process and an accusative of it, which, like these, are coordinate in generality I shall call respectively *connately coordinate* (or coordinately connate), and *alienly coordinate* (or coordinately alien).

On the other hand, the relations "connate with" and "alien to" are *unsymmetrical* when the accusative of the process concerned is subordinate in generality to the process. Accordingly I shall say that an accusative — for instance a leap — which is subordinate in generality to a process which — like jumping — is connate with it, is *connately subordinate to* (or subordinately connate with) that process. And similarly I shall say that an accusative — for instance a fence — which is subordinate in generality to a process which — like jumping — is alien to it, is *alienly subordinate* (or subordinately alien) to that process.

6. Existence of an Accusative Connate With a Given Process Possible Only in Occurrence of the Process

Close attention must now be given to the implications as to existence which go, or do not go, with connate and alien coordinateness and subordinateness. There are four possible cases. I list and illustrate all four, but the last two will be the ones of special interest for the purposes of my argument.

(1) When an accusative, *e.g.,* an obstacle, is *coordinately alien* to a process, *e.g.,* jumping, then obviously this accusative may exist independently of existence, *i.e.,* of occurrence, of the process; obstacles exist which are not being jumped, have not been jumped, and will not be jumped. On the other hand, in so far as the process is of the kind represented by a transitive verb, it cannot occur independently of existence of an accusative alienly coordinate with it: jumping, in so far as transitive, obviously cannot

occur without existence of some obstacle — some distance or thing — being jumped. Similarly, striking, in so far as transitive, cannot occur without existence of some object — be it only empty air — being struck.

(2) When an accusative, *e.g.*, a fence, is *subordinately alien* to a process, *e.g.*, jumping, then again this accusative may exist independently of occurrence of the process: a fence, for instance, which is a species of obstacle, may exist which is not jumped at any time. But here the process, even when it *is* of a transitive kind, can occur independently of existence of a *given* accusative alienly subordinate to it: transitive jumping could occur even if, for instance, no fences existed but ditches did.

We now come to the two cases of special interest for the purposes of the argument — the two where the accusative is connate with the process.

(3) When an accusative, *e.g.*, a jump, is *coordinately connate* with a process, *viz.*, jumping, then this accusative cannot exist independently of existence, *i.e.*, of occurrence, of the process: a jump exists only in the jumping, a stroke in the striking, a dance in the dancing, etc. — the *esse* of a *saltus* is its *saltari*. But although this obviously is true, it may be well nevertheless to pause here a moment to point out why it is true.

To do so, we must ask what exactly is the logical relation between jump and jumping, between the dance and dancing, etc., *i.e.*, between the connately coordinate accusative of a process and the occurrences of that process. The answer is that the *nouns* "jump," "dance," "stroke," name each a *kind, viz.,* a kind of process, but considered independently of occurrence of cases of it; whereas the *verbs* "jumping," "dancing," "striking," are the linguistic entities which not only likewise name the kind but in addition refer to *existence, i.e., occurrence,* of a case of the kind of process they name. The various tenses of which the verb admits express the various possible time relations between the time *of* discourse about a particular occurrence of an event of the given kind, and the time ascribed *by* discourse to that particular occurrence: the time of that occurrence may be earlier or later than, or the same as, the time of our discourse about it. The noun form, on the other hand, wholly ignores these temporal relations because it denotes a *kind* of event — not a case, *i.e.,* not an occurrence, of that kind — and kinds as such have no dates. Yet the kinds we are here considering are kinds *of events, i.e.,* they are kinds the existence of a case of which consists in an occurrence — a particular event — at a particular time.

Attention to these considerations enables us to answer our question: The reason why no jump, for instance, can exist except in the jumping, and why jumping, at whatever time, is always and necessarily the jumping of a jump, is that *jump stands to jumping as kind stands to existence of a case thereof.*

(4) Let us now finally consider an accusative, *e.g.,* a leap, *subordinately connate* with a process, *e.g.,* jumping. It is obvious that the process can exist, *i.e.,* can occur, at dates when *the given* accusative does not: jumping may be of a jump of some species other than a leap; dancing may be of a dance of some species other than the waltz; striking, of a sort of stroke other than a jab; etc.

On the other hand, *an accusative connately subordinate to a given process cannot exist independently of that process:* a leap exists only in the jumping thereof, a waltz only in the dancing, a jab only in the striking. That this is true is again evident even without explicit mention of the reason why it is true; but in any event the reason is that leap, waltz, jab, etc., respectively stand to jump, dance, stroke, etc., each as species to genus; that a case of the species cannot exist without the existing of a case of the genus; and that, as pointed out above, existence of a case of the genera, jump, dance, stroke, etc., consists in, respectively, jumping, dancing, striking, etc., at some time.

7. Existence of a Cognitum Connate With the Cognizing Thereof Possible Only in the Cognizing

So much being now clear, it may next be emphasized that although the processes so far used as examples were processes both motor and voluntary, the distinctions pointed out — between connate and alien accusatives and between accusatives coordinate and subordinate in generality to a given process — in no way depend on the activities being motor and voluntary ones; and therefore that the implications as to existence which we found rooted in these distinctions do not depend upon these characters either. Rather, the distinctions and their existential implications are perfectly general: any sort of process whatever — whether it be a response or an activity — has a connate accusative, and any sort of process which is transitive has in addition an alien accusative; and further, *whatever the nature of the process, an accusative connate with it (whether coordinately or subordinately) exists only in the occurrences of the process.* Because this is true universally, it is true of, in particular, the sort of process which is of special interest to us in these pages — *viz.,* the one called "cognizing" or more broadly, "experiencing" — notwithstanding that it is not, like jumping, a motor activity and notwithstanding that some species of it, *e.g.,* sensing, are involuntary and are responses instead of, like jumping, being voluntary and being activities. If we now agree to call any accusative of the cognitive or experiencing process a *cognitum,* then, in the light of the considerations which precede, it will, I believe, be evident that *any cognitum connate (whether coordinately or subordinately) with that process exists only in the occurrences of the process.*

8. The Hypothesis To Be Opposed to Moore's

The question we now face, however, is whether such cognita as blue or bitter or sweet are connate with the species of experiencing called "sensing," or on the contrary are alien to it; for on the answer to this depends, as we have now seen, the answer to the question whether the *esse* of blue or bitter or sweet is their *percipi*. Moore believes they are what I have called alien cognita of the experiencing. My contention will be on the contrary that they are cognita connate with the experiencing. At this point, however, I shall not attempt to prove this contention but only, first, to explain its meaning more fully, and second, to dispose of two *prima facie* plausible objections to it. This will make evident that there does exist a genuine alternative to Moore's contention regarding the relation of blue to the sensing of blue, and will enable me to show that it is an alternative he neither disposes of nor considers. To show this, however, will only be to show that his argument does not prove what it claims to prove, *viz.*, that the blue can exist independently of the sensing of blue. Only after this has been done shall I give the positive evidence I have to offer in support of my own contention that the blue cannot exist independently of the sensing of blue.

The hypothesis, then, which I present as alternative to Moore's is that "blue," "bitter," "sweet," etc., are names not of objects of experience, nor of species of objects of experience, but of *species of experience itself*. What this means is perhaps made clearest by saying that to sense blue is then to sense *bluely*, just as to dance the waltz is to dance "waltzily" (*i.e.*, in the manner called "to waltz"), to jump a leap is to jump "leapily" (*i.e.*, in the manner called "to leap"), etc. Sensing, that is to say, is a mental process having to sensing blue the same logical relation which obtains, for example, between the process in a string called "vibrating" and a particular mode in which it vibrates — say, the middle-C mode. Obviously, it would similarly be appropriate to say of the string that it is vibrating middle-C-ly. Sensing blue, I hold, is thus a species or modulation of sensing — a specific variety of the sort of process generically called "sensing" which, however, unlike dancing or jumping, is an involuntary and nonmotor kind of process, and is itself a species of the generic process called "experiencing." In the case of sensing, as in all cases where the known is connate with the knowing, what is known by the knowing process is then its own determinate nature on the given occasion.

With regard to the relation between blue and sensing blue, I further contend that the same remarks apply that were made above concerning the relation of jump and leap to jumping: the noun "blue" is the word we use to mention merely a certain *kind* of process (just as are the nouns "waltz," "leap," etc.), whereas the verb "to sense blue" is the linguistic form we use when we wish not only to mention that same kind of process but also to mention at the same time some *case, i.e.,* some *occurrence,* of that kind of process — the various tenses of the verb expressing the various possible temporal relations between the time at which we mention some case of that kind of process and the time we mention as time of that case itself. I now turn to the two possible objections alluded to above.

9.   The Objection That What Is Sensed Is Not "Blue" But a Case of "Blue"

It might be urged — perhaps under the belief that it constitutes a difficulty precluding acceptance of my hypothesis — that what we sense is never blue or bitter in general, *i.e.,* a *kind,* but always *a* blue or *a* bitter, *i.e.,* (it would then be alleged) some *case* of blue or bitter.

To this I reply that "blue" and "bitter" are the names of certain *determinable* kinds, and that "*a* blue" or "*a* bitter" are expressions by which we refer not to cases but to *determinates, i.e.,* to *infimae species,* of these determinable kinds.[20] That a determinate shade

---

[20] W. E. Johnson, in his chapter on "The Determinable" (*Logic,* Vol. I, Chap. XI), misleadingly uses the names of the various colors as illustrations of names of determinates; whereas the fact obviously is that blue, for instance, is a determinable having as sub-determinables cerulean blue, prussian blue, etc., and that no names exist in the language for the truly determinate colors — for instance for a cerulean

of blue is logically not a case but a species, *viz.,* an infima species, of blue is shown by the fact that even a perfectly determinate shade of blue is susceptible of existing many times, or no times, or only once, etc.; that is, qualitative determinateness neither constitutes existence nor entails existence. Existence of qualitatively determinate blue, bitter, etc., is a matter of occupation by them of some determinate place at some determinate time. It is presence of such qualities *there* and *then,* which constitutes a case of them; but what is at the particular place-time still is a species — always, however, an infima species, *i.e.,* a completely determinate "what."

On the basis of these considerations, my reply to the objection mentioned above is then that we do not *sense a case* of blue, but that our *sensing* blue of a determinate species, *i.e.,* our sensing bluely-in-some-completely-specific-manner, constitutes occurrence of a case of blue. That is, it constitutes presence at a determinate place and time of blue of that determinate shade, and therefore of course, of blue; just as our waltzing — which if we do it at all we do in some completely determinate manner — constitutes presence at a determinate time and place of that determinate species of waltz, and therefore automatically also of its genus, the waltz.[21]

10. The Objection That One May Be Aware Without Being Aware That One Is Aware

If in any case of awareness of blue what one is aware of is, as I contend, the determinate nature of one's awareness on that

---

blue completely determinate as to hue and as to degree of brightness and of saturation. But we could if we wished assign names to the various infimae species of cerulean blue — calling a certain one, perhaps, Anna cerulean, another Bertha cerulean, etc.

21 That a species, *e.g.,* a species of blue, can be *sensed* is paradoxical only if a *determinable* species is meant, *i.e.,* an abstract species, but not if, as here, a *determinate* or *infima* species is concerned. Again, it would be paradoxical to say of two patches of blue that they are the same *patch,* but not that they are patches of the same *blue;* for qualitative identity is compatible with numerical, *viz.,* locational, diversity. To contend, as some do, that where there is no qualitative difference what one has is exact similarity of quality but not sameness of quality is to be guilty of confusion of categories, for it is, by implication, to be reifying qualities.

occasion, then, it may be objected, it would follow that being aware of blue would be one and the same thing with being aware that one is aware of blue; whereas obviously they are not the same thing. To meet this objection, I shall first analyze the nature of the difference which is felt and which I acknowledge exists, and then I shall point out why this difference leaves untouched the essence of my contention.

If on an occasion when one has asserted "I am aware of blue" one is asked or asks oneself whether this is really so, then, in order to answer, one has to make an additional judgment, which (if affirmative) one formulates by saying "I am aware that I am aware of blue." I submit, however, that this judgment concerns the appropriateness of using the concept "being aware of" to describe the fact one was attempting to describe when one said "I am aware of blue." Or similarly, if I have asserted "I know that Mary is eight years old" and I am asked or ask myself whether I really know it and conclude "I know that I know that Mary is eight years old," the question this answers is whether the concept labeled "knowing" fits the status conferred upon my belief that Mary is eight years old by the grounds I have for the belief. I compare the particular sort of relation between grounds and belief, called "knowing," with the actually existing relation between my grounds and my belief in the case of Mary's age, and ask myself whether this actually existing relation is a case of that sort of relation. This comparison — and not the examining of additional evidence as to Mary's age — is the ground of my assertion that I know *that I know* that Mary is eight years old. Just this sort of difference, I submit, is the difference between knowing and knowing that one knows, or being aware and being aware that one is aware.

But in the statement "I am aware that I am aware (of . . .)," which is a correct formulation of the sort of situation just illustrated, the accusative ". . . that I am aware (of . . .)" is, let it be noted, *alien to* the particular occurrence of awareness which, in that statement, the words "I am aware (that . . .)" formulate. The very fact that one can be aware — say, of blue — without being also aware "that one is aware" (of blue) shows that one's being aware (of blue) is not a connate but an alien accusative of the possible *additional awareness* "that one is aware" (of blue) — as alien to it, indeed, and existentially independent of it as would Mary's being 8 years old be alien to and independent of the awareness one may come to have that this is her age.

On the other hand, the words "that I am aware" (of . . . or that . . .) would not be a correct formulation of the *connate* accusative of the particular awareness I report whenever I say "I am aware" (no matter *of* what, or *that* what). The only correct formulation of the connate accusative of "I am aware" or of "I am conscious" would have a form which is unusual because, except in a discussion such as this, the need to employ it never arises. This unusual form is *"I am aware an awareness,"* or *"I am conscious a consciousness,"* (that . . . or of . . .) — these phrases to be construed as one would construe, for instance, "I am awarded an award" (say, of a scholarship), or "I am hungry a hunger" (for, say, fruit). In these cases "I am aware," "I am conscious," "I am awarded," "I am hungry," can be replaced without any alteration of meaning simply by "I have": "I am aware an awareness" (that . . . or of . . .) means I *have* an awareness (that . . . or of . . .); "I am awarded an award of a scholarship" means I *have* an award of a scholarship, etc. But where an *alien* accusative of "I am aware" is concerned, that substitution is impossible: "I am aware that Mary is 8," or "that I am aware of . . ." cannot be replaced by "I have that Mary is 8," or "I have that I am aware of . . . ."

Thus, the objection that on my premises it would follow that I cannot be aware of anything without being aware that I am aware of it, whereas the contrary is true, is invalid, since this consequence does *not* follow from my premises. What follows from them is only that whenever I am aware I have an awareness, *i.e.,* I am "aware an awareness," and indeed, am aware in some specific mode, *e.g.,* bluely; just as whenever I strike, I strike a stroke, and strike in some specific mode, *e.g.,* "jabbily."

Having now made clear the nature of my hypothesis as to the relation of blue to sensing blue, and defended that hypothesis from two *prima facie* plausible objections to it, I may add that the relation the hypothesis describes is the one I shall mean whenever I say that blue is "content" of sensing blue; that is, when I so use this term I shall mean that blue stands to sensing bluĕ (or more generally, that any given species of experience or awareness stands to experiencing or being aware) as kind stands to occurrence of a case thereof. With this understood, let us now turn to Moore's criticism of what he calls the "content" hypothesis.

11. Moore's Criticism of the Hypothesis That Blue Is "Content" of the Sensing of Blue

The only place at which Moore's criticism of the contention that blue is content of the sensing or awareness of blue could be considered relevant to the meaning of "content" I have stated to be mine is the place where he raises the question "whether or not, when I have the sensation of blue, my consciousness or awareness is . . . blue."[22] He acknowledges that offence may be taken at the expression "a blue awareness," but asserts that it nevertheless "expresses just what should be and is meant by saying that blue is, in this case, a *content* of consciousness or experience."

As to this, I can only reply that what I mean (as defined above) when I say that blue is the content of my awareness of blue is not properly expressible by saying that my awareness is then blue, *unless blue be taken as the name, instead of as an adjective,* of the kind of awareness which is mine at the moment. That is, what I mean when I refer to blue as content of my awareness of blue is that my awareness is at the moment of the determinate sort *called "blue,"* and not that it has, like lapis lazuli, the property

[22] Moore, *Philosophical Studies,* p. 26.

of being blue; for when I assert of lapis lazuli that it is blue, what I mean is that it is such that whenever I turn my eyes upon it in daylight it causes me to experience something called "blue"; whereas I mean nothing like this when I say of my awareness that at a given moment it is of the particular sort called "blue."

To speak of a blue awareness, I would insist, is improper in the same way it would be improper to speak of an iron metal. We can properly speak of a species of metal called "iron," but if we wish to use "iron" as an adjective, we have to apply it to something — for instance a kettle or a door — which stands to iron not, like "metal," as genus to species, but as substance to property.

I conclude here, then, that Moore's criticism of the contention that blue is content of the awareness of blue is not a criticism of the contention that blue is a species of awareness — which is what I mean when I assert that blue is content of the awareness of blue. His criticism does not consider this contention at all and therefore does not refute it.

12.   Does Existential Independence Follow From the Fact That the Awareness Is of Blue?

It is only because Moore does not in his paper consider as a possible meaning of "blue awareness" the hypothesis that blue is a species of awareness rather than a property of it, that he is able to dismiss the possibility that "awareness is blue" as unimportant even if true — saying that, in any case, the awareness is *of* blue, and "has to blue the simple and unique relation the existence of which alone justifies us in distinguishing knowledge of a thing from the thing known."[23]   For he believes this relation entails in all cases that the known may exist independently of the knowing of it.   But we have seen that this is so only in some cases.   We do indeed speak of the tasting *of* a taste — *e.g.,* of the taste called "bitter" — and also of the tasting *of* quinine, but although "tast-

---

[23] *Ibid.*

ing" in both cases denotes a species of knowing, it obviously does not denote the same species in both cases: the relation of tasting to taste (or to bitter) is not the same as the relation of tasting to cheese (or to Cheddar). Similarly, when we speak of the smelling of a smell and of the smelling of a rose, of the hearing of a tone and of the hearing of a bell, or — as Moore himself points out elsewhere[24] — of the seeing of a color, e.g., brown, and of the seeing of a coin, we are obviously using "smelling," "hearing," "seeing," each in two senses notwithstanding that in each sense each of these processes is a species of knowing, and notwithstanding that in each sense the knowing is of something. Were any proof needed that the senses are two, it would be provided by the following consideration.

The two sentences "I see red" and "I see a rose" each represents an attempt to describe in English a judgment made by the utterer — something he believes. Now it is possible that "red" or "a rose" are not the right words to describe in English what he believes he sees; that is, either sentence may be an incorrect wording of his belief. But in the case of the sentence "I see red" the belief itself, which he uses that sentence to describe, cannot possibly be a mistaken belief. It cannot be erroneous because that which he believes is not anything more at all than is actually and literally seen (i.e., intuited) by him at the moment.

In the case of the sentence "I see a rose," on the other hand, not only as before may the sentence be an incorrect wording of his belief, but now in addition his belief itself may be mistaken: that which he believes he sees may not be what he believes it to be. It may be something else which looks the same as what he believes to be there, but the other characters of which are very different; for these other characters, e.g., tactual, olfactory, gustatory ones, etc., of course cannot literally be seen. Odor, taste, hardness, can be "seen" only in the elliptical sense that the colors

---

[24] Moore, Philosophical Essays, p. 187.

literally seen predict to us a certain odor, taste, etc. But whenever what we believe is something the nature of which is predicted or signified even in part, instead of literally and totally observed at the moment, error is theoretically possible.

The relation between seeing and seen, or more generally between knowing and known or experiencing and experienced, is thus not as Moore's paper asserts "a simple and unique relation," but is of at least the two kinds just illustrated. Moreover if, as I contend, the first of these two relations between knowing and known is the very relation between cognizing and a cognitum connate therewith, then in no case of that first relation is the known existentially independent of the knowing thereof. Therefore, from the fact that in all cases of knowing the knowing is *of* something, nothing general follows as to the existential independence or dependence of the known upon the knowing.

To prove such independence in a given case it would be necessary to show that when we speak of, *e.g.*, the tasting of bitter or the seeing of blue, the tasting is existentially related to the bitter, or the seeing to the blue, not (as I contend) as cognizing is to cognitum subordinately connate therewith, but on the contrary as, for instance, green is existentially related to sweet. But this is not shown by anything in Moore's paper. As just pointed out, the fact that the sensing or seeing is *of* blue does nothing to show it and, as I shall now make clear, neither does a certain additional fact to which Moore appeals.

13. Does Existential Independence Follow From the Introspective Distinguishability of the Awareness From the Blue?

Moore asserts that in any case of awareness of blue it is possible (even if not easy) to distinguish by careful introspective observation the awareness from the blue. This I readily grant, but I deny that it constitutes any evidence at all of the existential independence it is adduced to prove, for the fact that the awareness is observationally distinguishable from the blue leaves wholly open the question which is crucial here. This question is whether the awareness is distinguishable from the blue as for instance green is from sweet — *i.e.*, as a case of one species from a case of a logically independent species — or on the contrary (as I contend) as a case of a genus is distinguishable (by abstractive observation) within a case of any one of its species — for instance, as a case of the generic activity "to dance" is by abstractive observation distinguishable within any case of the species of that genus called "to waltz." That is, we can observe that a person is moving with the specific rhythm and steps called "waltzing"; and then we can abstract our attention from the specific nature of the rhythm and steps and notice only the fact (common to the waltz, polka, one-step, fox trot, etc.) that he takes steps in a rhythmical manner, *i.e.*, that he is "dancing." Indeed, observation merely that the genus "dance" is the one to which belongs a case of activity concretely before us is what would normally occur if — perhaps through the rapid opening and shutting of a door — we had only a brief glimpse of the dancing going on in a room.

To prove that blue and awareness are distinct in the manner which entails existential independence, we should have to have the same sort of evidence on which is based our knowledge that green and sweet are existentially independent: we have observed, for instance, that some apples are green and not sweet, and that some are sweet and not green. That is, we should have to observe — *i.e.*, to be aware — that at a certain time blue exists but awareness does not, and that at a certain other time awareness exists but blue does not. Of the latter we have a case whenever what we are aware of is something other than blue, for instance, sweet or green, etc.; but of the former it is impossible that we should ever have a case, for to be aware that one is not at the time aware is a contradiction.

This situation, it is true, does not prove that blue is existentially dependent on awareness of blue; yet just that sort of situation is

what would confront us if blue were existentially dependent on
awareness of blue; therefore that the situation we do confront *is*
of that sort is circumstantial evidence, so far as it goes, of such
dependence.

14.   Comment on Some Relevant Remarks of Broad's

It might be claimed, however, that the introspective observation
by which in awareness of blue we distinguish the awareness from
the blue is not of the abstractive kind I have described, but on the
contrary of the same "total" kind for the awareness as for the
blue.   This is perhaps what Moore means to assert when he says
that "to be aware of the sensation of blue is . . . to be aware of
an awareness of blue; awareness being used, in both cases, in
exactly the same sense."[25]

Some light will perhaps be thrown on the issue by examination
of certain remarks made by C. D. Broad.   He observes that a
sensation of red (the case would of course be the same with blue)
seems obviously to involve an act of sensing and a red "object";
but it is of particular interest to note his further remark that it
does not seem similarly obvious "that a sensation of headache
involves an act of sensing and a 'headachy' object."[26]

To me also it is evident that there is a difference between the
two cases, and the important point is that on Moore's view there
ought not to be any.   Both cases ought to be introspectively
analyzable alike into an awareness — a sensing — and an "object,"
viz., respectively, red and headache.   The explanation of the difference is, I submit, as follows:

The eye, which is the sense organ with which the sensation of
red is connected, is an organ susceptible of being oriented and
focused; that is, the eye is capable of *looking,* and it does look
in this sense whenever any color is seen or even imaged, for the
eye always has some orientation and some accommodation.   But

---

[25] Moore, *Philosophical Studies,* p. 25.
[26] C. D. Broad, *Scientific Thought,* p. 254.

with any orientation and accommodation of the eye there go kinesthetic sensa of a certain sort (the sort connected with the muscles of the eyeball and of the lens). And these kinesthetic sensa, I submit, are what Broad finds present in the sensation of red but absent in that of headache; for the latter is not, like the former, connected with an organ susceptible of orientation and accommodation and is therefore not, like the former, accompanied by characteristic kinesthetic sensa. The difference Broad notices is really present, but it is not rightly described as presence in the one case of an "act of sensing" absent in the other. What he calls an "act of sensing" (or we can say more specifically of "seeing") is in fact only the kinesthetic sensa which accompany the physical act of *looking, i.e.,* of orienting and accommodating the eye. Similarly, one must distinguish between the hearing, smelling, etc., and the kinesthetic sensa which always accompany the physical acts of listening, sniffing, etc.

The red, indeed, is existentially independent of the accompanying ocular kinesthetic sensa; for on the one hand a completely blind person (who of course does not see even black) has them, and on the other hand if the eye muscles of a normal person were anesthetized he could undoubtedly nevertheless sense red. But kinesthetic sensa are not an "act of sensing" the red. The genuine sensing process, on the contrary, is distinguishable in the sensation or sensing of headache as well as in that of red; but it is not distinguishable from the red and the headache as red is from kinesthetic sensa or from sweet, but — I now urge again in the light provided by removal of the confusion just discussed — as the act of dancing is distinguishable within the event of dancing the waltz. The red is no more an "object" of sensing or seeing than is the waltz an "object" of dancing.

The point is now reached where the first part of the task I undertook has, I believe, been accomplished. That is, I submit, the preceding pages have shown that Moore's argument to prove that blue can exist independently of the sensing or the being aware of blue neither proves this nor proves it to be more probable than not.   I now therefore turn to the second part of my task, which is to show that blue, bitter, or any other sensa cannot exist independently of the experiencing thereof.   This will be proved if I prove that blue, bitter, etc., are, as I have asserted, species, not objects, of experiencing.

15.   The Hypothesis That Bitter, Blue, etc., Are "Directly Present" to the Mind

For this positive attempt I shall take as starting point a fact already mentioned.   It is that if, in answer to the question "What do you taste?" we answer at one time "I taste bitter" and at another time "I taste quinine," the relation of the tasting to bitter is different from that of the tasting to quinine.   Or, to take another example, if having been asked "What do you see?" we answer at one time "I see blue" and at another "I see some lapis lazuli," it is obvious that the relation of the blue to the seeing of it is not the same as that of the lapis lazuli to the seeing of it.   Or again, if to the question "What do you hear?" we answer "I hear middle C," and at another time "I hear a bell," it is evident that the relation of middle C to the hearing of it is different from that of a bell to the hearing of it.

That it is different is obvious, but if it needed any proof it would be found in the fact that the judgment expressed by "I hear a bell" is the judgment that the object which is causing me to hear the tone I hear at the moment is a thing of the kind called a bell; or that the judgment "I see lapis lazuli" is the judgment that the object causing me to see blue is a substance of the kind called lapis lazuli; or that the judgment "I taste quinine" is the judgment that the substance presence of which on my tongue is causing me to taste the bitter taste I am tasting is a substance of the kind called quinine.   That is, in these examples, to taste or see or hear an "object" is to take a taste or color or tone one is experiencing as sign that the object which causes the experiencing of it is, respectively, something of the kind called quinine, lapis lazuli, a bell. To have this relation to one's experiencing of a taste, color, or tone is, in these examples, what being "object" tasted, seen, or heard consists of.

Therefore if bitter, blue, and middle C were also to be spoken of as "objects" respectively tasted, seen, and heard, it could be only in some other sense, not yet considered, of the word "object"; for obviously it could not be maintained that "I taste bitter" means (as in the case of quinine) that the cause of my tasting the bitter I taste is presence on my tongue of a substance called bitter taste, for "bitter" is not here the name of any kind of substance but of a kind of taste.

Our situation is then this. We have considered so far two sorts of relation a cognitum may have to the cognizing of it: one, the relation I have called "content of," and the other, the relation ordinarily called "object of," illustrated by the example of quinine as cognitum of tasting. This sense of "object of" I shall label "sense *A*" for convenience of reference. Now our problem was: is bitter (or blue, etc.) *content of,* or *object of,* the tasting (or the seeing, etc.) thereof? Admittedly, it is not "object of" the tasting in sense *A*. But this does not necessarily force us to conclude that bitter is (as I maintain) "content" of the tasting; for there might happen to be some third sort of relation, which a cognitum could have to the cognizing of it — a relation perhaps also called "object of" but constituting what we might now label "sense *B*" of "object of." The question therefore now is whether there is such a third sort of possible relation, and if so what exactly it is. The epistemologists who believe there is, usually describe it as "direct presence" of the blue or bitter to, or "immediate apprehension" of these by, the mind or consciousness. As against them I maintain that either these phrases are only other names for what I have called being "content of," or else they are figures of speech for which no literal meaning that is not absurd is available. I shall now attempt to make the latter evident.

The facts which, without our noticing it, suggest to us the employment of the words "direct" or "immediate" in the phrases mentioned consist of examples of directness or immediacy such as the direct contact of quinine with the tongue, or the immediate presence of a piece of lapis lazuli before the eye. The presence is in these cases "direct" or "immediate" in the sense that *there is nothing discernible between* the object and the sense organ — no medium or instrument discernible at the time between them. And when these same words — "direct" or "immediate" presence — are used to describe also the relation between bitter or blue and the mind, the only *literal* meaning they can have there is that the latter relation resembles that of the lapis to the eye or the quinine to the tongue in the respect that, in both relations, *there is nothing discernible between* the terms they relate.

But if (as of course we must where blue or bitter and the mind are the terms) we divest the word "between" of the only sense, *viz.,* the spatial sense, which it had when quinine and the tongue or lapis and the eye were the terms, then, I submit, no sense is left to them, and the words "nothing between" describe no hypothesis at all as to the nature of the relation of the blue or bitter to the mind. This means that when one of the terms of a certain relation is the mind, then — since the mind is not, like the head or sense organs, an entity having a place in space — nothing whatever is being said as to the nature of that relation by employing the words "direct presence" to describe it unless some definite meaning other than the spatial one is explicitly provided for those words. But everybody seems either to have assumed their meaning to be obvious and not incongruous to the cases concerned, or else to have defined the words ostensively only, as meaning the sort of relation there is between blue or bitter, etc., and consciousness of these. But of course to define "direct presence" thus only ostensively is not in the least to analyze the sort of relation the words apply to. In particular, it is not to offer the least evidence that analysis would not reveal it to be the very relation I have called "content of."

Aside from this, however, even if one supposes that bitter tastes are entities which would exist even if no minds existed, and one should be willing to accept the absurdity that not only minds but also bitter tastes (and likewise, of course, nauseas, dizzinesses, fears, etc.) have, like tongues and quinine, places in space and can move about or be moved about independently of each other so that a bitter taste or a nausea could become "present" to a mind in the sense of travelling to its spatial neighborhood until nothing remained spatially between them — even then, I submit, one would have to accept the further absurdity that this mere spatial juxtaposition without that mind's being itself in any way affected by it, *i.e.,* without any change being caused in that mind by it, would constitute cognition of bitter by that mind. For if one were to say that the juxtaposition does cause in the mind a specific change, *viz.,* one to be called not "smelling" or "hearing" etc., but specifically "tasting," this would amount to erecting bitter taste into as strictly a physical substance as quinine, and therefore to saying that tasting bitter taste and tasting quinine are both "tasting" in essentially the same (causal) sense. Yet it was obvious and admitted from the start that "tasting" does not have the same sense in both cases.

But further still, even if "presence of bitter taste in the spatial neighborhood of a mind" were not an absurdity, and even if such "presence" did cause in that mind a change called "tasting," even then there would still remain to give an account of that mind's intuitive cognition of its own tasting at the time it occurs, *i.e.,* of its cognition of the event *in that mind itself* caused to occur by the advent of the bitter taste in the spatial neighborhood of that mind. And this would face us then anyway with the need for my hypothesis that "tasting bitter taste" is the name of a specific variety of the activity called "tasting," *viz.*, the variety called "tasting *bitterly*" (in the literal not the figurative sense of this adverb), and that what the activity cognizes on every such occasion is its own specific nature on the occasion.

But everything for the doing of which we need a relation of a kind other than that of quinine to tasting is, I submit, adequately done for us by the relation just described, which I maintain is the one of bitter to tasting; and this relation does not entail the absurdities which would be required to give a literal sense *B* (distinct from both "content of" and sense *A* of "object of") to the "direct presence" hypothesis. Moreover, because the two relations "content of" and "object of" (in sense *A*) adequately account for every case, Occam's razor enables us to dismiss the still other nominal supposition — which might be resorted to *in extremis* — that bitter is "object of" tasting in some unique and indefinable other sense *C* of the words.

16. Taste a Species, Not an Object, of Experience

If the discussion in the preceding section has succeeded in what it attempted, it has shown that the phrase "direct presence to a mind" either is but another name for the relation between cognitive activity and the cognita connate therewith, or else is only a figure of speech for which no literal meaning not ultimately involving absurdities is forthcoming. If this has been shown, then the allegedly third hypothesis, which *prima facie* seemed meaningful and was the only one seeming to offer an acceptable alternative to mine, has been disposed of.

I shall not rest my case here, however, but will now attempt to show that, when the issues are sharply presented, my assertion that blue, bitter, etc., are not objects of experience nor species of objects of experience, but species of experience itself, is the **very** assertion common sense then finds itself ready to make. What is needed for this is only to put the question in a manner making it impossible for our judgment to be confused by the ambiguity which may still cling to the phrase "object of" in spite of what was said in the preceding section. To make the meaning of the question unmistakably clear, I then ask first what would be indubitable examples of the four possible kinds of accusatives of "experiencing." I submit the following:

The *alienly coordinate* cognitum of "experiencing" is "object" or "objective event."

The *connately coordinate* cognitum of "experiencing" is "experience."

An *alienly subordinate* cognitum of "experiencing" is "quinine," or "a rose," etc.

A *connately subordinate* cognitum of "experiencing" is "taste," or "smell," etc.

I believe the first three examples will be readily accepted as correct; but the fourth might be disputed, for if it is accepted my case is won.

"Taste," "smell," etc., I may be told, are not as the above would imply *species* of experience but *"objects"* of experience. If this is said, however, I ask what then would be right examples of connately subordinate cognita of experiencing? or — which is equivalent since experience is the connately coordinate cognitum of experiencing — what then would be right examples of *species* of experience? I believe it would not be disputed that tasting, smelling, etc. are species of experiencing; and I submit it is equally natural and proper and indeed unavoidable to say that taste and smell are species of experience, or that there is a species of experience called "taste." For the only alternative to this is to say that taste is an "object" of experience in the same sense that quinine is an object of experience, and this is plainly false.

Moreover, one who would deny that taste is a species of experience is called upon to say what then would be the cognitum coordinately connate with the species of experiencing called "tasting." If it is not taste, what then might it be? I for one can no more think of an answer than if I were asked what would be the coordinately connate accusative of striking if it were not stroke.

17. Bitter a Species, Not an Object, of Taste

To emphasize the point of the considerations just advanced, they will now be reiterated, but at the more determinate level where the relation of bitter to tasting is in question instead of that of taste to experiencing. Again I ask, what would be indubitable examples of the four possible sorts of cognita of tasting, and I submit the following:

The *alienly coordinate* cognitum of "tasting" is "physical substance."

The *connately coordinate* cognitum of "tasting" is "taste."

An *alienly subordinate* cognitum of "tasting" is "quinine."

A *connately subordinate* cognitum of "tasting" is "bitter."

Here again, to say that bitter is not a species but an "object" of taste is to say that bitter is related to tasting in essentially the same manner as quinine is to tasting, and this is patently false. Moreover, one who would deny that when bitter is tasted what is tasted is a species of taste is called upon to say what then would be examples of cognita *connately* subordinate to tasting. If bitter, or sweet, or sour, etc., are not such cognita, what then might be one? Again here, I can no more think of an answer than I could to the question what might be a subordinately connate accusative of striking if jab, uppercut, swing, etc., were not such.

18. Linguistic Inertia Responsible for the Error That Taste Is Object of Experience

It is easy to see how one is led into the error that taste is an object of experience or bitter an object of taste. What leads one into it is the tendency — which we may call linguistic inertia or linguistic optimism — to believe that when a word is the same it means the same, and that when it is not the same it does not mean the same. The sameness in this case is that of the word "of," which occurs equally and in grammatically similar positions when we speak of the experiencing of taste and of the experiencing of quinine; or of the tasting of bitter and of the tasting of quinine. The temptation to believe that "of" means the same in both halves of each pair is likely to vanish only when we realize that we likewise speak of the striking *of* a jab and of the striking *of* a man — in which case it is quite obvious that the two "of's" do not mean the same relation.

On the other hand, because the two words "experiencing" and "taste," or "tasting" and "bitter," are not *linguistically* connate, linguistic inertia tempts us to believe that the cognitive process and the cognitum in each case, for which those words stand, are not themselves connate either. And again, this temptation is likely to vanish only when we realize that "dancing" and "waltz," or "striking" and "jab," or "jumping" and "leap," etc., are not *linguistically* connate either, but that in each of these cases the accusative nevertheless is, beyond doubt, connate (subordinately) with the process.

19.   "Bitter" as Name of a Species of Taste, vs. as Name of a Property of Some Substances

One can speak of a bitter taste, and also of a bitter substance. Linguistic inertia therefore tempts one to believe that "bitter" is used in the same sense in both cases, but this is not so. As applicable to substances, "bitter" is the name of a *property,* and a property P of a substance S is an "If . . . then . . ." sort of thing: to say that S has property P is to say that if, in circumstances of kind C, S is treated in manner T, then S behaves in manner B. As applied to a taste, on the other hand, "bitter" is the name of the gustatory quality which the given taste *is,* not of a property

which the taste *has.* Thus, when one says of quinine that it is
bitter one is stating a property of it — a capacity it has — namely,
that if under ordinary circumstances quinine is placed on one's
tongue, this causes one to experience the gustatory quality called
bitter.[27]

20. Special Sources of Confusion When Visual Sensa Are Taken as Examples

My argument has been formulated at most places in terms of
gustatory sensa, but if it is valid for them it obviously is equally
so for sensa of any other kinds. The reason for having presented
the argument in terms of an example from the realm of taste
rather than from the favorite one of sight was that the question
at issue being a very difficult one, its exact nature could be exhibited more clearly by a simple example than by one where — as
in the case of sight — special risks of confusion are present.

The chief of these arises from the fact that the organ of sight,
viz., the eye, yields to us not only color intuitions but also place
and shape intuitions. This fact means that when our eye is
focused upon, for instance, an apple, we see not only a color
(say, green) but also "see" a place at which the color is. But
simultaneously (because our own nose as well as the apple is in
front of our eye) we see, although inattentively, also another
color (say, pink) and a place at which it is, different from the
place of the green. And the fact that the place at which the
green is seen and that at which the pink is seen are literally, *i.e.,*
spatially, external to each other seems to provide for some phi-

---

[27] Moore, in commenting on my criticism of his "Refutation of Idealism"
(*The Philosophy of G. E. Moore,* p. 656), says that I seem to be supposing that
there is some one and the same entity, to which I give the name "bitter," such that
when we say that quinine is bitter we are saying that this entity is "a property of"
quinine, whereas when we say of a taste which we are tasting that it is bitter, we
are saying of this same entity that that entity is "a species of" the taste which we
are tasting. Moore adds that this seems to him to be nonsense, and I wholly agree
that it would be nonsense. But I hold no such doctrine and am quite at a loss to
understand how Moore may have come to think I do. The only entity which is "one
and the same" in both cases is the *word* "bitter," and one of my chief contentions is
precisely that the *sense* in which it is used is radically different in the two cases.

losophers an irresistible temptation to believe that the green attended to (and the pink too if attention is called to it) are "external" also in the *metaphorical* sense the word has when we speak of externality to the mind, *i.e.*, are existentially independent of their being experienced. Obviously, however, spatial externality to each other of the places at which two colors are seen, or of the places of two physical things such as our own eye and an apple, is something totally irrelevant to the question whether the colors (or, for that matter, the physical things) are "external to the mind" in the sense of existing independently of their being experienced.

21. Summary of the Argument

The essential points of the foregoing discussion of Moore's article may now briefly be reviewed. First, attention was called to the distinction between accusatives connate with and alien to a given process and to the fact that an accusative of either sort may be either coordinate or subordinate, in respect of generality, to the corresponding process. It was then pointed out that any accusative connate with a given process exists only in the occurrences of that process and therefore in particular that any cognitum connate with a given cognitive process exists only in the occurrences of it; that is, the *esse* of any cognitum connate with the cognizing is its *cognosci*. The question as to whether a sensum, *e.g.*, blue or bitter, can or cannot exist independently of the *percipi* of it then reduces to the question whether the blue or bitter is a cognitum (subordinately) connate with or on the contrary alien to the cognizing thereof. My contention, I then stated, is that the sensum is a cognitum (subordinately) connate with the cognizing of it, *i.e.*, that what is cognized or experienced in cognition of it is the determinate nature the sensing activity has on the given occasion; and that, in just this sense, blue or bitter are "contents" of sensing and not "objects," *i.e.*, not alien cognita, of sensing. It was next pointed out that Moore's criticism of the "content" hypothesis concerns a hypothesis other than the one just described, which therefore remains a possible alternative to his own hypothesis that blue or bitter are "objects" of sensing. But since Moore's paper does not disprove or even consider that alternative hypothesis, and that hypothesis entails that the blue or bitter would exist only in the sensing thereof, his paper does not prove what it seeks to prove, *viz.,* that there is *no* cognitum of which it is true that its *esse* is its *percipi.* I then passed to the attempt to show that blue, bitter, etc., *are* cognita connate with the sensing thereof, and therefore that their *esse* is their *percipi.* To do so, I first pointed to the fact — stated by Moore himself in another paper — that seeing brown and seeing a coin, hearing middle C and hearing a bell, tasting bitter and tasting quinine, are not "seeing," "hearing" and "tasting" in the same sense in both cases; and therefore that if the coin, the bell, and the quinine have to the seeing, hearing and tasting the relation "object of," then brown, middle C and bitter either are not "objects of" these processes at all, or else are "objects of" them in some other sense of the term. The allegation that "direct presence to the mind" describes such an other sense was then examined and shown to be false; and this left, as the only answer in sight concerning the relation of sensa to the sensing of them, the one I had advanced. I then further attempted to show that it is the very answer common sense renders when the question is thoroughly freed of its ordinary ambiguity. Finally, some explanations were added to show how the error that sensa are "objects" of cognition arises. The upshot of the argument is that the distinction between sensing and sensum, to which appeal is commonly made nowadays and for which Moore's paper is generally regarded as the original warrant, is an invalid distinction if it is taken as the one from which would follow the possibility of existential independence of the sensum from the sensing. On the other hand, there is a valid distinction between sensum and sensing, but it is the one I have described, and from it what follows is that the existence of the sensum consists in the sensing thereof.

22. Moore's Allegation That the Argument Does Not Prove Its Contention

Moore offers two criticisms of the argument by which I have attempted to prove that the sensible quality "blue" — or, more generally, any sensum — can exist only in the sensing of it. He states that he is now inclined to agree with the contention itself; and he concedes that *if* the sensible quality "blue" is related to the seeing of it as the kind of cricket stroke called a "cut" is related to the striking of it, *then* it is a contradiction to suppose that the sensible quality "blue" exists without being seen. But — and this is his first criticism — he says that he cannot see that I have given any good reason for supposing that the relation is the same in the two cases.[28]

The retort here is that, in the course of the argument, each of the hypotheses commonly advanced as to the nature of the relation between the sensible quality "blue" and the seeing of it has been scrutinized and shown to be untenable. At least, Moore does not challenge the validity of the criticisms which were made of them. The situation is then that the hypothesis the argument offers as to the nature of that relation is the only one left in sight. It is true that this does not prove that no other is conceivable; but it does make incumbent on any one who rejects it either to advance a tenable alternative hypothesis, or else to point to some specific difficulty in the way of it.

The latter is what Moore's second criticism attempts to do. The difficulty, as he sees it, is that one cannot see the *sensible* quality blue without *directly seeing* also something else (called by him a sense datum) which *has* that quality but *is not* itself a quality — for example, a blue patch, or a blue speck, or a blue line, or a blue spot, etc., in the sense in which an afterimage, seen

---

[28] *The Philosophy of G. E. Moore*, p. 659.

with closed eyes, may be any of these things. Moore rightly says that any complete account of how the sensible quality "blue" is related to my seeing of it must include an account of how the afterimage, which has that quality, is related to my seeing of that afterimage. He then points out that my account of the former does not include any account of the latter, and adds that he cannot see at all how my account of the former could be consistent with any plausible account of the latter.[29]

The account Moore calls for, which I shall now offer, of the manner in which the afterimage is related to the seeing of it, is, I believe, completely consistent with the one already given of the relation between the quality "blue" and the seeing of it. Moreover, so far as I can discern, it is the only one in sight, for Moore himself does not offer any, and, as will be evident when it has been given, the criticism made in Section 15 of the hypothesis of "direct presence to the mind" is equally fatal where a blue-patch afterimage is concerned as where the sensible quality "blue" is concerned.

The account I now offer is, in brief, that a blue afterimage is a complex, and that all the elements of it are related to the seeing of them in the same way as the blue quality element is related to the seeing of it. In more detail, this means, first, that a blue afterimage "has" the quality blue in no other sense than that in which one can say of any complex that it "has" its elements — the sense, namely, in which one can say, for instance, that a heap of bricks "has" a given brick; that a chord "has" any one of its constituent tones; that an army "has" its general, or its artillery; that a tone "has" the pitch of middle C; etc.[30]

Secondly, in the case of a blue patch and of any other entity of the kind Moore calls a sense datum, the complex, which it is,

---

[29] *Op. cit.,* pp. 659–660.
[30] The relation of the elements of a complex to one another and to the complex may, as W. E. Johnson points out (*Logic,* Vol. I, pp. 110–2), be of various kinds, but the differences between them have no bearing on the use made here of the relation of the elements of a complex to the complex.

consists wholly of such elements as, not only sensible *color,* but also, sensible *extent,* sensible *quantity,* sensible *position,* sensible *duration,* etc., *i.e.,* wholly of *sensibilia,* no matter whether or not we choose to call these others too, like the blue, qualities (or *qualia*). This means that each and everyone of the elements of the "blue afterimage sense datum" may (or, in the absence of any alternative conception, must) be conceived, like the blue element, as a species or modulation of awareness; so that we then may or must speak of being aware not only *bluely,* but also *briefly* (or perhaps lengthily), *extensionally* (or perhaps punctually), *here-ly* (or perhaps there-ly), *abundantly* (or perhaps scantily), etc.

But then, because the elements of the complex sense datum are all of them *sensibilia,* one can in the case of each give arguments, exactly parallel to those given in that of "blue" or "bitter," to show that each is a cognitum connate with the cognizing of it, and therefore can exist only in the cognizing. And evidently the existential status of the sense datum, *i.e.,* of the complex they together constitute, can be no other than that of its elements.

In this connection, a few additional words of comment are called for by Broad's statement that he does not "find the slightest intrinsic difficulty in conceiving the existence of unsensed red patches or unsensed noises," or, in general of unsensed sensa.[31] I believe that the reason why he finds no difficulty in doing so is that the "sensing" which he finds it easy to abstract in thought from them is in fact, as already suggested, only the kinesthetic sensations accompanying the accommodation or the orientation of the eye or the ear.

The mistaking of these kinesthetic sensations for acts of sensing colors or sounds easily leads to an illegitimately physicalized conception of sensa; for orientation, and in the case of the eye accommodation also, is to the place of a *physical* thing. Sensa thus

---

[31] C. D. Broad, *Scientific Thought,* p. 262.

come to be thought of as having some of the properties of physical substances, and therefore as themselves quasi physical substances. Broad says, for instance, that sensa "are extended, and have shapes, sizes, colours, temperatures, etc."[32] Again, he mentions as example of a sensum, a "red patch," and says that it may be triangular; and he speaks of the sensum which enters into perception of a penny, as a patch which seems "to have a certain determinate ellipticity and a certain non-uniform distribution of various shades of brown."[33] This mode of speech carries with it the implication that "the patch" or "the sensum" is something which has to the sensible color, temperature, shape, etc., the same kind of relation that, e.g., a penny or other physical object has to these. Indeed, Broad states that sensa have in this way "some of the characteristics of physical objects";[34] and when the sensa he considers are, as usually they are, visual sensa, it would seem that a sensum is for him little different from what would be a physical object that lacked only the depth dimension; for example, the surface of a photograph.

Now, as I have argued in this chapter, color, temperature, taste, etc., as predicable of a physical object, are properties not qualities. They are, that is to say, like malleability, fusibility, etc., capacities — analyzable in terms of causation — which a physical object has, whether or not it be manifesting them at a given time (this itself depending on what the circumstances happen to be at the time). And no sensum can be said to have the property of being red, or being long, or being hot, in the sense in which on the contrary a rose, or a stick, or a potato, can be said to have these properties. What we can say of a given sensum is not that it *has* redness or length or temperature, but that it *is* a (determinate) redness-intuition, or length-intuition, or hotness-intuition; and that these several sensa are "one sensum" only in the sense that they are

---

[32] *Op. cit.*, p. 259.
[33] Broad, *The Mind and Its Place in Nature,* pp. 295–6.
[34] Broad, *Scientific Thought,* p. 259.

occurring together. Thus, if we say of a red sensum that "it is hot," we cannot (without contravention of the status of "sensum" which we assign to "red") be saying it in the same sense as if we were saying "it is hot" about a piece of iron. In the latter case, what it would mean would be that the piece of iron has the capacity to cause certain other substances to burn, or to melt, etc., and to cause in sentient beings the occurrence of a heat-intuition. But to be able to say about a red sensum that "it is hot," we have on the contrary to construe the assertion as meaning that a determinate redness-intuition and a determinate heat-intuition both have the same locus in time-intuition and space-intuition.

On the basis of that which has, I believe, been established in this chapter with regard to sensa, and more particularly, of the manner in which it has been established, it will be possible in the next to define introspection, inspection, and the mental, with greater precision than has hitherto been possible. Before we turn to this, however, something must be said concerning the "problem of the speckled hen," which I believe, is implicitly disposed of by the considerations which precede.

23. The Problem of the Speckled Hen[35]

It concerns the sense datum one has when looking at or imagining a speckled hen. The question is whether this sense datum can have speckles that are *merely* many, *i.e.*, numerous, but of no determinate numerousness. Ayer regards the problem as arising from the fact that it is worded in language inappropriate to sense data and appropriate only to objects. His position is that, in view of the nature of the problems that led to the introduction of the term "sense datum," there is no point in employing it at all unless one agrees to mean by it something that (*a*) cannot appear to

---

[35] This problem, in terms of a different example, was suggested by Gilbert Ryle to A. J. Ayer, who, in his *The Foundations of Empirical Knowledge,* proposes a solution of it. His solution was criticized by H. H. Price (*Mind,* Vol. L, No. 199, pp. 280 ff.) and the matter further discussed by R. Chisholm (*Mind,* Vol. LI, No. 204, pp. 368 ff.).

have characters it does not have, and (*b*) cannot have characters it does not appear to have. This position is, I believe, sound; but one must not forget that if one thus starts with a word and defines it to suit one's purposes, the question at once arises as to whether anything exists that conforms to the definition one has laid down. It is not and cannot be answered by the definition itself, but only by empirical scrutiny of the entities alleged to be instances of "sense data" as defined.

Concerning the speckles in the sense datum, Chisholm remarks that to say they are many, yet of no specific number, "is very much like saying that victory will come in 1943, but not in January or February or any other particular month up to and including December." This, however is a false analogy. The true one would be with *knowing* (or believing, or disbelieving, or supposing) that victory will come in 1943, and yet *not knowing* (or having no opinion, or making no supposition as to) what particular month it will occur in. In this, no paradox is involved. Thus, the essential point ignored by Chisholm's analogy is that a sense datum is essentially a *cognizing,* and more specifically, a cognizing of the kind, described in this chapter, which I have proposed to call an "intuiting." That is, a sense datum is not an *object* of consciousness but a *content* of consciousness — a determinate *modulation of consciousness itself;* and more specifically, a determinate modulation of the species of consciousness called "sensing." Consider, for example, a certain one of the completely determinate blues — say, blue of precisely the hue, brightness, and saturation of the blue I intuit as I now look at a certain spot on my tie; and let us agree to call that *infima species* of blue, say, "arral blue." The sense datum I have as I look at that spot is then a being-conscious *sensingly,* and further *bluely,* and still further *arrally-bluely.* A sense datum, thus, is a being-conscious, determinately adverbiated in a certain manner such as just illustrated.

Now, two things need to be noticed. One is that if, for example, someone says to me: "John wore a blue tie with his bathing suit," the sound of the word "blue" instantly causes in me a certain psychological event, namely, occurrence of a certain "abstract idea," the occurring of which as effect of hearing (or seeing) the word "blue" constitutes *understanding* this word. Under certain other circumstances, hearing the word "blue" might cause me in addition to intuit (imaginally) some determinate blue; but my understanding the word "blue," which occurs instantly when I hear it, does not consist in or depend on this. For this would constitute passing from the abstract, *i.e.,* determinable, idea which is the psychological meaning of the word "blue," to a particular one of the determinates under it. Such an activity would constitute imagining a concrete example of what one has abstractly conceived.

The second thing to be noticed is that the converse of what has just been described can and does occur, and that this is what disposes of the "speckled hen" kind of problem. More specifically, it is quite possible and indeed common to intuit some determinate blue, and yet *not engage on that occasion in the different and additional mental activity of classifying what one is intuiting, i.e.,* of deciding the (possible) question whether the determinate quality being intuited belongs under the determinable called "blue." To intuit a determinate color, or a determinate numerousness, is one thing; and it is quite another thing to judge whether that determinate color is classifiable as "a blue," or that determinate numerousness classifiable as "many." This second thing may not, and often does not, occur at all when the first occurs.

Moreover, judging whether the determinate color intuited is classifiable as "a blue" is easier and more likely to occur spontaneously than is judging whether it is classifiable, less indeterminately, as "a cerulean blue"; and this in turn easier and more likely to occur of itself than is judging whether it is classifiable, determinately, as "arral blue." Similarly, judging whether the determinate numerousness intuited in the case of the speckles is classifiable as "many" is easier and more likely to occur spontaneously than is judging whether it is classifiable, less indeterminately, as "two or three dozen"; and this in turn, than judging whether the intuited determinate numerousness is classifiable, determinately, as 47. Thus, it is perfectly possible that (*a*) one should be *sensing* a determinate numerousness of speckles; (*b*) that one should also be *judging* that this numerousness is classifiable as "large," *i.e.*, as "a manyness"; and yet (*c*) that one should *not also be judging* whether or not it is classifiable, determinately, as 47. For when the determinate numerousness sensed is as large as this, to judge which of the numerals is its appropriate verbal tag is *to count;* and the counting judgment — the matching of each of the speckles sensed with one and only one of the numerals up to and including "47" — may not, and ordinarily does not, occur at all. On the other hand, when the determinate numerousness sensed is very small — for example, is twoness, or threeness — then judging that the numeral which is its proper tag is "2," or "3," is practically automatic. Even then, however, *sensing* twoness is one psychological process, and *tagging* the twoness sensed with the numeral "2" or the word "two" is another psychological process. The tagging operation (whether the numerousness tagged be small or large) does not discover within the sense datum a character until then hidden. What it discovers is a relation, *viz.*, that of equality between the determinate numerousness sensed and the determinate numerousness of the collection of numerals up to and including the numeral "47."

This, I assume, is essentially what Price, in his review of Ayer's book, has in mind when (p. 288) he says that "there is a difference between being acquainted with something and verifying a proposition about it." Chisholm comments that "questions about the psychological machinery of cognition are not relevant to the . . . problem, for we are concerned, not with the nature of the act, if there is such, by which we apprehend and judge the number of speckles, but with its general reliability and with what is thus apprehended" (p. 370). But the distinction made is not between two different possible psychological processes for the cognition of one objective fact distinct from both, but between two psychological facts — one, a determinate *sensing,* and the other, a *classificatory judging* of that determinate sensing. Both, indeed, are cognizings, but of different sorts; and whereas the first has no "object" but a "content," *i.e.,* as defined earlier in this chapter, a cognitum connate with that sensing; the second, on the other hand, has an "object," *i.e.,* a cognitum alien to, not connate with, that judging activity — this object of the judging consisting of the content of that sensing.

Chisholm, it should be noticed, begs the question when he speaks of (italics mine): "*the* act — by which we *apprehend and judge* the number of speckles." For *two* acts, or at least two processes, are what we have if we not only "apprehend" but also "judge." The apprehending, *i.e.,* the sensing or intuiting, is not itself a judging at all, whether "basic" or not. He defines a basic judgment as belief or disbelief of a basic proposition, and "basic proposition" as synonymous with "sense-statement." But a *sensing* is not belief or disbelief of any *statement;* words do not enter into the sensing itself. They enter only when one attempts to *state* the content of one's sensing; and to state it is to utter, or at least think of, certain words (whose meaning had antecedently been fixed), which one judges applicable to that content.

Chapter 14

WHAT IS MENTAL?

So long as the distinction between experiencing and experienced does not receive the critical examination to which we have subjected it, Alexander's hypothesis that it defines the difference between mental and nonmental appears plausible. As we have seen, however, Alexander is able to avoid contradiction only by availing himself of the distinction between connate and alien *-eds*, and this entails that the definition of mental "acts" and nonmental "objects" in terms simply of the distinction between experiencing and experienced has to be abandoned; for it was the unqualified statement that in experience "the *-ed* is nonmental," which, together with the fact that all mental acts are *experienceds* as well as *experiencings*, gave rise to contradiction. To avoid it, that unqualified statement has to be replaced by the qualified one that the experienced is nonmental only when it is alien to the experiencing,[1] and is on the contrary mental when it is connate with the experiencing. But although Alexander himself uses the distinction between connate and "objective" (*i.e.,* alien) accusatives to avoid the contradiction mentioned, he does not heed its implications or appear to have even considered them, for he rests his contention that sensa are nonmental merely on the fact that sensa are *-eds,* whereas, to support that contention, what would have had to be shown is that sensa are *-eds* of the alien not the connate sort. In Chapter 13, however, compelling reasons were given for believing that the bitters, the blues, and all the other sensa

---

[1] Although, as we shall see, not always even then.

are connate not alien accusatives of tasting, seeing, and the other species of sensing; and therefore that the *esse* of sensa consists in the sensing.

This state of affairs, it is interesting to note, would be exactly expressed by saying that sensa are *sensations*. Hence, the fact that the word common usage employs is "sensations" does not evidence, as some have alleged, a common failure to distinguish between the sensing process and *objects* of it, called "sensa" — a distinction which, we have seen, is invalid. Common usage evidences on the contrary a sound even if unanalyzed recognition that sensa are but completely determinate forms of sensing. I shall therefore not hesitate, from this point on, to use the ordinary word "sensations" rather than "sensa"; for the former correctly expresses the true state of affairs, whereas the latter only tends to imbed in language the radical error which the meaning commonly attached to the word "sensa" constitutes.[2]

1. The Basic Criterion of the Mental

If in Chapter 13 we succeeded in establishing that sensa are sensations and are mental, the point has then been reached where the implications of the manner in which we established it can be stated in the form of a positive account of the nature of the mental, of introspection, and of "inspection."

We need to remember first, however, that it is hardly possible to discern and formulate the differentiating character either of the mental or of the physical unless one duly heeds the distinction between primitive and derivative facts; for what is basic for that purpose is the character which differentiates the primitive mental facts, or the primitive physical facts. The derivative facts, on the other hand, are reckoned as mental or as physical not through detection also in them of the character which identifies the primi-

---

[2] Cf. the errors — by this time, however, innocuous because recognized — similarly incorporated in language by such words as *duodenum* (*viz.,* that the part of the digestive tract it denotes is twelve inches long) or *melancholia* (*viz.,* that the state of mind so labelled is caused by black bile).

tives as mental or as physical; but, originally and in most cases only, because they are derivatives from primitives that were themselves somehow already identified as mental, or as physical.

Keeping in mind these considerations as well as the outcome of the preceding chapter, we are now able to define the basic criterion of the mental or psychical by saying that *if something being experienced is connate with the experiencing of it, then it is a mental primitive.* It may be well to emphasize at this point that such an accusative of experiencing may but need not be *noetic* in kind as, essentially, it would be whenever it happened to be a sensation, an image, a percept, or a concept. It may be instead essentially *conational, i.e.,* be a volition, a desire, an impulse, or an attitude; or again, it may be essentially *affective, i.e.,* be an emotion, a passion, a feeling, or a mood.

All these mental processes, however, are mental primitives as identified by the criterion just given; but there are also mental derivatives. The physical world, let it be remembered, includes not only perceptually public facts — which are its primitives — but in addition many other things, such as laws, various kinds of particles, energy, etc., which are not themselves perceptually public but are implicit in what is so, and knowledge of which is derived from what is so by inductive abstraction, by theoretical construction, or by interpretation of perceived facts in some other scientific manner. In the case of the psychical world, the situation is similar. In addition to the various introspectively observable processes mentioned above — which are psychical primitives — it includes also such things as habits, dispositions, aptitudes, latent memories. All these are *properties* (whether native or acquired) of minds, just as fusibility, ductility, elasticity, etc., are properties of certain physical substances; for a property, whether physical or psychical, is an "if . . . then . . ." sort of thing and thus is not itself directly observable, although knowledge of it is derivative, inductively, from events which are observed.

The mental, moreover, doubtless includes also much beyond this — in particular, subconscious or unconscious constituents. Unfortunately, psychological theory, as compared with physical theory, is still in its infancy, and therefore what it tells us about the subconscious or unconscious is as yet crude, fragmentary, and unreliable as compared with what physical theory tells us about the submicroscopic. But what must be emphasized here as strongly as possible is that to restrict the mental — as many psychologists think one should — to what introspective observation is able to find would be very naive — as naive as it would be to restrict the physical to what observation of the perceptually public is able to find; for it would be to recognize only the primitive facts of either realm. The truth is that invention of theoretical entities, for the purpose of explaining facts empirically ascertained but not empirically explainable, is quite as scientifically legitimate and as necessary in the case of the psychical as in that of the physical — provided, however, that the realness of the invented theoretical entities is tested in the former case, as normally it is in the latter, by trial of their capacity to serve as instruments for the making of inferences that eventual observation verifies.

2. Intuition, Introspection, Inspection, and Sensations

The meaning of the basic term *mental* (or psychical) having now been analyzed, definitions of a number of related other terms may next be offered.

One of these is *intuition*. I shall use it to mean at once the experiencing of an accusative connate with the experiencing, and that accusative itself; for, as the argument of the preceding chapter has shown, that which is intuited on a given occasion is the determinate nature which the very intuiting has on that occasion. "Intuiting," or "an intuition," is thus a broad term meaning occurrence of a mental primitive — occurrence of an event of the kind where *esse* is *percipi*.

Intuition, however, may be clear (attentive) or, in various degrees, obscure. That is, awareness of mental facts, like awareness of physical, ordinarily has a focus and a margin, and the contrast between focus and margin may be relatively sharp, or on the contrary gradual. *Introspection* then is intuition in so far as attentive; and *inspection,* if one wishes to distinguish it from introspection in general, would be intuition of the particular kind called sensation, in so far as attentive.

Sensations, or more broadly mental "impressions" (Hume's term), may be defined as those intuitions whose proximate cause is not some other intuition, or at least not some other intuition in the same mind. Perhaps there are no other mental impressions, in this sense, than those ordinarily called sensations, but considerable evidence exists that, occasionally, "telepathy" takes place, and if so the process induced in a given mind "telepathically" by another mind would be a kind of mental impression different from those commonly called sensations.

To this definition of "a sensation" it might be objected that sensations, for example certain kinesthetic ones, are sometimes caused by an intuition in the same mind, for example, by a volition to flex the arm. In such cases, however, the causation is not proximate but remote. What the volition proximately causes is the muscle contractions, or more strictly the nerve currents that cause them; and the contractions, or more strictly the nerve currents they cause, are the proximate cause of the kinesthetic sensations. The case is thus essentially similar to one where volition to experience, say, the sensation called sweet taste causes one to open a box of candy, pick out a piece, and put it on the tongue. Both are cases where a psychical event causes another psychical event remotely, through an intermediary chain of physical causations. The only difference is that, in the latter case, the chain is longer and includes some events outside the body.

A number of other terms — activity, response, voluntary and involuntary activity, deliberate and cursory volition, voluntary and involuntary deed —which necessarily enter into any discussion of either mental or bodily processes, were defined earlier in connection with our inquiry into the nature of freedom of efficacy.[3] We need add here to the list only the term *mental habit* — a mental habit being an acquired causal connection in a given mind between mental events of given kinds. That is, a mental habit consists in this, that occurrence of a mental event of a kind A in a mental context of a kind B regularly causes proximately occurrence of a mental event of a kind C.

3. The Possibility of Introspective Analysis

In connection with these remarks and with those made in Section 23 of the preceding chapter concerning the problem of the speckled hen, it is necessary to consider explicitly the question whether, or rather in what sense, introspective analysis of one's mental processes is possible. Some writers have alleged that it is not possible because, for one thing, to be feeling, say, hunger is one mental state, and to be interested in and perhaps trying to analyze that feeling is another and different mental state; so that the feeling which is the topic of interest when the latter is occurring is then past, and what is actually being introspected is only one's memory of it. Again, it has been contended that introspective analysis is impossible because analytical attention to a mental state automatically alters its nature; for example, analytical attention to one's anger alters or even terminates the anger.

This contention, however, is paradoxical, for it tacitly presupposes the possibility of what it explicitly declares impossible: if one indeed knows that analytical introspection of one's mental state alters its nature, it is only by analytical introspection that one

---

[3] Chapter 11, Sec. 9.

can have discovered this, and such introspection is then genuinely possible.

Again, if what one is presently analyzing introspectively is only a memory of a mental state already past, that memory itself, at least, is *present;* and if it is possible to be analyzing it introspectively while it is present, no reason appears why this should not be equally possible when a present feeling, *e.g.,* hunger, instead of a present memory, is concerned.

Moreover, it would follow from the allegation that the statement "I am hungry" would *always* be a misstatement of a fact which would be correctly statable only as "I was hungry." I submit, however, that when one says "I am hungry" one does *not* mean "I was hungry." There is a certain state of affairs for the reporting of which the statement "I am hungry" is the correct one in English; and also a different state of affairs, which in English is correctly reported as "I was hungry." The semanticist's business is not to deny this because it is inconsistent with some arbitrary conception he may have of what "introspective analysis" means; his business is to examine the difference between the two states of affairs the two statements respectively report, and then to formulate an account of the nature of introspective analysis that will be consistent with the manner in which the information each statement reports is actually obtained.

At all events, even in instances where what is analytically introspected really is only a present memory of some past mental state, even then, in so far as the present memory is faithful, whatever analytical introspection reveals in it is then also true of the mental state itself of which it is a memory; just as, if a photograph of a man's profile shows a so-called Roman nose, it follows if the photograph is faithful that the man himself had a Roman nose. The question as to whether, or how far, or when, memory is faithful is of course interesting and important;[4] but it is not

---

[4] Concerning this question, see C. I. Lewis's *An Analysis of Knowledge and Valuation,* Ch. XI passim.

relevant at this point since the ordinary assumptions concerning it are made alike by those who assert and by those who deny that only memories of one's mental states can be introspectively analyzed.

The tacit but false assumption which underlies the contention that only memories of mental states already past can be introspectively analyzed is that mental events have no duration at all but are instantaneous, and that two or more mental events cannot be simultaneous either wholly or in part. The truth is, on the contrary, that, as emphasized earlier, mental events — for instance, experience of the feeling called hunger, and likewise occurrence of the process called analytical introspection — do, like all other events, *take time;* that is, they are not instantaneous but all occupy some segment of time. Hence, "the present time" means in this connection not the mathematical, strictly durationless present, but the psychological, so-called specious present, which comprises always a segment, not a single point, of time. It follows that no contradiction is involved in the contention that some mental events overlap others in time; for instance, that analytical introspection of the hunger feeling begins *after* the beginning of the feeling, and takes place *while* the feeling itself, not a memory of it, is still present.

Finally, with regard to the nature of the process of analytical introspection itself, I submit that it is what I described in the section of the preceding chapter devoted to the problem of the speckled hen, namely, it is intuition *plus conceptualization* of such features of the intuition as one is curious about. The conceptualizing, as described in detail in that section, is what the analyzing consists in.

4. Epistemological Introspection

Broad points out that there is a difference between analyzing, for instance, one's perceiving-a-penny, and recognizing that the perceiving (whether veridical or not) refers to a certain "epistemological object," *i.e.*, recognizing what sort of thing it is which we are perceiving. The analysis of perceiving is, he would say, based on "psychological" introspection; but recognition of what kind of thing it is that we perceive should be called "epistemological" introspection if it be introspection at all.

Broad, however, believes that the alleged epistemological introspection turns out to consist of two parts. One part, which is not introspection at all, consists of "the statement in words of certain propositions which are judged or supposed," or in accordance with which we adjusted ourselves or acted. These propositions determine the "epistemological object" of the situation, *e.g.*, what we understand by a penny. The other part, which is a case of psychological introspection, consists of attention to our attitude towards these propositions and to the relations of that attitude to the other factors of the perceptual situation. But, Broad adds, "the recognition that the situation has such and such an epistemological object is not an additional cognitive process which may or may not be superinduced on the original situation; it is an essential part of the original situation itself . . . we cannot help knowing what we are judging," although we may find it difficult to state it accurately.[5]

It is quite true, of course, that, when we judge or perceive or desire, we know what we judge the thing judged to be, or what we perceive it to be, or what our desire is desire of. We do know, for instance, what we mean by "a penny" when we judge or perceive that something is a penny, or desire a penny. But this does not settle what is here the essential question, *viz.*, Of what specific sort is this knowledge we have of it? Is it introspective, or inspective, or inferential? And is it formulated knowledge, or unformulated? Nor does it settle the question as to whether it is by introspective observation, or otherwise, that we are able to clarify our knowledge of *what we mean* by "a penny," or of

---

[5] C. D. Broad, *The Mind and Its Place in Nature*, p. 292.

what a certain elliptical brown patch *means to us,* sufficiently to describe this meaning.

Now, it seems to me obvious that the meaning which the word "penny" has for me, or equally the meaning which the sight of a certain sort of brown elliptical patch has for me, is something which I know and can know only in the manner I have proposed above to call intuition. For the psychological *meaning for me* of a word, *e.g.,* of the word "penny," or equally of a certain sort of brown elliptical patch, consists in a specific sort of mental event regularly caused to occur in my mind by the sound or sight of that word or by the sight of such a patch; and the nature of that specific mental event at the moment it occurs is itself known to me intuitively, just as is the nature of any other mental event of mine at the moment of its occurrence. Moreover, if I am asked to *state* what the word "penny" means to me, I find that in order to do so the instances of my psychological response to the word "penny," of which I must avail myself, are instances where that response is focal rather than marginal, *i.e.,* attentive rather than inattentive; and attentive intuition is introspection. To illustrate: If someone says to me, "I was hungry but there wasn't a penny in my purse," I understand his statement and, among the words of it, the word "penny." But in such a case the psychological event — the intuition — which occurs in response to that word, is marginal not focal in my attention, and is therefore of but little utility for the purpose of translating it into concepts and stating the translation. On the other hand, if someone says to me instead, "translate into concepts the intuition caused in you by the word *penny,*" then the intuition caused in me by this word *as so uttered* is focal in my attention, and therefore relatively easy to translate into statable concepts. Thus, it is by introspection — by intuition in instances where it is attentive — that I *observe* the likenesses and differences between the meaning to me of the word "penny," and that of the words "dime," "shilling," "coin," etc., and these introspected likenesses and differences are what I then attempt to conceptualize and state in the form of a definition of "penny."

I conclude, then, that there is a process rightly called epistemological intuition and, in so far as attentive, epistemological introspection: *Intuition and introspection are epistemological whenever the mental event intuited or introspected has the psychological status of "meaning of" some other mental event.* As emphasized above, formulation in language of the content of epistemological introspection is something additional. To know what phrase would accurately formulate it is to know, no longer merely ingenuously but now also analytically, what the given word, or odor, or sight, etc., means to us.

5. The Allegation of Direct Acquaintance with "Universals"

Some philosophers believe they have "knowledge by acquaintance" of "universals" — the universals allegedly so known being objective in some such sense as Plato's. But the truth is that the direct scrutiny of them, which they assert they are able to make, is only epistemological introspection as just defined; that is, the analysis of a given "universal," which they are able to make on the basis of direct observation, is analysis solely of the abstract *idea* in their minds, connected with the name of the "universal" concerned — it is analysis of the *meaning to them* of that name. Were the scrutiny on the contrary, as they believe, direct scrutiny of an *objective* universal, then it should be capable of revealing to them in the case, say, of the universal, "silver," its various component properties; for example, that it is ductile, is a good conductor of electricity, etc. But the alleged direct "acquaintance" with and observation of that universal is of course quite incapable of finding in it these properties unless one has previously obtained knowledge of them by physical experiment with particulars or from a book, and incorporated that knowledge into one's *idea* of the nature of silver; for it is only one's idea of it which later one is directly scrutinizing.

Two things are responsible for such plausibility as attaches at first sight to the allegation that direct scrutiny of objective universals is possible. The first is the practice of applying the noun "universals" both to general *ideas* and to the general *objects or objective characters* the ideas are of. The second is the choosing as examples universals such as "red" and "color" which, as we have shown but is commonly overlooked, are *contents* not *objects* of consciousness, and which — because their being consists in their being thought — can be scrutinized directly. But the direct acquaintance, which is a fact in the case of the universals that are contents of consciousness, is a myth in the case of objective universals. These are knowable only indirectly and imperfectly by abstractive induction from the particulars in which they inhere.

6. Mental Objects

In the preceding chapter, the difference between *content* of consciousness and *object* of consciousness (or of awareness, or experience, etc.) was defined as that between an accusative connate with, and one alien to, the kind of mental process occurring at a given moment. The meaning of "connate with" was analyzed at length, but "alien to" was assigned no meaning other than "not connate with," although examples of alien accusatives were given sufficient to give an idea of the denotation of the term. An account of its meaning in positive terms is reserved for the next chapter, but at this point attention must be called to the fact that a *mental* event, *i.e.,* an *experienced* which is connate with the mental process occurring at the time and is thus *content* of consciousness, may *also* be alien to a mental process occurring at another time in the same mind, or to one occurring in another mind — thus being *object,* not content, of this other mental process. Hence, although the rule holds that if something being experienced is connate with the experiencing thereof it is mental, this does not entail that something necessarily is nonmental if it is alien to the experiencing of it: some *objects* of experience are mental, and others non-mental; for example, when I taste a bitter taste, the bitter taste being tasted is connate with the tasting occurring at the moment. It is therefore mental and is *content* of my consciousness at that moment. But when an hour later I remember the bitter taste I tasted an hour before, it is, although mental, nonetheless *object* of my consciousness at this later moment. The later mental process, *viz.,* the *remembering* process, has that taste as alien accusative, *i.e.,* as object; and, as connate accusative, *i.e.,* as *content,* has the remembrance being remembered (whose *object* is the taste the remembrance is of). Again, if — whether by empathy or inference — I can ever be said to know by interpretation of clues some mental state of another person, then the knowing of it constitutes a case where a mental state (*viz.,* one in another mind) is object, not content, of my knowing process.

Thus, the only mental events anyone intuits at a given moment are the ones occurring in his own mind at the moment. His own intuitions at other moments, and the intuitions of anyone else at any moment, are at the given moment not *contents* of his awareness but, if he is aware of them at all at that moment, *objects* of his awareness. On the other hand, there are objects of awareness, *e.g.,* of perception or of remembrance, which are not and were not mental, but physical. The tree being perceived, or the flood being remembered, would be examples. We now turn to the consideration of such objects.

Chapter 15

OBJECTIVE REFERENCE, OBJECTS, AND THE PERCEPTION OF NATURE

We experience the mental events occurring in our minds, and, as we have now seen, their existence consists in the experiencing of them; but we also experience, in a different sense, events and things which are "objective," and whose existence, common sense tells us, is independent of whether or not they are being experienced. Our task in this chapter is to inquire more particularly than we have yet done into the nature of experiencing in this second sense, into its relation to experiencing in the first sense, and into the meaning of the "objectivity" we ascribe to what is experienced in that second sense.

1. Some Statements of the Problem of Objective Reference

That many of our sensations and other mental states "refer to objects" is generally accepted; but it seems to many philosophers that this objective reference is paradoxical. How it is possible is therefore a question often regarded as perhaps the central one in the theory of knowledge. What the paradox is conceived to be may be shown by some illustrations.

W. Savery, for instance,[1] describes it as "the mystery of how a state in experience can report what lies beyond experience. . . . How can anything be the thought of something else? How can a mental state report not what it is, but what it is not?" And A.

---

[1] Savery, "On the Nature of Objective Reference," *Jour. of Philos.*, July 22, 1936.

O. Lovejoy[2] formulates the problem by saying that it "consists in that peculiarity of knowing which philosophers call 'meaning' or 'transcendent reference'; that is, in the fact that when we know we appear somehow to have within the field of our experience at a given moment objects which we must at the same time conceive as existing entirely outside that field — for example, as having their being at a time other than the time of the knowing of them."

The paradox is put most briefly by G. W. Cunningham[3] in the question, "If objects are outside of mind, how can they ever be known by it?" He goes on to remark, however, that the paradox "is based upon the assumption that the mind is sharply sundered from objects," and "when once this separation between mind and objects is made, the question concerning the possibility of knowledge of objects becomes inevitable," but also unanswerable. He believes he avoids it by maintaining that "the objective reference of judgment means that, in the act of knowing, mind and object are bound together and are not separate and distinct. Knowledge, then, is primarily a relation between mind and objects, and exists only when that relation exists. No object, then no judgment; no judgment, then no knowledge. How can the mind know objects? is a question which thus seems to be meaningless; it is impossible for the mind to know anything else but objects."

The comment suggests itself here, however, that if with Cunningham we say that whatever the mind knows is an object, then we are forced to distinguish between what might be called "subjective objects" (viz., states of mind, such as our feelings called pain, or nausea, or our conception of Julius Caesar, or of the 7th decimal of π, etc.) and "objective objects" (such as Julius Caesar himself, or the 7th decimal of π itself, etc.). The relation of the mind to "subjective objects" perhaps constitutes no problem,

[2] In a paper entitled "The Anomaly of Knowledge," *Univ. of Calif. Publications in Philosophy*, Vol. 4, 1923.

[3] Cunningham, *Problems of Philosophy*, Henry Holt & Co., New York, 1924, p. 102.

but the mind's relation to "objective objects" is in any case a radically different one and is the one specifically in view when "objective reference" is discussed. But Cunningham's quoted denial that mind and object are "sundered" when knowledge of an object is occurring, is only an assertion that at such times there is a relation, called knowing, between the mind and "objective objects." This may well be granted, but to have asserted it or granted it is not in the least to have described the specific nature of that relation. And elucidation of its nature and of the nature of its "objective-object" term is the very task with which the problem of "objective reference" confronts us. On the other hand, if the problem is formulated only as in the statements quoted from Lovejoy and Savery it is truly insoluble; for it then amounts to that of explaining how something *ex hypothesi* impossible nevertheless does occur.

2. The Proper Statement of the Problem

Proper formulation of the problem of objective reference is perhaps best approached in terms of the case of reference presented by our perception of physical objects, such as a book, a coin, etc. It will be useful in this connection to consider certain important passages in G. E. Moore's paper on "The Status of Sense Data,"[4] of which the following is a paraphrased summary: Moore there supposes himself to be looking at two coins flat on the ground at a distance from him, one of them a half-crown and the other a florin, and the half-crown so much farther away than the florin that the half-crown's visual image (its "visual sensible") is visibly smaller. Under these circumstances he, or anyone else similarly situated, would ordinarily assume that he knows — more specifically, perceives — certain objective facts, *e.g.,* that he is really seeing two coins, that although their sensible appearances are elliptical the coins are really circular, that the

---

[4] Moore, *Philosophical Studies,* pp. 185–90.

coins have another side and an inside, that the half-crown is really larger than the florin, and that both coins continue to exist if he ceases to look at them.   To know such facts under such circumstances is to "see," *i.e.,* to perceive visually, a physical object; and this is obviously "seeing" in a sense different from that in which "seeing" means merely to apprehend directly a "visual sensible."

In a case such as this, the knowledge Moore has of the objective facts mentioned is, he states, certainly "based, in the last resort, on experiences of mine consisting in the direct apprehension of sensibles and in the perception of relations between directly apprehended sensibles.   It is *based* on these, in at least this sense, that I should never have known any of these propositions [*i.e.,* any of these objective facts] if I had never directly apprehended any sensibles nor perceived any relations between them."

The fact pointed out by Moore in the last quoted sentence is, I believe, the one from which a right formulation of the problem of objective reference in perception must start.   Borrowing for the time being his term, "sensibles," I would state what I conceive that problem to be as follows: That apprehension of sensibles and of their relations is necessary to perception — and indeed even ultimately to conception — of "objective" facts of the kind mentioned implies that such "objective" facts are connected in some way with sensibles and the relations of sensibles.   The problem is then, just how are they connected.   Or we may put it otherwise as follows: "Objective" facts of the kind mentioned have to sensibles a certain relation R, such that unless sensibles were apprehended "objective" facts of that kind would not be known at all. The problem then is, what specifically is that relation R?   When we are in position to specify it, we shall then be in position to say that, in cases of the kind mentioned, to be "objective" is to have to sensibles the relation R.

This formulation of the problem, however, directly concerns only such objective reference as enters into perception.   To state the problem comprehensively we must, in the formulation of it, replace "sensibles" (*i.e.,* in ordinary language, "sensations") by the genus of which sensibles are but one species. For this genus I have already proposed the name "intuitions."

3. Two Possible Objections to the Proposed Formulation of the Problem

Before attacking the problem itself we must consider two objections which might be urged against the formulation of it just offered, for if they were well founded the problem as so formulated would be a pseudo problem. They are objections mentioned in connection with H. H. Price's theory of perception by L. E. Hahn in an article entitled "Neutral, Indubitable Sense-Data as the Starting Point for Theories of Perception."[5]

I shall not consider Hahn's contention that "sense-data" are not "neutral," for (although for reasons different from Hahn's) I agree they are not "neutral." I hold that they are mental, and in the two preceding chapters I have stated both what exactly I mean by this term, and what reasons I see for believing that this meaning is a true analysis of the implication the term has in its ordinary applications. The only two of Hahn's allegations with which I need to deal are that sense data are not indubitable, and that they are not the true starting point for a theory of perception. I begin with the latter.

Hahn writes: "If one accepts the pragmatic contention that in perception we start, not with sense-data as described by Mr. Price, but rather with empirical things, perceptually accepted objects, moreover, it becomes clear that sense data are not data *simpliciter,* but data abstracted out for a certain purpose." Now the words "what we start with in perception" (which occur also, and in this order, in the sentence following the one just quoted) are ambiguous: They may voice equally (*a*) the question as to what we start with when we set about *analyzing* the process of perceiving

---

[5] Hahn, in *Journal of Philosophy,* Vol. XXXVI, No. 2, October 1939.

objects; or (*b*) the question as to what the *process itself* of perceiving objects, starts with. Question (*a*) concerns the datum of the process of *analyzing* perception; and question (*b*) concerns the datum of the process of *perceiving*. The answer to question (*a*) is that instances of the perceiving of objects are the datum — the "raw material" — for the process of analyzing perception. This appears to be Hahn's contention, and to be what would here be meant by the pragmatist's contention that analysis must start *in medias res*, "where we are." It is, of course, quite correct *as regards analysis*. But the question which Price, I take it, and I myself, ask, is not question (*a*) but question (*b*); and the answer to it (which he and I contend is yielded by the analysis question (*a*) calls for) is that sense data are the datum — the "raw material" — for the process itself of perceiving objects. Hahn's discussion, unfortunately, does not clearly distinguish the two questions. Hence, his criticism of Price in the passage quoted amounts in fact only to this, that Price's answer to question (*b*) which is the one he was asking, is not the correct answer to question (*a*) which is the one Hahn is asking.

The problem any theory of perception attempts to solve is problem (*a*) above, *viz.*, that of *analyzing* the process called perception of objects. Its *datum* may be stated more fully as follows: There does occur a process, called perception of objects, of which the perceiving of a tomato, of a tree, of a piece of iron, etc., would be instances. This process is capable of succeeding or failing. Ordinarily, it succeeds and yields knowledge; but sometimes it fails and yields error. In the latter case that process is called, more specifically, illusory or hallucinatory perception; and in the former, veridical perception. The *quaesitum* of the problem, on the other hand, is: What exactly does the process of perceiving consist in generically? how does it differ in the cases where it yields error from those where it yields knowledge? and what is, in either set of cases, the datum — the "raw material" — which the process, called "perceiving," processes into "perception of an object"?

That the process is one of interpretation of certain clues — which are the data or "raw material" for it — would, I take it, be something the pragmatists would be the first to assert: the infant has to learn, through various later experiences, that what he saw when he first looked at a tomato was a tomato; for "to be a tomato" is to have a certain variety of characters (*e.g.*, a certain taste, a certain odor, etc.) other than and additional to the sort of visual appearance which, after experience, comes to serve as sign of them — as clue to their presence at times when they are not themselves being experienced.

Our question (*b*) above concerned the nature of these signs or clues, upon which the interpretive process called "perception of an object" proceeds. We answered it by saying that, ultimately, they consist of "sense data," *i.e.*, of sensations. But from Dewey's essay on "A Naturalistic Theory of Sense Perception"[6] to which Hahn refers, it may be gathered that what both he and Dewey would answer is that when an infant is confronted with, say, a tomato, he indeed does not perceive a tomato as such, but only a certain color and shape at a certain place; but that the color and shape he perceives are as truly objective as the tomato he eventually learns to perceive, although they are simple objects instead of complex like the tomato.

Such an answer, however, wholly ignores the distinction between the *quality* red, and the *property* red, and the consequent difference in the meaning of "seeing" or "perceiving" when one speaks of seeing or perceiving *red,* and of seeing or perceiving *something red, i.e.,* a red object. I maintain — in accordance, I have tried to show, with what common sense assumes — that seeing red, tasting bitter, etc., are modes or species of seeing, tasting, etc., and are experiences of subjective events, whereas

---

[6] In Dewey, *Philosophy and Civilization,* Minton Balch & Co., 1931.

seeing something red, tasting something bitter, etc., are experiences of objective facts. The truth or falsity of this contention cannot be decided by ignoring the difference between quality and property and asserting dogmatically that "seeing" red is perceiving an object, but only by furnishing some theory of the distinction between "objective" and "subjective."[7] This means that a theory of objectivity and objective reference is not just a piece of needless trouble which epistemologists other than pragmatists wish upon themselves, but is on the contrary something which the pragmatist, like anyone else, needs to fall back upon as soon as the propriety of his applications of the terms "object" or "objective" is challenged.

The next thing calling for comment is Hahn's statement that in perception sense data are "abstracted out for a certain purpose." Even apart from the ambiguity of "in perception" pointed out in what precedes, this statement of Hahn's misrepresents what in many cases is the true state of affairs. If, for example, someone behind me unexpectedly pricks my arm with a pin, the pain I feel thrusts itself on my attention by its own power without any need for me to "abstract it out" and irrespective of any epistemological or other purposes of mine. And the sense datum consisting of that pain is what I start with in perceiving that my arm has been pricked. Similarly, the loud sound sensation with which I start in perceiving thunder, or the bright light sensation with which I start in perceiving lightning, are patently not "abstracted out for a certain purpose" by me, but emerge spontaneously into my consciousness. They are not post-analytical data, but *pre-interpretational data*. Similar remarks apply to the many cases where smell or taste sensations, or feelings of thirst, hunger, itch, dizziness, etc., thrust themselves on our attention unsought and unexpected. We do not, for instance, first perceive a beetle crawling on the back of our own neck, and then "abstract out" from this objective

---

[7] The theory furnished, if it is not to constitute only a piece of linguistic anarchy, must, let us remember, fit the applications commonly made of these terms.

fact the feeling of itch; what in fact we do is the exact converse.

What is to be granted is only that in the majority of cases our interpreting of the sensation we experience is automatic and immediate, like our understanding of any familiar word such as "table." We do not first attend to the word, then wonder what it means, and then understand it. Rather, when we see or hear the word, understanding of it comes immediately, that is, without any interval whatever occupied perhaps with "effort to understand," as on the contrary occurs when the word is unfamiliar. In cases where the word is immediately understood, attention to the word itself does not normally occur without some purpose to abstract it out from the complex, already present, consisting of the word together with the understanding of it. Similar remarks apply when the interpretand, instead of being the word "table," is a set of visual sensations we have when, on a given occasion, we open our eyes. To understand these sensations is to "perceive an object" — perhaps a table; and the understanding of them may be again either immediate and automatic or, sometimes, delayed and the product of a more or less prolonged effort to understand what it is we see, *i.e.,* what these sensations mean.

Coming, lastly, to Hahn's contention that sense data are dubitable, it is unfortunate that he nowhere makes clear exactly what he contends is dubitable in connection with them. To return to the example used above — of the pain I feel if I have been stuck with a pin — I ask what exactly is dubitable on such an occasion. So far as I can see, only two things. One is the relations of what I am then feeling to various other facts; for instance what caused it. The other is whether the word "pain" is the correct one in English to describe the sort of feeling I feel. But obviously doubt as to the latter, or doubt as to the cause of my feeling, is not at all doubt of the "sense datum" consisting of the feeling itself which is then occurring no matter what its correct name or its cause may be. For me to doubt the feeling itself or the occurrence of it at the moment it is occurring — and similarly as regards the taste being tasted, the smell being smelled, etc., — is, I submit, quite impossible.

What is possible, of course, is to doubt whether the pain I feel or the taste I taste has a given epistemological status — perhaps one labelled "sense datum" by certain persons. Just that, for example, is what Dawes-Hicks doubts, whose doubt is mentioned by Hahn as proof that sense data "are dubitable." That is, as Dawes-Hicks himself makes clear, what he doubts is whether there are entities having the characters which for him are theoretically implied by the words "sense data." When I, on the other hand, assert that sense data are indubitable, I use the words "sense data" purely ostensively; that is, if I am asked what I mean by them, I answer, not by mentioning some stipulated set of characters, but by saying that I mean for instance a pain being felt, a taste being tasted, a smell being smelled, etc. And, I submit, it is simply absurd to speak of doubting *these* at the time they are being felt, tasted, smelled, etc. Any doubt present at that time is not *of* them but *about* them.

Let us, however, now return to the problem of objective reference itself.

4. Removal of Some Possible Sources of Confusion

Not a little of the difficulty presented by the problem arises from the fact that, in the cases one usually takes as examples, certain questions, other than and additional to that of the nature of objective reference, easily inject themselves without being recognized as other. This both greatly complicates the task one then actually attempts, and obscures the true nature of the problem of objective reference. To avoid such complications and confusions it is necessary at the outset to point out the principal of these other questions. Only thus can we isolate adequately for examination the problem of objective reference.

(*a*) One of these other questions is as to *whether the kind of object one perceives or thinks of exists*. For the nature of objectivity is one thing, and the existence of cases of a given objective kind is another thing. For example, when I think of a centaur my thought is not thought of a mental, subjective sort of entity, but is on the contrary thought of an objective, and a physical, kind of entity just as truly as when a horse is what I think of. Only, in the instance of the centaur cases of that kind of object do not exist, whereas in the instance of the horse cases of the kind do exist. On the other hand, *thinking of* something is a species of subjective activity, and a case of that activity exists at the moment I perform it whether what I think of be horse or centaur. Thus cases exist of kinds (*e.g.,* of the kind "thinking") which are not objective but subjective kinds; and on the other hand no cases exist of some kinds (*e.g.,* of the kind "centaur") which are objective kinds. Where perceiving instead of conceiving or imagining is concerned, the situation is similar. When for example the dipsomaniac "perceives" a pink elephant, his *perceiving, i.e.,* his act of interpreting as appearances of a physical object, the pink color and shape he intuits, is a mental activity and exists at the time he performs it. His perceiving, however, is not of a mental activity but of an entity of a kind just as truly both objective and physical as the kind of which he perceives cases when he watches the circus parade. Only, in the instance of the pink elephant, a case of the kind of physical object he perceives does not exist there and then and his perceiving is therefore classed as hallucinatory; whereas in the instance of the circus, cases of the kind of physical object he perceives do exist there and then and his perceiving is therefore classed as veridical.

(*b*) Another question, distinct from that of what it means to class the kind of entities called elephants (whether pink or gray) as objective, and distinct also from that of what it means for cases of an objective kind to exist, is the question as to *how we discover* whether a case of a kind of object we perceive does or does not there and then exist — for instance, how we discover that the pink elephants perceived do not exist, and the gray ones do. This question is not especially difficult to answer, for we need but observe how we actually proceed to remove such doubts as we may have on a given occasion as to the existence of the kind of object we perceive. At this point, however, we are not attempting to answer that question but only to make clear that it is distinct from that of the nature of objectivity.

(*c*) Another question also distinct from that of the nature of objectivity is the question whether a given kind of object is a kind of *physical* or of *mental* object. For although whatever kind is physical is objective, the converse is not universally true. As pointed out earlier, entities of a mental kind sometimes have subjective status and sometimes objective status: subjective always at the time of their occurrence for the mind of which they are part; but objective for that mind at all other times, *viz.*, when they are remembered, anticipated, or otherwise thought of, and objective also at all times for other minds thinking of them. For example, if I now remember having felt fear yesterday, my past fear experience is object of my present (and subjective) remembering activity. The fear, at the time of its occurrence, is subjective, for it is (subordinately) connate with the experiencing thereof; but when at a later time I am remembering it I cannot at that later time say of the fear remembered that it is now subjective, but only that it *was* subjective. Thus something which earlier had subjective status now has objective status, *viz.*, is object of present remembrance. But there are kinds of entities, classed by us now as objective, which never had nor ever will have subjective status for us. This is the case with all kinds of entities called physical.

(*d*) When objectivity is discussed in connection with perception, it is natural to take as examples of objective kinds of entities books, or pieces of iron, or trees, *i.e.,* instances of some kind of substance. But *objectivity must not be confused with substantiality* or with physical substantiality. For the realm of the objective includes not only kinds of substances but also kinds of events and of properties. Indeed, as we have seen, the various kinds of substances are analyzable into systems of properties, and properties themselves into regular connections between events of certain kinds. The notion of *event* is therefore epistemically the basic one. Hence, what we must now discover is what exactly it means to speak of an event as objective, for when we know this we shall know also what constitutes objectivity of properties and of substances.

Events are entities that occupy some segment of time or both some segment of time and some region of space. To say this, however, is not to say what an objective event is, for the question as to objectivity or subjectivity can be asked concerning times and places themselves also. It appears, therefore, that the nature of time and space and the relation of objective to subjective time and space are the first questions we must consider.

5. Intuited Time

Let us first consider intuited (or "sensible") time, which is what is called "subjective" time.

If we intuit a certain *quale* at a certain place, and also do *not* intuit it there, then we are intuiting *two times.*[8] The relation intuited between them is called *succession.* This experience constitutes a psychological "clock" of two beats, one positive and one negative — the negative, however, always having a quale of its own, which is "negative" only in the sense of negative of the other, that is, it is different from and exists instead of the other. The sets of positive and negative intuitions which are connected

---

[8] I use the term "a *quale*" as synonymous with the awkward term "a *what*" (as contrasted with "a *that*"). My use of "quale" is thus broader than that of C. I. Lewis, who means by it "sense quale" (*Mind and the World Order,* p. 60).

with physiological processes such as breathing and heartbeat constitute psychological clocks which beat throughout the bodied life
of a mind.

Of two times intuited as successive, one is called *earlier,* or
past relatively to the other; and the other *later,* or future relatively
to the one. Between the quale at one of them and the quale at
the other, there is always a quantitative difference in a peculiar
respect, which is not intensity and is not clearness in the sense in
which being clear means being attended to. This peculiar respect
of difference may be called, perhaps somewhat arbitrarily, *liveliness.* Of the two qualia, the one which is the livelier is called
later, and the other, *earlier.* The respect of difference here called
liveliness is not susceptible of analysis, but is identifiable without
difficulty. Suppose, for example, that the word "relatively" is
being heard. Then liveliness is the intuited character, of which,
at the time the syllable "ly" is heard, this syllable has most, the
syllable "tive" somewhat less, the syllable "a" still less, and the
syllable "rel" least, irrespective of what may be the loudness, *i.e.,*
the intensity, of any one of them. We might call this character
"recency" or "lateness," instead of "liveliness." If we do so,
however, we must be clear that these are but other names for a
peculiar simple character, which is intuited but cannot be defined;
for it is on the contrary only in terms of it that "nearness to the
present time" (which might be thought of as defining it) can
itself be defined: of several times the successiveness of which is
being intuited, the one whose quiddative content has *most* liveliness (or, if you will, is intuited as "latest" or most "recent") is
called *now,* or *strictly present;* and the times, preceding and
including it, over which extends the span of the intuition of successiveness, comprise what is called the *specious present.* Its
peculiarity is that the qualia occurring at the earlier parts of it
so persist — although with diminishing grades of "liveliness" or
"recency" — that they are intuited together with the quale occur-

ring at the strict present, and yet are intuited then as having begun earlier.

If two qualia are intuited as neither of them successive to the other, they are said to be intuited *simultaneously* or at the same time. If a quale is intuited as earlier than another, and no third quale is intuited as both later than the one and earlier than the other, then they are said to be intuited *at contiguous times* — the second quale being *immediately successive* to the first. Otherwise, the occurrence of either is said to be *separated by an interval of time* from that of the other.

If a given quale is intuited as simultaneous with every one of several other qualia, which are themselves intuited as at contiguously successive times, then the given quale is said to *persist, last, continue,* or *endure,* from (and including) the time of the first to (and including) the time of the last of these others (or throughout the time they take). And intuition of the time of the given quale is said to be intuition of a *duration,* a *segment of time,* a *quantity of time,* or *some* (*vs.* a) time. If, on the contrary, at the time at which we intuit a given quale we *do not* intuit simultaneously with *it* any two or more other qualia as at successive times, then intuition of the time of the given quale is said to be intuition of *an instant,* or *a* (*vs.* some) time. Intuition of an instant, that is to say, is intuition of the time of a quale not simultaneous with any intuited succession of other qualia.

Although the distinction between intuition of *a* time and of *some* time, *i.e.,* of an instant and of a duration, is indispensable and perfectly definite, it is nevertheless essentially relational; that is, intuition of the time at which a given quale is intuited is intuition either of a duration or of an instant according as, respectively, a succession of other qualia is, or on the contrary is not, intuited simultaneously with the given quale.[9]

Duration is neither intuitable, nor definable, otherwise than as

---

[9] An *absolute* or mathematical instant is the time of any quale which is conceived as, by stipulation, not simultaneous with any succession of other qualia.

simultaneity of some given quale with several beats of some
"clock." The question whether the beats of a given clock are
of equal duration therefore cannot be either defined or decided
otherwise than in terms of the beats of another clock beating
either faster or slower. The beats of the given clock are said to
be of equal duration if the same number of beats of a faster clock
are simultaneous with each one of the beats of the given clock;
or if the same number of beats of the given clock are simultaneous
with each beat of a slower clock. Theoretically, then, we can
take as *standard* clock any clock we choose, and then define and
decide the equality or inequality of duration of the beats of other
clocks by comparison with the standard clock. But with regard
to the standard clock itself, the question of equality or inequality
of duration of its beats is absurd (as implicitly denying that it is
the standard clock).

The fact that the earlier-later relation as it was defined is unsymmetrical is what gives *intuited* time an intrinsic direction.
Although we have not yet defined "physical" time, we may here
state parenthetically that physical time — the order of "physical"
events — has no intrinsic direction. A non-arbitrary direction can
be specified in it only by correlating it with intuited time, *i.e.*, only
in so far as physical time is *perceived*. Thus, inasmuch as "now"
or "the present time" is definable only in terms of a certain intuition (*viz.*, that of maximum "liveliness"), these words have no
applicability to physical time apart from correlation of it with
intuited time. In physical time itself, there is no past, present, or
future. Indeed, apart from such correlation, the terms "earlier"
and "later" cannot, for physical time, be given meaning except
relatively to some arbitrarily selected pair of physical times A and
B, with reference to which it is then true of a third time C that:
either C is beyond B from A; or C is beyond A from B; or C is
between A and B. We could then assign a physical meaning to
"earlier" and "later" in physical time by specifying, arbitrarily,

e.g., that any physical time *C* shall be called "later" than *A* if it is beyond *A from B,* or if we prefer, no less arbitrarily, if it is beyond *B from A.*

6. Objective Reference in the Remembrance or Expectation of Mental Events

The meaning of the principal time categories having now been analyzed in terms of intuitions we pass to objective reference in time, that is, to what occurs when one thinks of times other than those intuited in the specious present. These may be the times of mental events past or future to the specious present, or they may be the times of physical events. Discussion of the latter will be postponed until after space has been considered.

Examples of reference to mental events belonging to one's own mind that are objective, *i.e.,* that are other than those comprised in one's specious present and therefore are not *being* intuited, would be: remembering having worried, believing that one did worry, expecting that one will worry, etc. Several questions concerning such events present themselves. The first is as to just what it means to think of them *as past,* or *as future.* Another — which will be considered in the next chapter — concerns what exactly it is to *think of* instead of actually *experiencing* an event, no matter what its time; and, more particularly, how thinking of an event in the sense of *imagining* it differs from thinking of it in the sense of *conceiving* it abstractly. Still another question — to which we shall offer an answer here — has to do with the difference between *believing* that one has, say, worried, and *remembering* that one did worry.

The "reference" to objective times, which occurs in remembrance or expectation or in merely thinking of past or future times, depends on employment of the "before-after" relation. To think of an event as past, or as future, is to think of it, respectively, as *before* the earliest part of what is speciously present at the moment of such thinking, or as *after* the latest part of it, *i.e.,* after the part of it strictly present. Such employment of the "before-after" relation constitutes *reference* to past or to future; and this relation is available to us for this or any other employment because, as pointed out in the preceding section, we have previously intuited it within the specious present, where it orders the events comprised therein. This is our original experience of it, on which ultimately depends every use we make of it. Having experienced that relation there, we then *abstract* it from the specific events which happened to be its terms there, and we are then able to employ the abstract idea of it in the manner described above, which constitutes "reference" to past or future times.

Thus, to think of *having worried* is to think of — imagine or conceive — the kind of event called worrying, and think of it as occupying some (unspecified) time *before* what is speciously present at the moment of such thinking. To believe that one has worried is to think of one's having worried, and in addition *believe* what one is thus thinking of. In the case of *remembering* having worried, three factors additional to this enter. One is that the worrying one thinks of is not generic worrying but worrying *more specific in quality,* even if perhaps not completely so. Another factor is that, with this more or less specific nuance of worry (thought of, and believed to have been experienced in the past) are associated, *as context simultaneous with it in the past,* certain other also more or less specific kinds of experiences, and that this context too is being thought of. The third factor is that certain other likewise more or less specific kinds of experiences, associated with the worrying thought of *as antecedent and sequent context of it,* are also being thought of, thus making more or less determinate the place in past time to which it is referred. "Remembering" is what occurs when all these factors operate jointly.

The logically next step in our discussion of objective reference would be analysis of the space categories similarly in terms of the basic intuitions; but before we can do this, certain remarks concerning method, which have important bearing on the conduct of that analysis, must be introduced.

7. Remarks on Method, Relevant to the Discussion of Space Intuitions

In our discussion of space intuitions, we shall have to use *merely as names* certain phrases ordinarily used as descriptive, and a few words must be said at this point as to the legitimacy of this procedure.

Since in this chapter our task is to discover what it means to call a time, or a place, or an event, a relation, a substance, etc., "objective," then, obviously, the definition we seek of this cannot be framed in terms of entities themselves objective. It must be framed in terms of intuitions, and of relations among, or to, intuitions. But it might seem that this requirement is occasionally violated in what follows.

The situation, however, is this: Among the many species of intuition, only a few have names of their own — warmth, thirst, fear, lust, pain, bitter, etc. Because of this, when we consider a species of intuition which happens to be nameless, the only way to let someone else know which species we are considering is for us either (if we can) to employ an *object* adequate to cause in him at that moment an intuition of that species, or else to use a phrase that will cause him to think of that species; that is, either a phrase descriptive of the kind of *object* the presence of which would cause such an intuition in a normal person (*e.g.,* the odor "of roses," the taste "of cinnamon," etc.), or a phrase descriptive of the kind of *objective* occurrence in which would normally eventuate an intuition of the species concerned (*e.g.,* feeling "about to sneeze," feeling "like taking a walk in the woods," etc.).

Now, what must be emphasized is that, notwithstanding the nature of our task in what follows, it is perfectly legitimate for us to use such phrases there, provided we use them *merely as practical devices* for making someone else think of the species of intuition we desire him to consider — as legitimate as, for instance, it would be for us to put a rose under his nose and tell him that the species of intuition we speak of is the one he will experience if he now sniffs. Those phrases *as so used* are *virtual proper names,* for they function only as do tags. What, on the contrary, would be illegitimate for the purpose of this chapter would be to use them definitionally, as we should be doing if, for example, we were to say that being caused by the presence of a rose is the very essence of what we mean when we speak of "rose-odor" (whereas what we do mean is a certain species of odor itself, experience of which can, indeed, be caused in this way, but conceivably might and perhaps actually can be caused also in other ways).

This matter being clear, let us now address ourselves to the analysis of space intuitions.

8. Space in Terms of Tactual Intuition

The problem of the nature of objective space and of the relation of place-intuition to the perception of objective space is so difficult that we can hope to deal with it successfully only if we consider it first at the simplest imaginable level. Accordingly, we shall for the time being leave out of consideration altogether what is doubtless the favorite example of space-intuition and space-perception for all of us, *viz.,* the visual, and shall consider instead and by itself first the tactual.

Let us then place ourselves in imagination in the position of a person blind from birth — indeed, to simplify matters still more, devoid not only of visual sensations but also of all others except those called "pressure" sensations and "kinesthetic" sensations;[10] and let us consider how, out of these intuitive experiences, the

---

10 This is the first of the occasions on which we shall be using — legitimately, as pointed out in the preceding section — certain words (in this case "pressure" and "kinesthetic") not, as ordinarily, as descriptive of the kinds of stimuli causative of them, but merely as names of certain species of sensations.

conception and perception by him of a world both "objective" and "physical" would emerge.

Let us suppose that the pressure intuition occurring at a given time is of the kind we may call "right-index-finger-tip pressure."[11] Simultaneously with this intuition, we would be experiencing also an equally specific "right-arm" kinesthetic intuition complex; and what we must now note is that, from the two together, there emerges an intuition of particular *place* as being at the time "occupied" by a pressure intuition of that specific sort. If the kinesthetic intuition complex remained the same, but the particular quality of pressure intuition experienced were some other than the right-index-finger-tip one — say, the right-elbow-tip one — the particular place intuition we should then experience would also be a different one. And likewise, if the quality of pressure sensation remained the right-index-finger-tip one, but certain changes occurred in the kinesthetic intuition complex — say, it included the "raised-right-arm" quality of kinesthetic intuition, instead of the "hanging-right-arm" one — then the place intuition we should experience would again be a different one.[12] Thus place intuition does not consist of kinesthetic intuition nor of pressure intuition; rather, it is an *emergent* of the simultaneity of the two, and is *sui generis*. And to say that a given quality of pressure sensation "occupies" or is "at" a certain intuited place means that the given quality is one of the two components out of which emerges that place intuition or intuited place.[13]

---

[11] These words are here used only as, again, the *name* of a certain species of pressure intuition and not as descriptive of the sort of conditions under which it is experienced. All that is assumed here is the introspectively verifiable fact that "pressure" intuitions are somewhat unlike, as well as somewhat alike. For instance, if the tip of my nose, and the tip of my right-hand index, are both pressed in the same manner, the two sensations I get are introspectively alike enough to be both called by the same generic name (*viz.*, "pressure" sensations), but they are nevertheless qualitatively distinguishable just as a sensation of "red" is distinguishable from one of "blue," although both are sensations of "color."

[12] The meaning of place "on the body," and the distinction between it and place "relatively to the body," will be analyzed in due course.

[13] These two expressions, as we have seen, mean the same thing, although linguistic inertia suggests they do not; for an intuited place does not subsist in-

Place intuition, let it be noted, is originally "absolute" in the sense that, conceivably, a person might intuit one place, and his consciousness then be extinguished without its ever having included intuition of any other place and, *a fortiori,* without its ever having included intuition of the relation of the one place he intuits to any other.   Intuition of *space* is intuition of the relation of one place to other places, and is thus essentially relational; but intuition of a *place* is independent of intuition of any other place, although to it may be added intuition of its relation to some other intuited place.   Tactual intuition of the place which at a given moment we call "there" is prior not posterior to intuition of the relation of it to the place of our body at the moment.   What is said below concerning the discovery of "our own body" will make this evident.

A place is tactually intuited as *empty* if we have the same kinesthetic intuition complex as when it is intuited as occupied, but intuition of the specific pressure quality concerned has the inferior degree of intensity which gives it the status of "image" instead of that of "sensation."   If both the pressure and the kinesthetic intuitions have only imaginal status, then we are *imagining* the place they jointly determine.

If the right-index-finger-tip pressure intuition, for instance, persists while certain alterations are occurring in, for instance, the right-index-finger kinesthetic intuition complex, then the place first intuited after the original one is said to be *contiguous* with it, and what is intuited *while* these alterations are occurring is said to be *motion* of the right-index-finger-tip pressure intuition.[14]   The intuited places to which that right-index-finger-tip-pressure intuition is found susceptible of moving are classifiable, on the basis

---

dependently of the intuiting (as does, on the contrary, a physical place independently of the perceiving).   An intuited place is an intuiting "there-ly," or "here-ly," etc.

[14] Contiguity may also be defined in terms of a supposition somewhat different from the one made above: If pressure intuition persists but alters gradually in quality while the kinesthetic intuition complex remains unaltered, the place intuited first after the original one also is said to be contiguous with it.

of particular species of intuited alterations in the kinesthetic sensa-
tion-complex, as being "above" or "below," or/and "to the right"
or "to the left," or/and "nearer than" or "farther than," the
original place.[15] Intuited space, which is the relation of each
intuited place to every other, is in this manner discovered to be
three-dimensional.

The relations just named become known to us within what we
may call the "specious here," that is, known to us as between
places intuited within the duration of the already discussed
"specious now"; and — just as the before-after relation which
becomes known to us within the "specious now" enables us to
think of times "objective" in the sense of being times before or
after the "specious now" — so the above-below, nearer-farther,
contiguous-with, etc., relations (once they have been abstracted
by us from the "specious here" where we discovered them) enable
us to think of places that are objective in a similar sense, *viz.*, are
(for instance) farther than the place being intuited at the moment.

9. Comments on James's Criticism of Wundt's Theory of Space Perception

The theory of our intuition of space just outlined is in certain
respects similar to Wundt's view (which, however, he states in
terms of visual perception of space), that "we can ascribe a
spatial constitution only to *combinations* of retinal sensations with
those of movement. . . . In its psychological nature this is a process
of associative synthesis: it consists in the fusion of both groups of
sensations into a product, whose elementary components are no
longer separable from each other in idea."[16]

James dismisses this view on the ground that the "associative
synthesis" or "psychic fusion" or "combination" in which its

---

[15] These relations *originally* are dyadic, not triadic; that is, the intuited relation
of a place *A* to a place *B* is first *simply* (for instance) *nearer than*, and only later
if at all, nearer *to the place of my body* than —. The words "above," "below,"
"nearer than," etc., are here names, not adjectives, of certain sorts of intuited alterations of intuition.

[16] Quoted by Wm. James in his *Principles of Psychology*, Vol. II, pp. 277–8.

essence lies is "an unmeaning phrase." Yet the sort of process
to which the phrase refers is well recognized today under the
technical name of "emergence." James's offhand dismissal of it
as mythical appears especially blind in view of the fact that,
according to his own view of the emotions, an emotion would not
itself be anything but the emergent of a complex of visceral and
other sensations, none of which, admittedly, contain it. If he
were to adhere to the logic of his statement that "Retinal sensations *are* spatial; and were they not, no amount of 'synthesis' with
equally spaceless motor sensations could intelligibly make them
so," that logic would then compel him to say also that visceral
sensations must have anger as an element of them, for had they
not, no amount of synthesis with pectoral and other angerless
sensations could beget the feeling of anger. Indeed, by that
logic, James would be forced to say also that some of the parts
of an automobile must have the character of automobility for
otherwise no amount of synthesis with other parts equally lacking
it could beget it!

James's own view was that in each and every sensation, though
more developed in some than in others, there is discernible, beside
the element of intensity, also an "element of voluminousness,"
and that this element is *"the original sensation of space,* out of
which all the exact knowledge about space that we afterwards
come to have is woven by processes of discrimination, association,
and selection."[17]   The first comment this suggests is, of course,
that if there is no such thing as a "psychic synthesis" by which
the intuition of voluminousness could arise out of other intuitions,
then psychic analysis must be equally mythical, and no process of
"discrimination" can be called upon by James to explain how the
intuition of *e.g.,* place, could arise out of an intuition of voluminousness, which is distinctly *other* than that of place.

Again, when the word "volume" is used literally, it refers to

<hr>

[17] *Op cit.,* Vol. II, p. 135.

something susceptible of three-dimensional analysis. But when I have for example a sensation of sound, I find as impossible to discriminate in it an upper and a lower part, a near and a far, a right and a left, as I would to discriminate such parts in the feeling of anxiety, in the beauty of poetry, or in the science of logic. What is susceptible of such space-dimension analysis is always a set of contiguous places. Sound sensations have places, and a set of sound sensations at contiguous places would be susceptible of space-dimension analysis. But it is only if, while I intuit a sound, I *move* forward and backward, up and down, right and left, that I get the intuition of three dimensionality of the sound. Similarly, if I am enveloped by a uniform mist or smoke, or if, in the laboratory, I look at "film color," I do not get the intuition of voluminousness — three dimensionality — unless I alter the convergence, accommodation, and direction of my eyes (the color sensation remaining the while unaltered).

A sensation has extensity, whether one-, two-, or three-dimensional, only when it is intuited at several contiguous places simultaneously or within the specious present. The sound sensation, apart from intuition of motions back and forth, etc., by myself, does not, I submit, have voluminousness in any literal sense, any more than a so-called "high" tone is literally farther from the center of the earth than a "low" tone. In both cases, those terms are applicable only in some elliptical sense, involving, in the case of the greater so-called "voluminousness" of low tones, some sort of association with greater volume in the literal sense, just as in the case of "high" or "low" tones there is association with the fact that, in uttering them, the head is naturally tilted up, or down, respectively.

According to the analysis in the preceding section, our intuitions of place, of extensity, of volume, etc., are genuinely novel in the sense that the intuitions out of which they emerge are not themselves, *individually,* intuitions of place, extensity, etc. But although novel, those intuitions are not elementary but emergent; that is, their occurrence is strictly dependent upon the presence of certain other intuitions, whereas such intuitions as those of blue, of bitter, of pressure, etc., are not similarly dependent upon the presence of others and are in this sense elementary.

10. Physical Objectivity in Tactual Terms

Physical objectivity, like objectivity of, *e.g.,* our own past mental states, is to be defined in terms of a relation to certain of our intuitions. These, in the situation we have assumed to be ours, would necessarily be pressure and kinesthetic intuitions; but the relation concerned in the case of *physical* objectivity is not, as in the other case, merely that of "before-after," but is the *causal* relation.

It, too, is one the nature of which is first known to us through instances of it among our intuitions in the specious present, but it is important to realize that this is no reason for assuming that the causal relation can relate only terms consisting of intuitions. The use we shall make of this relation in defining physical objectivity would be illegitimate only if, with Hume, we were to define causation as a relation *among our impressions and images,* or, with Kant, as a form of synthesis the employment of which is valid *only within experience;*[18] but so to define it is only to restrict gratuitously its possible scope. All that the causal relation really presupposes concerning the nature of its terms is that they be *events* — that they be entities of the kind susceptible of taking place in time, or in both time and space — but not that the times and places concerned be subjective rather than objective ones, nor that the events there occurring be intuitions rather than of some

---

18 Kant's view that things-in-themselves *cause* our sensations (*e.g., Critique of Pure Reason,* Max Mueller's trans., p. 403) was early objected to on this ground by Jacobi and Schulze, and, as Höffding remarks (*Hist. of Philos.,* Vol. II, p. 61), "From Kant's standpoint, this objection admits of no answer."

other kind. For, let it be recalled, we found ourselves able to define "objective times" and "objective places" without making use of the causal relation, *viz.*, in terms of certain other relations (abstracted by us from the specious present) to certain intuitions; and as regards the events which may occur at these objective times and places, there is no reason why they should themselves *have to be* intuitive. Of course, it might be asked what sort of nature we are able to suppose a nonintuitive event to have, if, as we did, we start with intuitions only. The answer, as we shall see, is in terms of the causal relation.

Still proceeding under the supposition that we are limited to pressure and kinesthetic sensations, let us now develop in terms of that relation the account of the nature of physical objectivity just suggested.

Among our pressure sensations there would be some which could not be traced by us to any proximate cause consisting of some other of our intuitions (such perhaps as a volition), and, basically, a "physical" event would then mean for us an event *other than any of our intuitions, and having to these otherwise unexplained pressure intuitions the relation of cause to effect.* Neither more nor less than this is what, under our assumed limitation, we should mean by "being pressed by something," or "undergoing physical pressure." Thus, far from defining "pressure" intuition as the kind of intuition caused by the kind of physical event called pressure, *we are here on the contrary defining "physical pressure" as the kind of nonintuited event which causes intuition of the kind called "pressure" intuition.*

Our basic notion of a physical event is thus in part positive and in part merely negative: *positive* in that it is framed in terms of a relation already familiar to us, *viz.*, the causal relation, which is a relation between events; and in terms also of an effect-relatum consisting of an intuition, *viz.*, here a "pressure" intuition; but *negative* in that the event functioning as the other relatum, *viz.*, as the cause-relatum, is, aside from this, conceived by us only negatively, — only as being an event *other than* any intuition of ours.[19]

It may be asked how we can then ever know that there are events other than intuitive, or what their nature is. As regards the second question, the answer is that the *generic* nature of "physical" events — or at least of those which are basic to our conception of any other physical events — is the very one we have just been describing; and that to be a specific kind of such basic "physical" events similarly consists in being *a nonintuited event capable of causing a given specific sort of intuitive event.* For example, to be the sort of physical event called "physical pressure on us" is to be "a nonintuited event capable of causing in us the sensation called 'pressure'."

As regards the other question, *viz.,* how we can ever know that physical events as defined exist, the answer is that strictly speaking their existence has the same status as that of the universality of causation, namely as we attempted to show in Chapter 9, the status of fact analytically known. If, however, the demonstration there offered should be thought invalid, then the universality of causation — and therefore the existence of a cause in any instance where we do not actually observe one — would be only a postulate. But whether we know or only postulate that a given intuition which had no cause among our other intuitions nevertheless had some cause, in either case the question arises whether that knowledge or postulation is not wholly idle if the nature of that cause is conceived *merely* as "whatever event did cause the given intuition"; that is, if no other effect than the given intuition can be inferred from our conception of that cause. The

---

19 Although intuitions for which we find no cause among our other intuitions are what first lead us to postulate nonintuited events as causes for them, postulation of such events is extended to some other cases. If, for instance, intuition of a certain place causes pressure sensation at a given time, but does not do so at another time, we postulate a difference in nonintuited conditions between the two to account for the fact that the same effect does not both times result from intuition of the same place.

answer to this objection will appear farther on in some detail but is essentially to the effect that, in terms of physical events in the sense defined, physical properties and physical substances can be defined; that property and substance are predictive notions; and hence that the reality of the physical properties and substances we infer or postulate, and on the basis of which we predict intuitions not otherwise predictable, can be tested by observing whether these intuitions do or do not occur as predicted.

11. Perception of Physical Events

In any case, *perception of physical pressure,* as distinguished from intuition of the quality called "pressure," consists in *unformulated belief that an occurring pressure-intuition is being caused by an event which is not itself one of our intuitions* — such an event being what, basically, we mean by a *physical* event. If, throughout a given time, we are perceiving physical pressure as just defined, but the pressure-intuition involved alters gradually in quality, while the kinesthetic intuition-complex persists unchanged, what we are then perceiving is *motion* of physical pressure.

Perception of physical pressure, or of motion of it, is thus a special instance of what, in the next chapter, we shall describe generically as *interpretation.* Whether the interpretive process which figures in perception is to be described as "inference" is a matter of whether one wishes to reserve this term for interpretive activities that are discursive or, at least, that engage the attention. If so, perception is not inference. In the contrary case it is inference, but "telescoped" and unconscious or subconscious.[20] But in either case perception, like inference, involves passage from an *interpretand* (here, intuition of the pressure quality at an intuited place) to an *interpretant* (here, unformulated belief that that intuition is caused by a nonintuited event at a contiguous

---

20 Cf. the excellent discussion by W. T. Stace of "The Problem of Unreasoned Beliefs," *Mind,* Vol. LIV, Nos. 213, 214, Jan. and April 1945.

objective place). By an "unformulated" belief is here to be understood a belief which is not at the time put into words or other discursive symbols, either overtly or imaginally, but which is nonetheless occurrent; that is, not latent as are, on the contrary, those numberless beliefs of ours which at the time are not opera-tive (*e.g.,* my own belief, a moment ago wholly latent, that 7 times 12 is 84). A clear example, although one drawn from a different situation, of unformulated yet occurrent belief would be that in which a clerk unrolls paper to wrap a parcel: there comes a moment when he *believes* that the length unrolled is enough. But for this belief to occur and operate in him, there is not the least need that the words "This length is enough" should be uttered or even thought of by him. In fact, they seldom would be.

Whether perception of physical pressure, as defined above, is in a given case "veridical" or "hallucinatory," and what these terms themselves mean, is another question, but one which need not be considered at this point.

12. Perception of Physico-Psychical Properties, and of Physical Substance

As pointed out in an earlier chapter, the nature — the "what" — of any substance analyzes ultimately into a complex or set of complexes of properties; and properties themselves analyze into "if . . . then . . ." connections between kinds of events. Having just defined what (in terms of relation to the two kinds of sensa-tions to which we are assuming ourselves limited) a "physical event" basically consists in, we are now in position to define physical properties and perception of them; or at least to define the kind of physical properties, *viz., physico-psychical* properties, which are basic in the sense that, without them, perceptual or other knowledge of properties of the kind we shall call *physico-physical* would be impossible.

The only physico-psychical property which, under our assumed limitations, we could perceive would of course be tangibility.

Perception of it (whether "veridical" or "hallucinatory") would consist in *unformulated belief that, at an objective place contiguous with a certain intuited place at which pressure is at the moment intuited by us, there is occurring throughout a certain period a physical event which is such as to cause in us a pressure intuition whenever during that period we intuit that certain place;* that is, that objective place is believed by us to have during that period the *capacity* to cause pressure intuition in us whenever we intuit the certain place with which that objective place is contiguous. Such belief constitutes perception (whether "veridical" or not) of *tangibility of an objective place;* and this, under our assumed limitations, would be the same thing as perception of *something tangible,* as perception of *tangible substance,* and as perception of *a tangible objective place.*

Three remarks are called for by the preceding paragraph.

(*a*) The first has to do with the use of "perceiving" as applied not only to events, but also to properties (and substances). It was pointed out earlier that the perceiving of a physical *event* consists in the occurrence of a certain interpretive activity: an occurring intuition (which under our assumed limitations would be a pressure intuition) is interpreted as effect of some event that is not itself any of our intuitions. Now, the perceiving of a (physico-psychical) property consists in an additional act of interpretation: perception of a physical event one or more times at one place is interpreted as evidence that throughout a certain period that physical event is occurring there; that is, as evidence that whenever during that period we were to intuit the place contiguous with the place of that event, something occurring at the latter place would cause in us a (pressure) intuition. This additional act of interpretation is thus inductive — it is one of interpolation and extrapolation. It constitutes "perception" of the property, tangibility.

As to the propriety of terming it "perception," we need only point out that the case of tangibility is in this respect no different from that of, say, brittleness or elasticity; and that it is commonly regarded as perfectly proper to speak of *perceiving* the elasticity of a rubber band or the brittleness of a piece of glass. The essential point is thus only that although properties as well as events are "perceived," and although "perceiving" in both cases is interpreting, nevertheless what is interpreted, and the particular interpretation put upon it, are different in the two cases.

(*b*) The second remark to be made is that the adjectives corresponding to the various *physico-psychical* properties are predicable without incongruity not only of existing instances of physical substances, but also, and first, *of regions of space during a time*. Thus, for example, there is no incongruity in speaking of a warm place, a smelly place, a hard place, a dark place, or a noisy place; and these adjectives are predicable of places (during a time) not elliptically but literally. On the contrary, the adjectives corresponding to the various *physico-physical* properties are congruously predicable only of existing instances of physical substances: it would be incongruous to speak of a malleable place, or of a fusible, or ductile, or fragile place.

This entails that physical substances are necessarily conceived first, and basically, in terms of only their physico-psychical properties; and are of course perceived always through manifestness of one or another of such properties. How physico-physical properties are definable in terms of physico-psychical ones will be considered in detail in Section 13; but we can come to incorporate physico-physical properties into our concept of a physical substance only after we have observed how that substance affects or is affected by other physical substances. Hence we must have conceived and perceived physical substances *antecedently to, and therefore first independently of,* any knowledge or conception by us of such physico-physical properties as they may have; and this means, first in terms of only physico-psychical properties.

A physical substance thus may be conceived in one or another of three ways:

(1) in terms of *only* its physico-psychical properties. This is the original and basic conception.

(2) in terms of *both* its physico-psychical and its physico-physical properties. This is a later and richer conception.

(3) in terms of *only* its physico-physical properties. This is the conception employed by the physical sciences, and although incomplete it is all that is needed for their purposes. It is, of course, a conception that never could have been reached either by observation or by theoretical construction if physical substances, or at least some of them, had not possessed physico-psychical properties, since these alone make a physical substance observable. But so long as the only question asked (and it is the only one the physical sciences ask) is as to what physico-physical properties the various physical substances possess, only such properties need be listed in the answer. Physico-psychical properties are no part of the answer to that question, notwithstanding that, had it not been for them, that question could not have been answered at all.

(*c*) The third remark called for by the paragraph in which perception of tangibility was defined concerns the "contiguity of a physical place and an intuited place" referred to therein. *Prima facie* such contiguity may seem paradoxical, but the following considerations show that it is not really so.

We need to recall first that an "objective" place is an intuitable, though not at the moment intuited, place that is specified as having to a place intuited at that moment an ordinal relation of one or another of the kinds (*e.g.,* "beyond," or "next to," etc.) which we have been able some time to observe as obtaining between certain intuited places.

Now, to speak of an objective place as "physical" means only that we think of it as one where a "physical" event (as defined above) is occurring. At least, this is our first and basic conception of a physical place. As in the case of a physical substance, so here in the case of a physical place, we find three possible ways of conceiving it:

(1) in terms *only* of some specified ordinal relation of it to an intuited place. This is the way just described and it is the fundamental one.

(2) in terms *both* of its relations to some particular set of other physical places arbitrarily chosen as reference frame (coordinates), *and* of specification of these in terms of their relation to our intuited place, as in No. 1.

(3) in terms *only* of its relations to the physical places constituting such a reference frame; that is, without considering at all the question as to where these places are — a question which, ultimately, can be answered only in manner No. 1, but the answer to which need not be brought in if the only question being asked at the time is how a physical place one is speaking about is related *to that reference frame.* And, of course, this question is legitimate as far as it goes, even if, as will be pointed out in Section 15, the answer to it has no practical utility unless we know in addition (in way No. 1) where the reference frame itself is.

13. Perception of Physico-Physical Properties

Still under the limitations we have assumed, perception of change of physico-psychical property — specifically, of tangibility — can be defined, for this would consist in change from hardness to softness, or the converse, (or of smoothness to roughness, or the converse), and perception of such change is analyzable as interpretation (as described) of quantitative variations in pressure intuitions and kinesthetic intuitions. But now in terms of perception of changes in physico-psychical properties, we can define perception of *physico-physical* properties, *i.e.,* of properties in the case of which the "then . . ." term also (of the "if . . . then . . ." connection) consists of a *physical* event (instead of a psychical, as in physico-psychical properties). The definition would be as follows: If a given sort of change A of physico-psychical property at one place is observed to be regularly attended by a certain sort of change B of physico-psychical property at another place, then what is being observed is a physico-physical property. That is, the first place is being perceived to have, through a given period, this property: it is such that occurrence of a change of kind A of property there causes a change of kind B of property at the other place.[21]

It is observation of this sort of connection which provides us with our *basic* conception of physico-physical properties. But these in turn may conceivably be related by similar laws to certain others of themselves, and a law relating two physico-physical properties would describe the content of what might be called a *derivative* physico-physical property. In this way, physico-physical properties may be conceived, and be discovered, in the case of which the physico-psychical properties at the basis of the conception are quite lost sight of and forgotten, or deliberately abstracted from. But ultimate analysis of a physico-physical property can always exhibit them, since otherwise we could have no knowledge or even conception of it.

14. Which Perceived Body is "Our Own"?

Having now an account of the nature of tangible substance or body, and of the nature of (tactual) perception of it, we may next pass to an account (still in tactual terms only) of the distinction between "our own" body and other bodies. A body perceived is said to be "our own" if occurrence of the kinesthetic intuition complex involved in the perceiving results automatically in occurrence of a double, instead of a single, pressure sensation; for instance, in occurrence not of only a right-index-finger-tip-pressure

---

[21] A physico-physical property may concern one place only, the law constituting the property then being a law of coexistence (instead of a law of succession) of the two (or more) physico-psychical properties involved.

sensation, but also of, let us say, a middle-of-forehead-pressure sensation. Perception of the *shape* of the body we thus call "our own" is an additional step, as follows:

A shape is a set of places each of which is contiguous with some of the others. Intuition, within the specious present, of the variations (in, for instance, the "arm-and-hand" kinesthetic sensation complex) which yield uninterruptedly, say, the right-index-finger-tip-pressure sensation, yields to us the intuition of touch-shape; and this touch-shape intuition is the intuitive basis of perception (in the sense already defined) of tangible physical shape, *i.e.*, of the shape of a (tangible) body.

Any given one of these intuited variations in the kinesthetic sensation complex constitutes the intuitive basis of perception of the spatial relation (*i.e.*, distance plus direction) of the initially perceived place on the body touched to the place on it terminally perceived. It is in this way that (tactually) we discover the shape of, in particular, the body we call "our own" and the spatial relation to each other of any two or more places on it.

15. Physical Places of Origin

For each of us, some place or set of places on our own body is the basic or absolute physical "here" and the natural place of physical origin; that is, it is the place each of us has actually used as origin in developing knowledge of the places, and of the mutual relations of the places, of physical objects other than his own body. Of course, some origin other than this could be used; for instance, I could use the place now perceived by me of a certain corner of a certain desk as origin. That is, I could inquire only into the spatial relations to the place of that corner, of the places of physical bodies other than my own; thus, let us suppose, never even discovering the body called my own. When our purposes are purely natural-scientific we often use such conventional origins, *e.g.*, the pole star, the Greenwich meridian, etc. But it is to be noted that knowledge of the place of an object relatively to such conventional origins is wholly useless to us for any *practical* purpose unless supplemented by knowledge of the spatial relation of the used place of origin to the place of our own body at the time. For example, we could make no practical use whatever of a knowledge that an escaped tiger is at the moment in a clump of bushes 952 feet due north of the northernmost point of the city limits of New York unless we knew in addition the place of New York, and of the north, relatively to the place of our own body at the moment.

16. Enrichment of the Tactually Perceived Physical World on the Basis of Intuitions Other Than Tactual

Our assumed restriction to pressure and kinesthetic intuitions has now served its purpose and may be abandoned at this point. This will enrich for us the content of the perceived physical world, but will not in any way alter the nature of the general relation — described above specifically in terms of the minimal equipment we had assumed — of the world we call physical to the world of our intuitions.

Admission of the other sensations called "cutaneous" and their combinations, and of the sensations called "olfactory," "gustatory," "auditory," and "visual" will furnish the basis for perceptual additions which will together supply its familiar richness and complexity to the content of our perception of the physical world. Physical substances, for example, will then be perceived by us no longer merely as tangible, but also as having temperature, odor, sapidity, sound, color.

The manner in which the additional kinds of sensations furnish the basis for perception of such additional physical properties is essentially identical with that already considered in the case of pressure sensations and the perception of (tangible) substance. But, since our ordinary perception of the physical world is so largely visual, it will be appropriate now to take visual instead of pressure sensations as starting point, and to sketch again, but this time in terms of the former and more briefly, the relation of intuition to the perception of physical properties and substances; and also to make clear in what sense a physical substance tactually perceived and one visually perceived, or a place tactually intuited and one visually intuited, can be said to be "the same." Here again the problem has two parts: first, we must give an account of space in terms of visual intuitions, *i.e.,* more specifically, an account of the nature of visual place, direction, and distance, and of color-shape both two- and three-dimensional; and second, we must give an account, still in terms of intuitions and of relation to intuitions, of the nature of physical events, physical properties, and physical substances as visually perceived.

17. Space in Terms of Visual Intuitions

Here again the basic intuition is not vaguely of "space" but of place, and of place absolute in the sense already considered. As before it is the emergent of two factors, one of them consisting of kinesthetic intuitions; for color intuitions (including under color also white, black, and the grays), no less than pressure intuitions, are always accompanied by kinesthetic intuitions of certain characteristic kinds — specifically those we may call "eye-convergence," "eye-direction," and "eye-accommodation" intuitions.

The second factor, however, is one peculiar to visual intuitions: There is a certain character, admitting of degrees, which is possessed in superior degree by some of the constituents of the complex of color intuitions at any given moment, and in various inferior degrees by the other constituents. This peculiar character we may call *distinctness.* Identification of it will be easy if we state that, in the case of color constituents that have it in superior degree, we are able more readily and confidently to decide whether they are alike or unlike, to conceptualize them or their parts, etc., than in the case of constituents that have it in inferior degree.[22]

Now the basic intuition of visual place — the visual there-intuition — is the one which emerges from these two factors together: one, intuition of the superior distinctness of certain of the constituents of the color complex intuited at the moment, and the other, intuition of a complex of kinesthetic sensations of the kinds mentioned. Just this is what it means to say that the color constituents which are distinct are intuited as *at* a specific place, or that a specific place is intuited as *occupied* by the color constituents which are distinct at the moment.

If the given ocular kinesthetic intuition complex alters, then, from the one replacing it, together with the intuition of superior distinctness (no matter to what color intuitions it may attach at the moment), there emerges intuition of a "different" visual place. Intuition of the *quality and quantity of the change* in the given ocular kinesthetic intuition complex, through which is reached a certain other such complex, yields (as conjoined with intuition of superior distinctness) intuition of the specific "spatial relation" between the visual place initially intuited and that terminally intuited; that is, intuition of a "direction" and "distance" of the second from the first.

On the basis of the various qualities of change found possible in a given ocular kinesthetic intuition complex, the *directions* from the place intuited are classifiable as "above" or "below," or/and "to the right" or "to the left," or/and "nearer" and "farther." Intuition within the specious present of a number of contiguous places in one, two, or all three, of these dimensions yields to us the general intuition of *extent* and (in conjunction with intuition of the colors at the places intuited) intuition of one-, two-, or three-dimensional *color-shape*.

---

[22] Subsequently acquired knowledge of the eye and its structure permits us to say that the color intuitions possessing this superior distinctness at a given moment are those resulting from stimulation of the part of the retina called the fovea.

18. Intuition of Color Without Place or Extent

Intuition of absolute place (visual) was defined above as the emergent of, together, any given ocular kinesthetic intuition complex, and the character of superior distinctness attaching to some of the constituents of the color complex intuited at the moment. It may be asked, how then about the places of the color constituents that are *indistinct* at the moment? As to this I believe that originally, and perhaps in some measure even now, these indistinct color constituents are intuited without any place intuition, or therefore any extent intuition, attaching to them. This contention may appear paradoxical since we are now usually so conscious of the places, relatively to the place of the superiorly distinct color constituents, of some at least of the inferiorly distinct ones. Moreover, to some persons it appears obvious that if color is intuited at all it is intuited as extended.

To deal with the latter allegation first, I submit that it is possible to intuit color at a place within which we are unable to discriminate different places. Such a place, which constitutes a psychological *point,* is psychologically extensionless.

As regards the other objection, I believe that, when we intuit simultaneously a number of places as having certain relations to a given one, what takes place is that, within the specious present, there occurs in the kinesthetic complex the variety of alterations which are the bases for the intuition of the relations of those other places to the given one. These alterations in the ocular kinesthesia are susceptible of having either the degree of intensity that would determine us to call them "sensory," or the inferior intensity that would lead us rather to call them "imaginal." At least, this is what I believe occurs when the other places concerned are places in the "spread-out" dimensions as distinguished from the "third" or "nearer-farther" dimension.

In the case of the latter the quantities of change in the "convergence" and "accommodation" intuitions (which are the kinds at the basis of our intuitions of "nearer" and "farther") very early become associated with changes in the *degree of doubleness* of the "nearer" and "farther" color-shapes (and with kinds of disparity of portions of certain color-shapes in depth); and these are thereafter capable of arousing the intuitions of "nearer" and "farther" without actual occurrence of the changes in the "convergence" and "accommodation" kinesthesia that constitute the original bases of those intuitions.

That the intuition of depth, and even the intuition of spread-out-ness, although indeed each *sui generis,* are emergent rather than elementary may, I believe, be shown by performing the following simple experiment. If, while looking at a given thing at some distance from us we shut one eye (thus eliminating double images), we are immediately aware of a marked weakening of our intuition of the distances (in the third dimension) of other things relatively to the thing looked at. If we are careful to avoid moving the head or eyeball (so that no slightly disparate view arises that we could synthesize with the given one) and, by prolonging the contemplation, allow time for the fading of our consciousness of the nature of the objects having the color appearances we intuit, then very soon we find that all intuition of relative distances in the third dimension ceases. Moreover, if we prolong the contemplation, and are especially careful to *avoid attending to things in the periphery* (for attention to them is cheating since it involves, if not actual motions of the eyeball, at least alterations in the relative tensions of the eye muscles and corresponding changes in the kinesthetic intuitions) then we find that even the intuition of place-in-spread-out-ness relatively to the place of fixation ceases. Complete unchange of eye-muscle tensions for more than a very short time is difficult to achieve, and the experiment is therefore not easy to perform with full success; but a measure of success sufficient to give considerable support to the contention the experiment is intended to test is reasonably attainable.   It is especially necessary to bear in mind, however, that when we reach the point in the experiment where we ask ourselves whether the intuition of place-in-spread-out-ness has really ceased, what we find ourselves automatically doing in order to make sure is to attend to something peripheral — which means moving the eye or at least altering eye-muscle tensions — *and this is cheating;* for of course doing this does bring that intuition back, as the theory predicts it should.

19. Physical Objectivity in Visual and Other Terms

What now is the difference between intuiting color-shape — even three-dimensional color-shape — and perceiving a colored physical thing?   Here as before, introduction of the relation of cause and effect is the first step towards the answer.

Among our intuitions of color, just as among those of pressure, there are many for which we are unable to find a cause among our other intuitions.[23]   In these cases we infer or postulate as cause for them an event, conceived by us negatively as nonintuited, occurring (as the causal proximate relation demands) at a place contiguous with that at which the color is intuited.   Then in a manner exactly similar to that considered in the case of pressure intuitions and therefore in no need of being described again here, we pass from these nonintuited causal events to *properties* of the physico-psychical sort; and then to physical *substances* conceived first only as complexes of physico-psychical properties, and later also of physico-physical properties.   This passage depends only on the general relation between event, property, and substance, and on the postulation or knowledge that our intuitions have causes and that there are causal regularities, and not at all on whether the events concerned be causes of intuitions of the

---

23 Cf. Berkeley's statement in the *Principles of Human Knowledge:* "When in broad daylight I open my eyes, it is not in my power to choose whether I shall see or no, or to determine what particular objects shall present themselves to my view; and so likewise as to the hearing and other senses; the ideas imprinted on them are not creatures of my will."

pressure kind, or of the color kind, or some other. Thus, perception (solely in terms of color) of a physical substance having the *property* "being green" consists in (*a*) intuition of the *quality* green, plus (*b*) unformulated belief that immediately beyond the intuited place P occupied by the intuited green, there is occurring throughout a certain time a nonintuited event which is such as to cause us to intuit green whenever during that time we intuit place P. The green physical substance so perceived is thus simply a region of space (objective in the sense of *beyond* a certain intuited place) which, during a certain period, has the capacity to cause us to intuit the quality green.

The nonintuited events which cause our various sensations are eventually described by us in terms of the behavior of such occult entities as "molecules," "atoms," or "subatomic particles," which are postulated for the purpose (ultimately) of accounting for the specific sensations we do have on given occasions, and especially of enabling us to predict the sensations we shall have on certain other occasions. The definitions specifying the properties of the occult physical entities we postulate are at least — to use Karl Pearson's term — "conceptual shorthand." But if postulation that entities having these properties exist does enable us to make regularly true predictions, this is evidence that such entities *really* exist. For we may well ask in what else could possibly consist the difference between existing only in imagination and existing "really." I submit that if the hypothesis, for instance, that a given man is a scoundrel invariably enables us (in circumstances to which it is relevant) to predict successfully how he will behave, then he *really* is a scoundrel.

20. Visual Identification of the Body We Call "Our Own"

Among the variety of physical substances we perceive visually we distinguish one of them as being "our own body," and the next question is, on what basis do we do so; for in the case of visual perception no such mark is available to us as was provided by doubleness of pressure sensations when tactual differentiation of "our own" body from other bodies was the problem.

For visual identification of a perceived substance as being "our own body," we are fortunately able to lean on tactual identification of it. The manner in which we do so may be formulated in the following rules:

(1) If, simultaneously with visually perceived single contact between two visually perceived physical substances, there occurs regularly a *double* touch sensation then *both* of the visually perceived contacting substances are said to be (parts of) "our own body."

(2) If, simultaneously with visually perceived single contact between two visually perceived substances, there occurs regularly a *single* touch sensation, then *only one* of the two substances is said to be "our own body."

(3) Which of the two it is is determined by noting which one is such that, when contact of it with a third substance is visually perceived, a touch sensation (whether single or double) regularly occurs simultaneously.[24]

21. "Sameness" of Something Visually Perceived and Something Tactually Perceived

Perception of regular simultaneity of tactual perception of a substance, and of visual perception of contact between a part of our own body and a substance, is what constitutes perception of "sameness" of the tactually perceived substance and the visually perceived substance, and of "sameness" of the place of each. A similar criterion is used for identification as "the same" of substances perceived also otherwise than tactually and visually.

---

[24] These are the sorts of experiments we spontaneously make and the sorts of criteria we spontaneously use in learning to distinguish the body we call "our own" from other visually perceived substances. But obviously, at the time we learn it, which is very early, the experiments are not undertaken by us deliberately. They just happen to occur. Nor are the criteria we use formulated at the time. They merely are the sorts of differences there are to be observed between a certain physical body and all others.

Our own body as visually perceived by ourselves, and in particular the part of it which (except when it is "in the dark") is seen by us whenever we see anything else, *viz.,* our nose and orbital arch, is the physical object the place of which is used by us as natural place of visual origin, to which we refer directly or indirectly the visually perceived or conceived places of all other physical objects. The remarks made earlier concerning conventional origins, however, apply here also.

22. Externality to Our Body and Externality to Our Mind

When we speak of the trees, houses, mountains, and other physical objects we perceive, as being "out there" or "external to us," this means, then, at a distance from a certain other physical object we also perceive, *viz.,* the one called "our own body." As pointed out earlier, this meaning of "external to us" is obviously wholly different from that in which the physical world, *including our own body,* can be said to be "external to us," for, as applied to the physical world, these words mean other than psychical, or, since other minds too are "external to us," *other than our own mind.*

23. Fourfold Classification of "Real" Properties

It has been pointed out above that our first and basic conception of physical substances is in terms of their physico-psychical properties; and that it is only on the basis of a conception of physical substance so obtained that physico-physical properties can be conceived by us and can further enrich our conception of a given physical substance. The natural sciences, however, abstract just as far as they can from physico-psychical properties and seek to include in their accounts of the nature of physical substances only physico-physical properties. This is a perfectly legitimate aim, but it should be clearly recognized as manifesting only the fact that natural scientists, as such, interest themselves in none but the physico-physical properties of physical substances. That only these properties are of concern to natural science, however, does not imply that physical substances do not also have physico-psychical properties; nor that, without the latter, neither the physical substances themselves nor their physico-physical properties could ever be perceived or conceived by us.[25]

In the course of the foregoing account of the nature of the physical world and of its relation to the world of our intuitions two sorts of properties have been distinguished, viz., physico-psychical and physico-physical; but on the same basis of classification two other kinds of properties, viz., psycho-physical and psycho-psychical properties, have to be mentioned, yielding a fourfold classification of "real" (as distinguished from "verbal" or "logical") properties.

That account of four kinds of properties is, I believe, in complete agreement with W. E. Johnson's views as to four kinds of cases of causation, described by the same adjectives (physico-psychical, etc.) in sections 9 and 10 of the Introduction to Volume III of his Logic. Johnson, however, takes throughout the notions of physical event and physical object for granted, whereas I have, on the contrary, attempted above to analyze them.

The analyses, as we have seen, are partly in terms of either inference or postulation of a nonintuited cause of certain intuitions. But it should be noted that, once physical events and objects are perceived at all, then cases of physico-psychical causation additional to the one which according to our analysis is either inferred or postulated in perception are, not additionally either inferred or postulated, but observed in the same sense of this term in which cases of physico-physical causation can be said to be observed. For example, I may have until now perceived a certain physical substance only visually and tactually. Then, however, I am in position to observe experimentally what kind

___

[25] As noted in an earlier chapter, the distinction between physico-psychical and physico-physical properties, as defined, is the one which Locke's untenable account of the difference between "secondary" and "primary" qualities was really groping for.

of taste intuition, if any, is caused by placing that substance on my tongue. If I discover in this way that the substance has the physico-psychical property, "being bitter," I discover it by means of an experimental, *i.e.,* cause-revealing, procedure of precisely the same nature as that by which I may have discovered that the substance has the physico-physical property of, *e.g.,* being inflammable. For, as regards the nature of the terms the causal relation can relate, the definition of that relation specifies nothing at all except that they be events. It leaves completely open the possibility that both the cause-event and the effect-event may be physical, or that both may be psychical, or that either may be physical and the other psychical, or indeed that they be events of whatever other kinds might be conceivable.

24. Epistemic Status of the Analyses Offered in This Chapter

The objection might be made to some of the psychological analyses we have offered that introspection reveals no such psychical entities, events, or operations as were described, and therefore that these are nonexistent and the accounts of them mere inventions. This sort of objection, moreover, might also be advanced at more than one place in the chapters to follow. It may therefore be well at this point to say something as to the possible epistemic statuses of such psychological analyses. Three sorts of cases may be distinguished.

One concerns "telescoped" responses. It is a characteristic of associated or "conditioned" responses that, when well established, intermediary steps in them drop out. One kind of psychical event A comes to generate another D directly instead of, as at first, only through the generating of B, itself generating C, itself finally generating D. In such cases, introspection of the state of affairs ultimately established reveals only the direct sequence of D upon A; and the hypothesis that the sequence originally was of the form $A–B–C–D$ then has the status of an explanation — an explanation of the otherwise unexplained fact that A, although not natively connected with D, nevertheless now directly causes D. That hypothesis, of course, may be right or wrong, but it is not to be dismissed *a priori* simply on the ground that it appeals to factors not now observable; for very often explanations that are perfectly sound do this.   Rather, its worth is to be decided by one or another of the tests applicable to explanatory hypotheses in general, no matter in what field.   For example, the hypothesis that the sequence had earlier the form A–B–C–D may happen to be verifiable empirically by appeal to early memories; or, in the absence of these, observation of present phenomena of a more or less similar nature may corroborate the hypothesis.

In a second class of cases, the objection mentioned above is to be met by pointing out that it is there being based on a confusion; that is, that the analysis objected to is questioned not because it really is introspectively unverifiable, but because its *account* of what occurs — which necessarily is discursive, *i.e.,* verbalized — is mistaken by the objector for a claim that the *process* itself, which the account describes, is discursive — the objector then concluding that, since introspection reveals that the process is in fact not a discursive one, the account offered of it is untrue to the facts.

For example, the question why one cuts corners in walking might be answered by the statement that a straight line is the shortest distance between two points, and that one inclines to avoid useless expenditure of time and energy.   If this answer is taken to claim that one's cutting corners is the outcome of a piece of discursive reasoning, which one performs, it is then properly rejected as obviously untrue to the introspectable facts. Yet the answer is correct if taken, as it is intended to be, as a formulation, *i.e.,* a verbalization, of the beliefs and inclinations — in practice ordinarily remaining unformulated even to oneself — which automatically determine one's action in the given sort of case.   This illustration is borrowed from F. C. Sharp, who,

contending that "right" as the ordinary man uses the term means
that which arouses approbation under certain conditions, goes on
to say that we must not expect to discover what these conditions
are by asking the ordinary man to enumerate and describe them.
"The man in the street does not carry about with him in his mental
kit a set of formulae covering these conditions any more than
when he cuts a corner he says to himself, 'A straight line is the
shortest distance between two points.' But that the conditions
in question represent real forces may be shown empirically by
what he does when in doubt, or when he changes his mind, or
when the correctness of his predication is challenged by others."[26]

In a third class of cases, the reply to the objection that introspection fails to corroborate a psychological analysis proposed
would be that the latter in these cases has the status of *theory-
construction*, and therefore that the postulation in the course of
it of unobservable psychical entities — for instance, the censor or
the complexes of Freudian psychology — is as legitimate whenever this really explains and predicts as, in physical theory-con-
struction, is the postulation for the same purpose of unobservable
physical entities such as electrons, fields, etc. The *prima facie*
difficulty that in the case of psychical entities *esse est percipi*, and
therefore that an unconscious mental event is a contradiction in
terms, arises only from failure to keep in mind the distinction

---

[26] F. C. Sharp, "Voluntarism and Objectivity," *Philosophical Review*, Vol. L,
No. 3, May 1941, p. 256.

A psychical process which is not itself discursive, and perhaps is not even introspectable, may yet be parallel in form to, and therefore itself as rational as, the
discursive process which would be a verbalization of it and would thus describe it.
This fact seems to me to be overlooked by Stace in the article already referred to,
on "The Problem of Unreasoned Beliefs." The paradoxical character of his contention that a process whose steps are logically irrelevant to one another and to the
conclusion may nevertheless be valid in the sense of yielding truth more often than
chance would (p. 32) arises from the tacit, but I believe gratuitous, assumption
that relevance and rationality are characters which can belong only to *logical*
processes, *i.e.*, to processes whose terms are discursive entities — words or other
utterable symbols. The gratuitousness of this assumption, however, does not
invalidate either the argument or the conclusions of that admirable article.

between "derivative" and "primitive" entities, and to remember that derivative psychical entities are classed as psychical not because the character which identifies the primitives as psychical is observed in the derivatives also, but only because the derivatives are derivative *from primitives that are psychical.*

Chapter 16

The Mental Operations

The nature of intuition was considered in Chapters 13 and 14; and in Chapter 15 it was shown that, in ultimate analysis, to perceive an event in nature is to interpret a sensation as effect of a nonintuited event, which we denominate "physical." That nonintuited events occur is a corollary of the fact, whether known *a priori* or postulated, that every event and therefore every sensation has a cause, *i.e.,* is the effect of some other event; and of the fact that no proximate cause for our sensations is to be found among our other intuitions.

Fundamentally, then, nature — that is, the world called "physical" — is known to us by interpretation of our sensations in terms of certain constructs. But to say that nature is *known by construction* does not entail, as sometimes is assumed, that nature itself *is a construct.* For only when we use our hands or other parts of our bodies to make things do we literally construct physical objects, and we do this then out of other physical objects. On the other hand, when what we do is to construe our sensations as effects of nonintuited causes, the only thing we then literally construct is the idea we use in such construing, *viz.,* the idea "effect of a nonintuited cause." And, in so far as this construing happens to be valid, it constitutes discovery, not construction, of a physical object. In this respect, the epistemic situation here is analogous to that in which we construe certain perceived physical events as effects of certain conceived but unperceivable atomic events: the existence and properties of atoms are inferred, not generated, by us; and the inference, in so far as it happens to be valid, constitutes discovery, not creation, of the existence and properties of atoms.

In this chapter we shall consider the nature of interpretive activity in general, its kinds, and its relations to meaning and to language. To begin with, however, something must be said about mental operations.

1. Mental Operations

In Section 9 of Chapter 11, "operation" was defined as causation, by an event C in a substance S, of an event E in a substance Z. If Z is identical with S, the operation is *internal* to the given substance; whereas if S and Z are distinct substances, the operation is an *external* operation of S upon Z.

These definitions, together with those of other terms defined there also, imply that an operation may be either mechanical or purposive, and that a purposive operation may be successful or unsuccessful and may be unskilled or skilled in various degrees. The definitions, moreover, allow classification of operations under four headings, according to the nature — physical or psychical — of the cause-event and the effect-event entering in the operation. That is, an operation may be:

1. Physico-physical, or
2. Physico-psychical, or
3. Psycho-physical, or
4. Psycho-psychical.

No operation other than a "psycho-" one (*i.e.,* a psycho-physical or a psycho-psychical one) can be purposive.[1] But there can be mechanical operations of the two "psycho-" kinds, as well as of the two "physico-" kinds.

---

[1] Unless one should, arbitrarily, redefine "desire" and "belief" as consisting of such physiological events as are assumed or perhaps known to be invariable correlates of the psychological events the words "desire" and "belief" normally denote.

Examples of mechanical operations of kind 3, *i.e.,* psycho-physical, would be causation of fainting by pain, or by the perceiving or thinking of blood; causation of blushing by the feeling of shame, or of trembling or pallor by fear; causation of winking, or of dodging, or of automatic screening of the eye with the hand, by the sudden perceiving of an approaching missile; etc.

Examples of mechanical operations of kind 4, *i.e.,* psycho-psychical, would be all instances of simple association of ideas (*e.g.,* causation of the idea of snow by the idea of winter); again, instances of causation of a feeling, or of an impulse, by a sensation or an idea (*e.g.,* causation of fear, and possibly of the impulse to run, by the hearing of a sudden loud sound; or of feelings and impulses of lust by the imagining of the situations described in erotic literature, etc.).

The *internal* mental operations are the psycho-psychical ones, whether mechanical or telic. They are what *interpretation* consists in, and interpretation — especially semeiotic interpretation — is what we shall discuss in the remainder of this chapter.

2. Interpretation

Interpretation is the kind of mental event consisting in this, that one mental event causes another in the same mind. Either or both of the two events may have, or may not have, objective reference as described in Chapter 15. But in either case the definition of interpretation in general, just given, holds; for even when our consciousness at a given moment is consciousness of an object, interpretation consists in causation of another event in our consciousness by our *consciousness* of that object, not by that object itself independently of consciousness of it by us. For example, although we say that a mark consisting of a little cross causes us to think of addition, the fact is of course that at times when that mark is not perceived or imagined by us it does not cause us to think of addition or of anything else. On the other hand, if presence, perhaps near a person's head, of a design in the form of a cross had in itself, *i.e.,* even when he is not in a position to perceive it, the capacity to affect his consciousness — as for instance the taking of alcohol even when he is not conscious of having taken it — then such a case of causation would of course not be a case of interpretation.

Again, although we say that approaching black clouds are a sign that it will rain soon, the fact is that they function as sign only when somebody *perceives* (or otherwise knows) their approach and is thereby caused to *believe* that it will probably rain soon. The relation between the clouds themselves and the rain is one of physico-physical causation, and not, as in every case of interpretation, one of psycho-psychical causation.

It might be objected, however, that the approach of black clouds is a sign that it will rain soon, *whether or not* anybody actually perceives their approach. But, as will be explained in greater detail farther on, this is true only in the sense that even when it is not perceived, it is *potentially* a (more or less reliable) sign of rain; *i.e.,* is such (*a*) that there is a (more or less constant) objective connection between black clouds and rain; and (*b*) that if a person who knows this perceives black clouds he is thereby caused to expect rain. On the other hand, the approach of black clouds *actually* functions as a sign only when it is being perceived and causes expectation.

3. Interpretation of Perceptions Distinguished from Interpretation in Perception

Inasmuch as, in interpretation, the cause-factor is probably in the majority of cases a state of consciousness that is consciousness of an object, rather than a state of consciousness having no objective reference, it will be well to attend for a moment to what takes place on occasions of the former kind.[2]

---

2 Consciousness of an object, it should be remembered, is one thing, and real existence of an object such as one is conscious of is another thing. Reference to dreams and other hallucinations makes this evident.

Consciousness of an object is, as we saw in the preceding chapter, itself a case of interpretation: a given sound intuition, for example, for which we find no cause among our antecedent intuitions, causes us (in conjunction with our belief that no event occurs without a cause) to believe that some event other than any intuition of ours is causing that sound intuition. An objective event of the sort we denominate "physical" is for us originally nothing more than such a nonintuited causative event. We saw how on such a basis the idea of a physico-psychical property is reached; then, in terms of only such properties, our first idea of a physical substance; then, in terms of interaction with one another of physical substances so conceived, the idea of a physico-physical property; and lastly how our first idea of a given physical substance is itself thus eventually enriched by addition to it of our ideas of the physico-physical properties of the substance. It is a rich (but ordinarily unanalyzed) idea of this sort that, in an adult, is caused to arise when he reads or hears the word "bell," for instance.

When it is aroused in a person by the word bell (or by some equivalent expression) he is then *conceiving* a bell. When on the other hand it is aroused by some sensation, *e.g.*, a sound or a sight sensation of the kind a bell normally produces, then occurrence of that idea constitutes interpretation of that sensation as sound or sight "of a bell"; and if, together with the idea of the bell, there occurs also belief in the nearby existence of a bell, then the two together constitute *perceiving* (auditorily) that a bell is ringing, or (visually) that a bell is there. This perceiving, of course, may or may not be veridical in a given case. If the sound sensation were in fact caused not by the ringing of a bell, but by a phonograph record, and one had at the time no way of knowing this, one would perceive the ringing of a bell, but one's perceiving would then be not veridical but illusive.

If now we symbolize by S the sound sensation which is the

interpretand in such a case of objective perception, and by B the interpretant consisting of the idea of a bell and of belief in the nearby existence of a ringing bell, then we may symbolize perception of the objective fact that a bell is ringing, in this way: $S \rightarrow B$. Ordinarily, this act of interpretation would be instantaneous. That is, no time — occupied by puzzlement or curiosity or effort to understand — would elapse between S and B; rather, the interpretant would follow the interpretand instantly and, because the interpretand still endures when the interpretant arises, the latter seems to be, and *in part* is, simultaneous with the former in the specious present. But when the S is ambiguous or somewhat unfamiliar, or when we are so tired or sleepy that the functioning of our interpretive apparatus is delayed, or when, under laboratory conditions, the S is made so short as not to endure still while the B arises, then the essential distinctness and successiveness of the S and the B become unmistakably evident.

Now, however, in *further* interpretation, *i.e.,* in interpretation of the perceived *objective fact* that a bell is ringing, the S and B components of the perceiving of that fact function together as a unit. Accordingly, interpretation of that perceived fact by, let us say, belief that lunch is now ready (LR) may be symbolized thus: $(S \rightarrow B) \rightarrow LR$ — the latter belief being then perhaps in turn interpreted, conationally, by impulse to go to the dining room. With repetition, however, consciousness that a *bell* is ringing can easily cease to occur — the sound intuition coming to have directly as interpretant the impulse to go to the dining room.

4. Interpretation — Ideative, Affective, or Conative

That an interpretant may thus consist of an impulse implies that it would be a great error to think of interpretation as concerned only with what we may broadly call *ideas* (*i.e.,* sensations, images, and abstract ideas), as distinguished, on the one hand, from *affections* (*i.e.,* emotions, feelings, moods, sentiments) and, on the other, from *conations* (*i.e.,* volitions, impulses, desires, in-clinations, cravings). Rather, interpretation may equally well be ideative, or affective, or conative. The state of our consciousness, of course, — whether it be functioning as cause or as effect of a given other conscious state — is at most times in part idea, in part feeling, and in part conation. But, in most cases, one or another of these constituents is more intense or clearer than the others, eclipses them more or less, and dominantly determines the nature of the sequent state of consciousness. To overlook the fact that the interpretant of a given interpretand may be dominantly a feel-ing or an impulse rather than an idea would be to conceive erroneously the mental life of man as exclusively ideative. What is true is only that ideative interpretation is most often what is being referred to when "interpretation" is spoken of. The error that interpretation is *essentially* an ideative and cognitive process is traceable to the fact that emotions and conations (no less than sensations, images, or other ideas) are states of *consciousness,* *i.e.,* are "known" in the sense of intuited in the very occurrence thereof. But from this it does not follow that an impulse or a feeling is to be subsumed under the heading of "idea" or of consciousness cognitive of objects. Such a *non sequitur* appears to be at the basis of, for instance, theories which, like those of Stace and of Greene, claim that the esthetic experience is "cognitive."[3]

5. Interpretation an Irreducibly Tetradic Affair

The definition of interpretation given above might suggest that it is a dyadic affair, involving only an interpretand and an inter-pretant, but the truth is that *four* factors always are involved, as follows:

(*a*) The *interpreter,* namely, the complex of mental habits,

---

[3] W. T. Stace, *The Meaning of Beauty,* London, 1929; T. M. Greene, *The Arts and the Art of Criticism,* Princeton University Press, 1940. Cf. V. A. Tomas, "Has Professor Greene Proved that Art is a Cognitive Process?" *Jour. of Philos.,* Vol. XXXVII, No. 17, 1940.

dispositions, etc., of the person concerned. These constitute the kind of mind he *is*.

(*b*) The *context of interpretation,* namely, the kinds of things (whether subjective or objective) of which he is conscious at the time, whether clearly or obscurely.

(*c*) The *interpretand,* namely, a change of some kind supervening in the context of interpretation and thus functioning as cause.

(*d*) The *interpretant,* namely, a change of some other kind following it immediately and functioning as effect.[4]

That these four factors all are involved may be made evident by further examination of an illustration already used. It is obvious that perception or imagination of a little cross does not cause in a mind the thought of addition unless this mind has been trained in a certain manner; for no such effect results in the mind of the proverbial Hottentot or of any other wholly illiterate being. But even when the mind which is conscious of a little cross is one trained as our own minds have been, consciousness of that mark does not cause the thought of addition unless the mental context at the time is of a certain kind, namely mathematical. If the context at the time is, for instance, religious instead, then consciousness of a cross causes us to think of something very different from addition.

6. Semeiotic Interpretation

The definition of interpretation, given in the second section of this chapter and explicated in the fourth and fifth, concerns the generic meaning of "interpretation"; but, in the great majority of instances the meaning the word is intended to have is much narrower. For one thing, interpretation that is *functional* rather than idle is usually meant — interpretation thought of not

---

[4] The two words, interpretand and interpretant, sound so much alike as to be ordinarily indistinguishable as spoken, and are therefore best replaced in oral discourse by the Latin originals, *interpretandum* and *interpretans.*

merely as occurring, but in addition as having some function to perform. This entails that the interpretant that occurs is then, in one specific sense or another, right, or wrong — appropriate and more or less adequate, or not, in the existing circumstances, to certain demands of the interpreter.

It may be asked whether functional interpretation and telic interpretation are then one and the same thing. The answer is that they are not: telic interpretation is functional essentially; but mechanical interpretation, when functional, is so only adventitiously. More explicitly, interpretation of an event C by an event E is telic and (automatically) functional if, as we have seen, the cause-event C in it consists of a desire for occurrence of something D, together with belief that acting in manner M would cause D. Then the effect-event E is evaluated as "success" or "failure" on the basis of whether it does or does not satisfy the desire *that caused it, viz.,* the desire that it be or include D. Arithmetical addition would be an example of interpretation that is functional and telic.

On the other hand, interpretation of an event C by an event E is mechanical yet (adventitiously) functional if it is evaluated on the basis of whether it does or does not satisfy a desire (say, a desire that E should be or include D), *but this desire was no part of* C. An instance of interpretation that is thus functional yet mechanical would be one where the sight of something reminds one of something else, which it was important one should think of. One then evaluates one's having been made to think of it by the sight of the given thing as having been "useful."

What most often one has in mind when one speaks of interpretation, however, is interpretation which is not only functional, but functional *semeiotically;* that is, interpretation where the interpretand is a "symbol" or a "sign."

Semeiotic interpretation is the species of *ideative* interpretation where the interpretand is expected to function as, in some way, a *representative* of the kind of entity the interpretant is the thought of.[5] In the case of the interpretands called *symbols,* this representativeness means that for certain purposes they can be *substituted* for what they symbolize — some operations among the symbols (*e.g.,* arithmetical operations) then enabling one to infer what would be the outcome of certain operations or processes among entities of the kinds symbolized.

An interpretand of the kind called a *sign,* on the other hand, represents the entity of which it is a sign in the sense that it is an *informant* — a herald, precursor, trace, or otherwise a revealer — *of the existence of that entity as in some particular relation* (temporal, spatial, or other) *to the interpreter.* That is, a sign "represents," not in the sense of functioning as a substitute for the entity it is a sign of, but in the sense of revealing to the interpreter the *relation* in which he is standing to the time, or place, or other sort of *situs,* of that entity's existence. Hence a sign causes, at the time or/and later, in a rational interpreter, not the responses he would make to the presence of the entity itself, but the responses which, in the light of his total purposes, would, he believes, be appropriate to the relation in which he stands at such times to the existence at a certain *situs,* of an entity of the kind concerned. For example, perception of approaching black clouds — which are a sign of rain — causes in us, at the time of perception and at subsequent moments, the responses which, in the light of our purposes, would, we believe, be appropriate *at such moments* to the occurrence *in the near future* of rain at the place where we are.

The classification of species of interpretation described in what precedes may, for the sake of clearness, be put in schematic form as follows:

---

[5] Here and elsewhere in these pages the word "entity" is used as the noun corresponding to the participle "being" in its broadest possible sense. That is, "an entity" simply means "something," and thus, as the case may be, a substance, or an event, or a characteristic, or a relation, etc.

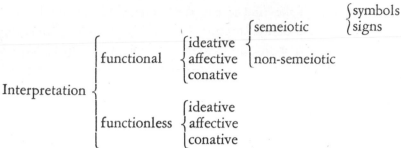

I shall not undertake a discussion of all forms of interpretation, but only of semeiotic interpretation. Yet a word must be said at this point to make clear the nature and importance of interpretation that is ideative and functional but *non-semeiotic*. An illustration of it would be what occurs in connection with the strings of nonsense syllables used in psychological laboratories in studies of memorization. The syllable "kak," let us say, causes the person who is subject of the experiment to think of another — say, "lal." If this is the next in the string originally given him it is the *right* interpretant of "kak"; if not, then the *wrong* interpretant. Interpretation in such a case is thus functional and also ideative; but it is not semeiotic since obviously the interpretand "kak" is to its interpreter neither a symbol nor a sign of "lal": it does not function as a substitute for "lal," and it does not *announce* to him the occurrence of "lal," but *causes* it.[6] It is the cue which causes "lal" to come to mind.

This example makes clear that the function of the interpretand in this kind of interpretation is only *presentative*: its function is simply to present a certain idea itself, and not, in addition, to represent something which the idea it presents would be idea of. But the importance of interpretation of this non-semeiotic type is brought home to us by examples of a less artificial kind, and is especially evident when interpretation happens to fail. Let us suppose that one needs the name of a person one has known, and

---

[6] I am indebted to Prof. L. J. Lafleur for having called my attention to strings of nonsense syllables as an instance where interpretation is non-semeiotic.

recalls that its first syllable is "Hol" but not whether the rest is "lingworth," "worthy," "linshead," "gate," "loway," or something else. To seek to recall the rest of the name is to seek the right non-semeiotic interpretant of the interpretand "Hol."

The common name for interpretation which is thus functional, ideative, and non-semeiotic is *rote recollection*. Its importance is commensurate with that of the functions of the various strings of ideas that happen to be concerned, which we need to remember in addition to, or without at the time any need of, remembering what the ideas are ideas of (if of anything). These strings are in most cases strings of *verbal* ideas; for example, the combination of a safe, the multiplication table, numerous mathematical and chemical formulae, the strings of syllables of which ordinary words consist, the foreign-language equivalents of given words. Another instance, perhaps hardly classifiable as verbal, would be rote memory of the notes of a piece of music.

7. Signs

Let us now consider signs and symbols more particularly than was done in the preceding section, and also something related to them, *viz.*, signals.

The word *sign* is often used nowadays by writers on semeiology in two senses, and, unfortunately, it would seem without always having clearly in mind which of the two senses the term has on a given occasion. One of the two senses is the broad one, in which "sign" is synonymous with "interpretand," and in which, therefore, names and other symbols are a species of signs. The other sense is the narrower and more usual one in which signs, as diagnostic interpretands, are contrasted with names and other symbols, which, simply as such, are not diagnostic. This is the sense "sign" has when, in ordinary language, the approach of black clouds is said to be a sign of rain, wrinkles on a man's face a sign of age, or the ringing of a bell a sign that lunch is ready. In ordinary language, on the other hand, it is not said that the word unicorns is a sign of unicorns (as the spoor of one would be), nor that the word rain is a sign of rain. Hence, to use "sign" nonetheless in the inclusive sense which requires us to say that the name of that kind of animal and the word "rain" are signs too, is a fertile source of confusions and misunderstandings. These can easily be forestalled by using for that inclusive sense the term "semeiotic interpretand," which expresses it exactly. I shall therefore myself use "sign" only in its most common, narrow sense, illustrated by such statements as that black clouds are a sign of rain, smoke a sign of fire, etc.; and, for the broadest sense, I shall always use "interpretand." It is the word "sign" as so used that I shall now attempt to define.

It is essential to notice first that the meaning of the assertion that, for instance, smoke is a sign of fire is in part objective and in part subjective. The objective part of its meaning is that a more or less regular objective connection obtains between fire and smoke — specifically, that smoke is always or generally an effect of fire, and fire always or generally the cause of smoke. But the objective relation of effect to cause, or of cause to effect, or of constant conjunction, is not itself the sign-signified relation. It is necessary to it, but not sufficient. There is needed in addition a subjective relation: In order that smoke be a sign of fire, it is necessary also (*a*) that the smoke be perceived or otherwise known by some mind to be occurring, and (*b*) that that mind be thereby caused to think of fire and to believe that it is occurring.

It is possible to *interpret* an event or character A as a sign of another, B, even when objective connection between A and B is lacking. Some persons, for example, interpret the number 13 as a sign of misfortune, although, because of the lack of objective connection between them, it is not truly so. Thus, to interpret A as sign of B means merely (1) to be aware of A and (2) to be caused thereby to think of B and to believe that B occurs or exists (or, as the case may be, has existed, or will exist). But that *A is* a sign of *B* means not only that it is interpreted as being such, but in addition that *A* and *B* are more or less regularly connected objectively. The qualification "more or less" is called for to allow for the fact that a sign is not necessarily a *certain* sign of what it signifies, but perhaps only a more or less *probable* sign of it. Signs, in other words, admit of various degrees of reliability: black clouds are a sign, but not a certain sign of rain.

Against the contention that without interpreters there are no signs, it might be urged that "smoke is a sign of fire even when no one happens to be interpreting it as such."[7] To do justice to the element of truth in this statement it is necessary to distinguish between being *actually* a sign of, and being *potentially* a sign of; for whenever something *A* is an effect of something *B*, or a cause of it, or is in some other way more or less regularly associated objectively with it, there exists the *possibility* for *A* to function as sign of *B*.

To say that *A actually* is a sign of *B* means:

(1) that *A* is more or less regularly associated objectively with B; and,

(2) that some mind is actually aware of *A*'s presence, and is actually caused thereby to think of *B* and to believe (or to incline to believe) that *B* exists (or, as the case may be, has existed, or will exist).

On the other hand, to say that *A* is *potentially* a sign of *B* means:

(1) that *A* is more or less regularly associated objectively with *B*; and

(2) that if at any time when *A* is present a mind

  (*a*) familiar with the objective fact that *A* is more or less regularly associated with *B*; and

  (*b*) not engrossed at the moment with matters ex-

---

7 Cf. J. Wild, "An Introduction to the Phenomenology of Signs," *Jour. of Philos. and Phenomenol. Research,* Vol. VIII, p. 222, and the discussion, pp. 234–44, between Wild and myself, of some of the contentions of that paper.

traneous to this, should become aware of the
presence of *A*, then that mind would be caused
thereby to think of *B* and to believe (or to incline
to believe) that *B* exists (or, as the case may be,
has existed, or will exist).

Thus, that a mind actually interprets *A* as a sign of *B* is a
provision intrinsic to the definition of *A*'s being *actually* a sign
of *B*; and that, under certain conditions, a mind would interpret
A as a sign of *B* is a provision intrinsic to the definition of *A*'s
being *potentially* a sign of *B*. Hence, the statement that "smoke
is a sign of fire even when no one happens to be interpreting it
as such" is true if "is a sign" is taken in the sense of "is potentially
a sign"; but is false if those words are taken in the sense of "is
actually a sign"; and this notwithstanding that, in both cases, it
is assumed that a more or less regular objective connection exists
between smoke and fire.

8. Symbols

What precedes means that, psychologically considered, *i.e.,* considered apart from the question of reliability, a sign is a semeiotic
interpretand the interpretant of which consists of an opinion.
More explicitly, a sign (*e.g.,* smoke perceived) causes its interpreter to think of a proposition (*viz.,* that fire is occurring) and
to believe or incline to believe it; and to say that a psychological
effect is of this kind is to say that it consists in occurrence of an
opinion.[8]

In the light of this analysis, we may now say that a *symbol* is a
semeiotic interpretand which, unlike a sign, is *not opinative.* That
is, what a symbol causes us to become conscious of either is not
a proposition, or, if it is, the symbol does not cause us to believe

---

[8] What I conceive to be the relations between propositions, opinions, judgments,
beliefs, sentences, and facts is set forth in an article entitled "Propositions, Opinions,
Sentences, and Facts," *Jour. of Philosophy,* Dec. 19, 1940, Vol. XXXVII, No. 26.
This article makes clear that to think of a proposition is not the same thing as to
think of a sentence.

it or to take towards it any other opinative attitude. The *name* of anything, thus, is a discursive symbol of the thing, and if we were to take the word "name" in a sense somewhat broader than is usual, we could say, conversely, that any discursive symbol is a name of what it symbolizes.

Between a symbol and a sign there is also this difference: A symbol causes one to think of what it symbolizes, and a sign, likewise, of what it signifies; but an interpretand is a symbol only if, or only in so far as, it is capable of functioning for some purpose as *substitute* for what it causes one to think of. As we shall see, this means that a symbol must, in some respect, be formally similar to what it symbolizes; but this is not true of a sign, except in those cases where the psychological context happens to make a combination of symbols function as a sign.

Symbols are of one or the other of two great kinds. Those we may call *indicative* (or monstrative) orient our attention to some certain "where," *i.e.*, to some place in some order system (*e.g.*, in space, or in time, or in the series of the whole numbers, etc.) no matter what in particular, or whether anything, occupies that place. On the other hand, the interpretands we may call *quiddative* (or descriptive, or characterizing) symbols make us think of some certain "what," no matter at which place or whether at any in a given order system this "what" exists. Some writers, it is true, reserve the word "symbol" exclusively for certain characterizing interpretands, and call an indicative interpretand simply an *index* — usually, it may be added, overlooking the important fact that what an index indicates is essentially a place and only derivatively what, if anything, happens to be at that place. But so to limit the use of the word "symbol" seems an arbitrary and therefore needlessly confusing departure from its ordinary usage.

An indicative and a quiddative symbol may be combined to form a complex symbol, such as that of existence of some species of state of affairs. Also, something which in a certain context functions as sign may in a different context function only as symbol. For example, the words "It is raining!" as now seen on this page and under present circumstances cause the reader to think of occurrence of rain at the moment, but do not cause him to believe what he is thus made to think of. That is, they function merely as symbol of a certain kind of state of affairs and of a certain variable time (*viz.,* whatever the time at which he reads them may be). On the other hand, were the reader in the same room with another person — the latter looking out of the window — and were this other person to say "It is raining!" the reader would normally then not only think of, but also believe in, occurrence of rain at the moment. That is, the same words but in these different circumstances, would for him then function as a sign that it is raining.

9. Signals

Moreover, utterance of that sentence under those circumstances by the other person would constitute a case of signalling; for *signalling* consists in purposive utterance, whether vocal, graphic, or other (within what the utterer believes to be the present or eventual field of perceptual attention of another person), of something the perceiving of which the utterer believes will cause in the other person a belief — or, as the case may be, an idea, an impulse, or a feeling — which the utterer is thereby attempting to cause in the other person. The person to whom a signal is addressed may of course be the utterer himself as existing at a later time.

A *signal,* then, is an utterance (in the above broad sense) intended by the utterer to be perceived by another person and thereby to cause in that person a certain belief (or, as the case may be, a certain idea, or impulse, or feeling) which the utterer desired to cause in him. And that a person P *interprets something as a signal* means that he believes another person *U* caused that thing in order that he should perceive it and that his perceiving it should cause in him a certain belief (or idea, etc.) which *U* desired to cause in him. Something that is not a signal may nevertheless be interpreted as being one by those who perceive it; and, conversely, they may not interpret as a signal something that actually is one.

Although signalling is attempting to communicate, not all communication is signalling; for unintentional communication of belief would not ordinarily be called signalling — for example, communication, to those who hear an instinctive cry of fear, of the belief that danger is present.

Signalling, it should be noticed, is an external operation, whereas interpreting (whether as symbol, as sign, or as signal) is a psycho-psychical operation, essentially internal.

10. Discursive Entities

The point has now been reached where we must make among interpretands a very important distinction — that, namely, between those which are discursive and those which are not. For this, however, we must first state in general what is to be understood by a "discursive entity," irrespective of whether or not such an entity happens at a given time to be playing a role in interpretation. By discursive entities — entities of discourse — I propose to mean any entities satisfying the following conditions:

(1) They are utterables; that is, they are entities susceptible of being readily "uttered" whether vocally, graphically, or otherwise. By "readily" is meant that they are such that perceptible utterances of them can in ordinary circumstances be caused by the mere wish.

(2) They are entities recognizable each as the same in the various utterances of it; or we may put this by saying that the various utterances of each are recognizable as "equal."

(3) They are entities of which cases occur only as results of human (or, exceptionally, of animal) utterance; that is, cases of them are almost always man-caused, artifactual — never, or only by the rarest accidents, caused by nature independently of human (or animal) intervention.

The first of these conditions, *viz.,* readiness of utterability, is relative to the means of utterance happening to be at our disposal. The means of vocal utterance are virtually always at our disposal, but those of graphic or other modes of utterance less often. Hence, when utterance is mentioned, we are likely to think primarily of speech and to regard other modes of utterance, such as writing, as substitutes for speech.[9]   But the priority of vocal over graphic or other modes of utterance is only practical or historical, not theoretical, and we therefore need take no account of it here.

From what has now been said it is evident that the entities called words, phrases, and sentences, and also those commonly called mathematical, logical, heraldic, astronomical, and other technical "symbols," are discursive entities as defined above — irrespective of whether they happen in addition to be at the time functioning semeiotically or not, and, if they are so functioning, irrespective of whether they are then serving as symbols, or as signs, or as signals.   For the convenience of brevity, I shall from this point on use the nouns "word" or "vocable" in the broad sense in which either of them is virtually synonymous with "discursive entity" as defined, and the adjective "verbal" or "vocable," similarly as synonymous with "discursive."   This means that such tachygraphs as $+$, $=$, 3, $\sqrt{}$, $\supset$, etc., are "words" as genuinely as are "plus," "equal," "three," "square root of," "implies," etc. Also, such things as groans, laughter, sobs, and various cries, would have to be called words in that broad sense.   This would, admittedly, be somewhat arbitrary, although Jespersen and some

---

[9] See for instance L. Bloomfield's "Linguistic Aspects of Science," *Internat. Encycl. of Unified Science,* Vol. 1, No. 4, pp. 6–8.

other linguisticians hold that words, in the usual narrower sense of the term, evolved out of such natural utterances, so that a sharp line between the two is hardly possible to draw. Also, the non-sense syllables used by psychologists in the study of rote learning would be "words," notwithstanding that — unlike ordinary words — they symbolize nothing. Indeed, even the syntactical order of words would have to be reckoned as at least a constituent of dis-cursive entities consisting of several words. Compare, for instance "friend of enemy of John" with "enemy of friend of John." Again, letters, punctuation and quotation marks, etc., would be discursive entities as defined, whether or not we chose to speak of them too as "words."

But although the sense in which I propose to use "word" and "verbal" is broader than the usual this will not deprive us of any needed distinctions. It leaves unaltered, for instance, the fact that such a "verbal" utterance as a moan is a *natural* sign of pain, whereas such another as the sentence "It hurts!" is a *con-ventional* sign of pain.

11. Verbal and Real Interpretands

Symbols and signs, evidently, may be either discursive or non-discursive — either verbal or, as we may say, real, if we now agree that in this context "real" shall simply mean nondiscursive. For example, a cloud shaped more or less like a human head would be a real symbol of a human head; whereas the words "human head" would be a verbal symbol of the same thing. Again, the crepitant sound I hear at certain times (such as ordinarily is caused by raindrops on the roof) is for me a sign, and a "real" sign, that it is raining. Whether it is in addition a reliable sign of it is, as we have seen, another question. On the other hand, the declarative sentence, "It is raining," uttered by someone within my hearing, is for me also a sign, but a verbal sign, of the same thing.

The utterance of discursive entities constitutes almost always, but not always, a case of signalling. An exception would be the case of a person who writes something which he does not intend to read later or to have others read, but which he writes solely because the process of writing helps him to clarify his thoughts. Another exception, already noticed, would be a spontaneous cry of fear, or, similarly, a groan of pain, etc., as also the solitary babbling of young children, on which S. K. Langer, G. de Laguna, and others have commented.

12. Technical and Nontechnical Terms

The distinction between technical and nontechnical terms is a matter of the way in which a discursive symbol has acquired its meaning. A technical term is a discursive symbol which has come to have the interpretant it has as the result of an explicit convention made or accepted by us in order to fit the term to be an *instrument of precision* for symbolizing and for the ulterior purposes to which precision of symbolizing is indispensable. In consequence, a technical term is very often also an esoteric term; that is, a term used and understood by only a limited group of persons and constituting a part of what we call the jargon, or lingo, or cant, of their particular field of endeavor. But a jargon term is not automatically also technical, for many jargon terms do not owe their meaning to an explicit convention, and lack the precision otherwise seldom possessed by a term.

A nontechnical term, on the other hand — whether it be a jargon term or be "vulgar" in the sense of being a part of common language — is a discursive symbol which has not acquired its interpretant through an explicit convention, but simply as a result of our repeatedly hearing or seeing the term employed in certain situations but not in certain others, by persons who themselves learned in the same way to interpret the term. This is of course the way in which we first learn to understand the words of our mother tongue. The meaning a word acquires for us in this way is usually unprecise in greater or less degree, and this is a fatal defect if one attempts to use the word for technical purposes, *e.g.,* as an instrument for remote inferences. Yet there can be technical language at all only by grace of our possessing to begin with a nontechnical, unprecise language wherewith to formulate the stipulations by which technical language is created. The situation is here as with the highly accurate machine tools industry makes today: they, or the tools with which they were made, or the tools with which these tools themselves were made, originally were made with the weak and inaccurate tools consisting of man's two hands and of the crude sticks and stones and so on found in nature.

13. Four Types of Semeiotic Interpretation

Interpretands, and likewise their interpretants, may be verbal, or else "real" in the sense of nonverbal. This suggests a fourfold classification of cases of semeiotic interpretation. Such interpretation may be *rei-real, rei-verbal, verbo-real,* or *verbo-verbal.* Let us consider the most important of the mental operations under each of these headings.

14. Rei-Real Interpretation: Perceiving, Imagining, Remembering

Rei-real interpretation is interpretation in the case of which both the interpretand and the interpretant are nonverbal. Examples of it have been discussed, although without being so labeled, earlier in this chapter and in the preceding ones. One of them was the *perceiving* of physical events and substances — our sensations, in such cases, functioning as interpretands. Another important example of rei-real interpretation is *remembering,* in those cases where neither the interpretand nor the interpretant is verbal — as, for instance, where the sight of some object causes us to think of the occasion on which we acquired it. Again, *imagining* — say, that a bell is ringing — would be an example of rei-real interpretation. This would differ from perceiving that a bell is ringing, on the one hand in that the interpretand is an auditory image instead of an auditory sensation, and on the other, in that the ringing of a bell — which is what the sound imagined means, *i.e.,* causes us to think of — is not here believed by us to be occurring; whereas, in the case of perceiving, it is so believed.

Again, *inferring* the imminence of rain from the perception of approaching black clouds, or the occurrence of fire from the perception of smoke, would be examples of rei-real interpretation. Some philosophers, it is true, would deny the name of inference to this kind of interpretive activity, because its terms are nondiscursive. But a name is needed for it, and, rather than to coin a special one, it would seem better to call also inference, but more specifically *nondiscursive inference,* what occurs in such a case and in the other sorts of cases considered by Stace in the article on "The Problem of Unreasoned Beliefs" mentioned earlier. For although both the interpretand and the interpretant are here nondiscursive, the interpretive process is essentially the same as when they are discursive, and is at least theoretically capable of being as rational and valid as in the cases where the process is "logical" in the sense that the terms in which it is carried on are purely verbal or at least are verbalized, *i.e.,* formulated. Ordinary usage seems to mean by "inference" any case where one belief generates another, irrespective of whether or not the beliefs concerned are verbalized, and irrespective also of whether the passage from the one to the other is valid or invalid.

15. Rei-Verbal Interpretation: Formulating, Describing, Counting

Rei-verbal interpretation is the process that would commonly be called formulating or putting into words. It consists in this, that consciousness of something of a given real kind (*i.e.,* nonverbal), in mental contexts of some particular kind, brings to consciousness some particular verbal entity(which we may or may not then utter physically). At least, this is what formulation *psychologically considered* consists in. But a verbal entity is not a correct formulation — a symbol, name, or description — of the given real entity, unless the verbal entity meets a certain formal requirement, alluded to earlier in this chapter. This is, that the linguistic properties the verbal entity has in the language to which it belongs be formally *parallel* to the real properties of the given real entity, to the extent necessary to enable the verbal entity to function as *substitute* of the real entity for certain purposes, *e.g.,* for purposes of valid inference, or of communication.

This is not to say that only then is the verbal entity *correctly called* a formulation of the real entity; but that only then is it a *correct formulation* of it. For, to take an analogous case, we do not refuse to call something a reasoning, or an inference, or a syllogism, unless it happens to be valid — else the predicates "invalid" or "fallacious" would always lack a subject. Similarly, then, we say that a verbal entity can correctly be called a *formulation* — *e.g.,* a description — of a real entity even when the verbal entity happens to be an *incorrect* formulation of it.

How important a mental operation rei-verbal interpretation is becomes evident when we notice that it is the operation we perform not only when we think of the name of something, but also when we describe, *i.e.,* formulate analytically, the nature of something. Indeed, also when we count or measure anything; for counting is a method for bringing to our minds the same word — specifically, the same numeral — whenever the multitude we are perceiving has the same numerousness, even in cases where we could not directly have distinguished its numerousness from that of certain other multitudes. And measuring, although it makes use of such physical intermediaries as yardsticks, balances, clocks, etc., is ultimately a device for insuring that the same verbal interpretant — *viz.,* the same numeral — shall be presented to our minds whenever the magnitude of the observed real interpretand is the same.

16. Verbo-Real and Verbo-Verbal Interpretation: Understanding Words, Calculating

No less important than formulating is the converse operation, *viz.*, verbo-real interpretation. When the discursive entities concerned happen to be written rather than spoken the operation is specifically called *reading*. The words in common use that would perhaps most nearly describe its general nature are "deciphering" or "decoding," although these words are ordinarily applied chiefly to instances where the operation is more or less laborious and slow rather than, as ordinarily, automatic and instantaneous. Those words, moreover, are oftenest applied specifically to an operation which is really translating — from an artificial or more or less unfamiliar language into our natural language or into an otherwise familiar one; and translating, of course, is not verbo-real interpretation, but rather — or in addition — is verbo-verbal interpretation.

Verbo-real interpretation is "understanding" words in the ordinary way, which we may call the notional way as distinguished from the verbal way. Its nature will be discussed farther on (Sec. 18), but the word "time" illustrates the distinction as well as any. That it is understood — notionally — by everyone is shown by the fact that we all utter and understand such expressions as "He did not have time to go to the library," "They came at the same time," "Time passes quickly when one is busy," etc. On the other hand, that few of us know — verbally — what the word "time" means to us is shown by the fact that hardly one man in a million could give an adequate statement of what he understands by it. One who could do this would understand the word "time" discursively, *i.e.*, verbally, as well as notionally.

But there is also such a thing as *merely* verbal understanding of a word. In such understanding, the interpretant cannot strictly be said to be the *meaning* of the word, and the interpreting is therefore understanding only in the sense in which thinking of "dabra" upon seeing "Abraca" constitutes understanding of the latter. It is understanding, namely, in the sense of interpretation which, although non-semeiotic, is nevertheless functional and is therefore either right or wrong — either understanding or mis-understanding. Thus, we may speak of "the verbal meaning" of a word; but this expression must be understood as elliptical for "the word or set of words that has the same meaning, if any," as the given word; *i.e.,* the word or set of words that is the verbal equivalent of the given word.

Other examples of merely verbal understanding of a word would be that of a person who happened to know neither French nor Spanish, but who, from a French-Spanish dictionary, had learned that "perro" is the right Spanish verbal interpretant of the French "chien," "gato" of the French "chat," etc. Again, a person ignorant of the meaning of English words could learn from Webster's dictionary that in English a verbal equivalent of the words "to bet" is the words "to stake upon the event of a contingent issue." Still other examples would be the abbreviatory, biverbal definitions of a logical calculus where we do not inquire what nonverbal entities, if any, are represented by the verbal entities used. And the transformations of numerical or algebraic expressions in conformity with the rules of a calculus would be still another and highly important example.

One's understanding of a word — whether merely notional, or merely verbal, or both notional and verbal — may be either in-genuous (*i.e.,* naive) or analytical. *Ingenuous* knowledge of the *verbal* meaning of a word would be knowledge of synonyms of it; for instance, knowledge that "to wager" is a verbal equivalent of "to bet." On the other hand, *analytical* knowledge of the *verbal* meaning of "to bet" would be knowledge that it means the string of words quoted above from Webster's.

The difference between analytical and ingenuous *notional* un-derstanding of a word is that between, for example, the understanding a locksmith has of the word "lock" and the understanding of it most of us have. Ours is ingenuous; his, analytical even if he is not able in addition to give an adequate *statement* of what he understands by "a lock."

17. Discovery vs. Prescription of the Meaning of Words

Knowledge of the meaning of a word may have been acquired in either one of two ways: through empirical discovery of the meaning of the word, or through prescription of a meaning for it. To have acquired it by discovery is (if intensional meaning is concerned) to have come to recognize certain characteristics, all of which are possessed by each of the entities conventionally indicated by the word but not all of which are possessed by any of the entities conventionally denied the name the word constitutes. It is in this way that the word "tree," for instance, comes to mean (discursively) for us in intension "having a woody trunk, roots, branches, bark, etc."; or, if extensional instead of intensional meaning is concerned, to have acquired understanding of it by empirical discovery is to have noticed certain mutually exclusive groups of entities all of which possess all the characters conventionally connoted by the word, but each of which groups is conventionally called by a familiar distinctive name of its own. It is in this way that the word "trees," for instance, comes to mean (discursively) for us in extension "oaks, maples, pines, birches, etc." When the intensional meaning of a word is what we seek to discover, an extensional convention is what furnishes the datum that we are to scrutinize; or, when the extensional meaning of a word is in question, then an intensional convention provides the datum.

When the word is one belonging to ordinary language, the convention concerned in either case is simply a prevailing semantic custom and is incompletely definite: it definitely includes certain classes of entities (or, as the case may be, certain characters) and definitely excludes certain others, but it leaves yet others not definitely either included or excluded. In consequence of this, the results of empirical scrutiny of the data furnished by merely customary intensional or extensional use of a given word are bound to remain themselves indefinite beyond a certain point, notwithstanding that some genuine gain in definiteness of understanding does result from careful empirical scrutiny of even such data. A remainder of indefiniteness is inevitable whenever our understanding of a word has been acquired thus empirically.

On the other hand, prescription, and more specifically, verbo-verbal prescription, is what generates the greatest definiteness of meaning. This is what we have in pure logic and pure mathematics — pure in the sense that the question as to what non-discursive entities, if any, their vocables symbolize is left completely open and in no way affects the development of their calculi. These sciences, in other words, are in essence exclusively concerned with verbo-verbal interpretations that originate in prescriptions. They take as their primitive facts certain prescriptions or stipulations as to the discursive interpretants of certain discursive entities. Stipulations of this kind are commonly called biverbal definitions and defining postulates. The latter may be regarded as in effect including the various rules of formation and transformation of the expressions included in the discursive system one implicitly creates by the stipulations, for these rules are statements of the discursive properties prescribed for the discursive entities entering into the system. Furthermore, development of a calculus consists in step by step discursive interpretation, according to the stipulated rules, of the primitive verbal facts created by the stipulations, thus making their verbal implications explicit.

Prescription of meaning, however, is not restricted wholly to the fields of mathematics and logic. It is also what creates technical terms in the natural sciences. But in such cases, the meaning prescribed for a term is not arbitrary. Rather, as Whewell long ago pointed out, there are some empirically ascertained propositions which the prescribed meaning is intended to fit,[10] or some theoretical interest the prescription is designed to serve. To illustrate this point, let us take the vulgar term "fish" and consider the manner in which, by prescriptive definition, it is made into a technical term of zoology.

Ordinary usage applies the word fish alike confidently to trout, shark, sardine, tarpon, bass, etc., because they are noticeably alike — although the respects of likeness between them ordinarily remain unanalyzed or only very superficially analyzed. Ordinary usage also confidently denies the name of fish to cows, elephants, hippopotami, dogs, etc. But there are other sorts of entities as to which ordinary usage vacillates, for example whales or porpoises. They are noticeably like the trout, shark, etc., which it unhesitatingly calls fish, but they also differ from these in certain respects, less obvious to the merely casual observation which guides ordinary usage in its application of words. Ordinary usage — employing as it does such words as starfish, cuttlefish, shellfish, whale-fisheries — simply has no definite answer to the question whether porpoises and whales are to be regarded as parts of the extension of the word fish. How then have zoologists come to know that porpoises and whales are no part of the extensional meaning of the word fish? Obviously, it cannot have become known to them by observation of, perhaps, the fact that "fishes" breathe by means of gills, or do not suckle their young, since the very question at issue is whether or not observation of "fishes" is to include observation of porpoises and of whales.

Observation that whales and porpoises suckle their young, whereas sharks, tarpon, herring, etc., do not, does not answer, but is on the contrary what raises, the question whether the former two are or are not fish. Obviously, then, the character of suckling the young came to be excluded from the intensional meaning of

___

[10] Whewell, *Novum Organon Renovatum*, Book II, Chap. II, Sec. II.

the word fish not by observation but by stipulation. The stipulation, however, was not arbitrary but was dictated by theoretical interest — by interest in the possibility of explanation and prediction. A character is important for theoretical purposes to the extent that it is a reliable sign of the presence or absence of other characters. Thus, the character of being susceptible of capture by the process called "fishing," or that of having a certain general shape, or that of living in the water, has little theoretical importance because few other characters are constantly conjoined with it that are absent from the things devoid of it. The character of suckling the young, on the contrary, is theoretically important because it is constantly conjoined with, and is therefore a reliable sign of, numerous other characters such as warm-bloodedness, breathing by lungs, viviparousness, etc., which are not jointly present without it. This is what determines zoological science to class porpoises and whales, which possess it, with cows and dogs as "beasts," and not with shark and herring, which lack it, as "fish"; in spite of the fact that, to superficial observation, porpoises and whales resemble sharks much more than they do cows.[11]

Let us now, however, return to the matter of notional understanding of words. Let us inquire particularly into its nature, and then consider the values and shortcomings characteristic, respectively, of notional and of verbal understanding of words.

18. Abstract Ideas and "Notional Understanding"

Nominalists have denied that there are abstract ideas. Here, however, it is maintained that abstract ideas essentially enter into what we have called notional understanding — whether it be of words, as in conceiving; or of sensations, as in perceiving. Something must therefore now be said to make the existence of abstract ideas evident and to clarify their nature and origin.

If we compare introspectively the experience of hearing pro-

---

[11] In connection with this matter see Whewell, *History of Scientific Ideas*, 1878, Vol. II, p. 102, from which my discussion borrows to some extent.

nounced a word of some language unknown to us with that of hearing pronounced a familiar word of our own language, a difference between the two becomes immediately evident. In the case of the word of our own language, the sound of the word instantly generates in us an intuition of a certain subtle kind — a specific such intuition for each different word; whereas this sort of psychological effect is absent when the word belongs to a language we do not know or is a novel nonsense word like those made up by psychologists for use in laboratory studies of rote learning.

These subtle psychological states — each having a quality of its own as truly unique as that of a color, a tone, or an emotion — are what commonly are called *abstract ideas or notions* as distinguished from sensations and images. And the psychological event we have called notional understanding of a word consists in the instant arousal by the word of the abstract idea — the notion — which is its semeiotic interpretant.

We cannot here consider the various kinds of abstract ideas and the mode of acquisition of each, but something which will be suggestive of the nature and origin of abstract ideas in general may be said as to our notions of physical substances. Let us suppose a person to be confronted by, let us say, a large stone. Then, if he were to attempt to walk through it, or to ask it questions, or to sprinkle it with sugar and eat it, or to deal with it in other inappropriate ways, we should say that he does not understand the nature of the object he sees. On the other hand, if he should treat it in ways conducive to the success of his purposes, we should say that he knows what kind of object he is dealing with.

"Knowing the nature of something," then, is a kind of psychological state intimately related in some way to one's possessing some specific set of habits — both receptory and operatory — relevant on the one hand to one's purposes, and on the other to the properties of the given thing.   By a *receptory habit* is meant here that certain sensations, caused in us by the thing, regularly make us anticipate certain other sensations from it.   For example, hearing the buzzing sound ordinarily caused by a mosquito makes us anticipate a sting and a certain visual appearance.   And by an *operatory habit* is meant that the sensations caused in us make us ready to perform certain operations appropriate to purposes of ours connected with the thing causing the sensations; for instance, in the case of the buzzing sound, such operations as slapping or shooing away, or otherwise effectively dealing with a mosquito. Thus, a mosquito generically is (originally) known to us solely as the sort of thing which is capable of causing certain sensations and is susceptible of being dealt with (adequately to certain ends) through certain acts.   This knowledge of what a mosquito is, however, is not present in us at most times in the form either of images or of words, but only as *a set of dormant habits.*

But when all the habits comprising the set are in one way or another stirred together from complete latency — made ready to function if and as need may occur — then a certain state of consciousness automatically arises: the complex of minimal sensory expectations and minimal volitional preparations, of which this total stirring consists, has an *intuited emergent "feel" of its own* different from that of any other such habit complex; and it is this intuited "feel" of it which constitutes our original *notion* or *abstract idea* of a mosquito.   This total but minimal stirring, let it be noted, is something very different from the getting ready to respond or to act in some one specific way; for the various types of response and of activity comprised in the set are largely incompatible with one another.   Only some of them are capable of being combined, made together.   Many of them are mutually exclusive, but are nevertheless co-members of the set because the circumstances and purposes to which a given one would be relevant are different from those to which the others would be relevant. To take an analogy, the total stirring might be compared to getting the *map* of a certain region; whereas readiness for one specific response or activity would be analogous to deciding on a specific *itinerary* through the region. Just as a map is a common basis for any number of different possible itineraries, each relevant to a different purpose and set of circumstances; so notional understanding of the nature of the thing a given word names is a common basis for any number of different specific expectations and plans of action, each relevant to a different aim and set of circumstances.

The intent of the foregoing account has been to throw light on the general psychological nature and origin of abstract ideas. For the sake of maximum perspicuity of essentials it has therefore abstained from mentioning certain factors of the example discussed, which complicate the account a little but do not alter its essence. A word about them must be added, however, to make clear that the abstract idea of a mosquito — to say nothing of others much more highly abstract — does not have only the anthropocentric basis which alone was mentioned in that account. The factors to which the account given traced that abstract idea were those habits of ours which bear on our personal, immediately practical relations to a mosquito — those having to do with what, directly, it can do to us or we to it. But the nature of a mosquito includes also characteristics that would remain if human beings had never existed — the mosquito's mating habits, its responses to light, to temperature, and to other conditions in its external and internal environment. Although man does not himself figure as an element of a description of these, he can nevertheless observe them. And their regularities too build up in him habitual expectations — expectations as to what a mosquito will do under various extrahuman circumstances, and as to what extrahuman effects its behavior will cause. Hence, what must be added to the account previously given of the abstract idea of a mosquito is that these impersonal expectations, no less than the personal ones and the readinesses for self-protective direct action, are part of the habit complex out of the minimal stirring of which emerges the unique "feel" that constitutes our abstract idea of a mosquito.

19. Perceiving, Conceiving, Imagining

In the light of what has just been said concerning abstract ideas and notional understanding, let us now return to, and examine in some detail, the fact mentioned earlier in passing that an abstract idea, once the mind has acquired it, may be aroused from latency in any one of several ways. Let us take again as example the abstract idea of a mosquito.

When what summons it is a *sensation* (of one or another of the kinds ordinarily caused by a mosquito), and in addition we *believe* (as ordinarily we then do) that the entity causing the sensation is one to which that abstract idea is appropriate, then this whole mental event constitutes *perceiving* a mosquito (visually, or auditorily, etc., and whether veridically or illusorily). To say that a certain abstract idea is "appropriate" to the entity causing a certain sensation means that the expectations, and the impulses related to them (of which together the abstract idea is the emergent), are — the expectations — probably, some of them, about to be fulfilled; and — the impulses — such that our carrying out certain ones of them in the present circumstances would affect the entity or its relations to us in a manner which would safeguard or foster those of our purposes or interests susceptible of being thwarted or promoted by the entity.

Appropriateness in this sense is what constitutes "correspondence" of our *idea of the nature* of the causative entity to the *objective nature* of the entity. Or we may put the matter by saying that the objective nature of a perceived entity, as distinguished from somebody's idea of its nature, consists in the entity's being such that a certain idea of its properties is appropriate (and certain other ideas of them inappropriate) in the presence of the entity — the appropriateness being defined in terms of conduciveness to fulfillment of specific kinds of purposes, interests or expectations related to the entity.

As pointed out earlier, perceiving, *e.g.*, perceiving a mosquito, comes under the heading of rei-real interpretation.

On the other hand, when the abstract idea of a mosquito is aroused in us *without belief* that a mosquito is present, by the *word* mosquito (or by other words, such for example as "a little buzzing insect that stings one on summer evenings"), then this constitutes *conceiving* (thinking of) a mosquito in general.

If, however, a set of words not only thus arouses in us the abstract idea of a mosquito, *i.e.*, makes us think of a mosquito, but in addition induces in us belief that a mosquito is present (as would, for example, another person's exclaiming "A mosquito!" or stating "There is a mosquito"), then these utterances of his are *verbal signs* for us — news, tidings — of the presence of a mosquito. In perception of a mosquito, on the contrary, the sensation (of the kind a mosquito ordinarily causes) which functions as sign of the presence of a mosquito is a *"real" sign* of it. In both cases, however, the interpretant of the sign is the same, consisting as it does of the thought (abstract idea) of a mosquito together with belief that one is present. The sign, of course, whether real or verbal, may be either illusive or veridical; that is, the belief it induces in us may be either erroneous or sound. In addition, the other person's *signal*, *i.e.*, the statement he made in order to induce the belief in us, may be either *mendacious* or *veracious*, according as he intended his statement to induce in us a belief which he himself held to be erroneous, or one which he held to be sound. And further, his *formulation* of what he intends to make us believe may (in respect to the particular language in which he intends to be speaking) be *correct* or *incorrect*; *e.g.*, he might, by mistake, use the word "mosquito" where "fly" would in English have been the correct word for what he meant.

The outcome of the preceding analysis is then as follows:

(1) A *concept* essentially consists of a word (or phrase) together with its semeiotic nonopinative interpretant;

(2) A *notional concept* consists of a word (or phrase) together with the abstract idea — the notion — which is its semeiotic nonopinative interpretant; and

(3) A *verbal concept* consists of a word (or phrase) together with the *words* (synonyms), or *phrase* (verbal definition), constituting the given word's semeiotic nonopinative interpretant. (The interpretant phrase contains no "opinator" word.)

Notional conceiving, *i.e.,* notional understanding of a word or phrase, comes under the heading of verbo-real interpretation; whereas conceiving verbally, *i.e.,* verbal understanding of a word or phrase, comes under the heading of verbo-verbal interpretation.

There now remains to ask what it is to *imagine something, e.g.,* a mosquito, as distinguished both from perceiving and from conceiving one.

"Imagining" is commonly used in one or the other of two senses. Sometimes it is used to mean illusory as distinguished from veridical perceiving; as, for instance, when, some one having said "I hear a mosquito," another person replies "No, you merely imagine it." The reply asserts in effect either that the interpretand was really an auditory image mistaken for a sensation — the interpretant being the same as in perception; or else that the interpretand was indeed a sensation, but one caused by something other than a mosquito, *i.e.,* the interpretant was inappropriate.

But sometimes "imagining" (or better, "imaging") is used in the sense of "forming an image of." In such imagining or imaging the interpretand is not, as in conceiving, the word "mosquito," but is an image — say, of the visual appearance of a mosquito — and the interpretant is the same as in the case of conceiving; that is, it consists of the notion of a mosquito without belief that one is present.

20. Merits and Defects of Notional and of Verbal Understanding of Words

Let us now consider the virtues and the shortcomings peculiar on the one hand to notional understanding of words, and on the other to verbal understanding.

We have seen that notional understanding of a word — at least in cases more or less analogous to the example we discussed — is rooted in our habits of expectation, and often also of action, in regard to things of the kind the word names. These habits, we suggested, were built up in us by observation or report of the various appearances of those things and of the regularities in their behavior — regularities as to the effects which, under various kinds of circumstances, are caused in, and are caused by changes in, those things. Let us note next that a word of which we have notional understanding may be either a vulgar or a technical term.

When it is a *vulgar* term, the habits at the basis of the notion it brings to our minds are chiefly habits relating to *ordinary* experiences of, and dealings with, entities of the kind the word names. To say these are "ordinary" means that they involve chiefly the capacities of such entities to affect us, and to do so directly or through but few and obvious intermediary steps; and the capacities of ourselves to deal with such entities, likewise directly or through but simple and familiar means. This is to say that, where vulgar terms are concerned, our understanding of them is mainly anthropocentric. Accordingly, the chief utility of notional understanding of a vulgar term is that it enables a person to shape his course in ordinary affairs by means of the commands, reports, opinions, counsels, or questions of other persons, in which the given term appears.

When, on the other hand, the word concerned is a *technical,* scientific term, notional understanding of it is chiefly exocentric — centered in external objects — for it is rooted in facts of the kind the sciences mainly seek, namely, facts as to what objective entities can do *to one another* and be done to *by one another*. In view of the current vogue of the anthropocentric version of the pragmatist philosophy of science, it is worth insisting here parenthetically that the sciences search for facts of this type quite irrespective of whether the interactions between the objective entities concerned can be controlled by us, or on the contrary are beyond our control; and irrespective also of whether or not the behavior of those objective entities can ultimately affect our welfare at all either for good or ill.

The exocentric character of the basis of our notional understanding of technical terms entails that the utility of such understanding of them is chiefly *scientific* utility, as distinguished from everyday practical utility. It is utility for the guidance of the investigator, as such, in his exocentric observational and experimental tasks, rather than utility for the guidance of the plain man in the ordinary, anthropocentrically practical tasks, which are his typical concerns.

It should be noted that the contrast emphasized above between scientific and practical utility is perfectly compatible with the fact that exocentric scientific knowledge, after it has been obtained, often turns out to have, indirectly, great practical utility. What is here maintained is only that, in many and probably most cases, the ordinary practical needs, to the satisfying of which such knowledge eventually turns out to be useful, were not what drove the scientist to embark on, or what directed him in, the search for that sort of knowledge. The fact that the search for knowledge is a problem-solving enterprise and that the problem solver himself is a living being and dwells in a society does not imply, as often seems tacitly assumed, that the problems he seeks to solve are *eo ipso* themselves biological or social. Not all the "problems of men" are problems *about* men. In man, as Schopenhauer rightly insisted, curiosity is capable of being disinterested — disengaged at times from its usual concern with biologically or socially practical problems. At such times its problems are purely scientific; that is, they are problems simply of knowledge-getting, investigated without extra-heuristic preoccupations. This means that the utility or instrumentality which a scientist, as such, demands of a hypothesis is utility *to the satisfaction of curiosity;* *i.e.,* what he demands is that the hypothesis be a valid answer or a means to a valid answer to the question he asked. But the question can be about anything. And the control, which genuinely scientific knowledge is alleged always to confer but actually confers only in some cases, is often only control over scientific events, *i.e.,* laboratory events, which may have no bearing or no known bearing on anthropocentrically practical problems.

We have now seen that the utility typical of notional understanding of words is its capacity — in ordinary matters, or in scientific research — to shape automatically our expectations and our actions suitably to the nature of the things the words name. On the other hand, the typical defect of merely notional understanding is its inadequacy for discursive purposes — for the purpose of making clear to others the meaning of words they do not understand, and for the purpose of long yet dependable trains of reasoning. Merely verbal understanding of words, on the other hand, has the sort of utility notional understanding lacks and lacks the sort of utility the latter possesses. One's understanding of a word, of course, is seldom exclusively notional or exclusively verbal.

In connection with verbal understanding too, we must consider both vulgar and technical terms. When a given word is a *vulgar* term, verbal understanding of it is again chiefly anthropocentric. The other words the given one brings to mind are either synonyms or loosely descriptive phrases, mostly in perceptual terms, such as would enable several persons cooperating in some task to identify the kind of thing the given word refers to if they lacked notional understanding of it as used in the commands, suggestions, or questions that pass between them.

When, on the other hand, the word is a *technical* term, verbal understanding of it, like notional, is then mainly exocentric. The other words the given one causes to come to mind are, typically, those formulating such of the properties of the object the word names as relate to the interactions of it with other objects. The inferences, of which scientific inquiry makes so much use, virtually require that these properties be *formulated*. That is, these inferences depend on *verbal* more than on notional understanding of the word which names the entity possessing the properties; and, moreover, on verbal understanding of it which is *analytical* rather than ingenuous. That scientific inferences are thus largely verbo-verbal is most obvious in the instance of those consisting of mathematical calculations. These often do not require notional understanding of the symbols entering into them, but only capacity to perform according to rule various transformations or substitutions in symbolic expressions. This is shown by the fact that sometimes calculating machines perform the required operations more quickly and accurately than does the mind.

The data which are fed into such machines, or, in some other instances, into the logical mechanism of the human mind, are not so much notions as words — specifically, numerals and certain other vocables. And it is in terms of verbal rather than of notional interpretation of these that the process of logico-mathematical inference goes on. One usually hopes, of course, and tries to insure by the operations called "counting" and "measuring," that the numerals represent adequately the real facts one is concerned with; and, otherwise, that the "operator" and "relator" symbols used represent adequately certain operations and relations among those facts. But the process of inference itself is, there, essentially verbo-verbal. It is this character of it which insures the rigor necessary for dependability where the conclusions to be reached by the inference are remote rather than proximate and turn on minute rather than on rough discriminations. In such instances it is only the verbal expression terminally yielded by the inference that needs to be "decoded," *i.e.,* interpreted notionally.

These remarks indicate that the scientific utility of verbal understanding of scientific terms and expressions is very great; for scientific inquiry, far from being solely an experimental task, relies to a considerable extent on inference both mathematical and other. Indeed, the farther a science progresses, the larger becomes the part of inference in it, and the more does experimentation then function as test of the validity of the inferences rather than as direct source of new knowledge. It must be remembered, however, that purely verbo-verbal inference is "blind," so that, if the verbal data we feed into its mechanism represent errors or absurdities, what it will yield to us — and as rigorously as in other cases — will only be the implications of those errors or absurdities.

21. Conditions Under Which Verbo-Verbal Operations Can Substitute for Rei-Real Ones

Mathematics and logic operate with verbal entities, and with rules set up by stipulation for the formation and transformation of verbal expressions. Their operations, thus, are autonomous in the sense that, for performance of them, it makes no difference at all whether the verbal entities figuring in them do or do not represent any nonverbal entities. It is therefore something of a puzzle that mathematics and logic should nevertheless sometimes be "applicable" — that their verbal operations should sometimes be capable of predicting what would be the outcome of physical and other real operations or processes. Such predictiveness, however, is possessed by verbal operations only when certain conditions are fulfilled. In the present section, I shall attempt to say only enough about the general nature of these conditions to make the predictiveness understandable.

In applying mathematics or logic to the solving of physical or other nonverbal problems, three kinds of operations are essentially involved. One is the rei-verbal operation of passing from given nonverbal facts to verbal entities representing each adequately for the purposes in view. This is the operation we have called coding or ciphering or formulating the given real facts. The second operation is essentially verbo-verbal, and may be called calculating, in the broad sense which includes not only arithmetical and algebraic operations, but also logical operations not ordinarily labelled mathematical. The third operation is verbo-real — that of decoding or deciphering the verbal expression in which the calculating eventuated, *i.e.,* of passing from that verbal expression to the notion of the sort of fact the expression symbolizes.

In order that the calculation, *i.e.,* the verbo-verbal operation, should be capable of predicting the fact that would result from the real operation or process for which it substitutes, it is necessary, for one thing, that the verbo-verbal operation should be formally similar or formally equivalent to the rei-real operation for which it substitutes. In the case of addition, for example, this means that the operation we call addition of numbers, and the one we call addition of, say, lengths, must equally possess the familiar set of formal characters — associativeness, commutativeness, etc. — which jointly define addition generically, *i.e.,* define addition irrespective of whether it be of numbers, or of lengths, or weights, or anything else.

Again, the verbal expression which formulates a nonverbal fact that is a datum of the problem must be formally similar to the fact it formulates; that is, the verbal relations of the expression to other expressions, and the real relations of the fact to other facts, must be similar or equivalent in form. To make clear what this means when, for instance, the verbal expression is numerical, a few words have to be said as to the nature of cardinal numbers, of numerals, and of numerousness. The following outline account of the nature of cardinal numbers makes no attempt at formal rigor, and largely follows Norman Campbell's.[12]

Let us first take a certain set of utterables, *i.e.,* of words, of one utterance of which the following are a part: 0, 1, 2, 3, 4, 5, 6, 7, 8, 9. The rule for constructing other entities of the set out of these may be assumed to have been already laid down. We then stipulate that the utterable entities constituting that set shall be called "the numerals," and that the numerals shall have a standard serial order, *viz.,* the order: 0, 1, 2, 3, 4, 5, 6, 7, 8, 9, . . . The rule for ordering the remaining ones in the standard manner may be assumed to have been already laid down.

We then select from among the numerals in their standard order the following standard sets, each of which, we stipulate, shall be called a "cardinal number":

0
0, 1
0, 1, 2
0, 1, 2, 3
0, 1, 2, 3, 4
etc.

But now, since each of the numerals is an utterable entity, *i.e.,* a word or set of words, we can stipulate finally that the last numeral of each of these standard sets shall be used as the name of the set.

A cardinal number is thus a collection of words related to a certain one of them, which is used as its name, in a manner fixed by stipulation — the collection of utterables which constitutes any given cardinal number automatically having to all the other such collections a unique set of relations in respect of including and included.

Now, formal similarity between a number (which, as we have just seen, is a certain sort of collection of numerals, *i.e.,* of words)

---

[12] Campbell, *What Is Science?* Methuen, London, 1921, Chap. VI.

and a collection of real entities (*e.g.,* a collection of units of length, or a collection of chairs, etc.) means *sameness of numerousness;* and this in turn means that the two collections are *matchable,* member for member. The operation, however, by which one passes from a given collection of real entities to a collection of numerals (*i.e.,* to a number) that will match it member for member, is the familiar operation called *counting* the members of the given real collection. The requirement of formal similarity means here, therefore, that the numeral we employ to represent the given real collection for purposes of calculation must be the numeral which counting of it yielded or would have yielded.

22. The Main Branches of General Hermeneutics

I propose to call General Hermeneutics the science that takes interpretation in general as its subject matter. It includes semeiology, but, since not all interpretation is semeiotic, its scope is broader than that of semeiology. In the light of the conception of functional interpretation set forth in this chapter, and of various distinctions we have had occasion to make, it is now possible to offer a list of the main branches of general hermeneutics.

First of all, under the heading of semeiology, three, or if we prefer four, systematic divisions of inquiry may be distinguished, as follows:

(*a*) *Syntactics.* This would be the study of the relations of discursive entities to other discursive entities, in so far as these relations are generated by conventional rules of formation and transformation of combinations of discursive entities; and wholly irrespective of what the discursive entities concerned stand for, or of whether they stand for anything at all. More briefly, syntactics is the study of semeiotic verbo-verbal interpretation.

(*b*) *Semantics.* This term is currently used in two senses — one broad and the other narrow. In the broad and more popular sense it is synonymous with semeiology, semeiotics. In the narrow and more technical sense it designates a branch of semeiology. For the broad sense, I propose to use exclusively "semeiology" or "semeiotics."

In the narrow sense, "semantics" is primarily the study of verbo-real interpretation, but may be conceived as including also the study of the converse type of interpretation, *viz.*, rei-verbal interpretation.

If, however, it should be regarded as desirable to distinguish each of these two types of interpretation by a name of its own, then "semantics" would designate only the study of verbo-real interpretation, *i.e.*, of the notional interpretation of words; and

(*c*) *Onomatics* would designate the study of rei-verbal interpretation, *i.e.*, of verbal formulation of nonverbal facts.

(*d*) *Alectics.* This name is here proposed for the study of semeiotic rei-real interpretation, *i.e.*, of semeiotic interpretation in which neither the interpretand nor the interpretant is a discursive entity. It is this nondiscursive, *i.e.*, wordless, character, which the adjective "alectic" connotes.

Mnemics. Since rote memory does not entail that the interpretand be capable of functioning as, for certain purposes, a substitute for what the interpretant is the thought of, nor even entails that the interpretant be the thought *of* anything, rote memory is not *semeiotic* interpretation, and the study of it or of the art of rote memorization is therefore not a branch of semeiology. Rote memory, however, is nonetheless *functional* interpretation; and the study of it and of the art of rote memorization is therefore a branch of general hermeneutics. It may be designated *mnemics.*

Semaphorics. This name is proposed for the study of signals. According to the analysis we have offered, a signal is an *attempt* by one person to communicate with another by means of some perceptually public utterance. If the signal is not interpreted as a signal by the person to whom it is addressed, the signalling is unsuccessful — the attempt to communicate fails. But although successful signalling thus implies an interpretive operation, signalling, being a psycho-physical not a psycho-psychical operation, is not interpreting; and if general hermeneutics is defined as the study of interpretation, semaphorics is not one of the branches of it. It is a branch of the study of the relations between minds — specifically, between one mind qua utterer of signals and another qua interpreter of them. It constitutes, perhaps, the "pragmatics" branch of an account of the operations of minds, as distinguished from the behavioral operations of organic bodies. C. W. Morris, who gave currency to the term "pragmatics" and who is throughout concerned with the behavior of organic bodies and therefore not of minds unless in the Pickwickian sense radical behaviorism puts on the word "mind," defines pragmatics as "that portion of semiotic which deals with the origins, uses, and effects of signs within the behavior in which they occur."[13] A critical examination of this definition need not be introduced here, since the operations of minds, not of organisms, is all we are directly concerned with in this chapter.

But in the light of the contents of Chapter 15 it appears that no semeiotic, such as Morris's, that is formulated wholly in terms of the behavior of bodily organisms, can be all-inclusive or indeed get at what is the very core of semeiosis. For, as we have seen, "material" substances and therefore "organic bodies" can ultimately be defined only in terms of "perception," and perception consists in *interpretation of an intuition* — specifically, of a sensation as effect of some nonintuited event. Interpretation in this case, however, cannot possibly be defined in terms of the behavior of "bodies," since these are themselves definable only in terms of such interpretation, *viz.*, of a certain psycho-psychical operation. Occurrence of it is thus presupposed, even if unawares, by any account of interpretation formulated in terms of the behavior of bodies.

---

[13] C. W. Morris, *Signs, Language, and Behavior*, p. 219.

Chapter 17

THE SUBSTANTIALITY OF MINDS

In the preceding chapters we have had many occasions to refer to minds. When so doing we have employed, simply as a matter of the ordinary usage of words, the various forms of speech appropriate in connection with substances, thus tacitly categorizing minds as substances. The hypothesis that a mind is a substance, however, is in little favor today. It suggests too readily the "something-I-know-not-what" of Locke, assumed to support — in some unanalyzed sense of the word — attributes observed to cohere. As so used, of course, "substance" is but a solid-sounding name for the answer to an unanswered question. But if, instead of such a gratuitous unknown, we are content to mean by "substance" simply what our analysis in Chapter 10 exhibited as distinctive of the kinds of entities — water, wood, trees, etc. — most commonly called substances, then, I submit, a mind too is genuinely a substance. To render this evident, however, we shall need to heed in the case of minds the same logical distinctions as in our discussion of material substances. We shall need to distinguish between the generic kind of thing called "a mind," the typical determinable kinds of mind, and the completely determinate kinds (*infimae species*) of mind. Then we shall have to ask what constitutes *existence* of such determinate kinds of mind as happen to exist.

The considerations set forth in Chapter 15 led us to the conclusion that physical objects — however firmly known and real — are in ultimate analysis known by us only through the interpreting, in the manner there described, of certain of the contents of our own minds. The description of that manner is our answer to the question as to the relation between the mental process that constitutes perceiving and the material events and substances perceived. That question concerns the *epistemological* relation between a mind and the world of material events and things (which includes that mind's body among other such things). But the question usually referred to as that of the relation between "mind and body," rather than between "mind and matter," is a different one.[1] It concerns the nature of the *ontological* relation between a given mind and the material object, unique among the many others that mind equally perceives, which it calls "its own" body. We have not so far directly considered this question, having decided that before we could do so fairly we needed to be clear concerning two preliminary questions: One, what is it to be "a material object"; and the other, what is it to be "a mind." Our answer to the first was offered in Chapter 15, and we are now to seek the answer to the second. To do so we obviously must proceed by observing the mind itself directly, that is, introspectively, and by reasoning inductively from what introspection exhibits; for if we were to proceed by assuming initially that the mind is a "function" of the body, and then mention only such facts as seem to accord with the sense we attach to that blessed word, we should be begging *ab initio* the whole question of the nature of the mind-body relation.

We shall therefore now attempt to say what a mind discovers itself to be when it observes itself introspectively and construes inductively what it so observes.

1. Mind as a Substance

Like the nature of any other substance, that of a mind analyzes into a system of what we have called "properties" or "capacities."

---

[1] Cf. W. P. Montague, "The First Mystery of Consciousness," *Jour. of Philos.*, Vol. XLII, No. 12, June 7, 1945.

They are such things as aptitudes, dispositions, proclivities, habits, tastes, powers, and other mental "traits"; for all these — like combustibility, brittleness, corrosiveness, etc. — analyze into "if . . . then . . ."causal connections. Some of them are innate, but the great majority are acquired by "conditioning." Some apparently are permanent, or virtually so, but others change after a longer or shorter time. A capacity is not itself an event but a causal connection between events qua of given kinds. On the other hand, the acquisition, continuance, or loss of a capacity is an event; it is not, however, an intuited event but is knowable only inductively by reflection upon such intuited events as are evidence of it.

The innate capacities of a mind, in contrast with the acquired ones (termed "habits") are those called "aptitudes," "dispositions," "instincts," etc. These are the very core of a mind, for on the framework consisting of a particular set of them are woven all the events which comprise the history of the particular mind concerned, including the acquisition of such habits as it does acquire. On that very same framework any one of many different histories were possible; and another history, more or less different from the actual one, would have been woven instead if certain external events, affecting the given mind but independent of its control, had occurred instead of those which did. Anyone of us who has attained middle life can easily imagine how different would have been the history of his mind notwithstanding the sameness of its individual core of aptitudes, dispositions, and instincts, if, perhaps, he had become an orphan at an early age, or had been born and brought up in a radically different environment, or had never met the woman who became his wife but had married another, and so on. In the light of such reflections, one's actual personality appears no longer as one's essential self, but rather only as a particular one of the many roles which the same basic actor was equally capable of personating, and bits of some of which he may in day dreams indeed occasionally play at personating.

Some of the properties of minds are psycho-physical: a given mind is such that, in circumstances of a certain kind, a mental event of a given kind (*e.g.,* a volition to raise the arm) causes a material event of a certain kind (*e.g.,* motion of the arm). Minds also have physico-psychical properties. These are the capacities a mind has under certain circumstances to experience sensations of various kinds upon stimulation of the sense organs of the material object called its body.

Minds have in addition endlessly numerous psycho-psychical properties. Memory and conceptual knowledge, for instance, are forms of mental habit — acquired capacities: psychical events of certain kinds come to cause regularly in a given mind psychical events of certain other kinds. At any given time, the vast majority of our memories, of our beliefs, and of the items of our conceptual knowledge are latent. They exist only as specific capacities. A moment ago, for instance, while I was not conscious of my knowledge that Aristotle was one of Plato's pupils, that item of knowledge existed in my mind only as an abiding causal connection — only in the sense that *if* the question as to whose pupil Aristotle was had come to my consciousness, *then,* under normal psychological circumstances, this would have caused the answer "Plato's" to arise in my mind. I had that knowledge not in the sense that I was thinking of that proposition and was conscious of believing it on good evidence — for at that moment I was not thinking of it at all — but in the sense that the *property* consisting of capacity to answer that question in that manner was even at that moment an intrinsic part of a complete account of the kind of mind which was mine over a certain period including that moment. Similarly, I have the capacity to remember under normal circumstances how much is 3 times 7; to calculate how much is 496 times 694, etc. The *exercise* of these and other mental capacities involves occurrence of particular intuitions, which are introspectively observable. But the *capacity* in each case is possessed throughout periods during which no occasion arises for it to be exercised; and the capacity here is not, any more than in the case of the capacities of physical things, directly observable. It is only inferrible, inductively, on the basis of observation of certain sequences of intuitions.

2. Determinable and Determinate Kinds of Mind

Just as various kinds of material substance can be distinguished, so can various typical kinds of mind; for instance, the artistic, the scientific, the mystical, the executive, etc. These labels, of course, mean only that, in the kinds of mind they designate, certain groups of capacities are relatively prominent.

Those labels, moreover, are names of determinable not determinate kinds of mind. An example of a determinate kind of mind would be the exact kind which happens to be, say, mine, or the reader's, or his aunt's, etc., at a certain time. It is the more or less systematically integrated set of mental capacities, each in its full specificity, which together constitute the nature of the given person at the time. It comprises, therefore, all the memories, beliefs, aptitudes, dispositions, tastes, and so on, which are his at the time considered and which would therefore have to be included in an exhaustive account of the kind of mind he individuates at the time.

3. What Constitutes Existence of a Mind of a Given Determinate Kind

But no matter how full and specific that account, what it would be an account of would be still a *kind* of mind, even if a determinate, not as before only a determinable, kind. It would be an *infima species* of the genus "mind." Hence, it would be theoretically possible that two or a dozen or a hundred minds of precisely the same determinate kind should exist at one or another time. Also, it is possible that there should cease to exist any mind of that determinate kind; and conceivable that none should ever have existed.

This poses the question as to what constitutes *existence* of a mind of a given determinate kind, and as to how one existent such mind would differ from another of the very same determinate kind. This is the question as to the nature of the so-called "principle of individuation" when the kind individuated is a kind of mind.

The answer is that one existing mind of a completely determinate kind would differ from another of the very same kind existing either at the same time or at some other time in that the history of each would be different. To say that an existing mind has a history is to say that a description of that mind includes not only *capacities,* which define the kind of mind it is at a given time of its existence, but in addition *events.* And it is these events that constitute the history, and the existing, of an "existing" mind of a given kind.

Those events are of two sorts. One comprises the acquirings, retainings, or losings, of one or another capacity. The other consists of the *exercisings* of one or another capacity. Each such exercise involves the occurrence of one or more intuitions. When the capacity concerned is a physico-psychical one, the intuition involved is a sensation. When the capacity is a psycho-physical one, the intuition involved may be of one or another of several kinds, but, typically, would be a volition — a volition to perform some bodily act. When the capacity is a psycho-psychical one, only intuitions are involved in the exercise of it. Exercise of it consists in occurrence of one or another of the mental operations discussed in Chapter 16. That is, exercise of it consists in this, that occurrence of a given intuition, in a context consisting of certain other intuitions, causes occurrence of a certain other intuition. And knowledge by the mind concerned that it possesses the particular psycho-psychical capacity concerned is an induction from its observation of such cases of causation among its intuitions. As regards physico-psychical and psycho-physical capacities, the sense in which a mind knows that it possesses them was explained in Chapter 15. In all cases, the knowledge a mind has of its capacities ultimately rests, in one way or another, upon its observation of its stream of intuitions. *These are therefore the existentially basic mental events.*

They are basic, moreover, also to our basic conception of "physical" events, to our knowledge of occurrences of these, and to our conception and knowledge of the history and therefore of the existence of any instance of a physical substance. All this follows from considerations set forth in Chapters 10 and 15, but the argument may be summarily stated as follows:

(*a*) The physical events which constitute the history of an existing instance of any physical substance S are conceivable only as changes or unchanges of *capacities* of S, or as changes in the spatial relations of S to some other physical substance Z.

(*b*) Change of location of a physical substance S, however, is itself describable as consisting in this: that at continuously successive times the set of properties defining the nature of S obtains at continuously different places.

(*c*) As we have seen, to say that a substance S has a capacity or property P is to say that S is such that *if* in circumstances of a kind K an event of a kind C should occur, *then* an event of a kind E would thereby be caused to occur.

(*d*) But further, if C, E, and K are conceived *in only physical terms,* then they too are conceivable only as changes or unchanges of *capacities,* which themselves analyze as "if . . . then . . ." causal connections between events themselves consisting of changes or unchanges of *capacities,* and so on, *ad infinitum.*

(*e*) It follows that, in terms of only *physical* events, it is impossible to make a historical statement about S (for instance, to say that at a certain time *T, S has* a capacity *P*) ; but only possible to say that, at time *T, S has P if certain physical conditions are then present.* For although *P* is itself of the "if *C*, then *E*" form, nevertheless to assert *P* categorically is a very different thing from asserting *P* conditionally; *i.e.,* it is one thing to say: "*S is* such that if *C*, then *E*," and quite another thing to say: "*S* is such that *if A, then S* is such that if *C*, then *E*." For example, it is one thing to say of a piece of wax that it *is* now *solid, i.e.,* is now such that if pressed it would resist penetration; and quite another thing to say of it that *if it is now cold,* then it is now solid, *i.e.,* is such that if pressed it would resist penetration.

(*f*) Hence the only facts that enable us to make historical statements about physical substances — *i.e.,* to escape from the *ad infinitum* conditionality of statement just described — are (1) that physical substances, or some of them, have physico-psychical capacities in addition to their physico-physical capacities; (2) that, at certain times, these physical substances exercise their physico-psychical capacities, *i.e.,* cause in us certain intuitions — specifically, certain sensations; and (3) that no intuition is itself a capacity or change of capacity, but is, in the experiencing of it, immediately and categorically known to be occurring; whereas changes or unchanges of capacities are known to be occurring only in the sense that occurrence of them is being signified or inferred — signified by or inferred from, ultimately, the immediately experienced occurrence of an intuition.[2]

The notion of event is basic and minimal, but employment of it leaves open the questions (*a*) as to whether the event one speaks of is mental or physical, (*b*) as to whether it is more particularly a change or an unchange, and (*c*), still more par-

---

[2] Cf. the role of what C. I. Lewis calls "terminating" judgments. My point here, is, I believe, essentially the same as his, notwithstanding the, as it seems to me, gratuitous pragmatic proviso he makes a part of his definition of terminating judgments. See his *An Analysis of Knowledge and Valuation*, pp. 179 ff. and (on pp. 274–5, *Philos. Review*, Vol. LVII, No. 3, May 1948, in the article already referred to) my criticism of his definition.

ticularly, whether it is a change or unchange of capacity, or of location, or of intuition. Further, among events, intuitions are basic in that they are the only events we directly and literally experience, as distinguished from inferring or postulating.

If we ask whether there may not be something more to a physical event than merely a change or unchange of capacity, or of location of a substance, the answer is that the only thing else, of which we have any positive conception, and which is available to us as content of such a supposition, would be *some intuition not our own,* connected somehow with the change or unchange of capacity or of location. This, in fact, is what we ordinarily suppose in the case of the physical events, in human bodies not our own, that we call *acts, viz.,* bodily events caused by a desire or volition of the mind we assume to be connected with the other body; for example, such a physical event as *jumping,* which is an act, whereas *falling* is not the sort of event called an act.

I see no necessity to suppose that rocks, water, etc., have an *an sich* consisting of intuitions; but even if we should suppose it, this would leave them no less material than are human bodies, and would lead us not to an idealistic monism but to a dualism of more or less the same type as that of body-mind; for the supposition of such an *an sich* for physical substances does not entail their being "not really" physical. They still have all the capacities we mean by "physical" capacities, and do not mean when we speak of "psychical" capacities.

It is worth noting further that when we think of the earth as it was before there were minds, we do so in terms of such landscapes as we find pictured in books on geology, or perhaps, at a remoter time, in terms of masses of incandescent gas. But either of these we conceive in terms either only of their physico-physical properties, or also of their physico-psychical ones; actually, chiefly in terms of the latter — and that is, in terms of what we should have seen, heard, etc., if we had been there. For if not so, then only as we now conceive the imperceptible and unimageable particles of physics and the events occurring among them; and that is, only in terms of physico-physical capacities and of changes in these capacities, or in their locations — such changes as somehow eventually cause changes in physical things that have physico-psychical properties; that is, in things that are perceivable.

4. The Stream of Intuitions

The intuitions, in the occurring of which the existing of a mind ultimately consists, are some of them clear and some obscure; some coexistent and some successive; some with objective reference and some without; some passive and some active. These intuitions are temporally related one to another much as are the notes which together make up a symphony. Some begin after certain others have ended; some, before others end, and during the time of coexistence interpenetrate with them, so that the intuited state of the mind at a given time is a complex of diverse intuitions.[3] Buddhist philosophers, to explain the continuity of the stream notwithstanding that none of the intuitions which make it up endures more than a finite time, are wont to compare the stream to a rope, in which none of the individual fibers extends through the whole length, but which is continuous nonetheless because the fibers overlap one another. The simile of the rope, however, is less adequate than that of a symphony, for in the rope the fibers do not interpenetrate; whereas the notes of a symphony sounding at a given time, although individually distinguishable by trained attention, nevertheless otherwise pervade one another much as do at a given time one's sensations, one's mood, one's thought, one's purpose, and one's impulses. Intuited

---

[3] Cf. D. H. Parker's *Experience and Substance*, p. 42, where he writes: ". . . the most diverse kinds of activities, not in any way necessary to each other, and sensa of the most diverse provenance and quality may be present together and interpenetrate. So a sorrow may exist not only side by side with but compenetrating each member of a series of reflections on the latest important European crisis, or equally compenetrating a medley of sounds coming in from the busy traffic of the city streets. . . ."

continuity of the stream is automatically insured by the fact that if there should be a gap in the stream it could not possibly be intuited, for intuition of it would fill it as effectively as would have any other intuition and there would therefore be no intuited gap.

5. Why No Two Minds Can Have the Same History

All mental events, like any others, have causes and effects. Some of these are internal to the given mind in the sense that they too are events in it, but others external in the sense that they are events outside it. For example, the proximate causes of those of a mind's intuitions called sensations are not any of its other intuitions and are therefore external. Again, some among those of its intuitions called "volitions" have some effects that are not any of its other intuitions but are either physical events or intuitions caused in some other mind and hence are external to the given mind. Each mind thus affects some other minds. It does so apparently sometimes directly, in the as yet ill-understood manner called "telepathy," but more commonly by voluntary or involuntary causation of material events that in turn cause sensations in the others.[4]

Now, from the fact that some of the events in each mind are caused by, or are contingent upon, some of the events in certain other minds, it follows that no two minds can have exactly the same history. If, for example, it happens to be an event in the history of mind A that it *taught* fact F to mind B at time T, then the history of mind B will be different from that of mind A in that, at time T, B *learned* fact F from A. Moreover, the sensations a mind has at a given time depend in part (so long as it

---

[4] I make no apology for thus referring to "telepathy" as a fact, even if one apparently rather rare. The evidence that it sometimes occurs is by this time both so abundant, and some of it so good, that anyone who rejects out of hand the possibility of telepathy can now fairly be regarded as simply uninformed. The term "telepathy," I should add, is used here without any theory as to how communication occurs in the instances so denominated, and only to mean communication between minds in some manner other than through movements causative of sensations.

has a body) on the place of its body at that time relatively to the places of the other material objects comprised in the physical world; and no two bodies — whether human, animal, or inanimate — can occupy the same place at the same time. Hence no two minds can have exactly all of the same sensations at every moment.

6. Location of Minds in Psychical "Space" and "Time"

In connection with the question as to what constitutes the "principle of individuation" where kinds of mind rather than of physical substance are concerned, it may be recalled that, when we were considering the problem of "action at a distance" in the case of physical substances, we found that physical "contact" and "distance" (spatial and temporal), and therefore, more generally, relative locations in physical space and time, had to be defined ultimately in terms of physical causation direct or indirect. In view of the question we are eventually to consider, as to whether it is possible that a mind should continue to exist after the death of its body — when the environment of that mind would then presumably consist only of other minds — it is interesting to ask what, if anything, "contact" and "distance" between thus disembodied minds might then mean. It seems possible to say that "psychical contact" between a mind A and another mind B would mean that A and B are so related that occurrence of a certain event E in A would cause occurrence of a certain event F in B directly, i.e., without intermediary causation by E of some event G in any third mind C. Psychical contact as so defined seems to be what occurs in instances of telepathy between minds whose bodies are at physical distance from each other.

On the other hand, to say that a mind A is "at a psychical distance" from a mind B would mean that they are so related that occurrence in A of a certain event E would cause occurrence of a certain event F in B, but would do so only indirectly, i.e., only through causation of some other event or events in one or more intermediary minds — the psychical distance between A and B being then said to be the greater as the number of intermediaries is greater.

These definitions of psychical contact and distance would in turn seem to provide an adequate basis for the conception of "relative locations of minds" in what we may call a psychical "space" and "time" that would be objective in the sense of *social,* as contrasted with the place-intuitions and time-intuitions of each mind. The "psychical location" of a given mind (whether embodied, or conceivably, unembodied) in objective, *i.e.,* social, "psychical space" and "psychical time" would thus be defined in terms of what that mind is and is not "in social position to" do to, and to be done to by, each of the other existing minds.

This conception of psychical position or location of minds as such, *i.e.,* of minds independently of whether embodied or not, appears to be precisely analogous to the conception, as we analyzed it, of position or location of material substances in physical space and time. Hence, in a sense parallel to that in which it is possible to say that occupation of a particular place in physical time and space is what constitutes existence of physical substance of a given determinate kind, it appears possible to say that occupation of a particular social position, *i.e.,* of a particular place in objective psychical time and space as defined above, is what existence of a mind of a given determinate kind consists in. "Occupation" in either case is defined in terms of causation, and thus implies having a history.

7. The Parts of Minds

A mind, like any other kind of substance, also has parts, for its capacities are integrated in a number of subsystems which, although normally connected and interacting with one another, nevertheless have each a degree of independence. Each of these subsystems of capacities is one of the organs or parts of the psychical organism called "a mind." Each of them is a "self" of a particular type — a playboy, or *pater familias,* or business man, or poet, or devotee, or moralist, and so on. Each, as existing, has its own interests, purposes, and will-to-experience-and-expression. Sometimes, one alone of these role-selves occupies the "stage of consciousness," *i.e.,* the intuitions then occurring manifest no other. Sometimes, two or more are in this sense on the stage, perhaps cooperating, perhaps contending for dominance or exclusive possession. At all such times, the other role-selves exist only "subconsciously," *i.e.,* the intuitions then occurring are not manifestations of them, or at least not direct manifestations; for if these other role-selves operate at all at such times, they do so only "from the wings," *i.e.,* only by inhibiting, or reinforcing, or modifying in some other manner what the manifestations of the role-self on the stage would otherwise be; not by manifesting themselves there directly in intuitions typical of themselves.

Like the members of a family, of a business organization, or of an army, or like the organs of a living body, or like the various economic, political, professional, and other groups in a nation, those various role-selves each have functions of their own in the life of the whole, with corresponding duties and rights. A mind, thus, is literally a society of semi-independent, semi-interdependent role-selves, which during life all use the same body and get along together more or less harmoniously and efficiently. Since their interplay is in large measure subconscious, and techniques for the investigation of the subconscious portion of the mind have only recently begun to be developed, our knowledge of it is as yet but meager.

But even after the preceding account of the states, the properties, and the parts of a mind, the question might still seem to remain as to what *is* this mind which *has* them. The answer is essentially the one given in Chapter 5 to the same question, but asked there about physical substances and about substance in general rather than specifically about minds. As regards the latter, the answer can hardly be put more tellingly than it was by the Buddhist sage Nagasena when answering King Milindha's same question.[5] He pointed out to the King that a chariot, which *has* wheels, axle, body, etc., *is* nothing other than these together in a certain relation to one another; and that this is true likewise of a mind and the states and other constituents it has. What these are has been described in detail above. Here we need only to repeat that what *has* any particular one of them is nothing other than the whole which they together constitute; and to add that the adjective corresponding to any given capacity — as "fusible" corresponds to fusibility, or "impatient" corresponds to impatience — are predicable, not of the kind of substance concerned, but only of existent instances of it.

8. Molecular Minds

In connection with the dissociations of personality which sometimes occur,[6] it is interesting to ask what is the least a mind could comprise and still be a mind as defined in this chapter. This question is of interest also in connection with the fact that such empirical evidence as there is that a mind may survive the death of its body is not only inconclusive but is also ambiguous in the sense that, even if it did establish survival, it would still leave open the possibility that what survives is only some portion of the mind concerned.

In the light of the preceding sections of this chapter it would seem that the simplest kind of mind theoretically possible would be a system consisting of only three capacities. One would be a capacity for "impressions" of some particular kind (whether caused by physical stimulation of a bodily sense organ, or caused

[5] *Milindapañha* (25¹), transl. by H. C. Warren in *Buddhism in Translations,* Harvard Oriental Series, Vol. 3, p. 131.

[6] See, for instance, the famous case described by Morton Prince in the book, *The Dissociation of a Personality;* also the booklet, *My Life as a Dissociated Personality* (edited by Morton Prince), which is the account another of his patients gives of her experiences.

telepathically, or clairvoyantly, or otherwise). A second capacity would be one for action, *i.e.*, for causation, by intuitions of the kind called impulses, of an external effect of some kind, which might consist of some bodily change, or of an intuition (impression) in some other mind, or conceivably of some material event other than a bodily one, produced "psycho-kinetically," *i.e.*, without the intermediary of a body. The third capacity would be a psycho-psychical one, to wit, a capacity for causation, by an impression of a given kind, of such an impulse as just described. It is to be noted that if, as now, a *minimal* mind is what we consider, then the effect caused by the impulse caused by the impression could not consist of some other intuition in the same mind, for such an other intuition in it would itself have an effect of one kind or another, and would thus evidence a fourth capacity (to wit, again a psycho-psychical one), and therefore the kind of mind so constituted would not be the simplest conceivable. The triadic, simplest kind, we may call "molecular"; and we may then say that the minimal *existence, i.e.*, history, of a molecular mind would consist of a single exercise of its three capacities. This would involve two intuitions: one, an impression; and the other, an impulse caused by it.

The "molecular" kind of mind just described, and likewise the "molar" kind of mind that is actually ours, may be called *participative,* in the sense that some of the intuitions of any such mind have causes external to it, and some have effects also external to it: it is to some extent affected by, and in turn affects to some extent, an environment of some kind, whether a physical or a psychical. But that a mind should thus be participative does not preclude, but rather entails, that, at certain times, a molar mind should actually not be participating. These would be the times at which only its psycho-psychical capacities are being exercised. Such times are often very short; but also often long, as when the mind's activity is solely reflective; for example, when it is occupied only in brooding over its memories, or in daydreaming, or in laboring systematically at imaginal or abstract constructions, without the intervening therein of sensations or other externally caused impressions or of externally causative volitions. Moreover, it appears conceivable without contradiction, although perhaps not normally possible, that such wholly nonparticipative mental activity should be prolonged for any length of time. If so, it would be one of the forms which a mind's survival of death, if it should be a fact, might take.

9. The Species of Consciousness

The preceding remarks suggest the need of analysis of the concepts of subconsciousnes, normal consciousness, dream-consciousness, and unconsciousness.

(a) *Subconsciousness and supraconsciousness.* As optional alternative to the term "subconscious" I shall employ "subliminally conscious," and contrast the subconscious or subliminally conscious with the supraconscious or supraliminally conscious. Within the supraliminally conscious I shall distinguish two species, namely normal waking consciousness and dream consciousness (whether night or day dream).

What I propose to mean by the subliminally conscious resembles to some extent what I think Dr. Morton Prince means by "co-conscious ideas."[7] He describes them as ideas which we have without being aware of them.[8] But the question this description immediately provokes is what exactly can be meant by our "having" ideas, if it does not mean our being aware of them at least "intuitionally." For, in Chapter 13, we contended that an "idea" (in the inclusive sense of any "intuition" — whether sensation, image, percept, craving, feeling, or other) is essentially a modulation of awareness or consciousness. Hence the ideas we have no awareness of can be only the modulations of other

---

[7] Prince, *The Unconscious*, p. 249.

[8] In a footnote, *op. cit.*, pp. 250–1, Prince quotes passages from several philosophers — Hartmann, Kant, Herbart — who have entertained such a notion.

consciousnesses, not those of our own consciousness. This is so, at least, unless being conscious and being aware are, contrary to what ordinary usage assumes, somehow not the same thing. But an explicit and definite account of the difference alleged would be needed to vindicate the allegation, and Prince makes no attempt to provide one.

Here we shall adhere to ordinary usage and continue to take "consciousness" and "awareness" as synonymous; and we shall accomplish otherwise and without the paradox of "ideas of which we are not aware," what Prince was trying to accomplish by means of it. We shall do it by distinguishing between subliminal and supraliminal consciousness (or awareness) as follows:

In supraliminal consciousness, that is, in normal waking consciousness and in dream consciousness, sensations and images are interpreted automatically and for the most part tacitly (*i.e.*, without verbalization, even subjective) as aspects, appearances, or symbols, of some kind of thing or event (though not necessarily always also as signs of the existence of some event or thing of the kind concerned). That is, in supraliminal consciousness, some meaning is always attached to one's sensations and images. For example, the set of sensations one has if one looks at this: ☞ is automatically and tacitly categorized — apperceived, interpreted, construed — as meaning a hand, or perhaps a pointer, or an ornament, or a design, or perhaps only as "a puzzling appearance." In supraliminal consciousness there is always an apperception-mass of one kind or another — a classificatory interpretant — to which the image or sensation gets spontaneously related.

Now this, I submit, is what the "supraliminal" character of supraliminal consciousness consists of: consciousness is "supraliminal" in so far as it is categorized, whereas in so far as consciousness is not so it is "subliminal," *i.e.*, is subconsciousness. Hence, to return to the speckled hen used as example in the last section of Chapter 13, what a person is conscious of supra- or on the contrary sub-liminally when looking at or imaging the hen will vary with the person and the occasion. For instance, what he is conscious of supraliminally might be only the color, or the shape, or the arrangement of the speckles; and their multitude would then be merely sensed or imaged, but not categorized at all, *i.e.*, not categorized even tacitly as many, or few, or over a dozen, or even as "some multitude." And this, I submit, is the sense in which their multitude can be said to be subconscious though sensed. One's sensations or image at the time would be potential data for recognition, *i.e.*, for categorization, of the speckles as many, or as the case may be, few, etc., but the recognizing or categorizing would simply not occur at all; the many-ness, or fewness, etc., though sensed or imaged, would not be *discriminated,* whether focally or marginally. Thus the limen, to which the words supraliminal and subliminal refer, is the difference between recognitive, categorizing consciousness and consciousness that is not so, and because of this is never supra-liminally remembered.

This account of what it is for sensations or images to be subconscious or subliminally conscious would apply in all essentials equally to intuitions of other kinds; for instance, to subconscious desires, attitudes, or feelings. At the root of it is the fact that, if one is going to speak of a "subconscious" at all, and mean by it not an unconscious but another sort or level of consciousness, then one must correspondingly speak of what is ordinarily meant by the "conscious" as the "supra" or "supraliminally" conscious, and say exactly how it and the subconscious differ. In this way one avoids the paradox of asserting that we have states of *consciousness* of which we are *not conscious;* for to say "not aware" instead of "not conscious" is, as noted earlier, only to use a synonym unless the difference one then must postulate between awareness and unawareness of one's states of consciousness is the same as that between supra- and subconsciousness as defined above. The difference between focus and margin of attention would, of course, not avail to escape the paradox, for it is a quantitative difference, in respect of clearness, *within the supraliminally conscious.*

(*b*) *Normal consciousness and dream consciousness.* Normal waking consciousness and dream consciousness are the two species of supraliminal consciousness. The essential difference between them, I submit, is that dream consciousness is uncritical, whereas normal consciousness is always more or less critical. This means that in normal consciousness, judgment, *i.e., belief or disbelief based on reason and past experience,* always plays more or less of a part; whereas dream consciousness is wholly naive — the dream content, generated by wishes, fears, or other emotions, being automatically believed so long as the dream lasts.

(*c*) *Unconsciousness.* Total unconsciousness is nothing one ever can actually experience, for to experience it would consist in consciousness of unconsciousness, and this is a contradiction. That one was totally unconscious at a certain time is only something one supposes in order to account for the fact that one has no memories relating to that time, although — as one has good indirect reasons to believe — stimuli were then playing upon one's body which would normally have caused sensations and perceptions intense or interesting enough certainly to be remembered. This is the situation when, for instance, the total unconsciousness one hypothesizes concerns a period during which — as one later learns indirectly — one's body was under anesthesia (perhaps for a surgical operation), or was in a faint, in coma, or in deep sleep.

But an entirely possible alternative hypothesis is that although one was indeed unconscious *of the events which those stimuli constituted or resulted from,* nevertheless one was not totally unconscious, but was dream-conscious, and that one has forgotten what and even that one was dreaming. Another equally possible hypothesis is that at that time one was not totally unconscious but was conscious only subliminally, and nothing that is not supraliminally conscious (though not everything that is so) ever is supraliminally remembered.

Lack of memories, again, is the only actual basis of the explanatory supposition one tacitly makes when what one asserts is, not that one was at a certain time totally unconscious, but that one was unconscious *of a certain event,* which one has since learned did occur in such relation to one's sense organs that it was capable of stimulating them.

That one was wholly unconscious of that event is a possible explanation; but others equally possible are that one was supraliminally, even if perhaps more or less inattentively, conscious of the event, but that it is not remembered; or again, that one was only subliminally conscious of the event. Probably the true explanation is sometimes one and sometimes another of these three.

There are cases, however, where what one reports is that one *is now* unconscious of anything of a specified kind; for instance, of any noise such as a cricket makes, or of any change in the temperature, or of any difference in the appearance of two things. Here, one possibility is that no such noise, or change, etc., is in fact occurring. Another, that it is occurring, but that one is indeed wholly unconscious of it, *i.e.,* that the stimulation of one's sense organ is too weak, or in some other way fails to cause any sensation. And a third possibility is that it does cause sensation, but that the sensation remains subconscious.

The distinctions made in this section evidently remove the paradox which, without them, would be involved in the supposition that, at no time during a person's life is he totally unconscious. They make it possible to suppose — although of course they do not prove — that he is *always* conscious, in one or another of the three modes we have distinguished; or indeed often at once partially conscious in each of two or of all three of them.

PART IV

The Mind-Body Relation and the Possibility of a Life After Death

Chapter 18

The Mind-Body Relation

The question which, at the beginning of Chapter 1, we stated we desired ultimately to answer was that of the relation between mind and body and the implications this relation may have as to the possibility that a mind survives the death of its body. We noted that the inconclusiveness of the classical treatments of the mind-body problem has been due in large measure to the looseness of the terms in which that problem has generally been formulated and discussed. Accordingly, in Parts II and III we have attempted to define sharply and in a nonarbitrary manner the difference between the "mental" and the "material," and to provide likewise objective analyses of the categories of Causality, Substance, and Property or Capacity, which are of basic importance in connection with the mind-body problem. We have also stressed the need of distinguishing between the problem of how material things and events are epistemologically related to the minds which know them, and the allied yet different problem of the ontological relation between a mind and the particular material object called its body. The latter is the one we are ultimately concerned with.

In the examination of it in which we shall now engage, we shall proceed on the assumption that the preceding chapters have demonstrated that a mind, as there defined in terms of facts introspectively observable and of theoretical interpretation of them, is a substance and more specifically a psychical substance; and that it is so in a sense exactly parallel to that in which a material thing, conceived in terms of facts perceptually observable and of theoretical interpretation of them, is a substance and more specifically a physical substance. Hence I shall assume that we are fully warranted in employing with regard to minds all the forms of speech appropriate in reference to substances in general.

To be kept in mind also as we enter upon our inquiry is the fact that our analyses of the meaning of the terms matter, mind, and causality have brought out nothing that would preclude interaction between minds and material objects and, in particular, human bodies. For, on the one hand, interaction between different substances does occur, as for instance between copper and nitric acid; and on the other, no evidence has appeared that interaction between two substances is possible only if both of them are physical. Rather, as pointed out in our discussion of the various logically possible kinds of properties of substances, certain psychical events, *viz.*, sensations, clearly appear to have bodily causes; and certain bodily events, for instance blushing, clearly appear to have psychical causes.

Our first step must now be to answer — more fully than we did in Chapter 15, where we considered it only from a special point of view and for a special purpose — the semantical question as to just what it means to refer to a particular human body as "one's own." Just what are the criteria by which I, for example, decisively identify as "my own" one and only one human body out of the thousands which exist and which I perceive?

1. Which Human Body Is One's Own?

One of the peculiarities of that body is, of course, that I never can see directly certain parts of it; for instance, most of its back, or any part of its head except a certain aspect of its nose, orbital arches, and cheeks, which I never similarly see in any other body. Moreover, although I seldom attend to this aspect of it, I always see it when it is illuminated if I see anything at all. A well-known drawing in Mach's *Analysis of the Sensations* represents what, in monocular vision, he was able to see directly of his own body while reclining on a couch.[1]

These peculiarities, however, seem to be accidental to, rather than of the essence of, my ownership of the body I call my own; for they might characterize a human body and yet, if certain others about to be described were absent from it, I would not call it my own; whereas if these others characterized it I would so call it even if it did not have the former characteristics.

The peculiarities which are thus criterial of my ownership of the body I call mine are four. One of them is that it is the only physical object in which certain activities of my mind directly cause or inhibit movements or other bodily changes: In only one human body is blushing directly caused by my feeling shame, or indigestion by my worrying. The most patent instance, however, is that of volition. I call mine the only body in which, for instance, my merely willing to raise an arm does, in normal circumstances, cause the arm to rise. That the volition *causes* the movement of the arm is something for which I have empirical evidence as good as, if not better than, for any of the other facts universally accepted as instances of causation. The experimental evidence that the volition causes the motion is of precisely the same form — Single Difference, and Regularity of Sequence — as for example the evidence I have that turning the switch of my lamp causes it to light, or that pressing a piano key causes the sound which follows.

Of course, some would object that the cause of the movement, or, to be more precise, of the excitation in the motor area of the brain, is not the volition but is some immediately preceding event in some of the brain neurons. But, as pointed out in Chapter 12, this is not something observed to be a fact, but only something

---

[1] English transl., Open Court Pub. Co., p. 16.

postulated. Moreover, it is postulated only for the sake of saving the dogma that causation of a material event is never by anything but some other material event — and, what is more, of saving that dogma in the face of instances where exceptions to it are on the contrary what observation according to the experimental Method of Difference appears to reveal.

It is essential in this connection to remember that the sciences called "natural" sciences are those which choose to inquire into none but the physico-physical properties of the objects they study; and that this choice automatically makes of every question as to cause a question as to physical cause. What that choice determines is thus only the horizon of those particular sciences; but, unfortunately, their practitioners often mistake this self-imposed horizon for the boundary of the universe. The fact, however, as I have insisted after Hume, is that, theoretically, anything might cause anything; and hence that, in any case where what experimental observation repeatedly testifies to is psycho-physical causation, there is no theoretical reason whatever for refusing to accept it.

Before turning to the other marks distinctive of the body each of us calls his own, something must be added to what has been said about it above. The statement that it is the only material object in which one can cause certain changes merely by volition probably needs to be qualified slightly in the light of certain facts for the reality of which psychical research has gathered rather impressive evidence, both of the spontaneous and the experimental kinds. I refer to the so-called *PK* or psychokinetic effect. The statistically treated results of experiments with dice mechanically cast seem to show that, under certain conditions, mere volition that a certain number shall turn up causes that number to turn up with a frequency significantly above chance. If this is so, we ought then to say that causation of a bodily movement directly by desire that it occur is simply a special instance of the *PK* effect — one where it is at its maximum.[2] It is essential to remember in this connection that causation, directly by a desire or a volition, of some change in the behavior of a material molecule is neither more nor less intrinsically intelligible, nor *a priori* more probable or improbable, when the molecule happens to be part of a brain than when it happens instead to be part of a physical object of some other kind, such as a piece of wood or a die. The molecules of certain brain tissues would simply happen to be a kind of physical object capable of responding more easily than any other to psychical stimuli.

But even if the reality of the *PK* effect is admitted, it remains true that for each of us there is only one material object whose behavior he can affect directly to any but a minute extent, when at all, by a mere volition, and that this unique material object is the one he refers to as *his* body.

Another of the marks of it is that it is the only one, physical stimulation of which in certain manners causes in his mind sensations of certain corresponding kinds. For example, I might be perceiving half a dozen hands protruding from under a cloth and that a pin is being stuck in each in turn, and I would call a particular one of them mine if and only if the pricking of it caused me to feel pain.

As in the instance of the criterion discussed immediately before, however, a minor qualification probably needs to be introduced here also, in order to take into account the evidence mentioned earlier that telesthesia, or "clairvoyance," sometimes occurs; that is, causation by physical events, without intermediary stimulation by them of the sense organs, of vivid images virtually the same as the sensations those physical events would have caused had they stimulated the sense organs. The existing evidence, both of the spontaneous and the experimental kind, that this phenomenon

---

[2] Cf. the highly interesting article, "The Psi Processes in Normal and Paranormal Psychology," by R. H. Thouless and B. P. Wiesner. *Proceedings, Soc. for Psychical Research,* Part 174, Vol. XLVIII, Dec. 1947, pp. 177–196.

sometimes really occurs is considerable; and we therefore find ourselves led to entertain the possibility of regarding sensation as a special instance of clairvoyance — the most frequent, and the one where the physico-psychical effect is steadiest, most capable of being prolonged at will, and most reliable. Then the sense organs, together with the corresponding nerves and cortical regions, would, like radio tubes and their connections, be specialized receptors and transformers of certain physical stimuli — the cortical events which are the terminal physical transformation of those stimuli being the kind of physical events somehow best capable, but not necessarily the only ones capable, of causing mental events of the kind called sensations. Here as before we should be clear that it is neither more nor less intelligible or probable *a priori* that vivid intuition of, for example, color should have for its immediate cause a molecular change in the brain cortex, than a molecular event in some physical object other than the brain or any part of the body.[3]

Besides the two marks just mentioned, there are two others which likewise single out a certain human body as one's own. They are less obvious to casual observation, but quite as significant theoretically. They too consist of unique capacities in respect to causation, but now capacities of causation of changes in the *capacities*, instead of only the states, of conscious mind and of brain.

One of these marks of a body as one's own is that it is the only one, certain mutilations of whose brain or its nerve connections ever directly cause alterations in the capacities of one's conscious mind. For example, the severing of afferent or efferent nerves destroys the mind's capacities to respond to the corresponding sense stimuli or to cause the corresponding bodily acts. Again, destruction of certain cortical areas destroys, at least temporarily, certain psycho-physical skills — for instance certain lin-

---

[3] See in this connection again the article by Thouless and Wiesner referred to in Note 2.

guistic skills.   Again, the surgical operation called prefrontal
lobotomy notably alters the conscious personality.

The remaining mark has to do with causation in the converse
direction.   There is only one body — and we call it our own —
in which certain changes of structure, *viz.,* the more or less
elaborate connections among brain neurons corresponding to
certain habits or skills, can be brought about by persistent firm
volition to acquire such habits or skills; for example, some linguistic or musical skill, or some code of manners, or some admired
and desiderated moral virtue.   It is true, of course, that acquisition of any of these depends on recurrent practice; but the
immediate determinant of the practising can be and is in such
cases the abiding firm purpose to acquire the skill.   The determinant need not be adventitious external stimuli, such as those
by response to which many of our other skills are gained.
Compare, for example, the deliberate learning of some dead
language with the automatic learning of one's mother tongue.
The first is willed in a sense in which the second is not so;
although, of course the willing of it, like every other event, is
determined — in this case, determined by certain desires, which
one believes knowledge of that language would enable one to
satisfy.

2. Mind-Body Interaction Analytically True

These remarks make evident that, when the meaning of the
question as to the relation between a mind and "its" body is
explicated, it turns out that the question means: *How is a mind
related to the particular human body with which alone it immediately interacts?*   Thus, analysis of the meaning of the question makes evident the answer to the question; namely, that the
mind-body relation, whose specific nature the question concerns,
is that of *direct causal interaction.*   That this is the basic relation
between a mind and its body is thus true as a matter of conceptual
analysis.   That relation is therefore tacitly postulated in the very

asking of the question. Indeed, it would be postulated equally in denial that a mind and its body are causally connected, since, once more, the expression "its body," which would figure in the denial as well as in the question, means "the body with which alone the mind concerned has direct causal connection." The denial, therefore, would be implicitly self-contradictory.

This conclusion could be escaped only if it were possible to show that the correlations by which a mind identifies a certain human body as its own are noncausal. But this cannot be shown, for to do so would require showing, for instance, that the pain felt immediately after a bee stings one's arm is not caused by the bee sting nor by any other physical event, but is caused by some psychical event simultaneous with the act of the bee and immediately antecedent to the pain. But no such psychical event is to be observed; nor is there any need to postulate that one occurs unobserved, for no valid reason exists to reject as cause of the pain the observable act of the bee. Rejection of it as cause is not demanded by any known fact, but only by the wholly gratuitous assumption that the cause of a psychical event always has to be another psychical event, and that the effect of a physical event has to be always another physical event.

3. The Alleged Mysteriousness of Psycho-Physical Interaction

That the principle — really, the postulate — of the conservation of energy does not preclude the possibility of interaction between mind and body was made clear already in § 9 of Chapter 12, and no more need be said about it here. But that a mystery, at all events, is involved in causation as between psychical and physical events seems to be believed by many persons — for instance by the British physiologist, E. D. Adrian, in his highly interesting little book, *The Physical Background of Perception,* and by Dr. J. R. Jones, who reviewed it in *Mind.* What needs to be repeated in this connection is that there is neither more nor less mystery in physico-psychical or in psycho-physical causation than there is in physico-physical causation. The causal relation, itself, is exactly the same. In no case does the particular nature of the event, which happens to function as cause in a given case, enable us to predict without previous observation what will be the particular nature of the event that will turn out to be the effect of the first. The causal relation is strictly neutral as regards the nature of the events figuring as terms in it. Whether the relation between two events is that of cause to effect does not depend on what *kinds* of events they are, but solely on the *form* of the relation actually obtaining between them. That form is specified in the canon of the experimental method of Single Difference. Causation of a sensation by nerve currents in the cortex, or of nerve currents there by a volition or a feeling, is no more mysterious than is causation of motion of one billiard ball by impact of another. It is causation in exactly the same sense in both cases, and that sense is the one the Method of Difference defines: That two events are cause and effect means that they are related as that "method" specifies, and the question as to *how* an event causes what it does cause is meaningless if *proximate* causation is in view. It is meaningful only as regards *remote* causation, since what the question "how?" asks for is an account of the causal steps intermediary between the two events concerned.

4. The Basic Relation Between a Mind and Its Body

Let us, however, now turn to a more detailed examination of the relation between mind and body. To say that the two interact is true but not specific enough. A more adequate statement is that there is between them a certain simple causal relation, which is basic in the sense that it is what ultimately makes possible several important more complex relations.

That basic relation may be stated by saying that for each mind there is normally one and only one physical object called its body, which is such that it, or more specifically its brain, is *the im-*

mediate physical patient of that mind, and the immediate physical agent upon that mind.

This relationship may be analyzed into the following several statements.

First, that, as we argued in the preceding chapter, a mind is a substance, and more specifically a psychical substance, and the brain is a physical substance.

Second, that in each of these two substances various events occur.

Third, that to say the brain is functioning at a given time as physical *patient* of the mind means that certain mental events are then causing certain brain events; and to say the brain at a given time is functioning as physical *agent upon* the mind means that certain brain events then occurring are causing certain mental events.

Fourth, that to say the brain is *immediate* physical patient of, and agent upon, the mind, means that the causation just mentioned is direct, *i.e.,* without intermediary.

And *fifth,* that to say the brain is *the* immediate physical patient of, and agent upon, the mind, means that *no physical substance other than the brain* so functions, or at least normally so functions.

5. Media of Action and of Response

The brain, however — or on many occasions the virtual unit consisting of it, of its nerve connections to motor and sensory organs, and of these organs themselves — has to the mind not only the relation just described, but also, by virtue of it, certain others. These are to be defined in terms of a certain concept, namely that of "medium of causation" or "causal intermediary," which we must now examine.

A *medium of causation* (whether automatic or purposive) is a substance functioning as one link in a chain of causation. More explicitly, a substance M is said to be a medium or intermediary in causation of an event E in a substance B, by an event C in a substance A, if and only if C in A causes in M some event D that in turn causes E in B. If, for example, the wind blows a tile off a roof, and the falling tile kills a man, the tile is then functioning as positive medium of causation of the man's death by the wind — it is the medium through which the wind *acts upon* the man in the particular manner called killing him; and, conversely, it is the medium through which the man *responds* to the wind in the particular manner called dying. More generally, if M is a medium of *action* by A upon B, it is automatically also a medium of *response* by B to A.

In the illustration just given, however, neither the action nor the response is voluntary or purposive. The tile is functioning as medium of *automatic, blind, nontelic* causation. But if the death-dealing tile had been, not blown off by the wind, but thrown by someone intending to kill the man, the tile would then have been functioning as medium of *purposive* causation. And this is what being an *instrument* or *implement of action* essentially means. The tile, however, would not have been for the man killed an *instrument* of response to his murderer's behavior, but only an *automatic medium* of response to it; for his response, *viz.*, his dying, was not something intended by him and he did not employ the tile as instrument to it.

But there are, of course, instruments of response as well as instruments of action. A microscope, a radio, or a hearing aid would be examples of media of causation which the user of them employs as instruments of visual or of auditory response — response, that is, by himself — to certain events which would not otherwise cause in him any response. Such objects can be described as *instruments* of response, instead of only as *automatic media* of response, because the person whose response is intended by the user is in such cases himself.

In this section, "medium of causation" is what has been defined.

On the other hand, "medium of prevention" (*i.e.,* preventive, insulant, obstacle, impediment, hindrance), again whether automatic or telic, would be defined as follows: A substance N is said to be a *medium of prevention* of events of kind E in a substance B when an event of kind C occurs in a substance A, if and only if, were it not for N's relation to the then state of affairs, C in A would cause E in B.

6. Purposiveness vs. Feed-Back Mechanism

Since the notion of purpose is inherent in that of instrument or implement as distinguished from medium of blind causation, it will be well to recall here briefly what was said earlier as to the nature of purposiveness, and to stress the difference between purposiveness and regulation effected automatically by "feed-back."

An act A is purposive if and only if the agent believes that the act may or probably will have a certain effect E, and if what causes him to do A is desire that the effect E shall occur. Desire and belief, however, are *mental* events. Hence, whenever we employ the category of instrument, we tacitly postulate that the ultimate agent acting through the medium of the instrument is a mind.

It is sometimes thought, however, that purposiveness can be defined in purely material terms; but this is an error arising from failure to distinguish between purposive action on the one hand and, on the other, automatic mechanical regulation, that is, regulation by what have been called *feed-back* or *servo-mechanisms.* The latter are what we have when disturbance of a state of affairs automatically actuates a mechanism that automatically restores that state of affairs. A simple example is that of a water tank whose intake valve is actuated by a ball float, and is therefore opened when the water level falls and shut when such opening has restored the level. The *existence* of a servomechanism is sometimes, though only sometimes, the result of somebody's purpose; but once the mechanism exists, and no matter whether it came to exist because it was desired to exist or independently of any such desire, its *functioning* is not itself purposive but quite automatic: the float does not fall nor the valve open because they desire to restore the level and believe their so behaving will do it. The float and the valve, having neither desires nor beliefs, do not themselves entertain any purposes. Their behavior is entirely automatic, whether or not its result happens to gratify some person's desire. This is true equally in the case of the purposively made tank-and-float mechanism, and in the case of such a purely adventitious mechanism as that by which the greater or smaller amount of water, which pours over the spillway of a mountain lake as its level varies, maintains that level constant within certain limits. Indeed, approximate maintenance, purely automatically and mechanically, of a state of affairs that otherwise would terminate unless purposive action happened to intervene, is precisely the feature distinctive of the kind of mechanisms called feed-back or servomechanisms.

7. The Body as Proximate Physical Medium of Extra-Somatic Interaction

The preceding remarks, concerning media of automatic and of purposive action and response, enable us now to describe with precision the chief special kinds of relation between mind and body which obtain by virtue of the basic fact that the body is the immediate physical patient of, and agent upon, the mind.

One of them is that the body, much of the time, functions as the mind's proximate physical medium of *automatic response* to physical events external to its body. This is what occurs in the instance of sensations caused by stimulations of the exteroceptor and the distance-receptor sense organs, in so far as response to such stimuli is not intended but is automatic. When on the contrary such response is *sought,* as in instances of perceptual curiosity, the body is then functioning specifically as *instrument* of response.

Again, the body functions sometimes as the mind's proximate physical medium of *automatic action upon* substances external to the body. This is what occurs in so far as bodily events that are effects of mental events cause unsought effects in the material world external to the body. An example would be footprints left in soft ground when walking, fingerprints left on objects handled, and so on. On the other hand, when the mental event causing the bodily behavior consists of a *desire to cause* the extra-somatic effect which one believes would result from such behavior, the body is then functioning not as automatic but as *purposive medium*, that is, as *instrument,* of action by the mind on the extrasomatic world. Examples where the body so functions would be in the pushing, or turning, or picking up of something, or in the doing of any other intended external deed, whether caused directly through the body's behavior, or only indirectly through the effect of its behavior on some other physical object, which then functions as *remote* physical instrument of the mind, whereas the body remains its *proximate* physical instrument.

It may be added that when the external physical object which, through the intermediary of the body, acts upon or is acted upon by the mind, happens to be itself *another human body,* then the body of the given mind functions as proximate physical *medium of communication,* either automatic or purposive, between the given mind and the mind of that other human body.

8. The Body an Integrative Medium

In what has now been said we have for simplicity's sake spoken throughout as if, in voluntary operation upon an extrasomatic object, the brain's response to the volition concerned caused contraction of just one muscle; and also as if the mind's response, mediated by the body, to extrasomatic objects stimulating a given sense organ, consisted just of the corresponding kind of sensations. What actually occurs, however, is usually much more than this.

The body is not merely a medium of causation between the mind and the extrasomatic world; it is in addition an *integrative* medium, which more or less elaborately *processes the nerve currents* initiated by volitions or by stimulations of the sense organs. Let us consider this important fact more particularly.

Even in an operation so simple as that of picking up a pencil many muscles in diverse regions of the body are involved, and their contractions and relaxations, simultaneous and sequential, have to integrate in one very complex pattern. Now, the point to notice is that in the majority of cases the integrating process is not itself willed or conscious at all, but is performed automatically by the nervous system. The mind's volition that the pencil be picked up merely switches on an already organized neuromuscular mechanism, which then performs its characteristic operation as automatically as does the record changer on a phonograph when it is tripped — the operation being automatically regulated throughout its course by the developments of the situation faced, which occur as the operation proceeds.

In some cases the mechanism needed is innate; as for example, in the human infant, the sucking mechanism; or, in the newborn chick, the pecking mechanism. But the mechanisms involved in picking up a pencil, or in tracing letters and words, or indeed in the vast majority of human voluntary operations, are not innate but acquired. They get built into the nervous system gradually, as a result of conscious attempts, repeated until the desiderated skill has been attained.

Attainment of it is marked by the fact that the integrating of the various movements involved no longer requires attention or volition, but occurs automatically in the (by then sufficiently "educated") brain and nervous system, in response merely to the mind's desideration of the objective effect it thinks of.

Ability to write, for example, was so built up. The various movements involved in the forming of letters were at first willed

movements, and coordination of them consciously and painstakingly effected. After much practice the tracing of letters and
words became an automatic response of the coordinative mechanisms which had finally become rigged in the brain, and which
were then part of its equipment, ready henceforth to function
without attention whenever switched on by the mere thought of
what one wants to say.

The process by which the nervous system becomes equipped
with an automatically integrative operatory mechanism may
roughly be compared to the gradual wearing of a rut by the
travel of a vehicle purposively guided again and again in a certain
course. The rut, which is an effect of this, becomes a cause when
it gets deep enough: it becomes a guiding mechanism, which, in
the absence of purposive guidance — or sometimes even in spite
of contrary purposive guidance — guides automatically in that
same course the vehicle whose earlier purposively guided travel
gradually created the rut.

Turning now to the perceptual side, we find that a state of
affairs obtains there which is similar to that just described on the
operatory side. Mechanisms exist in the nervous system which
automatically distribute and integrate the nerve currents initiated
by certain stimulations of a sense organ. Some of these mechanisms exist from birth, but most of them come into existence only
as effects of experience on the nervous system. That is, the
connections constituting those mechanisms are gradually instituted
in the nervous system partly by the repeated occurrence, together
or in close succession, of certain excitations of certain sense organs
— for example, excitations of the ear by the sound of an automobile horn, of the eye by the presence to it of the automobile,
etc. — and partly by the repeated mental association of the resulting auditory and visual sensations with relevant volitions, which
volitions in turn cause movements which excite the proprioceptive
nerve endings and hence the corresponding cortical area.

With sufficient repetition of this process, a direct neural connection gets established between, say, the auditory area in the brain and the motor area, without need of the intermediary volitions. And henceforth, excitation of the auditory area by such a sound automatically causes a minimal relevant motor response, and this in turn a minimal excitation of the cortical area for proprioceptive sensations.

Now, the essential point in that complex state of affairs is that, after such a pattern of connections has become established in the nervous system, stimulation of the ear by the kind of physical sound to which that brain pattern is conditioned has for its immediate psychical effect not simply the auditory *sensation* due to the stimulation of the ear by the horn, but rather the kind of mental event called a *perception* — specifically, *auditory perception* of the presence of an automobile. Such a perception consists of that auditory sensation *integrated with the idea of its meaning*. That is, what occurs is not the auditory sensation only, but also, simultaneously, the *understanding* of it. This is because the mental event which constitutes understanding of the sensation is not in such a case — as otherwise it would be — the conclusion of a mental process of interpretation of the auditory sensation as clue to imminent visual and other sensations and to appropriate impulses to act. Rather, the mental event that constitutes *understanding* of the auditory sensation is caused, *then as directly as the sensation itself,* and virtually at the same instant, *by the integrated pattern of brain excitation* automatically instituted by the nerve current from the ear. The understanding — that is, the apprehension of meaning — which would otherwise have been the conclusion of a mental process of diagnostic inference from the auditory clue, is now instead the *direct effect on the mind* of an equivalent but purely neural process. The difference is roughly analogous to that between, on the one hand, performing a calculation and thereby reaching a certain result, and, on the other, not performing it but being directly presented with that same result by a calculating machine that performed it.

This account of the automatic integration of nerve currents by a brain which, as a result of certain mental activities, has become equipped with appropriate operatory and perception-serving mechanisms is of course little more than a sketch. But its essential point is that, both in perception and in extrasomatic operations, the nervous system generally functions not as a merely transmitting intermediary between the mind and the extrasomatic world, but as an intermediary which, in the course of transmission, automatically *processes, i.e.,* distributes, in an elaborate manner the nerve currents initiated by mental events or by stimulations of the exteroceptive sense organs. This accounts for the fact that destruction of certain brain areas may not destroy capacity for sensations or for muscular contractions, and yet may destroy certain perceptual or operatory skills related to them; and this in turn can alter profoundly in various ways the manifest personality.

9. The Body as "Vehicle" of the Mind

Up to this point we have discussed only the body's function as proximate physical medium of communication, automatic or purposive, between the mind and the extrasomatic world. The body, however, has to the mind another and more intimate relation, for which it is difficult to find a wholly suitable name, but which, for reasons that will appear, I shall call that of physical "vehicle" of the mind.

The mechanism of the body's vehicular function is similar to that of its function as medium of interaction with the extrasomatic physical world, but in the case of the vehicular function, *only the intrasomatic physical world is directly concerned.* The two functions are in some degree interdependent, but they also have a degree of independence, so that each can up to a certain point be described separately.

The basic fact as regards the vehicular function is that the body is to a certain extent a self-contained little physical world. That is, some sensory stimulations originate within it, and some excitations of efferent nerve tracts result in processes that terminate within the body — motor or secretory processes that either do not affect the extrasomatic world at all or do so only indirectly. But these processes stimulate proprioceptive or interoceptive nerve endings and thus cause certain sensations, which in turn may cause impulses, emotions, or other mental events, and these in turn further intrasomatic events. There is thus to some extent a circular relation between mind and body. In respect to it, the two constitute a closed circuit; whereas, in their relation to the extrasomatic world, they constitute an open circuit.

Another fact, to which the notion of the body as physical vehicle of the mind has reference, is that the body not only is normally the only part of the physical world that interacts *directly* with the mind, but also is the only one that, except during coma or deep sleep, does so *constantly*. Other particular physical objects on the contrary interact with the mind only sporadically, adventitiously, and indirectly.

The body's vehicular function may be further explicated by calling attention to some of the more important corollaries of the circular relation on which it depends. One of these corollaries is the body's function as *material of physical self-expression* for the mind — such self-expression being either automatic, as in the blush of shame, or purposive, as, for instance, in expressive dancing.

Another of those corollaries is the body's function as *reflector* to the mind of such bodily effects as are caused by desires, volitions, feelings, and other mental activities. These effects are "reflected" through the sensory stimulations and resultant proprioceptive and interoceptive sensations which those bodily effects automatically generate. Were it not for this reflecting or, as we might say, mirroring activity of the body, we could not know, except through visual observation, whether, for instance, it is into our own pocket or into that of our neighbor that we are reaching, for we should have no kinesthetic perception of the position or movement of our hand.

Again, and in like manner, the body signals automatically to the mind also various general or local bodily states, such as exhaustion, inanition, vigor, weakness, health, illness, injuries, and so on. The sensations these bodily states generate, which function as mental signs of the presence of those bodily states, are either pleasant or unpleasant, and in so far become subjects of attention and generators of purposes as to the body.

In consequence, the ailing or defective body functions for the mind as an unpleasant and troublesome physical *abode,* and the healthy and efficient body on the contrary as a comfortable and convenient *vehicle;* and the mind correspondingly views its possession of the body as an affliction or an opportunity.

The hypothesis which has now been outlined as to the nature of the mind-body relation is in essence not novel, but is much more circumstantial and its terms more empirical and more precisely defined than in the case of the classical interaction hypothesis, which says little more than that mind and body interact. We have, moreover, pointed out that the theoretical difficulties which have commonly been supposed to stand in the way of interaction are illusory, as arising only out of a gratuitous assumption. And we have emphasized that the empirical evidence we possess, that some mental events cause bodily events and that some bodily events cause mental events, is of exactly the same form as in cases where the evidence is universally accepted as establishing causation. These conclusions as to the mind-body relation, and others we have reached as to the nature of a mind and of the various mental processes, largely remove the ambiguity which ordinarily infects the question as to the possibility that a mind, or some part of it, survives the death of its body. We may now proceed to consider what implications concerning that possibility those conclusions may have.

Chapter 19

The Case Against the Possibility of Survival

That a man's life continues in some form after the death of his body has always been believed by a large majority of mankind. Before we ask whether it is possible that this belief should be true, it will be well to ask first why it has so generally been held. But a word concerning two points of terminology is called for at the outset.

The first relates to the name by which we shall refer to the entity the possibility of whose survival is in question. It has been variously termed man's mind, personality, soul, or spirit — these words in most cases being defined either not at all or but loosely. For the present purpose there will be no need to take account of the more or less different meanings various writers have proposed for those terms; and since we have in preceding chapters reached a definite conception of the meaning implicit in the ordinary predicative usage of the term "mind," this term is the one we shall employ here. We shall assume that it includes such more special facts as the others may denote.

The other point of terminology concerns the common practice of describing as belief in "immortality" the belief that the human mind survives the death of its body. Strictly speaking immortality implies survival forever. But I believe few persons give much if any thought to the "forever" part of the hypothesis. It is survival of *death* that people are really interested in, and assurance of survival for some substantial period — say a thousand or even a hundred years — would probably have as much or nearly as much present psychological value as would assurance of survival strictly forever. Most men would be even less troubled by the idea of extinction at so distant a time than is a healthy and happy youth by the idea that he will die in fifty or sixty years. Therefore what I shall discuss will be the possibility that the human mind survives the death of its body for some time whether finite or not, rather than that it survives it specifically forever.

1. Why Belief in Survival Is Easy and Widespread

This being understood, let us now consider what apparently are the chief psychological determinants of the belief in survival. One of them is what may be called psychological inertia — the natural tendency to assume that what we are accustomed to find present will continue to be so. Each of us having had conscious life at all times in the past which he can remember, he tacitly assumes that this will continue. As J. B. Pratt has pointed out, the child takes the continuity of life for granted. It is the fact of death that has to be taught him. But when he has learned it, and the idea of a future life is then put explicitly before his mind, it seems to him the most natural thing in the world.[1]

It is worth noting in this connection that, although we sometimes say that we were unconscious at certain times or that some person we observe is unconscious, nevertheless, as pointed out in Chapter 17, unconsciousness is nothing we ever really observe in ourselves or in anyone else. What we actually observe when we say that another person is unconscious is only the fact that his body does not then react to certain stimuli which at other times elicit perceptible responses. He is unconscious of *those stimuli,* but for all we know he may be vividly dreaming. And

---

[1] Pratt, *The Religious Consciousness,* p. 225. Cf. C. D. Broad, *The Mind and Its Place in Nature,* p. 524.

as regards ourselves, we of course are never conscious of being unconscious, for this is a contradiction. When we assert that we were unconscious during a certain period, what we really know is only that we have no memories relating to that period. This is no proof, and is even hardly evidence at all, that our consciousness was totally extinguished during that period; for if this followed, then the fact that we have no memories whatever of the first few years of our lives, nor of the vast majority of our days since, would equally require us to conclude that we were totally unconscious at all those times. But we have plenty of indirect evidence to the contrary.

Consciousness thus is something we have had at all times we can remember; and psychological inertia therefore makes natural and easy the idea that consciousness survives the death, as it does the sleep, of the body.

Another psychological determinant of the belief in survival is the wish to survive. How subtle is this wish is shown by the fact that even persons who believe that death means complete extinction of the individual's consciousness often find comfort in various substitute conceptions of survival. They may, for instance, dwell on the continuity of the individual's germ plasm in his descendants. Or they find solace in the thought that, the past being indestructible, their individual life remains eternally an intrinsic part of the history of the world. Also — and more satisfying to one's craving for personal importance — there is the fact that since the acts of one's life have effects, and these in turn further effects, and so on, therefore what he has done goes on forever influencing remotely and sometimes greatly the course of future events. Gratifying to one's vanity, too, is the prospect that, if the achievements of one's life have been great or even only conspicuous or his benefactions or evil deeds have been notable, his name may not only be remembered by acquaintances and relatives for a little while, but may live on in recorded history.

But evidently survival in any of these senses is but a consolation prize — but a thin substitute for the continuation of conscious individual life, which may not be a fact, but which most men crave nonetheless.

The roots of this craving are certain desires which death appears to frustrate. For some, the chief of these is for union with persons dearly loved. For others whose lives have been wretched, it is the desire for another chance at the happiness they have missed. For others yet, it is desire for further opportunity to grow in ability, knowledge, or character. Often there is also the desire, already mentioned, to go on counting for something in the affairs of men. And again, a future life for oneself and others is often desired in order that the redressing of the many injustices of this life shall be possible. But it goes without saying that although belief in a future life is easy and desires such as these often suffice to induce it, they constitute no evidence at all that it is a fact.

2. The Hypothesis of Survival Logically Independent of the Hypothesis That a God Exists

Wishful thinking does not wish to regard itself as being that, and it therefore often protects itself from self-recognition, even if not from recognition by others, by clothing itself in argument. The so-called moral argument for immortality is, I believe, an instance of this and is therefore to be reckoned as rationalization of a wish-induced belief in survival, rather than as a statement of any genuine reason to pronounce the belief true.

The argument is that the annihilation of the individual would be incompatible with the goodness and power of God. As a philosophical correspondent of mine puts it, "Persons are intrinsic values, and a God who annihilated such a value would be no God any more." Again, "If value is metaphysically structural in the universe, and if value is real only in, of, and for persons, we have a high degree of systematic probability for immortality." Another philosopher puts it in the question, "If God is good and God is sufficiently powerful, how can such a God allow the values (potential or actual) bound up with individuals to become forever lost? . . . The world would be irrational if, after having brought into being human beings who aspire against so many almost overwhelming odds to achieve higher values, it should dash them into nothingness. . . . How solve the problem of evil unless there be a continued existence where shall obtain appropriate rewards and readjustments and further opportunities?"[2]

The argument, let it be noted, is conditional: *if* there is a God . . . *if* he is good and sufficiently powerful . . . *if* the existence of evil is reconcilable with the goodness and power of God . . . *if* value is metaphysically structural in the universe . . . etc. Much pious ingenuity has gone into attempts to prove those "ifs" or at least show them to be more probable than not. But it seems to me in spite of it that the propositions concerned still have the status only of postulates, that is — to use Charles Peirce's characterization of a postulate — the status only of propositions which we hope are true.

If there are extrahuman intelligences at all in the universe, then the most plausible hypothesis would seem to be that they are many, that they are variously limited in power and in knowledge, and that some are good and others evil in various degrees. That one of them is perfect at least in goodness, and is supreme even if not infinite in power, is a belief not based on impartial survey of the evidential facts but born rather of a longing for the remembered comfort of the young child's relationship to his father.

But further, it is a question whether annihilation at death would be an evil. Most persons, it is true, desire survival; but if there is no survival, there can be no frustration of that desire, for frustration is an experience and cannot occur if one is no longer

---

[2] Vergilius Ferm, *First Chapters in Religious Philosophy,* pp. 279–80.

there to have it. What death of a man's body does frustrate, whether or not his mind survives and whether there is one God or many or none, are the desires and interests of persons who survive him on earth, who valued him and his life there. If the existence of a God is somehow compatible with *this* indubitably experienced evil, it would be all the more compatible with nonsurvival, which, not being experienced, would not be an evil.

God, it is true, would perceive the nonsurvival of men's minds, but if *he* did not mind it, perception of it would then not be experience by him of an evil. As regards the assertion that "persons are intrinsic values" which a God could not allow to perish without ceasing to be a God, *i.e.*, to be good, it is obscure and, in such senses of it as suggest themselves, highly dubious. Does it mean that existence of a person has *positive* value, *i.e.*, is good, even if he happens to be a wholly or predominantly evil person? This seems the opposite of evident. Again, is existence of a good person — *i.e.*, of one disposed to do good — an *intrinsic* good, and if so in what sense of "good"? and who experiences the intrinsic goodness of his existence? Or is not rather the existence of a good person good only instrumentally, *i.e.*, good only in so far as he not only has the disposition to do good, but exercises it and does so successfully, not blunderingly?

The upshot of these considerations, I submit, is that no contradiction is involved in the supposition that there is a God, or several, and yet no survival; nor any contradiction in the supposition that there is no God and yet that there is survival. The supposition that a God exists has no more logical connection with the possibility of a life after death than it has with the possibility that life exists on the planet Mars. The after-death world, if there is one, is just another region of the universe. The belief that there is such a region has of course been employed in the service of religion, but it is no more intrinsically religious than is the belief in life on Mars.

3. The Case Against the Possibility of Survival

Although the belief in survival is easy, tempting, and widespread, critical reflection quickly brings forth a variety of *prima facie* strong reasons to regard that belief as illusory.[3]

There are first of all certain facts which definitely suggest that both the existence and the particular nature of consciousness at various times wholly depend on the presence of a functioning nervous system. Protagonists of the impossibility of survival remark, for example, that wherever consciousness is observed it is found associated with a living and functioning body. Further, when the body dies, or the head receives a heavy blow, or some anesthetic is administered, all the familiar outward evidences of consciousness terminate, permanently or temporarily. Again, we know well that drugs of various kinds — alcohol, caffein, opium, heroin, and many others — cause specific changes at the time in the nature of a person's mental states. The secretions of the endocrine glands, or deficiency of them, also affect the mind in various ways. Also, by stimulating in appropriate ways the body's sense organs, corresponding states of consciousness — namely, the various kinds of sensations — can be caused at will. On the other hand, cutting a sensory nerve immediately eliminates a whole range of sensations. Again, the contents of consciousness, perceptual capacities, linguistic skills, and various mental powers and personality traits, are altered in characteristic ways when specific regions of the brain are destroyed by disease or injury or are disconnected from the rest surgically as in prefrontal lobotomy.

That the nervous system is the indispensable basis of mind is further suggested by the fact that, in the evolutionary scale, the degree of intelligence of various species of animals keeps pace

---

[3] An excellent statement of them is given by Gardner Murphy in the article, "Difficulties Confronting the Survival Hypothesis," *Jour. of the Amer. Soc. for Psych. Research*, Vol. XXXIX, No. 2, April 1945, pp. 67–94. See also Corliss Lamont's *The Illusion of Immortality*, Putnam's, 1935; C. D. Broad's *The Mind and Its Place in Nature*, Harcourt Brace, 1929, Chaps. XI and XII *passim*, and especially pp. 526–33.

closely with the degree of development of their brain; and that in an individual human being a similar correlation is to be observed between the growth and decay of his brain, and that of his mind, from infantility to maturity to senility.

That continued existence of mind after death is impossible has been argued also on the basis of theoretical considerations. It has been contended, for instance, that what we call states of consciousness — or more particularly, ideas, sensations, volitions, feelings, and the like — are really nothing but the minute physical or chemical events which take place in the tissues of the brain. For, it is urged, it would be absurd to suppose that an idea or a volition, if it is not itself a material thing or process, could cause material effects such as contractions of muscles. Moreover, it is maintained that the possibility of causation of a material event by an immaterial mental cause is ruled out *a priori* by the principle of the conservation of energy; for such causation would mean that an additional quantity of energy suddenly pops into the nervous system out of nowhere.

Another conception of consciousness, which is more often met with today than the one just mentioned but which also implies that consciousness cannot survive death, is that "consciousness" is only the name we give to certain types of behavior which differentiate the higher animals from all other things in nature. According to this view, to say, for example, that an animal is conscious of a difference between two stimuli means nothing more than that it responds to each by different behavior. That is, the difference of behavior is what consciousness of difference between the stimuli consists in; and is not, as is commonly assumed, only the behavioral sign of something mental and not public, called "consciousness" that the stimuli are different.

Or again, consciousness of the typically human sort called thought is identified with the typically human form of behavior called speech; and this, again not in the sense that speech expresses or manifests something different from itself called "thought," but in the sense that speech — whether uttered or only whispered — is thought itself. And obviously, if thought, or any mental activity, is thus but some mode of behavior of the living body, the mind cannot possibly survive death.

A number of other difficulties of a different order also confront the survival hypothesis. Broad mentions two. One is "the apparently haphazard way in which men are born and die." Common sense rebels against the idea that, for instance, an unwanted child produced in a drunken orgy and dying of neglect or by infanticide six weeks after it is born is "a permanent and indestructible part of the universe, or indeed that it survives the death of its body at all." The other difficulty Broad mentions is "the continuity between men and animals." If the minds of men survive, why not also those of cats and dogs, and indeed those of lice and earwigs?

Still another difficulty becomes evident when one imagines in some detail what survival would apparently have to include if it were to be survival in any sense important enough to warrant giving it any thought. It would, one feels, have to include persistence not alone of consciousness, but also of personality; that is, of personal character, acquired knowledge, cultural skills and interests, memories, and awareness of personal identity. But even this would not be enough, for "survival" means to *live* beyond the body's death; and to live means to meet new situations and, by exerting oneself to deal with them, to broaden and deepen one's experience and develop one's latent capacities. But it is hard to imagine this possible without a body and an environment for it, upon which to act and from which to receive impressions. And if a body and an environment were supposed, but not material and corruptible ones, then it is paradoxical to think that, under such radically different conditions, a given personality could persist. To take a crude but telling analogy, it is past belief that, if the body of any one of us were suddenly changed into that of a shark or an octopus, and placed in the ocean, his personality could, for more than a very short time if at all, survive intact so radical a change of environment and of bodily form.

Such, in brief, are the chief reasons commonly advanced for holding that survival is impossible. Scrutiny of them, however, will I think show that they are not as strong as they first seem, and far from strong enough to prove that there can be no life after death.

4. Critique of the Case Against the Possibility of Survival

Let us consider first the assertion that "thought," or "consciousness," is but another name for subvocal speech, or for some other form of behavior, or for molecular processes in the tissues of the brain. As Paulsen and others have pointed out[4] no evidence ever is or can be offered to support that assertion, because it is in fact but a disguised proposal to make the words "thought," "feeling," "sensation," "desire," and so on, denote facts quite different from those which these words are commonly employed to denote. To say that those words are but other names for certain chemical or behavioral events is as grossly arbitrary as it would be to say that "wood" is but another name for glass, or "potato" but another name for cabbage. What thought, desire, sensation, and other mental states are like, each of us can observe directly by introspection; and what introspection reveals is that they do not in the least resemble muscular contraction, or glandular secretion, or any other known bodily events. No tampering with language can alter the observable fact that thinking is one thing and muttering quite another; that the feeling called anger has no resemblance to the bodily behavior which usually goes with it; or that an act of will is not in the least like anything we find when we open the skull and examine the brain. Certain mental

---

[4] F. Paulsen, *Introduction to Philosophy* (trans. by F. Thilly, 2nd ed.), pp. 82–83.

events are doubtless connected in some way with certain bodily events, but they are not those bodily events themselves. The connection is not identity.

This being clear, let us next consider the arguments offered to show that mental processes, although not identical with bodily processes, nevertheless totally depend on them. We are told, for instance, that some head injuries, or anesthetics, totally extinguish consciousness for the time being. As already pointed out, however, the strict fact is only that the usual bodily signs of consciousness are then absent. But they are also absent when a person is asleep; and yet, at the same time, dreams, which are states of consciousness, may be occurring.

It is true that when the person concerned awakens, he often remembers his dreams, whereas the person that has been anesthetized or injured has usually no memories relating to the period of apparent blankness. But this could mean that his consciousness was, for the time, dissociated from its ordinary channels of manifestation, as was reported of the coconscious personalities of some of the patients of Dr. Morton Prince.[5] Moreover, it sometimes occurs that a person who has been in an accident reports lack of memories not only for the period during which his body was unresponsive but also for a period of several hours before the accident, during which he had given to his associates all the ordinary external signs of being conscious as usual. As emphasized already in § 1, if absence of memories relating to a given period proved unconsciousness for that period, this would force us to conclude that we were unconscious during the first few years of our lives, and indeed have been so most of the time since; for the fact is that we have no memories whatever of most of our days. That we were alive and conscious on any long past specific date is, with only a few exceptions, not something we actually remember, but only something which we infer must have been true.

---

[5] *My Life as a Dissociated Personality* (ed. by Morton Prince), Boston: Badger.

We turn now to another of the arguments we mentioned against the possibility of survival. That states of consciousness somehow entirely depend on bodily processes and therefore cannot continue when the latter have ceased is proved, it is argued, by the fact that various states of consciousness — in particular, the several kinds of sensations — can, at will, be caused by appropriate stimulation of the body.

Now, it is very true that sensations and some other mental states can be so caused; but we have just as good and abundant evidence that mental states can cause various bodily events. John Laird mentions, among others, the fact that merely willing to raise one's arm normally suffices to cause it to rise; that a hungry person's mouth is caused to water by the idea of food; that feelings of rage, fear, or excitement cause digestion to stop; that anxiety causes changes in the quantity and quality of the milk of a nursing mother; that certain thoughts cause tears, pallor, blushing, or fainting, and so on.[6] The evidence we have that the relation is one of cause and effect is exactly the same here as where bodily processes cause mental states.

It is said, of course, that to suppose something nonphysical, such as a thought, to be capable of causing motion of a physical object, such as the body, is absurd. But I submit that if the heterogeneity of mind and matter makes this absurd, then it makes equally absurd the causation of mental states by stimulation of the body. Yet no absurdity is commonly found in the assertion that cutting the skin causes a feeling of pain, or that alcohol, caffein, bromides, and other drugs, cause characteristic states of consciousness. Common sense here accords with Hume's demonstration, to which we have repeatedly referred, that no logical absurdity is ever involved in supposing an event of a given kind to cause any other particular kind of event, and therefore that only experience can tell us what in fact can cause what. And as

---

6 John Laird, *Our Minds and Their Bodies*, London: Oxford University Press, 1925, pp. 16–19.

we have also seen, the so-called principle of the conservation of energy precludes neither psycho-physical nor physico-psychical causation.

As regards the fact that certain mutilations of the body rob the mind of certain of its powers, this too is a fact, just as it is a fact that destruction of one's motor car, if one can get no other, destroys, not one's capacity to drive, but at least the possibility of exercising it. But it is equally true that certain mutilations of one's mind make it permanently or temporarily impossible for the body to exercise capacities which it still physiologically possesses. Impotence, deafness, or blindness caused by some psychological trauma are examples.

What it is essential to bear in mind in connection with the type of arguments we have just been considering is this: The fact that two substances, Mind and Brain, interact entails that some events in each can cause some events in the other, and indeed that the development of each is greatly affected by such events in the other. But this is quite compatible with a considerable range of autonomy in the body, and likewise in the mind. Hence no more contradiction is involved in supposing that such activities of the mind as are autonomous, *i.e.,* psycho-psychical, still go on when the connection between it and the body is temporarily severed — or, at death, permanently — than is involved in the fact that the autonomous activities of the body — breathing, circulation of the blood, metabolism, etc. — still go on during coma, deep sleep, or anesthesia, *i.e.,* at times when psycho-physical and physico-psychical action is suspended.

A word, next, on the parallelism between the degree of development of the nervous systems of various animals and the degree of their intelligence. This is alleged to prove that the latter is the product of the former. But the facts lend themselves equally well to the supposition that, on the contrary, or at least in equal measure, an obscurely felt need for greater intelligence in the circumstances the animal faced brought about the variations which eventually resulted in a more adequate nervous organization. In the development of the individual, at all events, it seems clear, as we have pointed out, that the specific, highly complex nerve connections which become established in the brain and cerebellum of, for instance, a skilled pianist are the results of his will over many years to acquire the skill.

We must not forget in this context that there is a converse, equally consistent with the facts, for the theory, called epiphenomenalism, that mental states are related to the brain much as the halo is to the saint, that is, as effects but never themselves as causes. The converse theory, which might be called hypophenomenalism, and which is pretty well that of Schopenhauer, is that the instruments which the various mechanisms of the body constitute are the objective products of obscure cravings for corresponding powers; and, in particular, that the organization of the nervous system is the effect and material isomorph of the variety of mental functions exercised at a given level of animal or human existence. It is clear that epiphenomenalism, and likewise a hypophenomenalism that should assert psycho-physical but deny physico-psychical causation, would be not merely arbitrary, but would clash with facts which there are none but dogmatic reasons to refuse to take at their face value.

As regards the difficulty felt to arise from the haphazard way in which men are born and die, and from the continuity between men and animals, Broad, who in mentioning it says he is conscious that it affects him personally more than any others, nevertheless goes on to show with his usual admirable objectivity that these facts have no *logical* right to exert this influence. As to the first, he writes: "There is no logical transition from 'This [mind] is caused by the careless or criminal action of a human being' to: 'This [mind] is the kind of thing whose existence is transitory'." And as to the second, he concludes a detailed critique of it with the statement: "The alleged reasons for thinking it very unlikely that earwigs are immortal either are no reasons at all or they obviously depend on characteristics in which human beings and earwigs differ profoundly."

There remains the difficulty of forming any conception of some plausible form which a survival that would now seem to us significant could take. This difficulty can be dealt with, if at all, only by bringing forth such a conception. At this place no attempt will be made to do so, but a separate section farther on will be given to a survey of some of the chief forms, whether worth having or not, which survival might, without inconsistency with any known facts, be imagined to take.

5.   What Accounts for the Prima Facie Plausibility of the Arguments Against the Possibility of Survival

Our examination of the reasons commonly given for asserting the impossibility of survival has revealed that they are logically weak — far too much so even to show that survival is more unlikely than likely. The whole question will be placed in a useful perspective if we now ask why so many of the persons who advance those reasons nevertheless think them convincing.

This is, I believe, because they approach the question with a certain metaphysical bias. It derives from a particular initial assumption they tacitly make, namely, that *to be real is to be material;* and to be material, as we have seen, is to be some process or part of the perceptually public world.

Now the assumption that to be real is to be material is a useful and appropriate one for the purpose of discovering and employing the physico-physical properties of material things; and this purpose is a legitimate and very frequent one. But those persons, and most of us, do not ordinarily realize that the validity of that metaphysical assumption is strictly relative to that specific purpose; for what that assumption automatically does is to limit one's horizon to physical causes and physical effects, and thus to make the suggestion of any nonmaterial cause or effect of a material event seem incongruous — as indeed it is *under, but only under, that assumption.* Because of one's ordinary failure to realize this state of affairs, he ordinarily continues making that assumption out of habit, and it continues to rule his judgments of relevance and plausibility in matters of causation even when, as now, the purpose in view is no longer that of discovering or employing such physico-physical properties as material things have, but is a different one, for which that assumption is no longer useful or even congruous.

The point is all important here and therefore worth stressing. Its essence is that, as made clear in Chapter 6 and again in Chapter 12, the conception of the nature of reality that proposes to define the real as the material is not the expression of an observable fact to which everyone would have to bow, but is the expression only of a certain direction of interest on the part of the persons who so define reality — of interest, namely, which they have chosen to center wholly in the material, perceptually public world. This specialized interest is of course as legitimate as any other, but it automatically ignores all the facts, commonly called facts of mind, which only introspection directly reveals. And that specialized interest is what alone compels persons in its grip to employ the word "mind" to denote, instead of what it commonly does denote, something else altogether, namely, the public behavior of bodies that have minds; or makes it seem improbable or even absurd to them that any physical event could have any but a physical cause, or that anything but the material world and its processes should be self-sufficiently real. Only so long as one's judgment is swayed unawares by that special interest do the logically weak arguments against the possibility of survival, which we have examined, seem strong.

It is possible, however, and just as legitimate, as well more conducive to fair judgment as to the possibility that a mind or some parts of it survives the death of its body, to center one's interest for a time on the facts of mind as introspectively observable — ranking them for the time being as most real in the sense that they are the facts the intrinsic nature of which we most directly experience; that they are the facts which we most certainly know to exist; and moreover, that they are the facts without the experiencing of which we should not know any other facts whatever — such, for instance, as those of the material world.

The sort of perspective one gets from this point of view equilibrates that which one gets from the materialistic point of view, and is what I propose now to sketch briefly. For one thing, the material world is then seen to be but one among other objects of our consciousness. Moreover, one becomes aware of the crucially important fact that it is an object known by interpretation rather than strictly given. What this means has been stated in detail in Chapter 15, but its present bearing may be made clear by an example. Suppose that, perhaps in a restaurant we visit for the first time, an entire wall is occupied by a large mirror and we look into it without realizing it is a mirror. We then perceive, in the part of space beyond it, various material objects, notwithstanding that in fact they have no existence there at all. A certain set of the vivid color images which we call visual sensations was all that was strictly given to us, and these we construed, automatically and instantaneously but nonetheless erroneously, as signs or appearances of the existence of certain material objects at a certain place.

Again, and similarly, we perceive in our dreams various objects which at the time we take as physical but which eventually we come to believe were not so. And this eventual conclusion, let it be noted, is forced upon us not because we then detect that something called "physical substance" was lacking in those objects, but only because we notice, as we did not at the time, that their behavior was erratic — incoherent with their ordinary one. That is, their appearance was a mere appearance, deceptive in the sense that it did not then predict truly, as ordinarily it does, their later appearances. This, it is important to notice, is the only way in which we ever discover that an object we perceive was not really physical, or was not the particular sort of physical object we judged it to be.

These two examples illustrate the fact that our perception of physical objects is sometimes erroneous. But the essential point is that, even when it is veridical instead of erroneous, all that is literally and directly *given* to our minds is still only some set of sensations. These, on a given occasion, may be only color sensations; but they often include also tactual sensations, sounds, odors, and so on. It is especially interesting, however, to remark here in passing that, with respect to almost all the many thousands of persons and other "physical" objects we have perceived in a lifetime, vivid color images were the only strict data our perceiving activity had to go by; so that, if the truth should happen to have been that those objects, like ghosts or images in a mirror, were actually intangible — that is, were only color images — we should never have discovered that this was the fact. For all we directly know, it may have been the fact!

To perceive a physical object, then, instead of merely experiencing passively certain sensations (something which perhaps hardly ever occurs), is always, as we have insisted in Part III, to interpret, that is, to construe, given sensations as signs of, and appearances to us of, a postulated something other than themselves, some event in which is causing them in us; and other events in which are capable of causing in us sensations of other specific kinds. This belief commonly is only tacit and instinctive; but when reflection considers it explicitly, it is vindicated by our belief — or as I have argued in Chapter 9, our knowledge — that every event has some cause and therefore that our sensations too must have one, although we find none for them among our other mental states.

Such a postulated extramental something we call "a physical object." We say that we observe physical objects, and this is true. But it is important for the present purpose to be clear that we "observe" them never in any more direct or literal manner than is constituted by the process of interpretive postulation just described — never, for example, in the wholly direct and literal manner in which we are able to observe our sensations themselves and our other mental states.

That perception of a physical object is thus always the product of two factors — one, a set of sensations simply given to us, and the other an act of interpretation of these, performed by us — is something which easily escapes notice and has even been denied. This, however, is only because the interpretive act is almost always automatic, instantaneous, and correct — like, for instance, that of thinking of the meaning of any familiar word we hear. But that an interpretive act does occur is forced on our attention when, in a particular case, we discover that the interpretation was incorrect — that is, we discover that we misconstrued the meaning of the sensations. Or again, the interpretive act is noticeable when, because the sensations are too scant and therefore ambiguous, we catch ourselves hesitating between two or more possible interpretations of them and say that we are not sure what object it is we see.

The remarks made in the present section have been intended to make evident that explanations in terms of material causes do not have the exclusive authoritativeness which they seem to many persons to possess, and that the tacit assumption of those persons that only material things, but not minds, can have independent existence, is quite gratuitous. We have supplemented those remarks by a sketch of the view of the universe obtained when one conceives oneself essentially as a mind rather than as a body. The enlarged perspective provided makes clear that no paradox at all is really involved in the supposition that some forms of consciousness may exist independently of connection with animal or human bodies.

Chapter 20

THE CASE FOR THE POSSIBILITY OF SURVIVAL

That the arguments commonly put forth to prove the impossibility of survival are logically quite insufficient to do so does not constitute a positive case for its possibility. A positive case has to establish that survival is both theoretically and empirically possible.

The *theoretical* possibility can be established only on the basis of an analysis of what it is to be a mind: if no incompatibility appears between what the analysis reveals and the supposition of a mind's existing without a body, then the contention that survival is theoretically possible is in so far vindicated.

Such vindication, I submit, is supplied by the contents of Parts II and III of the present work, for nothing in the conception of the nature of a mind reached by us in the light of those contents appears to render it logically necessary that a mind should cease to exist when its body dies. What that conception logically entails is only that when the body has died the life of the mind then can no longer include exercise of certain of the capacities it had, namely, its physico-psychical and its psycho-physical capacities. But it remains conceivable without contradiction that the mind should still then exercise its psycho-psychical capacities — both its internal ones and, if any, also its external ones, such as telepathy would involve.

As regards the *empirical* possibility of survival, on the other hand, the only sort of evidence ultimately capable of establishing it would be empirical evidence that, in some instances at least, survival *actually* occurs. Accordingly, what we must consider in this chapter is the empirical evidence there may be that survival has actually occurred. But as soon as one undertakes this task, three questions thrust themselves forward. One of them is whether the alleged facts, which are adduced as evidence of survival, really are facts. Then, if they really are facts, the second question is whether survival is the only possible or at least the most probable explanation of them. And if this appears to be so, the third question is: What then exactly is it, the survival of which those facts prove or make probable. A complete mind? or only certain parts or certain capacities of it? or only certain of its memories? or perhaps something else altogether?

As we turn to the first of these questions, the peculiar nature of the facts it concerns makes it necessary, if we are to consider the question fairly, that some remarks should first be made concerning the difference between *causes of* and *reasons for* belief or disbelief.

1. Credulity and Credibility, Incredulity and Incredibility

The facts which are offered as empirical evidence of survival are of relatively rare occurrence, and they are of kinds that clash with the tacit assumptions as to what is and what is not naturally possible, which have been gradually built up in us by ordinary experience both lay and scientific. They are of some of the kinds which what is now known as paranormal psychology or psychical research has made it its business to investigate, and which it calls psychical phenomena, or for short, Psi phenomena. The rarity and extraordinary nature of facts of this general kind makes them psychologically hard to believe, irrespective of such solidity or lack of it as they may actually have. Hence many persons, without careful study of, or even any acquaintance with, the original reports of those facts, deny them out of hand, ridicule them, or dismiss them *a priori* as being reports only of instances of mere fraud, of malobservation, or of misinterpretation of what was actually observed. This attitude is more common and stronger among scientists than among laymen, for the latter, being more

ignorant of the laws of nature, have less of the intellectual ortho-
doxy and pride which firm knowledge of some of those laws and
of the manner in which these were discovered easily generates in
scientists.

Credulousness is readiness to believe — and incredulousness, to
disbelieve — without having investigated; and, when one cites to
an incredulous person the report of some fact of the out-of-the-
ordinary kinds here in view, what he commonly replies is "Do
you really believe it?" But the question which alone would be
scientifically relevant would be as to what *reasons* there are for
believing or for disbelieving the report; that is, is the report
rationally credible *on the evidence available*. What one happens
to be psychologically able to believe is one question; and what,
as a rational being, one ought to believe in view of the evidence
is another question. The latter is the important one in the search
for truth.

If, as in the instances here in view, the occurrence reported is
of a highly abnormal kind, then previous experience of occurrences of normal kinds constitutes no basis for an assumption of
antecedent improbability. For example, that normal musicians
who hear only once an elaborate and lengthy musical composition
are not capable of then reproducing it constitutes no rational basis
for assuming an antecedent probability that persons whose musical
endowments are highly abnormal — for instance, Mozart — could
not do it.

Further, if circumstantial evidence of the occurrence of the
facts reported is lacking and only testimonial evidence is available,
then the credibility of the report of them — *i.e.,* the then probability that they did occur — depends solely on the form and detail
of the report, the number of witnesses reporting, and such knowledge as we have as to their honesty, as to their competence to
observe critically and report accurately facts of the kind concerned,
as to their opportunity to do so on the occasion in view, and so on.

These are the factors which determine the scientific weight — the rational credibility — of testimonial evidence. In the absence of circumstantial evidence and of antecedent improbability of a reported fact, disbelief (or equally belief) of a report of it is *irrational* if it is not determined by those factors.

But in matters of judicial proof, and in meteorology, astronomy, history, and some other fields besides that of psychical research, the events in which one is interested often are not reproducible at will. Then, if circumstantial evidence of their occurrence is lacking, the testimony of such persons as claim to have witnessed the event is the only way of establishing its occurrence. And, that testimonial evidence can sometimes be such as to carry great weight in the eyes of unprejudiced persons is shown by the fact that on the basis of it many men have been sentenced to death.[1]

How difficult it actually is even with the best of intentions to be really unprejudiced, *i.e.,* to be completely rational, as regards reports of Psi phenomena may be evidenced by means of a concrete instance. The one I shall employ has no bearing directly on the matter of survival, but only indirectly in that what is true of it as regards belief and disbelief is true of Psi phenomena in general and therefore of those which seem to constitute empirical evidence of survival.

The report about to be cited is by the distinguished chemist and physicist, Sir William Crookes.[2] He states explicitly at the outset that the occurrences he reports "have taken place *in my own house,*

---

[1] Although it is customary to contrast circumstantial and testimonial evidence, the fact is, of course, that testimonial evidence is simply a particular kind of circumstantial evidence. Concerning the criteria of reliability of testimonial evidence, see J. H. Wigmore, *The Principles of Judicial Proof,* Part II.

[2] It originally appeared, together with reports of many other equally arresting occurrences, in an article entitled "Notes of an Enquiry into the Phenomena Called Spiritual During the Years 1870–73," *Quarterly Jour. of Science,* January 1874. This article, with a number of others by Crookes on the same general subject, has since been reprinted in a little book entitled *Researches in the Phenomena of Spiritualism,* Manchester and London, 1926. They all relate to observations and experiments made by him with various so-called spiritualistic mediums. In the instance now to be cited, the medium was D. D. Home. An additional article by Crookes, entitled "Notes of Seances with D. D. Home," appeared in the *Proc. of the Soc. for Psychical Research,* Vol. VI, 1889–90, pp. 98–127.

in the light, and with only private friends present besides the medium." He groups these occurrences under various headings and, under that of "The Levitation of Human Beings," he writes:

> "On one occasion I witnessed a chair with a lady sitting on it rise several inches from the ground. On another occasion, to avoid the suspicion of this being in some way performed by herself, the lady knelt on the chair in such manner that its four feet were visible to us. It then rose about three inches, remained suspended for about ten seconds, and then slowly descended. At another time two children, on separate occasions, rose from the floor with their chairs, in full daylight, under (to me) most satisfactory conditions; for I was kneeling and keeping close watch upon the feet of the chair and observing that no one might touch them."

This report, which is but one of many Crookes gives, is detailed; the conditions of observation are stated and were good; the fact reported is of a kind Crookes was competent to observe, namely, motion of a physical object; the forces that are known to physicists, by which physical objects can be caused to move, were known to him; his honesty is beyond question; and the opportunities for the tricks by which the motions he perceived could have been produced on the stage were nonexistent in Crookes's own house.

Furthermore, the fact that when the causes of motion known to physicists are not acting such occurrences do not happen if normal persons only are present creates no antecedent improbability (or probability) as to their happening where a highly abnormal person, such as Home certainly was, is present.

Now, I myself find the fact reported by Crookes psychologically hard to believe; but the only question here scientifically relevant is whether I have any *rational* grounds for not believing it, and in the light of the considerations just recited I cannot think of any such grounds. If, then, I am unable to believe it, this shows, not that the fact did not occur as reported, but only that in me belief and disbelief are in this case determined *not by evidence and reason, i.e., not scientifically, but by extrarational factors;* that is, by factors that have no logical bearing on the truth or falsity of the proposition disbelieved.

This point is of cardinal importance as regards impartiality in the matter of reports of Psi phenomena, and I shall therefore further quote what Crookes himself, and a scientific friend of his, say about it. In the article already cited, Crookes writes:

> "The phenomena I am prepared to attest are so extraordinary and so directly oppose the most firmly-rooted articles of scientific belief — amongst others, the ubiquity and invariable action of the force of gravitation — that even now, on recalling the details of what I have witnessed, there is an antagonism in my mind between *reason,* which pronounces it to be scientifically impossible, and the consciousness that my senses, both of touch and sight — and these corroborated, as they were, by the senses of all who were present — are not lying witnesses when they testify against my preconceptions."

Crookes, then, in a footnote quotes some remarks on the subject of belief and disbelief, which, he says, occur in a private letter from an old friend he does not name, to whom he had sent an account of some of the occurrences he had witnessed, and whose "high position . . . in the scientific world renders doubly valuable any opinion he expresses on the mental tendencies of scientific men." The latter's remarks, quoted by Crookes, are as follows:

> "Any *intellectual* reply to your facts I cannot see. Yet it is a curious fact that even I, with all my tendency and desire to believe spiritualistically, and with all my faith in your power of observing and your thorough truthfulness, feel as if I wanted to see for myself; and it is quite painful to me to think how much more proof I want. Painful, I say, because I see that it is not reason which convinces a man, unless a fact is repeated so frequently that the impression

becomes like a habit of mind, an old acquaintance, a thing known so long that it cannot be doubted. This is a curious phase of man's mind, and it is remarkably strong in scientific men — stronger than in others, I think. For this reason we must not always call a man dishonest because he does not yield to evidence for a long time. The old wall of belief must be broken by much battering."

We must not, indeed, call him dishonest, but we must call him in so far irrational; and when he approaches the subject of Psi phenomena, not like Crookes with the will to find out, nor like his friend with the wish to believe, but as more often happens with a wish to disbelieve made emotional by his vested intellectual or professional interests; then he is likely to be not only irrational, but as obstinately incredulous in the face of evidence as are obstinately credulous those who accept all reports of Psi phenomena uncritically because of their wish to believe or their love of the marvellous.

As Dr. W. F. Prince remarked, "It is the extremest test of human nature to be quite just and entirely governed by reason in relation to what one does not like." In a book aptly entitled *The Enchanted Boundary*,[3] he quotes from the writings of numerous physical scientists, psychologists, physicians, and others who have attacked the whole domain of psychical research, and the passages he quotes show that every one of them as he enters that domain with general hostile intent, drops at its boundary the principles of scientific method and instead abandons himself to emotion, bias and prejudice — resorting to *a priori* assumptions, refusal to face and discuss calmly the main issues, attacks on men of straw, arguments *ad hominem*, distortions of fact, and the like. The book is excellent prophylactic reading for anyone sincerely desirous of appraising scientifically what he may find when he crosses that seemingly enchanted boundary.

A number of writers distinguished in various fields, however,

---

[3] Boston, 1930, pp. ix, 7, 8.

have proved immune to the magic of that boundary and have commented upon it. Charles Richet, for example, in an address entitled "Des Conditions de la Certitude,"[4] discusses much more extensively than does Crookes's unnamed scientific friend the psychological determinants of belief, and like him concludes that "one has absolute belief only of habitual facts," that "to believe completely a phenomenon, one must be used to it"; and he notes the curious fact, also reported by others, that even when one has observed a paranormal fact under unexceptionable conditions and has been absolutely convinced that it occurred as observed, one's conviction tends, *without reasons,* to diminish gradually with the mere passage of time.

Another open-minded writer, C. D. Broad, commenting on the prevailing attitude towards Psi phenomena, writes:

> It has always seemed to me most strange and most de-plorable that the vast majority of philosophers and psychologists should utterly ignore the strong *prima facie* case that exists for the occurrence of many supernormal phenomena which, if genuine, must profoundly affect our theories of the human mind, its cognitive powers, and its relation to the human body.[5]

Again, Camille Flammarion in his book, *The Unknown,*[6] devotes the first chapter to incredulity and the second to credulity. In the first, he mentions instance after instance in which learned men of their day, some of them still famous for distinguished scientific work of their own, ridiculed and rejected *a priori* as impossible newly discovered facts of science or of technology that eventually became universally admitted — the rotation of the earth, the chemical elements, meteorites, current electricity, hypnosis, steam navigation, railroads, transatlantic cables, flying machines, etc. An amusing instance of such neophobia, which

---

[4] *Proc. Soc. for Psych. Research,* Vol. XXXV, 1926, pp. 422–444.
[5] Broad, "The Philosophical Implications of Foreknowledge," *Proc. of the Aristotelian Society,* Suppl. Vol. XVI, 1937, p. 177.
[6] Harper and Bros., 1900.

Flammarion witnessed, occurred when Edison's phonograph was introduced to the French Academy of Sciences by one of its members. Another one of them rushed forward in a rage, accusing him of trying to dupe the academicians by ventriloquism; and indeed declared again six months later that after a close examination he could find nothing in the invention but ventriloquism! In the second chapter, on the other hand, Flammarion cites some of the innumerable instances on record, of credulity on the part of the learned as well as of the ignorant, which are especially edifying in the cases where belief is maintained even notwithstanding flagrantly adverse evidence.

In the face, then, of reports of Psi phenomena — whether ones allegedly evidential of survival, or others — it is essential to be on one's guard against irrational credulity and, equally, against irrational incredulity. There is no doubt that many or most of the phenomena mediums claim to produce are fraudulent. But, as an experienced investigator, Harry Price, has remarked, the ability to discriminate between genuineness and fraud "thrives best when it gets a reasonable amount of exercise in *both* directions."[7] On the other side, as careful study of the history of Psi phenomena shows, reports that a puzzling phenomenon was eventually accounted for in a natural manner, or that a medium was exposed as fraudulent, often have *themselves* been fraudulent or at least dictated by the will to disbelieve; for emotion is just as strongly engaged, if not more so, on the side of disbelief as

---

[7] *Confessions of a Ghost Hunter,* p. 311. An edifying description of many of the extraordinarily ingenious tricks and devices to which fraudulent mediums resort is to be found in Hereward Carrington's *The Physical Phenomena of Spiritualism, Fraudulent and Genuine.* This author, who is himself an able amateur conjurer and was led thereby to an interest in Psi phenomena, has stated that it was only after eight years of investigation of hundreds of supposed "physical" mediums that he came upon any phenomena which he could be certain were genuine. That a great deal is to be accounted for by trickery is certain. On the other hand, as V. Schrenck-Notzing remarks somewhere in his *Phenomena of Materialisation,* to postulate that trickery can defeat any precautions whatever which one could take is to endow conjurers *a priori* with powers quite as marvellous as those claimed for mediums, and thus gratuitously to assume that all investigation is futile.

on that of belief, and with a resulting equal lack of objectivity. Most people are highly disturbed by unexplained occurrences, especially if these relate to matters of practical import. Hence any assertion that the occurrence has been accounted for along familiar lines is easily accepted from eager desire for the intellectual comfort it brings. This state of affairs makes it necessary to scrutinize, no less critically than the others, reports of fraud or of other easy explanation of well attested paranormal occurrences.

With this general introduction to the out-of-the-ordinary kinds of facts to which the case for the possibility of survival appeals as empirical evidence, let us now state the case itself.[8]

2. The Empirical Evidence for the Possibility of Survival

As pointed out earlier, evidence for the empirical *possibility* of survival can consist only of empirical evidence that, at least in some instances, survival *actually* occurs. This evidence, which is of a variety of kinds, was reviewed and discussed by Professor Gardner Murphy in two articles, published in the *Journal of the American Society for Psychical Research*,[9] on which the present exposition is largely based.

The first category of evidence he mentions consists of apparitions of a person dying or having just died but not known to have been ill or in danger. Although there are also apparitions of the living, Professor Sidgwick's report on the Census of Hallucinations showed that nearly three-quarters of the apparitions are of persons at or shortly after the time of death, and that the

---

[8] Two excellent introductions to the field of psychical research are G. N. M. Tyrrell's *Science and Psychical Phenomena,* Harpers, 1938, and his *The Personality of Man,* Penguin Books, 1946. Both are admirably sober, lucid, and documented, and each has a chapter (XI and 26 respectively) on the prevailing attitude towards psychical phenomena and the psychological determinants of belief and disbelief.

[9] G. Murphy, "An Outline of Survival Evidence," *Jour. of Amer. Soc. for Psychical Research,* Vol. XXXIX, No. 1, Jan. 1945; and "Difficulties Confronting the Survival Hypothesis," *loc. cit.,* No. 2, April 1945.

frequency of such apparitions significantly exceeds what chance coincidence would account for. There are also cases of apparitions months or years after death, sometimes to persons ignorant of the death. The article referred to cites striking instances of the various categories.

Sometimes the apparition brings, either automatically or by exercise of initiative, knowledge of facts until then unknown to the percipient. An example is that of the apparition of a girl to her brother nine years after her death, with a conspicuous scratch on her cheek. Their mother then revealed to him that she herself had made that scratch accidentally while preparing her daughter's body for burial, but that she had then at once covered it with powder and never mentioned it to anyone. Another famous case is that of a father whose apparition some time after death revealed to one of his sons the existence and location of an unsuspected second will, benefiting him, which was then found as indicated. Still another case would be the report by General Barter, then a subaltern in the British Army in India, of the apparition to him of a lieutenant he had not seen for two or three years. The lieutenant's apparition was riding a brown pony with black mane and tail. He was much stouter than at their last meeting, and, whereas formerly clean shaven, he now wore a peculiar beard in the form of a fringe encircling his face. On inquiry the next day from a person who had known the lieutenant at the time he died, it turned out that he had indeed become very bloated before his death; that he had grown just such a beard while on the sick list; and that he had some time before bought and eventually ridden to death a pony of that very description.

Other striking instances are those of an apparition seen simultaneously by several persons. It is on record that an apparition of a child was perceived first by a dog, that the animal's rushing at it, loudly barking, interrupted the conversation of the seven persons present in the room, thus drawing their attention to the apparition, and that the latter then moved through the room for some fifteen seconds, followed by the barking dog.[10]

Another type of empirical evidence of survival consists of communications purporting to come from the dead, made through the persons commonly called sensitives, mediums, or automatists. Some of the most remarkable of these communications have been given by Mrs. Leonard in London, and by the celebrated American medium, Mrs. Piper, who for many years was studied by the Society for Psychical Research with the most elaborate precautions against all possibility of fraud. In several instances, the evidences of identity supplied by the dead persons who purportedly were thus communicating with the living were of the very kinds, and of the same precision and detail, which would ordinarily satisfy a living person of the identity of another living person with whom he was not able to communicate directly, but only through an intermediary, or by letter or telephone.[11] In communications through a medium, the only ones having any evidential value are of course those where the facts communicated were not known to the medium. That this was the case in many instances is certain. Sometimes the facts communicated and later verified were unknown to the sitter as well as to the medium, and sometimes were not all known by any one living person. In a few cases, indeed, they were not known by any living person or persons at all. Sometimes the purportedly communicating deceased had never during life been known either to the medium or to the sitter, but was later found to have existed and to have recently died, and the communicated facts to be true.

10 The documents obtained by the Society for Psychical Research concerning this case, that of the lieutenant's apparition, and that of the girl with the scratch, are reproduced in Sir Ernest Bennett's *Apparitions and Haunted Houses* (London: Faber and Faber, 1945), pp. 334–337, 28–35, and 145–150, respectively.

11 A summary of some of the most evidential facts may be found in the book by M. Sage, entitled *Mrs. Piper and the Society for Psychical Research* (New York: Scott-Thaw Co., 1904); and others of them are related in some detail in Sir Oliver Lodge's *The Survival of Man*, Sec. IV (New York: Moffat, Yard, and Co. 1909), and in A. M. Robbins's *Both Sides of the Veil*, Part II (Boston: Sherman, French, and Co., 1909). The fullest account is in the *Proceedings of the Society for Psychical Research*.

There are cases on record also where the same purporting communicator manifests through several mediums independently, identifying himself by using the same symbol, phrase, or message in each case. The most impressive, however, are those which have come to be known as "cross-correspondences," for they seem to indicate on the part of the communicator not only survival of memories, but also of the actively working intelligence needed for the devising of some ingenious proof of identity. In them, for example, two mediums sometimes thousands of miles apart give each a different communication, neither of which is intelligible by itself, but when put together they are found to constitute an unmistakable allusion to an obscure passage in some work of classical literature. Or again, one communication mentions that a specific and uncommon question which is being asked had been asked before through another medium, and mentions the name of the person who had asked it.

In some cases, the person who seeks to obtain communication does not himself have a sitting with the medium but is represented at the sitting by a proxy, who was not acquainted with the deceased from whom a communication is sought and also sometimes is unacquainted with the person seeking the communication, or indeed does not even know for whom he is acting as proxy. Under such conditions, communications *prima facie* strongly evidential of the identity of the purported communicator are nevertheless obtained.

Of course, when facts of these kinds are recounted, as I have just done, only in summary or in the abstract, they make little if any impression upon us. And the very word "medium" at once brings to our minds the innumerable instances of demonstrated fraud perpetrated by charlatans to extract money from the credulous bereaved. But the modes of trickery and sources of error which immediately suggest themselves to us as easy natural explanations of the seemingly extraordinary facts suggest themselves just as quickly to the members of the research committees of the Society for Psychical Research. Usually, these men have had a good deal more experience than the rest of us with the tricks of conjurers and fraudulent mediums and take against them precautions far more strict and ingenious than would occur to the average skeptic.

But when, instead of stopping at summaries, one takes the trouble to study the detailed original reports, it then becomes evident that they cannot all be just laughed off; for to accept the hypothesis of fraud or malobservation would often require more credulity than to accept the facts reported.

To explain those facts, however, is quite another thing. But it is worth recording that some of the investigators — for instance Dr. Richard Hodgson, Sir Oliver Lodge, Professor J. H. Hyslop — who approached the subject most skeptically and investigated it most painstakingly and critically over long terms of years, and who considered most carefully the hypotheses other than survival, which have been proposed to explain the facts, came eventually to the opinion that the balance of evidence was in favor of the survival hypothesis.

Two variants of the survival hypothesis may be mentioned here. One, which in the past had considerable vogue, is that the communicators are "demons" — spirits not human existing without physical embodiment — who take pleasure in deluding the bereaved and in occasionally inducing them to conduct their affairs foolishly. I call this hypothesis a variant of the survival hypothesis because, if it were confirmed, it would equally establish the empirical possibility of unembodied existence of minds.

The other variant of the survival hypothesis is that, not strictly a mind, but only a "psychic factor" survives the death of the "bodily factor," and that the psychic factor again gives rise to a mind properly so called when united with the bodily factor of a medium.[12]

12 C. D. Broad, *The Mind and Its Place in Nature*, pp. 535 ff., 550, 651–3.

An explanation of the facts, which obviously suggests itself as alternative to survival, is fraud, *i.e.,* that the medium obtained in a natural manner information given out. This, however, is ruled out in the best cases — *e.g.,* Mrs. Piper's, Mrs. Leonard's, and some others — by the elaborate precautions which were taken to preclude it. Much the most plausible alternative to the survival hypothesis is that the veridical information given out is obtained telepathically by the entranced medium from the minds of living persons possessing it; that the medium's trance personality has histrionic powers as extensive as those which persons under hypnosis manifest; and that these powers, on the basis of the information telepathically obtained, enable the entranced medium to reproduce the voice, the handwriting, the tricks of expression and mannerisms of the deceased with sometimes striking verisimilitude. This hypothesis, however, requires that the medium should be able to pick up needed items of information not only from the subconscious as well as the conscious part of the mind of the sitter, but also from the mind of any other living person having the information, no matter in what part of the world that person may be. But Gardner Murphy points out that, farfetched as this seems, "we have *direct evidence* that this process of filching and sifting among the minds of the living does actually occur."[13] Even granting it, however, there remain still unaccounted for the few cases where the facts communicated were not known to any living person.

To many persons the hypothesis of telepathy, even if not welcome, seems more acceptable than that of survival — perhaps because radio communication suggests to them that telepathy may be explicable by "vibrations in the ether, resulting from and acting on nervous matter."[14]

Tyrrell, however, gives a number of strong reasons why telep-

---

[13] Murphy, "Difficulties Confronting the Survival Hypothesis," *loc. cit.,* p. 79.
[14] *The Evidences for the Supernatural* by Dr. I. L. Tuckett, p. 140, cited by G. N. M. Tyrrell in his *The Personality of Man,* p. 68.

athy cannot be a physical phenomenon analogous to radio. Moreover, after examining the facts which point to survival, he considers telepathy as alternative explanation of them,[15] and shows that if all the facts to be explained are taken into account, the implications of the telepathy explanation are even more extraordinary than is the survival explanation.

From this outline account of the empirical evidence for survival, let us now turn to the difficulties which confront it.

3. Critique of the Empirical Evidence for Survival

One difficulty is that, as just stated, survival is not the only hypothesis capable of accounting for the empirical facts, since telepathy, even if it too involves difficulties, provides an alternative explanation for most even if perhaps not quite all of the facts. But there are other difficulties in the survival explanation. For one, as emphasized by Professor E. R. Dodds,[16] the purported nature of the communicators seems to depend on what, according to the beliefs prevalent in the medium's milieu, that nature is expected to be: among spiritualists, the spirits of the dead; in medieval times, demons or the devil; in classical antiquity, sometimes gods or goddesses, etc. And he points out that facts of the same kinds as those in communications purportedly from spirits have been obtained from psychics who have no "controls" or "communicators," and who do not regard themselves as media of communication with spirits. There are instances where persons purporting to have survived death and to be communicating were in fact still living; and instances where they had been invented out of whole cloth by the sitter. Again, although the communicators often strikingly reproduce characteristic traits of the deceased, they also at times manifest traits sharply at variance with some of those known to have been possessed by the deceased.

---

15 *Op. cit.*, Chapters 22, 23.
16 Dodds, "Why I Do Not Believe in Survival," *Proc. Soc. for Psych. Research,* Vol. XLII, 1934, pp. 147–172. The paper also contains a critique of Broad's "psychic factor" hypothesis and an impressive defense of the telepathy explanation.

As regards the evidence constituted by apparitions, a difficulty arises from the fact that the apparitions are not only of persons, but also of animals (*e.g.,* the lieutenant's horse), and of inanimate objects, such, in particular, as the clothing the apparitions wear. Furthermore, what, if anything, is proved to survive by the apparitions is not directly, if at all, the *mind* of the deceased, but some sort of appearance of his *body.* In some cases the apparition may be accounted for as a subjective hallucination in the percipient. This explanation, however, is not equally plausible in cases where several persons see the apparition. But some of the facts recorded by V. Schrenck-Notzing in connection with the medium Eva Carriere suggest that, strange as it seems, *images* in a medium's mind can sometimes become objectified in some manner sufficient to make them visible to others; so that such "ideomorphs," and not the deceased himself, may be what the apparitions really are. Moreover, as Gardner Murphy points out, when in day or night dreams one forms an image of a person, one's image is of the person as *doing something;* and as likely as not, something we subconsciously wish or fear he would do. This could account for the fact that sometimes the apparition behaves as if motivated by definite purpose. It would equally account for evidences of purpose and initiative in the personalities manifesting through mediums.

The empirical evidence for survival, when it is not merely mentioned more or less in the abstract as mostly was done in what precedes, but is considered in the full concreteness of the original reports, is sometimes very impressive. On the other hand, the difficulties which we have similarly mentioned, that stand in the way of the survival explanation of the facts, are, as Professor Dodds's article makes very clear, hard indeed to dispose of. In either case, it is virtually impossible in the present state of our knowledge to define the issues sharply, for the attempt to do so is complicated by the necessity of taking into consideration the strange Psi capacities — clairvoyance, precognition, retrocognition, besides telepathy — which in ordinary life do not function or do so to but a negligible extent, but which both the record of well attested spontaneous occurrences and the experimental demonstrations in recent years by J. B. Rhine, Whately Carington, and others, have shown to be parts of the latent equipment of at least some human minds.

When these three sets of considerations are taken fully into account, it seems to me that not only the empirical evidence, but the question itself as to whether it shows survival to be a fact more probably than not, is so ambiguous as to preclude answering the question "yes" or "no." We need to deal first with the question: What exactly is it, about which we ask whether "it" does or does not survive the death of the body? As Gardner Murphy puts it, "When I ask myself whether I personally accept these objections [*i.e.*, those we have mentioned], and repudiate the evidence for survival, I find myself answering that it is improbable that the issue has been correctly stated at all."[17] That what we might call a man's "noon-day personality," *i.e.*, the whole set of capacities ready to function in him as occasion calls for when he is at his best, survives intact the death of his body seems very unlikely indeed. The Psi evidence does not show that *that* survives; and ordinary observation shows that that noonday personality is a precarious thing, easily robbed of some of its component capacities by physiological and psychological accidents of various kinds; so that the times when a man is "really" himself — meaning the times at which he is at his best — are perhaps the exception rather than the rule even during life.

According to our analysis in Chapter 17, a mind is a composite of parts more or less well integrated, the parts, which we have denominated role-selves, being sets of systematically interrelated capacities or properties. These various parts too — down to what

---

17 Murphy, "Difficulties, etc.," *loc. cit.*, p. 93.

we have called molecular minds — are genuinely minds, though simpler, more specialized, less versatile than the whole of which they are parts. No reason has appeared not to regard as possible that any one of such parts should become more or less completely detached from the whole. And, with such parts as with the whole, no contradiction has appeared in the supposition that some of them may exist independently of connection with a material body, although without one the possibility of exercise of other than psycho-psychical capacities would be lacking. It is worth noting incidentally that, in the light of our analysis, not only would what are now currently called dissociations of personality be exceptionally possible,[18] but equally so the converse process, viz., one of *association* of some foreign "role-self" with a given personality — the sort of thing which the words obsession or possession used to be employed to designate, but which nowadays is assumed to be only a superstition. In the case of Morton Prince's Miss Beauchamp, the "Sally" personality gives the impression of independence, rather than of being a dissociated component of Miss Beauchamp's; and when he eventually succeeded in integrating the "Real Miss Beauchamp" out of the several dissociated components, Sally had no place in the integrated whole, but was simply eliminated — to use her own words, "squeezed out" and forced to "go back to where I came from."[19] So real and vital was the Sally personality that, Dr. Prince says somewhere, he felt somewhat as if he were committing a murder when he finally eliminated her!

The conclusion I now wish to submit is that no contradiction appears to be involved in the supposition that some parts or capacities of man's mind survive the death of his body, and therefore that such survival is theoretically quite possible. As to whether it is actually as well as theoretically possible, there is

---

[18] See, for instance, Dr. Morton Prince's well-known book, *The Dissociation of a Personality.*
[19] *Op. cit.,* pp. 519, 524.

strong *prima facie* evidence that in some instances *something* survives, which appears to be some part or some set of capacities of the mind whose body has died. But the demonstrated reality and occasional functioning of the paranormal capacities mentioned above — in particular, telepathy, clairvoyance, and retrocognition — so complicate the interpretation of the facts ordinarily adduced as empirical evidence of survival that, with our present very meager knowledge of the latent paranormal capacities of the human mind, and with the rather drastic revision of the ordinary ideas of our relation to *time* which the fact of precognition would appear to require, nothing both definite and well evidenced can yet be concluded concerning the actual, as distinguished from the theoretical, possibility of partial survival.

Chapter 21

Some Theoretically Possible Forms of Survival

It will be recalled that in Chapter 19 we mentioned as one of the difficulties in the way of the survival hypothesis that of imagining any definite form existence after death might take that would be both theoretically possible and significant enough to be worth our caring now whether it is a fact or not. We postponed discussion of this difficulty, stating that it could be met, if at all, only by actually describing one or more such forms. In the present chapter, we shall attempt to do this.

1. Status of the Descriptions to Follow, of Possible Forms of Survival

Let it be explicitly stated at the outset, however, that what we shall say will be only speculative. That is, no claim will be made that such evidence, if any, as could be adduced to point to one or another of the forms of survival we shall describe is sufficient to establish a positive probability that survival in that form is a fact. The only claims made will be:

(1) That the forms of survival we shall describe are *possible* in the sense of (*a*) consistent with the outcomes of our analyses of what it is to be "mental," to be "a mind," and "to exist"; (*b*) consistent with our findings as to the nature of the mind-body relation; and (*c*) consistent also with all empirical facts, whether normal or paranormal, now known; and

(2) That those forms, besides being possible, also are in various degrees *significant* enough to be of some interest to us now.

Substantiation of these claims would thus mean only that those descriptions of forms of survival have the status of articles of legitimate though optional belief; that is, the status of propositions for or against the truth of which there is at present no evidence or no preponderance of evidence, either theoretical or empirical — which propositions, therefore, it is legitimate to believe for the time being, if one finds oneself psychologically able to do so and if one finds more present value in doing so than in not doing so.

This conception of legitimacy of belief (or disbelief) of a proposition in the absence of a preponderance of evidence either for or against it accords in essentials with that enunciated by William James in the famous essay in which he discusses the conditions of the right to believe, but which he unfortunately entitled "The Will to Believe." Most of the criticisms of this essay seem to me to have missed its central, carefully qualified thesis, and to tilt in fact chiefly at what its regrettable title suggests. But when the qualifications which James makes an essential part of the thesis are taken fully into account, the soundness of that thesis seems to me evident.

2. The Simplest Theoretically Possible Form of Survival

The simplest form which survival, if it should be a fact, could take would consist in the continuation of a single state of consciousness after death. This state conceivably might be the last state of a person's consciousness immediately before death; or it might be one which, when bodily concerns are cut off, psychologically emerges out of the attitudes and feelings that have been prevalent in the person's life. It might be a state of blissful ecstasy similar to that of the mystic trance; or on the contrary one of anguish, or pain, or fear; or indeed any other single state of consciousness.

If some one state thus absorbed the whole consciousness and no change in it occurred, then no passage of time would be experienced and the given state would therefore be eternal in the sense of timeless, whether or not it were eternal also in the sense of enduring forever in the time of a possible external observer.

It is obvious that survival such as just described would not be *personal* survival. If, however, the persisting state of consciousness were of the kind the mystics have called union with God, the peace that passeth understanding, Samadhi, Nirvana, and by yet other names, it might well be better than anything which the activities and experiences of life in personal terms can yield. At least, so testify the mystics, who have tested both. Schopenhauer, who contrasted the two in terms of assertion and of abolition of the will, acknowledges that "what remains after the entire abolition of will is for all those who are still full of will certainly nothing; but, conversely, to those in whom the will has turned and has denied itself, this our world, which is so real, with all its suns and milky ways — is nothing."[1] But it goes without saying that even if survival in the form of continuation of a single unchanging state of consciousness should be a fact, no reason whatever appears for believing that it would be a state of the blissful kind just referred to rather than one of anguish, or some other particular sort of state.

3. Survival as Dream Consciousness

Another possible form of survival would consist in consciousness such as is now ours in dreams; that is, in images of various kinds of objects, and of situations in which we play some role — the content of the dream being determined at least in part by conscious or subconscious wishes or fears. Survival in this form would account for some of the communications concerning the nature of the afterlife obtained from mediums. In particular, it would account for reports as to scenery, houses, associates, and occupations virtually duplicating, though with improvements,

---

[1] Schopenhauer, *The World as Will and Idea*, tr. by Haldane and Kemp, Vol. I, p. 532.

those of ordinary life. It would account also for the fact that some of the reports deny what some others affirm; for where wish is architect and playwright, diversity of scenery and of drama is naturally to be expected from diversity of persons.

Afterlife as dream would also account for such *prima facie* absurd reports as that the deceased smokes cigars and drinks whiskey and soda.[2] For in our dreams we all do these or similar things, and so long as the dream lasts we take it as reality. Thus, if we were to report the dream while it is still going on — that is, without having become aware that it is but a dream — we should mistake the dream images for objects perceived and acts performed, or for memories of these, and thus report events precisely such as those seemingly absurd ones.

Again, afterlife as dream would account for communications to the effect that, the afterworld being so like this one, the deceased does not realize for some time that he has died. It would account also for the reports that the deceased has met persons (*e.g.,* Adam Bede) which actually are only characters in novels or other works of fiction; and it would account for the lack of firmness and precision which is general in the communications obtained by automatists.

4. Survival Consciousness as Reflective Reminiscence

A form of survival consciousness different from that just described would be one consisting of a reviewing of the memories of one's embodied life, of reflection upon them, and of distillation from them of such wisdom as reflection can yield. Something like this anyway occurs to some extent in old persons that are not fools, when, because only the embers of passion then remain, it becomes possible for them to view their own lives with the perspective of spectators. There is evidence from hypnosis and psychoanalysis that many if not all memories normally irrecover-

---

[2] Oliver Lodge, *Raymond,* pp. 197–8.

able are somehow subconsciously preserved; and if the after-death reminiscing we are now hypothecating should happen to include all of them, a much greater harvest of lessons from them could be extracted by reflection than is possible simply in old age. Nevertheless, since both the material for reflection and the penetration of one's reflective capacity would be finite, that process of distillation could hardly fail to exhaust its possibilities sooner or later.

5. Survival as Critically Controlled Creative Imagination

Still another possible form of survival consciousness would be one resembling to some extent the dream consciousness already considered, but differing from it by addition of the purposively critical activity characteristic of mental creativeness or discovery, whether poetic, pictorial, musical, mathematical, dramatic, philosophical, or other.

6. Survival as Including Objective Experience and Activity

Another possible form of survival would be one not wholly self-sufficient like that just described or like dream consciousness, but including adventitious images caused, like those we now call sensations, somehow externally (say, telepathically, or clairvoyantly) ; and, like sensations, resistant to alteration at wish except through external activity conforming to objective laws of some kind.

Even if such adventitious images were merely color shapes, they would, in virtue of their adventitiousness and possession of properties of their own, be taken by the critical beholder of them, as our visual sensations are taken by us now, as appearances of an environment independently existing. And if those images were not only of color, but also of sound, odor, temperature, pressure, and so on, and could be modified not by the mere wish like images of imagination, but, like our sensations now, only by volitions putting into play automatic agencies external to the mind concerned, then the mind or part of the mind surviving would have exactly the same reasons we now have for coming to regard itself as being in a material environment; although, of course, the material objects composing it might be as different in their specific appearance and properties from those of earth as the objects found in polar regions are different from those in the tropics, or as birds are from fish.

Then, evidently, the question would arise: What relation is there in space or time between that after-death material world and the material world we now know? The former might conceivably be some planet in one of the many other solar systems. But it might equally be this earth over again. And in either case it might be reached either immediately after death, or only after some interval, occupied possibly in some one or more of the manners we have described; for no reason appears for supposing that surviving consciousness might not have several stages — one, perhaps, merely of dream consciousness; another, of reminiscence and reflection; and so on.

7. Survival as Transmigration

The hypothesis of survival as rebirth (whether immediate or delayed) in a material world (whether the earth or some other planet) is of course not novel. It has been variously called reincarnation, transmigration, metempsychosis, or palingenesis; and, as W. R. Alger declares, "No other doctrine has exerted so extensive, controlling, and permanent an influence upon mankind as that of the metempsychosis — the notion that when the soul leaves the body it is born anew in another body, its rank, character, circumstances, and experience in each successive existence depending on its qualities, deeds, and attainments in its preceding lives."[3]

Although the hypothesis of such dependence is in large part logically distinct from and additional to that of rebirth in another

---

[3] W. R. Alger, *A Critical History of the Doctrine of a Future Life*, p. 475.

material body, it has in fact been virtually always conjoined with the latter — probably because the transmigration hypothesis then is, as Alger further says, "marvellously adapted to explain the seeming chaos of moral inequality, injustice, and manifold evil presented in the world of human life. . . . Once admit the theory to be true, and all difficulties in regard to moral justice vanish . . . the principal physical and moral phenomena of life are strikingly explained; and, as we gaze around the world, its material conditions and spiritual elements combine in one vast scheme of unrivalled order, and the total experience of humanity forms a magnificent picture of perfect poetic justice."[4] This conception of survival, moreover, is the most concrete. Because what it supposes is so like the life we know, it can be imagined most clearly.

Not only has it had wide popular acceptance, but it has also commended itself to some of the most eminent thinkers not only in the East but also in the West.[5] Among these have been Pythagoras, Plato, and Plotinus; and Origen and some others of the early Christian fathers. Indeed, the statement twice reported of Jesus[6] that John the Baptist was the prophet Elijah who was to come, suggests that Jesus himself perhaps held the doctrine. In more recent times, David Hume, although not himself professing it, asserts that it is the only conception of survival that philosophy can hearken to.[7] Schopenhauer's contention that death of the body is not death of the will, and that so long as the will-to-live persists it will gain bodily objectification, amounts to acceptance of the idea of rebirth. McTaggart regards earthly rebirth as "the most probable form of the doctrine of immortality."[8] And Alger, who in spite of the merits he finds in the doctrine apparently does

---

[4] *Op. cit.,* pp. 481–2.
[5] Cf. E. D. Walker, *Reincarnation, a Study of Forgotten Truth,* London, 1888.
[6] Matt. 11:14; 17:12, 13.
[7] Hume, *Essay on Immortality,* III.
[8] McTaggart, *Some Dogmas of Religion,* p. xiii, and Chap. IV.

not himself hold it, nevertheless declares — somewhat optimistically — that its "sole difficulty is a lack of positive proof."[9]

This difficulty, however, is one which attaches equally to rival conceptions of survival, and indeed, as we concluded in the preceding chapter, to the hypothesis of survival itself, irrespective of kind. But since, in respect of practical significance for us now, the transmigration hypothesis apparently would have in addition to concreteness the merits Alger describes, it will be worth while now to inquire in some detail whether it really is theoretically tenable, or on the contrary faces insuperable difficulties. Our purpose in this chapter — which, as stated at the outset, is only to meet the charge that no significant and theoretically possible form of survival can be clearly imagined — not only allows but requires that, in the coming discussion, we should state the transmigration hypothesis in such form, whether historical or not, as will best avoid the objections which suggest themselves. Their nature will, as we proceed, itself determine the details of that form.

8. Examination of the Transmigration Hypothesis

The hypothesis of survival as rebirth — let us say, on this earth — at once raises the question whether one's present life is not itself a rebirth; for logically, even if not in point of practical interest, the hypothesis of earlier lives is exactly on a par with that of later lives. Hence, assuming transmigration, to suppose that one's present life is the first of one's series of lives would be as arbitrary as to suppose that it is going to be the last, *i.e.*, that one will not survive the death of it although it is a survival of earlier deaths.

Now, the supposition that one's present life not only will have successors but also has had predecessors, immediately brings up the objection that we have no recollection of having lived before.

---

[9] Alger, *op. cit.*, p. 482.

But, as we have already several times had occasion to remark, if absence of memory of having existed at a certain time proved that we did not exist at that time, it would then prove far too much; for it would prove that we did not exist during the first few years of the life of our present body, nor on most of the days since then, for we have no memories whatever of the great majority of them, nor of those first few years. Lack of memory of lives earlier than our present one is therefore no evidence at all that we did not live before.

Moreover, there is occasional testimony of recollection of a previous life, where the recollection is quite circumstantial and even alleged to have been verified. One such case may be cited here without any claim that it establishes preexistence, but only to substantiate the assertion that specific testimony of this kind exists. Evidently, testimony cannot be dismissed here any more than elsewhere merely because it happens to clash with an antecedent belief the empirical basis of which is only that we have not met before with such testimony. So to proceed would be to become guilty of *argumentum ad ignorantiam*. If preexistence should happen to be a fact, it is obvious that the only possible empirical evidence of it would consist of verifiable recollections such as testified to in the case about to be described.

It is that of "The Rebirth of Katsugoro," recorded in detail and with many affidavits respecting the facts, in an old Japanese document translated by Lafcadio Hearn.[10] The story is, in brief, that a young boy called Katsugoro, son of a man called Genzo in the village of Nakanomura, declared that in his preceding life a few years before he had been called Tozo; that he was then the son of a farmer called Kyubei and his wife Shidzu in a village called Hodokubo; that his father had died and had been replaced in the household by a man called Hanshiro; and that he himself, Tozo, had died of smallpox at the age of six, a year after his

---

10 L. Hearn, *Gleanings in Buddha Fields,* Chap. X.

father. He described his burial, the appearance of his former parents, and their house. He eventually was taken to their village, where such persons were found. He himself led the way to their house and recognized them; and they confirmed the facts he had related. Further, he pointed to a shop and a tree, saying that they had not been there before; and this was true.

Testimony of this kind is directly relevant to the question of rebirth. The recollections related in this case are much too circumstantial to be dismissed as instances of the familiar and psychologically well-understood illusion of *déja vu,* and although the testimony that they were verified is not proof that they were, it cannot be rejected *a priori.* Its reliability has to be evaluated in terms of the same standards by which the validity of testimonial evidence concerning anything else is appraised.

A second objection to the transmigration hypothesis is that the native peculiarities of a person's mind as well as the characteristics of his body appear to be derived from his forebears in accordance with the laws of heredity. McTaggart, whose opinion that earthly rebirth is the most probable form of survival we have already mentioned, considers that objection and makes clear that "there is no impossibility in supposing that the characteristics in which we resemble the ancestors of our bodies may be to some degree characteristics due to our previous lives." He points out that "hats in general fit their wearers with far greater accuracy than they would if each man's hat were assigned to him by lot. And yet there is very seldom any causal connexion between the shape of the head and the shape of the hat. A man's head is never made to fit his hat, and, in the great majority of cases, his hat is not made to fit his head. The adaptation comes about by each man selecting, from hats made without any special reference to his particular head, the hat which will suit his particular head best." And, McTaggart goes on to say: "This may help us to see that it would be possible to hold that a man whose nature had certain characteristics when he was about to be reborn, would be reborn in a body descended from ancestors of a similar character. His character when reborn would, in this case, be decided, as far as the points in question went, by his character in his previous life, and not by the character of the ancestors of his new body. But it would be the character of the ancestors of the new body, and its similarity to his character, which determined the fact that he was reborn in that body rather than another."[11]

McTaggart's use of the analogy of the head and the hats if taken literally would mean, as a correspondent of mine suggests, that, like a man looking for a hat to wear, a temporarily bodiless soul would shop around, trying on one human foetus after another until it finds one which in some unexplained manner it discovers will develop into an appropriate body. McTaggart, however, has in mind nothing so far fetched, but rather an entirely automatic process. He refers to the analogy of chemical affinities in answer to the question how each person might be brought into connection with the new body most appropriate to him.

But although McTaggart's supposition is adequate to dispose of the difficulty which the facts of heredity otherwise constitute, the rebirth his supposition allows is nevertheless not personal rebirth if, by a man's personality, one means what we have meant in what precedes, namely, the habits, the skills, the knowledge, character, and memories, which he gradually acquires during life on earth. These, we have said, may conceivably persist for a longer or shorter time after death, but, if our present birth is indeed a rebirth, they certainly are not brought to a new earth life; for we know very well that we are not born with the knowledge, habits, and memories we now have, but gained them little by little as a result of the experiences and efforts of our present lifetime.

But this brings up another difficulty, namely, what then is there

---

11 McTaggart, *Some Dogmas of Religion*, p. 125.

left which could be supposed to be reborn? A possible solution of it, which at the same time would provide empirical content for Broad's postulated but undescribed "psychic factor," is definable in terms of the difference familiar in psychology between, on the one hand, *acquired* skills, habits, and memories, and on the other *native* aptitudes, instincts, and proclivities; that is, in what a human being is at a given time we may distinguish two parts, one deeper and more permanent, and an other more superficial and transient. The latter consists of everything he has acquired since birth: habits, skills, memories, and so on. This is his personality.[12] The other part, which, somewhat arbitrarily for lack of a better name we may here agree to call his individuality, comprises the aptitudes and dispositions which are native in him. These include not only the simple ones, such as aptitude for tweezer dexterity, which have been studied in laboratories because they so readily lend themselves to it, but also others more elusive: intellectual, social, and esthetic aptitudes, dispositions, and types of interest or of taste. Here the task of discriminating what is innate from what is acquired is much more difficult, for it is complicated by the fact that some existent aptitudes may only become manifest after years have passed, or perhaps never, simply because not until then, or never, did the external occasion present itself for them to be exercised — just as aptitude for tweezer dexterity, for instance, in those who have it, must remain latent so long as they are not called upon to employ tweezers.

There can be no doubt that each of us, on the basis of his same individuality — that is, of his same stock of innate latent capacities and incapacities — would have developed a more or less different empirical mind and personality if, for instance, he had been put at birth in a different family, or had later been thrust by some external accident into a radically different sort of environment, or had had a different kind of education, or had met and married

---

[12] Lat. *persona* = a mask for actors (*per* = through, and *sonus* = sound) ; thus, the mask or appearance through which the voice speaks.

a very different type of person, and so on. Reflection on this fact should cause one to take his present personality with a large grain of salt, viewing it no longer humorlessly as his absolute self, but rather, in imaginative perspective, as but one of the various personalities which his individuality was equally capable of generating had it happened to enter phenomenal history through birth in a different environment. Thus, to the question: What is it that could be supposed to be reborn? an intelligible answer may be returned by saying that it might be the core of positive and negative aptitudes and tendencies which we have called a man's individuality, as distinguished from his personality. And the fact might further be that, perhaps as a result of persistent striving to acquire a skill or trait he desires, but for which he now has but little gift, aptitude for it in future births would be generated and incorporated into his individuality.

A man's individuality, as we have here defined it, would to some extent function as would Broad's "psychic factor": it would be what remains of a man after not only the death of his body but also after the disintegration of his lifetime-acquired "personal" mind, whether at bodily death or at some longer or shorter time thereafter. On the other hand, although his "individuality" would not itself be a personal mind, it would be an intrinsic and indeed the basic constituent of what his *total* mind is at any time. Out of the union of this basic or seminal constituent with a living body there would gradually develop a personal mind, whose particular nature would be the resultant on the one hand of the experiences due to the circumstances of that body, and on the other, of the core of aptitudes and tendencies therein embodied. Such parts or activities of a personal mind as we described in earlier sections of this chapter can, without theoretical difficulty, be supposed to survive the body's death at least for sometime; and *these* could (as Broad suggests of his "psychic factor") be what, in the mediumistic trance, becomes temporarily united with the medium's "bodily factor," which then furnishes it the possibility of expression vocally or by writing. Thus, what would be so expressing itself in the trance communications would not be the whole personal mind of the deceased, but only so much of it as still persisted; and even this, more or less colored or distorted by the necessity for it of making use of the particular set of acquired neural connections (discussed in section 8 of Chapter 18) in the medium's brain, which are certain to be more or less different from those that had been built up in the brain of the deceased.

The hypothesis we are considering would thus appear to have the virtues of Broad's "psychic factor" hypothesis, but in addition to provide an account of the nature of that factor in familiar psychological terms, while avoiding the criticisms of Broad's "psychic factor" made by Dodds in the article already cited.

Another objection which has been advanced against the transmigration hypothesis is that without the awareness of identity which memory provides, rebirth would not be discernibly different from the death of one person followed by the birth of another. In this connection, Lamont quotes Leibniz's question: "Of what use would it be to you, sir, to become king of China, on condition that you forgot what you have been? Would it not be the same as if God, at the same time he destroyed you, created a king in China?"[13]

But continuousness of memory, rather than preservation of a comprehensive span of memories, is what is significant for consciousness of one's identity. Thus, for example, none of us finds his sense of identity impaired by the fact that he has no memories of the earliest years of his present life. And if, on each day, he had a stock of memories relating to, let us say, only the then preceding ten years, or some other perhaps even shorter period, this would provide all that would be needed for a continuous

---

13 Corliss Lamont, *The Illusion of Immortality*, p. 22; Leibniz, *Philosophische Schriften*, ed. Gerhardt, IV, 300.

sense of identity. The knowledge he would have of his personal history would, it is true, comprise a shorter span than it now does, but the span in either case would have an earliest term, and in either case the personality known would have a substantial amount of historical dimension. That the sense of identity depends on *gradualness of change* in ourselves, rather than on preservation unchanged of any specific part of ourselves, strikes one forcibly when he chances to find letters, perhaps, which he wrote thirty or forty years before. Many of them may awaken no recollections whatever, even of the existence of the persons to whom they were addressed or whom they mentioned, and it sometimes seems incredible also that the person who wrote the things they contain should be the same as his present self. In truth, it is not the same in any strict sense, but only continuous with the former person. The fact, as the Buddha insisted, is that one's personality, like everything else that exists in time, changes as time passes — some constituents of it remaining for shorter or longer periods, the while others are being lost and others acquired. Yet, because of the gradualness and diverse speeds of the changes between one's earlier and one's present personality, the sense of identity is at no time lacking.

One more difficulty in the conception of survival as transmigration remains to be examined. It concerns not so much the theoretical possibility of transmigration as its capacity to satisfy certain demands which death appears to thwart — such capacity being what alone gives to a conception of survival practical importance and interest for us in this life.

One of these demands, as we have seen, is that the injustices of this life should somehow be eventually redressed; hence, conceptions of survival have generally included the idea of such redress as effected in the life after death. And, when survival has been thought of as later lives on earth, the redress has been conceived to consist in this — that the good and evil deeds, the strivings, the experiences, and the merits and faults of one life, all would have their just fruits in subsequent lives; in short, that as a man soweth, so shall he also reap.

Now, however, it may be objected that, without memory of what one is being rewarded or punished for, one learns nothing from the retribution, which is then ethically useless. This, in fact, was the essential point of the passage from Leibniz quoted earlier. Leibniz was considering Descartes's conception of the soul as an immortal substance, and contending that "like matter, so the soul will change in shape, and as with matter . . . it will indeed be possible for this soul to be immortal, but it will go through a thousand changes and will not remember what it has been. But this immortality without memory is wholly useless to ethics; for it subverts all reward and all punishment." And then comes the passage quoted earlier: "Of what use would it be to you, sir, to become king of China, on condition that you forgot what you have been?"

But all this is obviously based on a tacit and gratuitous ascription to the universe of the twin human impulses, vindictiveness and gratitude. It is these only which lead one to conceive a just future life as one of punishment and reward. For punishment and reward, although they satisfy vindictiveness and gratitude, are morally defensible only in so far as they contribute to the moral education of the recipient. But the eye-for-eye-and-tooth-for-tooth mode of moral education is not the only one there is, nor necessarily always the most effective. If, for example, impatience caused Tom to do Dick an injury, the morally important thing as regards Tom is that he should acquire the patience he lacks; but the undergoing by him of a similar injury at the hand of Dick is not the only possible way in which he could come to do so. Indeed, it would contribute to this only in proportion as Dick's retaliation were prompt and were known to be retaliation for the injury resulting from Tom's impatience. Other ways in which Tom might learn patience are conceivable. He might, for example, eventually find himself in a situation psychologically conducive to the development of patience — one, for example, where his love for someone would cause him to endure year after year without resentment the vagaries or follies of the loved person — or, more generally, some situation which for one reason or another he would be powerless to alter or to escape and in which only patient resignation would avail to bring him any peace.

As regards Dick, on the other hand, compensation for his unmerited injury at the hand of Tom need not consist in the immoral pleasure of retaliation upon Tom. The injury, which as such robs him of certain powers or opportunities, might lead him to develop other and more significant capacities latent in him, or might awaken him to other and better opportunities of which he would otherwise have remained unaware. Compensation for injury can be paid in various kinds of coin, and can truly compensate no matter at whose hands the payment comes; and, on the side of the doer of injury, the ends of justice are truly served if the wages of vice turn out to be eventual virtue.

It is further conceivable that Tom's eventual landing into a situation forcing him to practice patience should be a perfectly natural consequence of his vice of impatience. Each of us that is old and mature enough to view the course of his life in perspective can see that again and again his aptitudes, his habits, his tastes or interests, his virtues or his vices — in short, what he was at a given time — brought about, not by plan but automatically, changes in his material or social circumstances, in his associates, in his opportunities and so on; and that these changes in turn, quite as much as those due to purely external causes, contributed to shape for the better or the worse what he then became. This, which is observable within one life, could occur equally naturally as between the present and the subsequent bodied lives of a continuous though gradually changing self.

These suppositions have been introduced here only to make clear that the *lex talionis* conception of the justice for which later lives would provide the opportunity is crude and limited, and is far from being the only imaginable form justice could take, or necessarily the most effective. Those suppositions have also made clear that, for the moral education and the compensation which are the ends of justice, memory of the injury done and knowledge that an eventual educative consequence or piece of good fortune is a consequence of the injury done or sustained, is not in the least necessary, as on the contrary it is, where the *lex talionis* is the instrument of justice employed.

We have now considered the chief of the difficulties in the way of the transmigration form of the survival hypothesis. In attempting to meet them and to take into account the survival possibilities described in earlier sections of this chapter, we have gradually defined a form of survival which appears possible and which, if it should be a fact, would have significance for the living. The main features of that conception may now be summarily recited. They would be:

(*a*) That in the mind of man two comprehensive constituents are to be discerned — one, acquired during his lifetime and most obvious, which we have called his *personality* or the personal part of his mind; and another, less obvious but more basic, which exists in him from birth, and which for lack of a better name we have called his *individuality* or the individual part of his mind;

(*b*) That this part, consisting of aptitudes, instincts, and other innate dispositions or tendencies, is the product gradually distilled from the actions, experiences, and strivings of the diverse personalities which developed by union of it with the bodies of a succession of earlier lives on earth (or possibly elsewhere);

(*c*) That, between any two such successive lives, there is an interval during which some parts of the personality of the preceding life persist — consciousness then being more or less dream-like, but perhaps gradually learning to discriminate between images of subjective origin and memory images, and between either of these and images of objective, *i.e.,* of telepathic or clairvoyant, origin, if any;

(*d*) That some time during the interval is occupied by more or less complete recollection of the acts and events of the preceding life, and of their discernible consequences; and that dispositions of various apposite sorts are generated thereby, in some such automatic way as that in which, during life, deep changes of attitude are sometimes generated in us by our reading or seeing and hearing performed a tragedy or other impressive drama, or indeed by witnessing highly dramatic real events;

(*e*) That, partly because the specific nature of a man's individuality automatically shapes to some extent the external circumstances as well as the nature of the personality he develops from a given birth, and perhaps partly also because what his individuality has become may determine automatically — through some such affinity as McTaggart suggests — where and when and from whom he will be reborn, justice is immanent in the entire process, though not necessarily in the primitive form of *lex talionis.*

In conclusion, however, let it be emphasized again that no claim is made that this conception of survival is known to be true, or even known to be more probably true than not; but only (1) that it is possible in the threefold sense stated earlier; (2) that belief or disbelief of it has implications for conduct; (3) that, if true, it would satisfy pretty well most of the demands which make the desire for survival so widespread; and (4) that, notwithstanding some gaps in that conception due to our ignorance of mechanisms such as certain of those it postulates, it is yet clear and definite enough to refute the allegation it was designed to refute, namely, that no life after death both possible and significant can be imagined.

INDEX

INDEX